GOVERNING WORK AND WELFARE IN A NEW ECONOMY

Governing Work and Welfare in a New Economy

European and American Experiments

Edited by

JONATHAN ZEITLIN AND DAVID M. TRUBEK

OXFORD

UNIVERSITY PRESS

*This book has been printed digitally and produced in a standard specification
in order to ensure its continuing availability*

OXFORD
UNIVERSITY PRESS

Great Clarendon Street, Oxford OX2 6DP

Oxford University Press is a department of the University of Oxford.
It furthers the University's objective of excellence in research, scholarship,
and education by publishing worldwide in

Oxford New York

Auckland Cape Town Dar es Salaam Hong Kong Karachi
Kuala Lumpur Madrid Melbourne Mexico City Nairobi
New Delhi Shanghai Taipei Toronto
With offices in
Argentina Austria Brazil Chile Czech Republic France Greece
Guatemala Hungary Italy Japan South Korea Poland Portugal
Singapore Switzerland Thailand Turkey Ukraine Vietnam

Oxford is a registered trade mark of Oxford University Press
in the UK and in certain other countries

Published in the United States
by Oxford University Press Inc., New York

Oxford is a registered trade mark of Oxford University Press
in the UK and in certain other countries

Published in the United States
by Oxford University Press Inc., New York

ISBN 0-19-925717-5

CONTENTS

Part 2. Experimenting with the Work–Welfare Nexus: The United States

Part 3. Governing Work and Welfare in a New Economy: Emergent Patterns and Future Possibilities

LIST OF FIGURES

LIST OF TABLES

NOTES ON CONTRIBUTORS

Joshua Cohen is Professor of Political Science and Philosophy, and Leon and Anne Goldberg Professor of Humanities, at the Massachusetts Institute of Technology.

Laura Dresser is Research Director of the Center on Wisconsin Strategy (COWS) at the University of Wisconsin-Madison.

Adalbert Evers is Professor of Comparative Health and Social Policy at the Justus Liebig University in Giessen and the Institute for Social Research (ISF), Frankfurt.

Maurizio Ferrera is Professor of Politics and Public Administration at the University of Pavia and Director of the POLEIS Center for Comparative Political Research at the Bocconi University in Milan.

Janine Goetschy is a senior research fellow at Centre National de la Recherche Scientifique (CNRS), attached to the University of Paris-Nanterre and to the Institute of European Studies at the Free University of Brussels.

Joel F. Handler is Richard C. Maxwell Professor of Law and Policy Studies at the University of California-Los Angeles (UCLA) Law School.

Anton Hemerijck is Deputy Director of the Netherlands Scientific Council for Government Policy (WRR) in the Hague and Senior Lecturer in Public Administration at the University of Leiden.

James S. Mosher is Assistant Professor of Political Science at Ohio University.

Paul Osterman is Professor at the Massachusetts Institute of Technology's Sloan School of Management and Department of Urban Studies and Planning.

Ida Regalia is Professor of Theory and Politics of Labor at the University of Milan and Deputy Director of the Institute for Social and Economic Research (IRES) of Lombardy.

Martin Rhodes is Professor of European Public Policy at the European University Institute, Florence.

Joel Rogers is John D. MacArthur Professor of Sociology, Law, and Political Science, and Director of the Center on Wisconsin Strategy (COWS) at the University of Wisconsin-Madison.

Charles F. Sabel is Professor of Law and Social Science at Columbia University Law School.

Robert Salais is the Director of the Centre National de la Recherche Scientifique (CNRS) Research Group on Institutions and Historical Dynamics of the Economy (IDHE) at the École Normale Supérieure in Cachan.

Alain Supiot is Professor of Law at the University of Nantes and the Maison des Sciences de l'Homme 'Ange Guépin'.

David M. Trubek is Voss-Bascom Professor of Law, Director of the Center for World Affairs and the Global Economy, and Co-Director of the European Union Center at the University of Wisconsin-Madison.

Louise G. Trubek is Clinical Professor of Law at the University of Wisconsin Law School.

Jonathan Zeitlin is Professor of History, Sociology, and Industrial Relations and Co-Director of the European Union Center at the University of Wisconsin-Madison.

PREFACE

This book is the fruit of a transatlantic dialogue on work, welfare, and governance organized by the European Union Center of the University of Wisconsin-Madison. Earlier versions of the chapters were presented to an interdisciplinary group of European and American scholars at two workshops held in Madison in April 2000 and May 2001. We are grateful to the participants in these workshops, including those whose contributions could not be included in this volume, for their stimulating comments and valuable advice. We would also like to thank the European Commission for its financial support of our EU Center, without which this project would not have been possible, especially the program officers in Washington (Jonathan Davidson, Bill Burros) and Brussels (Fernando Ponz, Roy Dickinson); and the International Institute and Office of International Studies and Programs of the University of Wisconsin-Madison, which provided equally vital material and administrative support. We are particularly grateful to the EU Center staff for their hard work and cheerful efficiency in coordinating the project, especially Crister Garrett, the Associate Director; Sebnem Ozkan, who managed the practical arrangements for both workshops; and Darya Vassina, who also played a crucial role in preparing the manuscript for publication. Both of the editors would like to acknowledge the splendid hospitality and intellectual environment of the European University Institute in Florence, especially its Robert Schuman Center for Advanced Studies, where Jonathan Zeitlin spent the spring of 1999 as a Jean Monnet Fellow, and David Trubek composed his chapter for this volume as a visiting scholar in the spring of 2001. Finally, we want to thank David Musson of Oxford University Press for his warm encouragement and support of this project from its inception.

1

Introduction: Governing Work and Welfare in a New Economy: European and American Experiments

JONATHAN ZEITLIN

1.1. Common Challenges, Convergent Responses?

Most recent discussions of work and welfare in Europe and the United States have tended to assume, implicitly if not explicitly, that little mutual learning could arise from transatlantic comparisons. According to one widespread view, common on the right, especially in the United States and certain international organizations, the 1990s saw the global triumph of a single dominant economic model, that of American free-market capitalism, whose superior efficiency was reflected in higher growth and lower unemployment rates than those of continental Europe. From this perspective, the main question raised by transatlantic comparisons was how to overcome the social, political, and administrative barriers to European emulation of the American model through the adoption of neo-liberal reform policies such as workfare and labor-market deregulation.[1] According to a second broadly-held view, common on the left, especially in Europe, such efforts to promote European emulation of the American model were both inappropriate and undesirable given the fundamental differences between the two regions in economic organization, social values, policy regimes, and political/institutional structures.

For helpful comments and advice in preparing this introduction, I am grateful to David Trubek, Louise Trubek, Charles Sabel, Joel Rogers, Robert Salais, Anton Hemerijck, Peer Hull Kristensen, Philippe Pochet, four anonymous reviewers for Oxford University Press, and the participants in the conference on 'Renegotiating the Welfare State: The United States in Comparative Perspective', Northwestern University, June 18, 2001.

[1] The *locus classicus* of this view is the OECD (1994); for a European statement, see Siebert (1997). This perspective remains dominant in much of the English-language international press coverage, especially the editorial pages of *The Economist*, the *Wall Street Journal*, the *New York Times*, and the *Financial Times*.

Not only were average levels of inequality within the European Union much lower than in the United States, but a number of European countries had sharply reduced unemployment without widening social divisions during the late 1990s through various combinations of homegrown reform efforts such as negotiated wage restraint, labor-market activation, and intensive training/retraining. Whatever its merits as a critique of the first view, from this perspective there might seem to be even fewer positive lessons to be learned by comparing work and welfare on opposite sides of the Atlantic.[2]

This book, the product of an interdisciplinary working group of leading European and American scholars convened by the European Union Center of the University of Wisconsin-Madison, starts from a contrasting premise. Despite the many evident differences between the United States and the European Union (as well as among EU Member States themselves), the contributions to this volume suggest that each have been struggling with a set of common challenges to which neither side has ready-made solutions. How to reconfigure labor-market institutions and welfare regimes designed for a previous era, based on very different patterns of productive organization, employment, and household/family structures, in a 'new economy', which as the essays in this book show has emerged in strikingly similar ways on both sides of the Atlantic over the past quarter-century? How to balance flexibility and security in this new economy, characterized by increased volatility and uncertainty, greater international openness and competition, a faster pace of innovation, more fluid boundaries between firms, and devolution of enhanced responsibilities to individuals and teams, resulting in rapidly shifting skill profiles and less-stable employment careers?[3] How to provide individuals with the complementary resources and institutional supports or 'capabilities' needed to navigate safely through the ensuing hazards and transitions of the labor market and the life course? How to recalibrate established

---

[2] For examples of this second view, which has gained ground as a result of recent improvements in European employment performance, see Auer (2000); Esping-Andersen and Regini (2000); Ganssmann (2000); Conseil d'Analyse Économique (2000); Bermeo (2001); Huber and Stephens (2001: 323–37). In December 2000, before the American economy turned sharply downwards, seven European countries had equal or lower standardized unemployment rates (US: 4.0%; Luxembourg: 2.4%; Switzerland: 2.5%; Netherlands: 2.8%; Norway: 3.6%; Austria: 3.6%; Ireland: 3.8%; Portugal: 4.0%), while three others had only slightly higher rates (Denmark: 4.7%, Sweden: 5.1%, United Kingdom: 5.2%): OECD Standardised Unemployment Rates, February 2002. Of these, only the United Kingdom had experienced a widening of wage and income inequality comparable to that of the United States during the 1980s and 1990s: see Scharpf and Schmidt (2000: table A.21, 358); Atkinson (1999).

[3] The 'new economy' in this sense thus long antedates the *fin-de-siècle* internet bubble and has continued to develop apace since its collapse. For an early and still influential analysis of the breakdown of the old order, see Piore and Sabel (1984); and for a review of the ensuing debates on the emergence of a new 'post-Fordist' production paradigm, see Hirst and Zeitlin (1991).

welfare programs and expenditures to cover changing distributions of social risk between generations and genders across the life cycle in response to demographic pressures such as population aging and increasing female labor-force participation? How to reconcile work and family life, in light of rising levels of women's paid employment, whose importance for economic growth and welfare state sustainability is widely acknowledged, but which requires expanded provision of complementary caring services for children and the aged, whether through public or private channels?

Beyond these common substantive challenges of reconfiguring work and welfare in a new economy, the contributions to this book further suggest that the European Union and the United States face similar problems of developing effective and legitimate arrangements for their governance. For on each side of the Atlantic, reform of what we may call the work–welfare (or employment–social protection) nexus constitutes a complex and thorny governance conundrum: among the wickedest of 'wicked problems' in British administrative parlance, combining both horizontal and vertical dimensions.[4]

On the horizontal dimension, welfare and employment reforms typically cut across formally distinct but functionally interdependent policy areas or governance domains, each involving a multiplicity of public and private actors. In the United States, for example, as a number of the chapters document, there is growing recognition that the long-term success of welfare-to-work programs may depend on complementary shifts in the provision of supporting services for low-wage employees like health care, child care, transportation, and training, as well as tax credits. In the European Union, too, as several of the contributors detail, activation and inclusion policies increasingly emphasize the value of an 'integrated approach' combining individualized social assistance, training, and employment placement services with broader initiatives aimed at stimulating urban and regional (re)development. Within the 'tightly coupled' welfare and labor-market regimes of continental Europe, similarly, recent efforts to promote job growth in the private-service sector have highlighted the need for conjoint reforms of wage determination, employment protection, taxation, social security, and pensions systems to make such initiatives effective.[5]

On the vertical dimension, as the essays in this book show, reforms of the work–welfare nexus typically cut across established divisions of labor between

---

[4] 'Wicked' or 'cross-cutting' problems, according to Sabel and O'Donnell's (2001: 76) account of recent British administrative reform debates, are those 'that both draw on the local knowledge of service providers and service users and require co-ordination of service provision across a wide range of formal jurisdictions'.

[5] On the need for and difficulties of coordinated reforms across multiple policy domains to encourage the expansion of low-wage service employment in the key case of Germany, see, in addition to Chapter 4 by Ferrera and Hemerijck, Scharpf (2001*a*) and Streeck (2001).

different levels of governance. In the United States, a central feature of recent welfare-to-work and health care reforms has been the devolution of broad discretionary authority over program design and implementation from the federal government to states and localities.[6] Europe, by contrast, has experienced a double (though far from complete) shift of competences in social and employment policy, downwards from the national state to local and regional governments and upwards to the EU level. In both cases, however, such reforms not only call into question existing distributions of powers and responsibilities among political and administrative units, but also pose a series of parallel challenges for the emergent system of multi-level governance in each region. How to coordinate policy-making and implementation across different levels of governance when comprehensive blueprints can no longer be designed and imposed from the center? How to avoid reform blockages by entrenched groups occupying strategic veto points? How to ensure accountability of local units and promote diffusion of promising solutions to common problems in a decentralized system of policy experimentation?

In an uncertain and rapidly changing environment like that of today's 'new economy', comprehensive, ready-made responses to these complex, multi-dimensional problems appear increasingly unsatisfactory. No country or region can plausibly claim to have worked out all the answers or to represent a optimal model for all others to follow.[7] Precisely for this reason, experimentation with the work–welfare nexus has become the watchword of reform on both sides of the Atlantic. Such experimentation, as the contributions to this book abundantly illustrate, may take a wide range of forms depending on variations in institutional settings, policy inheritances, and problem loads, not only between Europe and the United States, but also

---

[6] As is well known, US social welfare programs have generally remained less encompassing in scope, less generous in levels of provision, and more decentralized in their administration than in most European countries. But as Paul Pierson (1995) and others have argued, between the 1930s and the 1990s the United States experienced a 'creeping nationalization of income transfers' as a result of the more rapid growth of expenditures on national programs and the federal government's gradual assumption of increased authority over shared programs. The key element of the 1990s reforms of welfare and Medicaid, as in other policy areas such as education and transportation, was the relaxation of various grant-in-aid conditions accompanying federal financial assistance to state governments, which had been introduced during the previous phase of centralization. Yet, as scholars of American federalism have frequently observed, 'devolution' in this context is something of a misnomer, since the Constitution reserves to the states all powers not specifically delegated to the US government on the one hand, while Washington often continues to attach detailed conditions to states' use of federal money on the other. For authoritative overviews of recent developments within US federalism and the interpretive paradoxes associated with them, see Derthick (2001); Kincaid (2001); Donahue and Pollack (2001).

[7] For insightful discussions of the empirical and normative difficulties of identifying a single 'peak economy' or optimal model of labor-market institutions and social policies within contemporary capitalism, see Freeman (1998, 2000).

across and even within the Member States of the European Union itself. Yet, there are intriguing signs, as the essays in this volume also indicate, that analogous solutions to the challenges of governing work and welfare in a new economy may be nonetheless emerging from these experiments.

In the European Union, the most significant innovation has been the development of the so-called 'Open Method of Coordination' (OMC), based on mutual agreement of policy objectives by the Member States; development of common guidelines, indicators, and targets; benchmarking of performance and exchange of 'good practices'; formulation of national action plans; peer review and joint monitoring of implementation in an iterative, multi-year cycle. By systematically and continuously obliging the Member States to pool information, compare themselves to one another, and reassess current policies in light of their relative performance, the OMC appears to be a highly promising mechanism for promoting crossnational deliberation and experimental learning across the European Union. This approach, which also seems particularly well-adapted to the problems of pursuing broad common concerns under conditions of institutional diversity among participating units, was pioneered by the European Employment Strategy (EES) during the late 1990s. But the OMC in various forms has now become a virtual template for EU policy-making in other complex, politically-sensitive areas, including not only social inclusion, pensions, and health care, but also macroeconomic management, education and training, research and innovation, immigration and asylum.[8] Both the EES and the new OMC social inclusion process (inaugurated in 2001) likewise build on and at least potentially reinforce

---

[8] OMC processes vary in their modalities and procedures depending on the specific characteristics of the policy field, the Treaty basis of EU competence, and the willingness of the Member States to undertake joint action. Thus the Commission and the Council have the right to issue formal joint recommendations to Member States on their implementation of the Employment Strategy and the Broad Economic Policy Guidelines, but not concerning the common social inclusion and pension reform objectives. National Action Plans are prepared and reviewed annually for employment and bi-annually for social inclusion, while in the case of the new OMC process for pension reform (launched at the end of 2001), looser 'National Strategy Reports' will be presented for review only every three or four years, with regular updates incorporated into the annual Broad Economic Policy Guidelines. In the words of Frank Vandenbroucke, Belgian Minister for Social Affairs and Pensions, who oversaw the development of the social inclusion and pension reform OMC processes during his country's 2001 EU Presidency: 'open co-ordination is not some kind of fixed recipe that can be applied to whichever issue ... [It] is a kind of cookbook that contains various recipes, lighter and heavier ones': see Vandenbroucke (2001: 4). For a useful comparative analysis of coordination and cooperation procedures within the European Union by policy area and Treaty basis, see White Paper on EU Governance Working Group 4*a* (2001). For preliminary examinations of the new social inclusion process, see Ferrera, Matsaganis, and Sacchi (2002) and Pochet (2002); on the incipient OMC processes in pensions and health care, see de la Porte and Pochet (2002*b*); de la Porte (2002); Council of the European Union (2001); and Commission of the European Communities (2001).

established practices of social concertation and negotiated governance in reform of work and welfare at EU, national, and subnational levels, from the European social dialogue through national social pacts to territorial employment pacts and local or plant-level collective agreements. Yet, many unresolved questions remain, as several of the contributions to this book emphasize, about how exactly these coordination processes work in the absence of binding sanctions, their effectiveness in achieving common objectives, their contribution to crossnational learning, their transparency and openness to participation by non-state actors, and their impact on policies and practices at lower levels of governance.[9]

In the United States, as a number of chapters in this volume show, the most innovative initiatives toward building new systems of welfare provision and labor-market governance have come from state and local-level actors in response to devolution, privatization, and regulatory gaps in federal policies and programs. Some of these efforts involve local strategies of reconstructing training, job access, career transitions, and wage standards through community organizations, public–private partnerships, and other intermediary bodies, linked to but distinct from both unions and state agencies. In certain cases, like that of the Industrial Areas Federation (IAF) described by Paul Osterman, these strategies seek to connect problem-solving and organizational learning to the creation of new community-based collective actors powerful enough to demand a voice in reshaping the rules of the local labor market. Other state-level reform initiatives such as the expansion of health care coverage for low-income workers involve various combinations of information sharing, joint standard setting, and collaborative problem-solving by partnerships among state-level government agencies, advocacy organizations, and service providers, facilitated by flexible rules for the use of federal funding. As in Europe, moreover, these experimental approaches to labor-market and welfare reform are echoed by parallel developments in other policy areas such as public education, environmental protection, policing, and criminal justice, entailing decentralized, deliberative exploration of

---

[9] For assessments of the objectives, potential contribution, and initial achievements of the OMC by two of its major architects, see Rodrigues (forthcoming); Larsson (2002). Maria João Rodrigues, former special advisor to the Portuguese Prime Minister and coordinator of the March 2000 Lisbon European Council, is widely known as the 'mother of the OMC', while Allan Larsson, former Swedish Finance Minister and Director General for Employment and Social Affairs at the European Commission, may equally be considered the 'father of the EES'. Academic evaluations of the OMC are just beginning to appear. In addition to Chapters 2, 3, and 13 by Trubek and Mosher, Goetschy, and Sabel and Cohen, respectively, see: de la Porte and Pochet (2002*a*); Jacobsson (forthcoming); Jacobsson (2001); Hemerijck (2002); Scharpf (2002); Wincott (forthcoming); Sundholm (2001); Ahonen (2001); Hodgson and Maher (2001). For an internal review of the OMC prepared for the European Commission in connection with the Convention on the Future of the EU, see Romano (2002), and for the official mid-term review of the EES, see Commission of the European Communities (2002).

common problems, benchmarking and monitoring of progress, assistance and sanctions for poor performers, and diffusion of the most successful solutions.[10] But as in the European case, there are many open questions. In the United States, the most salient of these concern the sustainability of local experiments, their capacity for expansion on a wider scale, and their potential integration with national programs and policies.

Despite the many unresolved issues highlighted by the essays in this volume, the simultaneous emergence on both sides of the Atlantic of new forms of experimentalist governance may indeed represent, as Joshua Cohen and Charles Sabel suggest in Chapter 13, a convergent if accidental response to a common dilemma: 'the proliferation of a broad class of situations in which inaction is unacceptable but omnibus solutions are plainly unworkable'. And it is a striking, if perhaps paradoxical feature of the book's findings, that despite the vast differences in social, political, and institutional contexts, it is at the local level that experimentation with reform of the work–welfare nexus in the European Union and the United States appears most similar.

1.2. Regime-Specific Problems, Hybridization, and Crossnational Policy Learning

The United States and the European Union, this book argues, face common substantive challenges of reconfiguring work and welfare in a new economy. They likewise face common procedural challenges of coordinating reforms of the work–welfare nexus across interdependent policy domains and levels of governance, each involving a multiplicity of public and private actors. And on both sides of the Atlantic new forms of experimentalist governance appear to be emerging as convergent responses to these common challenges. But what are the prospects for mutual learning from the policy solutions being developed across the two regions? Can promising policy approaches or 'good' if not 'best' practices be transferred effectively from one national context to another, and if so, under what circumstances?

Much recent work on welfare states and labor market institutions has advanced strong reasons to believe that the possibilities for genuine crossnational learning and policy transfer are instead severely limited. Although developed capitalist countries may all face broad common challenges such as globalization, deindustrialization, or population aging, an influential

---

[10] For more extensive discussions of US experimentalist governance approaches in these policy areas, see, in addition to Chapter 13 by Cohen and Sabel, Dorf and Sabel (1998); Sabel, Fung, and Karkkainen (2000); Sabel (2001).

current of comparative research emphasizes that these manifest themselves in very different forms and intensities depending on pre-existing economic profiles, institutional configurations, and policy legacies. National welfare states, as several of the chapters in this book observe, are frequently classified into distinctive regime clusters or 'worlds', based on various criteria such as their principles of eligibility, structure of benefits, sources of funding, and organizational arrangements (Esping-Andersen 1990; Ferrera 1998; Esping-Andersen 1999; Huber and Stephens 2001). According to such typologies, for example, in the 'liberal' or 'Anglo-Saxon' world, tax-funded public welfare benefits and services are largely residual, flat-rate, and means-tested, with a predominant role reserved for private provision through the market and the family. In the 'social democratic' or 'Nordic' world, by contrast, tax-funded public welfare benefits and services are generous, extensive, and largely universal, with a limited role for private-market provision. In the 'conservative-corporatist', 'Christian Democratic', or 'Continental' world, relatively generous earnings-related welfare benefits are financed through employment-based social insurance schemes, often administered by the 'social partners' themselves, with a more limited role for public-service provision. Finally, some classifications (as in Chapter 4 by Ferrera and Hemerijck) distinguish a fourth 'Latin' or 'Southern European' world, with many institutional similarities to the Continental welfare regime, but characterized by greater fragmentation and unevenness of social insurance coverage, a larger role for public service provision (especially in health care), and heavier reliance on the family to compensate for persistent gaps in the social safety net.[11]

As a result of these pervasive institutional variations, such analyses often argue, universal trends like economic internationalization and post-industrialism affecting all advanced countries nonetheless confront each cluster of national welfare states with a distinct constellation of regime-specific adjustment problems. A particularly strong version of this thesis is the 'service economy trilemma', originally formulated by Torben Iversen and Anne Wren (1998), but elaborated in closely related forms by other leading

---

[11] The most influential of these typologies is Esping-Andersen's (1990), 'three worlds of welfare capitalism', based on variations in their degree of 'de-commodification' or detachment of social rights from market forces, modes of stratification, and socio-political origins. Other comparative social policy scholars like Maurizio Ferrera (1998) have proposed alternative systems of classification based more on divergences in institutional and organizational arrangements. Although Esping-Andersen has now shifted the focus of his typology from 'welfare-*state*' to 'welfare' regimes, conceived as distinctive configurations of state-market-family provision, he continues to insist on the conceptual and empirical validity of his original three worlds, while rejecting alternative candidates: see Esping-Andersen (1999: chapter 5). For a useful critical review of the debates around Esping-Andersen's typology and the shifts in his position, see Wincott (2001).

comparative social policy scholars like Fritz Scharpf (Scharpf and Schmidt 2000; Scharpf 2001*a*) and Gøsta Esping-Andersen (1996, 1999). The nub of this trilemma is the difficulty for national governments of simultaneously attaining budgetary restraint, earnings equality, and employment growth in an open economy, where international competition and technological innovation restrict job creation in the exposed (mainly manufacturing) sector, capital mobility inhibits fiscal expansion, and relative productivity remains low in the labor-intensive sheltered service sector.[12] Employment growth in advanced economies, on this view, may be achieved either in well-paid public services, thereby undercutting budgetary restraint, or in low-paid private services, thereby sacrificing earnings inequality; hence governments may pursue any two of these goals but not all three at the same time. Since each of the three major types of welfare regime occupies a different position in relation to this trilemma, each accordingly faces a distinct set of policy adjustment problems. Thus, the social democratic welfare states of Scandinavia have sustained high levels of both employment and equality by expanding public-sector service jobs, but encounter increased difficulties in financing the ensuing costs through taxation and borrowing. Liberal welfare states in Anglo-Saxon countries like the United States and the United Kingdom, conversely, have created large numbers of private-sector service jobs without threatening the stability of public finances, but experience widespread problems of poverty and social exclusion among low-wage workers and their families. The conservative or Christian Democratic welfare states of continental Europe, finally, have maintained their commitments to both budgetary restraint and earnings equality, but only at the cost of low levels of employment in both public and private services. With social insurance benefits and funding closely tied to stable jobs, this third configuration confronts not only growing divisions between labor-market insiders and outsiders, but also a vicious spiral of increasing payroll charges, rising indirect costs, and declining employment, which could eventually undermine the financial sustainability of the continental welfare states themselves.[13]

---

[12] Iversen and Wren place greater weight than Scharpf on the role of endogenous shifts in consumption patterns and the price elasticity of demand for manufactured goods as structural causes of the relative expansion of sheltered service-sector employment, though they also acknowledge the importance of labor-saving productivity growth in constraining the scope for job creation in exposed sectors like manufacturing.

[13] The conservative continental welfare states, as Esping-Andersen in particular emphasizes, also suffer from low levels of female employment and fertility which pose an added threat to their demographic and financial sustainability, primarily due to the difficulty for women of combining family responsibilities with careers outside the home in the absence of affordable public or private child and elder care services: see Esping-Andersen (1996) and Esping-Andersen (1999). See also the discussion in Chapter 4 by Ferrera and Hemerijck.

Not only the adjustment problems facing advanced welfare states but also the feasible responses available to them are often held to vary systematically as a consequence of differences in national institutional characteristics and capabilities. The crucial issue here revolves less around crossnational variations in welfare regimes *per se* than around divergences in production regimes and the linkages between the two. Thus a growing body of scholarship, pioneered by David Soskice and Peter Hall (Soskice 1999; Hall and Soskice 2001), distinguishes between two diametrically opposed 'varieties of capitalism': uncoordinated 'liberal market economies' (LMEs), in which exchange of goods and services is based predominately on arms-length, competitive market transactions, as in the Anglo-Saxon countries; and 'coordinated market economies' (CMEs), in which economic activity is orchestrated primarily through collaborative relationships and non-market institutions, whether organized around industry associations as in central and northern Europe, or around enterprise groups as in East Asia. Each variety of capitalism or production regime, on this view, depends on a different national framework of interconnected and mutually complementary institutions governing key dimensions of economic activity such as industrial relations, vocational education and training, corporate finance, and inter-firm relations. These different national institutional frameworks in turn systematically shape the production, investment, and innovation strategies adopted by economic actors, giving rise to distinctive patterns of comparative advantage in world markets, which further reinforce the internal coherence and external specialization of each regime.[14] The fundamental source of crossnational divergence in production regimes, according to this analysis, lies in the coordinating capacity of business, though its exponents also recognize the causal significance of variations in the organization of labor and the state emphasized by other cognate approaches to comparative political economy.[15] Where strong business coordinating capacity does not already exist, however, governments cannot create it, since the common understandings, mutual trust, and specialized expertise necessary for non-market coordination among firms 'takes typically decades to grow' (Soskice 1999: 46). Hence, policy solutions to common challenges facing advanced welfare states that depend on the encompassing character and coordinating capacity of business and labor associations, such as negotiated wage moderation or increased firm-based

---

[14] For discussions of possible 'elective affinities' and institutional complementarities between production and welfare regimes, see Ebbinghaus and Manow (2001); Estevez-Abe, Iversen and Soskice (2001); and Huber and Stephens (2001).

[15] For a related typology of national industrial relations systems based on variations in the coordination of collective bargaining and degree of state involvement, see Scharpf and Schmidt (2000).

training for transferable skills, will only be viable in CMEs. LMEs, conversely, can be expected to gravitate instead towards less institutionally demanding adjustment strategies such as deregulation, privatization, and welfare retrenchment.[16]

These theoretical approaches, which emphasize the radical diversity of national institutional contexts, lead to profound skepticism about the prospects for mutual learning and policy transfer across welfare and production regimes. Nations, on this view, are best able to learn from members of the same institutional family, which confront a common set of regime-specific adjustment problems. Following this logic, Scharpf has long advocated 'closer cooperation' within the European Union among subgroups of countries with similar welfare states and industrial relations systems, which he argues could gain far more than the Union as a whole from examining each others' experiences and coordinating their reform strategies, especially if they could make use of Community legislation for that purpose. Thus, for example, continental countries struggling to reform 'pay-as-you-go public pension systems might develop common solutions even if these would not apply to Member States relying to a large extent on either tax-financed basic pensions or funded public or private pensions', while 'Member States with national health systems might benefit from common solutions that would not apply in countries relying on compulsory insurance for the financing of privately provided health care, and vice versa' (Scharpf 2001b: 12–3). Over the past two decades, similarly, successive British governments and their academic advisers, both Conservative and Labour, have self-consciously looked to the United States and other liberal market economies or welfare regimes rather than to continental Europe as a model for reform initiatives across a wide range of policy areas, including welfare-to-work and education and training. Since 'the British and US welfare regimes have much in common' by contrast to their European counterparts, observes Robert Walker, a prominent UK social policy specialist, 'it is not surprising...that British politicians—even Labour ones—should look to the United States when in search of new policy ideas,' as in the case of the Blair government's 'New Deal' (Walker 1998; cf. also Deacon 2000; Peck 2001: chapter 7). And Soskice himself, who served as a policy advisor to the Blair government, has explicitly advocated that the United Kingdom should concentrate on the expansion of mass higher education along US lines as a means of upgrading young

---

[16] For a parallel argument about the polarization of national industrial relations systems between the 1970s and the 1990s into a bimodal pattern of coordinated and market-determined wage-setting systems in response to external economic pressures, see Scharpf and Schmidt (2000: esp. 317–24).

people's general skills, rather than seeking to develop continental-style apprenticeship programs, whose success would require levels of employer coordination unattainable in a British setting (Soskice 1993).

Yet, the empirical foundations for these views of radical institutional diversity as an insuperable obstacle to crossnational learning and policy transfer across regime types are surprisingly shaky. As Anton Hemerijck and his colleagues have persuasively argued, the advanced welfare states that adjusted most successfully to the challenges of the 1990s have departed from their original regime types by developing new hybrid policy mixes incorporating elements borrowed from foreign models. 'It seems that precisely those countries that are deviating from their original clusters in selected policy areas have proved particularly effective in addressing the most typical problems to emerge from regime-specific structures', observe Ferrera, Hemerijck, and Rhodes. 'It is their very "hybridity"', they further contend, 'that appears to work in their favor in achieving a *system-wide search* for a new, economically viable, politically feasible, and socially acceptable profile of social and economic regulation' (Ferrera, Hemerijck, and Rhodes 2000: 44; cf. also Hemerijck and Schludi 2000: 205).

Thus, as Ferrera and Hemerijck's Chapter 4 in this volume shows, within the Nordic social democratic regime cluster Denmark has relaxed the public budgetary constraint on its welfare state while simultaneously maintaining high levels of social protection, employment, and income equality by increasing the funded and earnings-related components of its pension system on the one hand and by stepping up individualized labor-market activation and training programs for the unemployed on the other. Within the Anglo-Saxon liberal regime cluster, similarly, Ireland has achieved extraordinary rates of economic and employment growth while sharply reducing absolute (if not relative) income poverty and deprivation through negotiated wage restraint, increased welfare spending, and new forms of social partnership at both national and local levels, which integrate representatives of the unemployed and excluded into deliberative problem-solving fora alongside unions and employers. Within the Continental corporatist or Christian Democratic regime cluster, the Netherlands has likewise dramatically improved employment levels, especially in the private service sector and among women, while avoiding any sharp rise in budget deficits or earnings inequality, through promotion of part-time and temporary jobs (which increasingly enjoy rights of equal treatment in pay and social benefits), restriction of access to disability pensions and sickness insurance (which had been widely abused by employers and unions to cushion the social effects of industrial restructuring), and long-term, consensual wage moderation. Even within the Southern European regime cluster, whose adjustment problems are widely considered the most

severe of all, Portugal has combined a strong employment performance with
a far-reaching recalibration of social protection through reform of unemployment insurance and pension systems, strengthening of the basic safety
net, expansion of active labor market and insertion programs, and sustained
wage restraint, all negotiated through a series of tri- and bipartite social
pacts. In none of these cases, moreover, has the absence of supposed institutional prerequisites such as business coordinating capacity, encompassing
unions, or corporatist traditions proved an insuperable obstacle to the sustained development of new forms of social concertation and negotiated
governance, including in countries such as Ireland and Portugal where these
had never previously existed.[17]

Most national cases, in fact, do not fully correspond to a single pure type
of welfare regime, but comprise instead an idiosyncratic and historically
contingent mix of institutions and programs derived from different models.
Their heterogeneous character emerges even more clearly when we also consider the intersection of divergent industrial relations systems and 'breadwinner' or gender regimes (Lewis 1992, 1997) with the various 'worlds of
welfare capitalism' themselves (Visser and Hemerijck 2001; Ebbinghaus and
Manow 2001; Wincott 2001). Thus the Netherlands, unlike the archetypal
Continental corporatist welfare state, provides a generous basic 'citizen's pension', which has facilitated the rapid expansion of 'atypical' jobs by ensuring
a modicum of old-age security for employees with irregular or interrupted
working careers. France, too, supports higher levels of female employment
and fertility than other Continental welfare states, largely because of the
country's historic commitment to subsidized public childcare, while also
retaining a 'statist' or 'contestational' rather than corporatist system of industrial relations. Both the United Kingdom and Ireland, unlike other Anglo-
Saxon welfare states, maintain universal national health services which are
neither residual nor means-tested, while a number of Southern European
countries such as Italy and Spain have adopted a more decentralized variant
of the same model. And even the ultra-liberal United States still runs major
earnings-related social insurance programs in the form of Social Security
and Medicare for the elderly. As Robert Salais's Chapter 12 demonstrates
using new international data, although the systems of rules governing social
protection in advanced economies are far from uniform, they vary more
by the type of risk covered than by country. Even those OECD countries

---

[17] On the resurgence of social pacts and concertation during the 1990s among European countries lacking the classic institutional prerequisites postulated by neo-corporatist and production
regime theories, see in addition to Chapters 4 and 5 by Ferrera and Hemerijck, and Rhodes, respectively, Rhodes (2001); Fajertag and Pochet (2000); Regini (1997).

most committed to a particular approach (universal, work-related, or means-tested) do not apply it to all social risks, and often combine multiple rules in tackling a single type of hazard such as old age, illness, disability, or unemployment.[18]

Such internal diversity within national welfare states and industrial relations systems may well serve, as Colin Crouch contends, as an adaptive resource in overcoming tendencies towards path-dependency and institutional 'lock-in' highlighted by regime theorists. Thus, as we have already observed in relation to the contribution of hybridization to welfare-state adjustment in the 1990s, what he calls 'mongrel' systems of mixed parentage may prove more robust and adaptable than purebred 'pedigree specimens' or regime types. But at a still deeper level, Crouch suggests, the sheer institutional complexity of most advanced industrial nation-states is likely to provide an alternative range of inherited characteristics which can be drawn upon by reflexive social and policy actors in developing opportunities for innovation when the dominant strand within their national systems no longer appears capable of resolving a particular set of problems (Crouch 2001*a,b*).

This empirical (re)discovery of historical contingency, internal hetero-geneity, and innovative hybridization as pervasive features of the comparative institutional development of welfare states and industrial relations systems points instead to an altogether more positive view of the prospects for cross-national learning and policy transfer than that postulated by the regime theor-ists. Appreciation of shared problems, from this perspective, opens up new possibilities for identifying promising policy solutions or good practices through crossnational comparisons, not only within Europe, but also between the European Union and the United States. Yet, the successful assimilation of models and practices borrowed from elsewhere, as the policy-transfer liter-ature among others emphasizes, demands close attention to national and local differences in institutional context, which may limit their direct applicability.[19] In order to be effectively transferred, most such practices or models must therefore be adapted or even transformed to suit local circumstances and fit with interdependent elements of existing labor market and welfare state

---

[18] Esping-Andersen himself is well-aware that 'there is no single pure case', since most countries contain elements drawn from multiple welfare regimes. But as Wincott points out, he and his fol-lowers nonetheless go on to argue that most national cases fall into one of the three major regime clusters on the basis of the 'over-dominating character of the whole welfare package', a concept which remains unspecified: cf. Esping-Andersen (1990: 28–9); Esping-Andersen (1999: 86–8); Wincott (2001: 417).

[19] For a recent review of the policy transfer literature, which underlines both the potential benefits in terms of crossnational learning and the risks of failure associated with 'uninformed', 'incomplete', and 'inappropriate' transfer, see Dolowitz and Marsh (2000).

institutions.[20] Such an approach in turn requires what Visser and Hemerijck (2001) call 'contextualized benchmarking', based on careful examination of both the institutional environment from which a given policy solution originated and the local conditions surrounding its proposed implementation elsewhere, as opposed to the decontextualized variant more commonly practiced by international organizations such as the OECD, based on the generalization of standard one-size-fits-all models of best practice. This experimental process of crossnational policy borrowing and transformation, moreover, may give rise in turn to the emergence of new 'good practices', whose adaptation to local contexts elsewhere would likewise become a condition for their wider diffusion, thereby setting off an iterative cycle of imitation and innovation which might draw the participants closer together without ever resulting in full convergence between them.

Some promising policy solutions to the problems of reconfiguring work and welfare in a new economy have already begun to travel in opposite directions across the Atlantic—at least at the level of ideas. Among the examples discussed in this book might figure the US Earned Income Tax Credit (EITC) as a solution to the problem of the working poor associated with the expansion of employment in low-wage, labor-intensive services, or European 'flexicurity' policies mandating equal pay and benefits for part-time and temporary workers in exchange for some relaxation of job protection for full-time, permanent employees as a solution to the problem of labor market segmentation between 'insiders' and 'outsiders'. But each of these examples also illustrates the necessity of adapting and modifying policy models borrowed from abroad to suit local circumstances and institutional contexts. Thus as Ferrera and Hemerijck point out in Chapter 4, the EITC has served as an inspiration for new or proposed policy initiatives aimed at containing the rise of the working poor while encouraging the growth of low-wage service jobs not only in liberal states like the United Kingdom and Ireland but also in a number of continental European countries, such as Belgium, France, the Netherlands, and Germany. In the latter cases, however, public subsidies for low-wage jobs have been targeted primarily on reducing employers' social security contributions rather than on topping up workers' incomes, in order to accomplish similar aims to those of the EITC under different circumstances by offsetting the disemployment effects of high payroll taxes and wage floors associated with conservative–corporatist welfare regimes.[21]

---

[20] For parallel arguments in relation to transfer and hybridization of productive models, see Zeitlin (2000); Boyer, Charron, and Jürgens (1998).

[21] For a detailed review of US research on the EITC, see Meyer and Holtz-Eakin (2001). On the German case, where the proposed employment subsidies for low-wage workers have not so far been implemented, see Scharpf (2001a).

And in the United States, similarly, where there are few legal or institutional restrictions on dismissals outside the shrinking unionized sector, the implementation of a 'flexicurity' approach would tend to focus more on improving standards of pay and benefits for 'atypical' or contingent workers than on reducing employment protection for labor-market insiders.[22]

If hybridization of national welfare states and labor-market institutions through intelligent adaptation of policy solutions developed elsewhere is indeed an effective way to blunt the horns of regime-specific adjustment problems like the 'service economy trilemma', then experimentalist governance mechanisms may have a special role to play in facilitating this process. The Open Method of Coordination (OMC) in particular is specifically designed to assist the European Union's Member States in learning from one another how to reconcile full employment, social cohesion, and budgetary stability through a continuous cycle of contextualized benchmarking, peer review, and exchange of good practices.[23] Following this approach, as we have already observed, Member States are expected to compare their progress towards common objectives and targets by adapting jointly agreed European guidelines to national circumstances, to submit their current policies and future plans to reciprocal scrutiny, and to share information about successful experiments which could help to improve each other's performance. Thus for example the Peer Review Programme of the European Employment Strategy (EES), which involves in-depth conferences and study visits on specific good practices hosted by individual Member States, explicitly emphasizes both the importance of understanding the original institutional environment surrounding such policies and the ensuing need for often substantial adaptation in transferring them to different national contexts.[24]

Contrary to the claims of Scharpf (2001c: 19) and others, therefore, the effectiveness of experimentalist governance mechanisms such as the

---

[22] For discussion of US policy proposals aimed at equalizing pay and benefits of part-time and temporary workers with those of their permanent, full-time counterparts, inspired in some cases by European examples, see Barker and Christensen (1998: chapters 11–12) and Carré *et al.* (2000: 16–17).

[23] As Caroline de la Porte and Philippe Pochet remark, the European Union has now introduced an OMC process targeted at each corner of the 'service economy trilemma': the Broad Economic Policy Guidelines (and associated Stability and Growth Pact) for fiscal discipline, the EES for employment growth, and the Social Inclusion process for earnings equality: see de la Porte and Pochet (2002a: 287–9).

[24] As Trubek and Mosher note in Chapter 2, it is still too early to gauge the precise impact of this program and other learning-promoting mechanisms associated with the EES on the participating countries. But a preliminary evaluation by the European Commission concludes that 'although Member States may not necessarily adopt the policies reviewed in an identical form, they are interested in adapting them to their own circumstances. In most cases, Member States have been inspired by their participation in the peer reviews to develop new initiatives or improve existing ones': see European Commission (2001: 3); ÖSB/INBAS (2001).

OMC may be improved rather than impaired by the variety of institutional arrangements and policy legacies among the participating units. In the words of a recent report of a high-level group on industrial relations in the European Union, chaired by Maria João Rodrigues, the 'mother of the OMC': 'Diversity in Europe should be treated as an asset (a natural laboratory for policy experimentation) rather than as an obstacle to integration' (European Commission 2002: 37). Opportunities for mutual learning through comparative exploration of alternative solutions to common problems, on this view, are enhanced rather than diminished by the breadth of variation among the participants because of the wider range of experiences and perspectives on which they can draw. 'Comparison of different projects by publics that are themselves diverse in their composition', Cohen and Sabel contend in Chapter 13, 'makes it possible to examine each concept both in the mirror of the others and from the varying angles presented by differing points of view. This kind of examination has been shown in many settings to bring to light deep flaws in individual projects that remain long undetected when they are pursued in isolation, and to reveal novel possibilities that are missed when many projects are pursued simultaneously but in willful indifference to each other'. The upshot, they conclude in relation to emergent forms of experimentalist governance or 'deliberative polyarchy' on both sides of the Atlantic, is 'to transform diversity and difference from an obstacle to cooperative investigation of possibilities into a means for accelerating and widening such enquiry'.

These last considerations indicate that experimentalist governance arrangements themselves may constitute a promising field for transatlantic learning. Thus the European Union and its Member States may be able to learn something from the United State's predominately bottom–up, horizontal approach to policy coordination, discussed in several of the American chapters in this book, about how to involve a wide range of civil society actors and to develop commonly accepted standards for their participation. The United States, on the other hand, may also have something to learn from the European Union's OMC about how to combine genuine devolution of program design and implementation with accountability of local units while supporting diffusion of promising solutions to common problems in a multi-level system of policy experimentation. In the case of welfare reform, for example, prominent critics of the Temporary Aid to Needy Families (TANF) program have advocated that 'the federal role should not be to impose detailed prescriptions for state approaches' (such as the minimum weekly work requirements for all recipients that the Bush administration is currently proposing to extend), 'but rather to establish national goals and hoped-for-outcomes, and to hold states accountable for making progress towards [them]' (Strawn, Greenberg, and Savner 2001: 235)—a system which if enacted would bear an unmistakable resemblance to the OMC.[25]

1.3. Reading the Volume

The volume proceeds in three parts. Part 1 focuses on experimentation with the work–welfare nexus in the European Union. Taken together, the essays in this section constitute a state-of-the-art overview of reform experiments, policy innovations, and new approaches to governance of work and welfare in the European Union at all levels from the Union through the national to the regional and local. Chapters 2 and 3, by David Trubek and James Mosher and by Janine Goetschy, respectively, closely examine the most important recent EU-level governance experiment, the EES, which has served as the model for the new OMC now emerging as the leading approach to European policymaking in social protection and other politically sensitive areas. After describing the origins, development, and operation of the EES, the authors then assess from different perspectives its practical impact on the Member States and potential contributions to EU social policy. Both Chapters 2 and 3 reach broadly positive conclusions about the EES within the limits of the available evidence. Trubek and Mosher highlight its promise as a novel governance mechanism for the European Union capable of encouraging crossnational learning and partial convergence around common objectives and outcomes without demanding an unrealistic degree of uniformity in policies and institutions, while stressing the desirability of expanded public participation in the process. Although concurring with much of this assessment, Goetschy underscores instead the need to combine the OMC with the more traditional binding instruments of the so-called 'Community Method' like legislation and social dialogue agreements in order to avoid any potential dilution of EU social regulation.

Chapters 4 and 5 deal primarily with developments at the national level. Maurizio Ferrera and Anton Hemerijck begin by surveying the multiple 'recalibration' challenges (functional, distributive, normative, and politico-institutional) facing European welfare states. They then go on to anatomize the different problem loads created by these challenges and the varying responses to them across the four 'Social Europes' or welfare-state clusters

---

[25] For a similar suggestion by the editors of a recent transatlantic volume on comparative federalism that 'the nation-states in Europe are increasingly using their "Union" to implement a principle of mutuality and horizontal "delegation" of competences or authorities from which the "United" States may have a lot to learn', with specific reference to the OMC, see Nicolaidis and Howse (2001: 6, 465–6).

(Nordic, Continental, Anglo-Saxon, and Southern). In each of these clusters, as we have seen, the countries that have adjusted most successfully to these challenges are those like Denmark, the Netherlands, Ireland, and Portugal that have deviated from their original regime type by selectively incorporating new hybrid elements from elsewhere. But the authors also argue that effective recalibration of welfare regimes is clearly underway to a greater or lesser extent across most European countries, including the larger ones, such as Germany, France, Italy, and Spain, where unemployment remains highest and the political obstacles to reform most formidable. Such recalibration, they conclude, has been fostered not only by innovative domestic adaptation of inherited institutional structures to fit new social needs, cultural values, and economic constraints, but also by EU policy initiatives, from Economic and Monetary Union (EMU) to the EES and other OMC processes, which increasingly shape the cognitive orientation, normative goals, and practical options of national reform efforts.

Martin Rhodes considers the national social pacts, which contrary to the expectations of many observers on the right and left alike have played a key role over the past decade in preparing national governance systems to meet the challenges of EMU across many of the EU's Member States. Despite these pacts' past successes in securing wage moderation and negotiated reform of labor markets and welfare states, he identifies a series of internal strains which may threaten their continuing capacity to serve as effective mechanisms for domestic adjustment to external pressures. Prominent among these strains are 'problem overload' or 'linkage stress' arising from the incorporation of an ever-wider range of policy issues and actors into 'augmented' mega-pacts; weakening vertical governability of bargaining systems in the face of intensified pressures for further devolution of negotiations over pay and employment conditions; ongoing tensions between the productivity and distributional aims underlying such pacts; and a resurgence of partisan politics and ideological conflict in several countries. At the same time, however, the imperatives towards continued concertation also remain strong, in terms of the obligation under EMU to sustain price/wage stability and budgetary consolidation, as does national actors' awareness of the high potential costs of unilateral action to achieve these goals. The resolution of these countervailing pressures, the author argues, may vary significantly from country to country, since the functional requirements of EMU are mediated through national institutional structures and politics. But where such national social pacts survive or are resurrected after a period of breakdown, as Rhodes considers probable in most EU Member States, their architecture is likely to become more complex, flexible, and articulated in order to mesh with an emergent double shift in the locus of bargaining towards enhanced cross-border coordination of sectoral demands across the Eurozone on the one hand and increased decentralization of negotiations to the local and company levels on the other.

Chapters 6 and 7 concentrate on developments at the local and regional levels. Ida Regalia explores current trends towards the decentralization of employment protection and labor-market governance through local-level concertation uncovered by a crossnational research project in the five largest European countries (France, Germany, Italy, Spain, and the United Kingdom). Although the 'territorial employment pacts' promoted by the European Union and financed through its structural funds represent the most prominent examples of such sub-national concertation, Regalia also identifies a plurality of parallel experiments, from bilateral contracts between public agencies and private-service providers through multi-employer con-sortia to local and company-level collective bargaining agreements, which differ from one another not only in organizational form, but also in their willingness to depart from the standard model of permanent, full-time employment in defining new rules for regulating the conditions of 'atypical' workers. The long-term success of such experiments, she argues, will depend both on the willingness of local actors to work together in devising joint solutions to common problems, and on the resources and incentives for such cooperation provided by national and European levels of governance, includ-ing *ex post* performance monitoring.

Drawing on the results of a crossnational research project, Adalbert Evers compares the evolution of local and regional labor-market and social inte-gration policies in three large European countries (France, Germany, and Italy), and assesses the influence of recent EU policies aimed at promoting local action for employment. In each of these countries, he reports, the research team found not only a clear trend towards decentralization of admin-istrative competencies but also widespread take-up of key EES concepts such as shifting from passive to active measures, building cooperative partnerships among local actors (including the so-called 'third sector' of community groups and non-profit organizations), and integrating labor-market programs with complementary initiatives in related policy domains like social assis-tance, economic development, and urban regeneration. At the same time, however, the project also uncovered a series of fine-grained local and regional variations across these countries in networks of cooperation, program link-ages, and policy objectives, which highlight the ambiguity of EU concepts such as an 'integrated approach' or 'local partnership' and demonstrate the contin-uing need for flexibility in their application.

Part 2 of the volume focuses on experimentation with the work–welfare nexus in the United States. Joel Handler critically reviews the most important and widely discussed shift in US social policy over the past decade: the end of 'welfare as we knew it' through the conversion of federal matching support for entitlement benefits to poor single-mother families into block grants to the states, with expanded local discretion in the use of these funds subject to stringent work requirements and time-limits for recipients. Although the reported 'success' of local welfare-to-work projects figured prominently in the case for changing national policy, US welfare reform, as Handler shows, has lacked many of the features necessary for promoting learning from decentralized experimentation, such as consistent information reporting, systematic performance monitoring, and rigorous program evaluation. Based on the available evidence, however, he concludes that the majority of welfare leavers have not escaped poverty, while factors other than the reforms themselves such as improved macroeconomic conditions and the increased work incentives provided through the EITC appear to account for much of the dramatic decline in national welfare rolls. Future welfare reforms, Handler contends, should build on those local experiments which have proved most effective in improving recipients' lives and decreasing poverty through a flexible mix of job search, education, training, and work activities, while avoiding punitive sanctions.

Paul Osterman analyzes the national policy problems created by the changing structure of the US labor market and investigates a set of innovative local responses to these challenges. As job tenures have become shorter, internal career ladders have eroded, wage determination has decentralized, and union power has declined, workers increasingly lack institutional supports needed to guide them through a more mobile and uncertain labor market. In the absence of national policy reforms, Osterman observes, some of the most promising labor market initiatives have come from networks of community organizations such as the IAF. Through various combinations of training, employment services, educational reform, living wage campaigns, and political mobilization, he demonstrates that IAF branches across the US Southwest have enjoyed remarkable success in improving the skills, job opportunities, and wages of their poor and disadvantaged constituents, thereby helping to reshape the structure of local labor markets. As a multi-organizational network which seeks to orchestrate and diffuse mutual learning among its members, while linking programatic initiatives with political mobilization, the IAF thus offers a possible model of how new national labor market policies may emerge from local experimentation, a recurrent pattern in US history.

Laura Dresser and Joel Rogers's Chapter 10 likewise takes its point of the departure from the conjoint effects of welfare reform and structural changes in the US labor market, which have expanded the ranks of the working poor while weakening established mechanisms for wage and career progression. In response to these developments, they examine a variety of new 'workforce intermediaries', linked to but distinct from both unions and public agencies, that have arisen at a local level to facilitate career transitions, supply training, and/or guarantee wage floors no longer provided by collective bargaining, legislation, or market forces. These new intermediaries, the authors argue, can help to resolve a range of supply and demand-side collective action problems-besetting US labor markets, while contributing creatively to the governance of work and welfare in a substantially altered economic and institutional context. But generalizing such local experiments to a wider scale, Dresser and Rogers note, would require supportive public policies of various kinds, such as the creation of a national technical assistance infrastructure to diffuse good practice and conditioning firms' access to subsidized training on their participation in the relevant intermediary bodies. The growing salience of these 'workforce intermediaries' in US local labor markets, they conclude, offers new opportunities for reinvigorating American unions, but this promise will not be realized unless unions also expand their understanding of membership beyond certified majorities under exclusive collective bargaining agreements.

In Chapter 11, Louise Trubek addresses innovative programs for providing health care services to low-wage workers which have emerged in Wisconsin and other US states in the wake of welfare reform and the failure of the Clinton administration's national health plan. Taking advantage of enhanced flexibility in federal regulations, BadgerCare and other similar state-level experiments link national Medicaid and children's health insurance programs to employer-funded health plans in order to provide expanded workplace coverage through a managed care system. To resolve the resulting coordination problems, Wisconsin and other states have fostered collaboration among a multiplicity of public and private actors through information-sharing networks and community-based delivery systems, underpinned by privately certified but statutorily required quality assurance standards. These local collaborations and community delivery systems are intertwined with broader government, advocacy, and private foundation networks which promote learning from shared experiences and encourage transfer of knowledge, funding, and influence across states, thereby providing a mechanism for scaling up experimental programs. As in other policy areas, however, Trubek also suggests that these developing forms of horizontal coordination will eventually need to be matched by complementary changes in federal legislation and funding.

The chapters in Part 3 of the volume survey emergent trends and reflect on future possibilities for the governance of work and welfare in a new economy. Robert Salais (Chapter 12) re-examines the effective operation of welfare systems across OECD countries using new international data bases. From this evidence, he finds a surprising degree of convergence in levels of social expenditure (calculated on a net basis including private as well as public benefit schemes). Though the systems of rules governing social protection are plural, they turn out to vary more by the type of risk covered than by country. In Europe as well as the United States, Salais observes that the centrality of participation in work as a foundation for welfare provision is increasing, without necessarily undermining (and in some cases expanding) universality of access to in-kind services. These developments, the author argues, call for a new approach to work and welfare, based on Amartya Sen's concept of 'capabilities', aimed at promoting each person's positive freedom to act and choose, which would entail an expanded conception of work beyond dependent wage labor and a more active and preventative form of security across the life cycle. Such a capabilities approach, he contends, is congruent with current transformations both of work, such as the spread of new forms of organization demanding enhanced responsibility and initiative from individuals and groups, and of welfare, such as the growing personalization of in-kind services and efforts to combat social exclusion by enabling those at risk to acquire all the means necessary for participation in work and community life. Since European countries vary significantly in the extent to which their welfare systems promote capabilities, Salais concludes, the generalization of this approach should be actively pursued by the European Union through the OMC, whereby Member States benchmark themselves against one another and seek to emulate the standards reached by the best performers. To perform this role effectively, however, the OMC would need to develop better indicators for evaluating the quality of work and welfare and to foster a more inclusive public debate on the integration of a capability approach into national social and employment policies.

In Chapter 13, Joshua Cohen and Charles Sabel scrutinize emergent forms of economic and social governance in the European Union from the perspective of democratic theory, focusing on their implications for the relationship between popular sovereignty and redistributive solidarity. They begin by establishing a series of theoretically significant 'facts' about the European Union, which they see as producing a regulatory framework for market integration without sacrificing public health and safety or social protection through new forms of comparison-based governance issuing in open-ended rules, such as comitology and the OMC. The authors then use these 'facts' as a benchmark for assessing four alternative readings of the European Union: as a regulatory technocracy, as a consociational or neo-corporatist association of functional associations, as a cosmopolitan democracy founded on a transnational public sphere, and as a deliberative polyarchy. Each of these readings, they observe, postulates a distinctive relationship between sovereignty and solidarity and between regulation and redistribution, while drawing on a particular view of US experience to buttress its arguments. The first two technocratic and associative readings, Sabel and Cohen contend, fall foul of the 'facts' about the European Union by underpredicting the scope and extent of social regulation on the one hand and the openness of the actors participating in the rule-making process on the other, while also misinterpreting US history. The third public sphere reading, in their view, alternatively ignores and impotently decries the evolving practice of political deliberation within the European Union as increasingly concentrated in delegated regulatory processes beyond the reach of conventional legislative oversight. Although many empirical questions remain unresolved, the authors argue that the progress and proliferation of new governance processes like the OMC in areas such as employment and social inclusion better supports the fourth reading of the European Union as a deliberative polyarchy. In such a polity, sovereignty in the sense of legitimate political authorship is devolved to problem-solving publics, solidarity is understood as mutual dependence and capacitation in addressing common challenges, rules are open and revisable, and redistribution flows from regulation aimed at reducing social risks by reordering markets rather than by correcting their undesirable outcomes. This reading of the European Union, they conclude, draws our attention to parallels with recent US experience of decentralized governance experimentation, such as the court-ordered reform of the Texas public education system, under which state agencies and individual schools themselves are obliged to monitor comparative performance in meeting their constitutional obligation to provide an 'adequate' education to all children and to take appropriate action to correct any shortfall. At the same time, this reading underscores the limitations of many European developments and shows the need to expand participation and accountability in order to ensure that the European Union's emergent deliberative polyarchy is genuinely democratic.

Chapter 14 by Alain Supiot looks beyond Europe and the United States to the broader international economy in a far-reaching reflection on the implications of current transformations of work and welfare for established categories and practices of labor law and social regulation. Increasing openness of borders, he observes, has produced a double movement toward economic globalization and localization which calls into question existing frameworks of solidarity based on the nation-state. One major response to the ensuing challenges, Supiot finds, has been the emergence of new forms of governance or *régulation* as states seek to compensate for their limited cognitive and practical capacities by retreating from fixing substantive rules for the achievement of public goals in favor of establishing general objectives and procedures for their attainment through negotiations among the social partners and other relevant actors. This approach, he notes, has enjoyed considerable success at a national, European, and even international level, as can be seen from examples such as the reform of French labor law through collectively negotiated implementation of framework legislation; the EES, with its EU-wide guidelines and national action plans; and the International Labor Organization's declaration on core labor rights, to be put into practice by each of its Member States in their own way. Yet, the effectiveness of these new approaches to governance, Supiot contends, depends on two fundamental conditions. The first is the existence of an international regulatory authority capable of orchestrating consensus around the objectives to be pursued (as the European Commission has arguably done in the case of the EES) and of determining when national systems of social security and collective bargaining should be exempted from international legal norms of free competition (as the European Court of Justice has also done in a series of well-known cases). The second condition is the restoration of a balance of forces between workers and employers, which the author suggests might be advanced by exploiting the enhanced public vulnerabilities of firms under globalization to influence their social policies through information campaigns, boycotts, and investment pressures by labor organizations in collaboration with consumers, environmentalists, and other advocacy groups. The role of nation-states in the governance of work and welfare, he concludes, is not disappearing but being redefined as their core task shifts from setting domestic rules to incorporating global and local norms into national models. This shift can only operate harmoniously if each country accepts that it has as much to learn from as to teach one other, while eschewing efforts to impose its own rules on the rest of the world. Such mutual learning, Supiot argues, could best be fostered through the creation of an independent social market authority, recognized by all and empowered to adjudicate case by case the disputes arising from the development of international exchange.

The essays in this volume demonstrate that Europe and the United States confront common challenges of responding to the transformations of work and welfare in a new economy. Some older approaches no longer work, and new policies are needed. Given the novelty and complexity of the issues, coupled with the degree of uncertainty concerning the best way to proceed, policy makers in the European Union and the United States have increasingly recognized the need to accept diversity, encourage experimentation, foster collaborative problem-solving, and link multiple levels of governance. The result has been a proliferation of new forms of experimentalist governance based on various combinations of devolved decision-making, information pooling and performance comparison, deliberative exploration of promising solutions, and redefinition of policy objectives in light of accumulated experience. Europeans are systematically studying and debating each others' policies and practices through the OMC, while American states and localities are likewise developing new mechanisms for information sharing and horizontal comparison. Hence, there is now an opportunity to expand the process of mutual learning to the transatlantic region as a whole. The book contributes to this project by tracing parallel trends in governance and showing how new policy options are emerging from such experimentation. Some of these options, like 'flexicurity' and the EITC, have already attracted attention from scholars and policy-makers from the other side of the Atlantic, thereby underlining the potential for future transatlantic learning.

References

AHONEN, P. (2001). 'Soft Governance, Agile Union? Analysis of the Extensions of Open Coordination in 2001', *EIPA Working Paper* No. 18.IV–2001. Maastricht: European Institute of Public Administration.

ATKINSON, A. B. (1999). 'The Distribution of Income in the UK and OECD Countries in the Twentieth Century'. *Oxford Review of Economic Policy*, 15/4: 56–75.

AUER, P. (2000). *Employment Revival in Europe: Labour Market Success in Austria, Denmark, Ireland, and the Netherlands*. Geneva: International Labour Office.

BARKER, K. and CHRISTENSEN, K. (eds) (1998). *Contingent Work: American Employment Relations in Transition*. Ithaca, NY: ILR Press.

BERMEO, N. (ed.) (2001). *Unemployment in the New Europe*. Cambridge: Cambridge University Press.

BOYER, R., CHARRON, E., JÜRGENS, U., and TOLLIDAY, S. (eds) (1998). *Between Imitation and Innovation: The Transfer and Hybridization of Productive Models in the International Automobile Industry*. Oxford: Oxford University Press.

CARRÉ, F., FERBER, M. A., GOLDEN, L., and HERZENBERG, S. (eds) (2000). *Non-Standard Work: The Nature and Challenges of Changing Employment Arrangements*. Champaign, IL: Industrial Relations Research Association.

Commission of the European Communities (2001). 'The Future of Health Care and Care for the Elderly: Guaranteeing Accessibility, Quality, and Financial Viability'. December 5. COM (2001) 723 final. Brussels: The European Commission.

—— (2002). Taking Stock of Five Years of The European Employment Strategy'. July 17. COM (2002) 416 final. Brussels: The European Commission.

Conseil d'Analyse Économique (ed.) (2000). *Réduction du chômage: les réussites en Europe*. Paris: La Documentation Française.

Council of the European Union (2001). 'Joint Report of the Social Protection Committee and the Economic Policy Committee on Objectives and Working Methods in the Area of Pensions: Applying the Open Method of Co-ordination'. November 23.

CROUCH, C. (2001a). 'Problems of the New Determinism: A Re-examination of Path Dependence and Embeddedness Theories'. Unpublished paper Florence: European University Institute, May.

—— (2001*b*). 'Welfare State Regimes and Industrial Relations Systems: The Questionable Role of Path Dependency Theory', in B. Ebbinghaus and P. Manow (eds), *Comparing Welfare Capitalism: Social Policy and Political Economy in Europe, Japan and the US*. London: Routledge, 105–24.

DE LA PORTE, C. (2002). 'The Soft Open Method of Co-ordination in Social Protection', in E. Gabaglio and R. Hoffmann (eds), *European Trade Union Yearbook 2001*. Brussels: European Trade Union Institute, 339–63.

——and Pochet, P. (eds) (2002*a*). *Building Social Europe through the Open Method of Co-ordination*. Brussels: PIE-Peter Lang.

——and POCHET, P. (2002*b*). 'Public Pension Reform: European Actors, Discourses and Outcomes', in C. de la Porte and P. Pochet (eds), *Building Social Europe through the Open Method of Co-ordination*. Brussels: PIE-Peter Lang, 223–50.

DEACON, A. (2000). 'Learning from the US? The Influence of American Ideas upon "New Labour" Thinking on Welfare Reform'. *Policy & Politics*, 28/1: 5–18.

DERTHICK, M. (2001). *Keeping the Compound Republic: Essays on American Federalism*. Washington DC: The Brookings Institution.

DOLOWITZ, D. and MARSH, D. (2000). 'Learning from Abroad: The Role of Policy Transfer in Contemporary Policy-Making'. *Governance*, 13/1: 5–24.

DONAHUE, J. D. and POLLACK, M. (2001). 'Centralization and Its Discontents: The Rhythms of Federalism in the United States and the Europan Union', in K. Nicolaidis and R. Howse (eds), *The Federal Vision: Legitimacy and Levels of Government in the United States and the European Union*. Oxford: Oxford University Press, 73–117.

DORF, M. C. and SABEL, C. F. (1998). 'A Constitution of Democratic Experimentalism'. *Columbia Law Review*, 98/2: 267–473.

EBBINGHAUS, B., and MANOW, P. (eds) (2001). *Comparing Welfare Capitalism: Social Policy and Political Economy in Europe, Japan and the US*. London: Routledge.

ESPING-ANDERSEN, G. (1990). *The Three Worlds of Welfare Capitalism*. Cambridge: Polity Press.

——(ed.) (1996). *Welfare States in Transition: National Adaptations in Global Economies*. London: Sage.

——(1999). *Social Foundations of Post-Industrial Economies*. Oxford: Oxford University Press.

——and REGINI, M. (eds) (2000). *Why Deregulate Labour Markets?* Oxford: Oxford University Press.

ESTEVEZ-ABE, M., IVERSEN, T., and SOSKICE, D. (2001). 'Social Protection and the Formation of Skills: A Reinterpretation of the Welfare State', in P. A. Hall and D. Soskice (eds), *Varieties of Capitalism: The Institutional Foundations of Comparative Advantage*. Oxford: Oxford University Press, 145–83.

European Commission, DG EMPL (2001). 'Employment Strategy: Peer Review Programme 2002–2003'. Brussels: European Commission.

——(2002). 'Report of the High Level Group on Industrial Relations and Change in the European Union'. Brussels, January.

FAJERTAG, G. and POCHET, P. (eds) (2000). *Social Pacts in Europe: New Dynamics*. Brussels: European Trade Union Institute/Observatoire Social Européen.

FERRERA, M. (1998). 'The Four "Social Europes": Between Universalism and Selectivity', in Martin Rhodes and Yves Mény (eds), *The Future of European Welfare: A New Social Contract?* Basingstoke: Macmillan, 79–96.

——, HEMERIJCK, A., and RHODES, M. (2000). 'The Future of Social Europe: Recasting Work and Welfare in the New Economy'. Lisbon: Report for the Portuguese Presidency of the European Union.

Ferrera, M., Matsaganis, M. and Sacchi, S. (2002). 'Open Coordination Against Poverty: The New EU "Social Inclusion Process"'. *Journal of European Social Policy*, 12/3: 227–39.

Freeman, R. (1998). 'War of the Models: Which Labour Market Institutions for the 21st Century'. *Labour Economics*, 5/1: 1–24.

—— (2000). 'Single-Peaked vs Diversified Capitalism: The Relation Between Economic Institutions and Outcomes', *NBER Working Papers* No. 7556. Boston: National Bureau of Economic Research.

Ganssmann, H. (2000). 'Labor Market Flexibility, Social Protection and Unemployment'. *European Societies*, 2/3: 243–69.

Hall, P. A. and Soskice, D. (eds) (2001). *Varieties of Capitalism: The Institutional Foundations of Comparative Advantage*. Oxford: Oxford University Press.

Hemerijck, A. (2002). 'The Self-Transformation of the European Social Model(s)', in G. Esping-Andersen with D. Gallie, A. Hemerijck, and J. Myles, *Why We Need a New Welfare State*. Oxford: Oxford University Press.

—— and Schludi, M. (2000). 'Sequences of Policy Failures and Effective Policy Responses', in F. Scharpf and V. A. Schmidt (eds), *Welfare and Work in the Open Economy, vol. I: From Vulnerability to Competitiveness*. Oxford: Oxford University Press, 125–228.

Hirst, P. and Zeitlin, J. (1991). 'Flexible Specialization vs Post-Fordism: Theory, Evidence and Policy Implications'. *Economy and Society*, 20/1: 1–55.

Hodgson, D. and Maher, I. (2001). 'The Open Method as a New Mode of Governance: The Case of Soft Economic Policy Co-ordination'. *Journal of Common Market Studies*, 39/4: 765–89.

Huber, E. and Stephens, J. D. (2001). *Development and Crisis of the Welfare State: Parties and Policies in Global Markets*. Chicago: University of Chicago Press.

Iversen, T. and Wren, A. (1998). 'Equality, Employment, and Budgetary Restraint: The Trilemma of the Service Economy'. *World Politics*, 50: 507–46.

Jacobsson, K. (2001). 'Employment and Social Policy Coordination: A New System of EU Governance'. Paper for the Scancor workshop on Transnational Regulation and the Transformation of States. Palo Alto: Stanford University, June 22–23.

—— (forthcoming). 'Soft Regulation and the Subtle Transformation of States: The Case of EU Employment Policy', in B. Jacobsson and K. Sahlin-Andersson (eds), *Transnational Regulation and the Transformation of States*.

Kincaid, J. (2001). 'Devolution in the United States: Rhetoric and Reality', in K. Nicolaidis and R. Howse (eds), *The Federal Vision: Legitimacy and Levels of Government in the United States and the European Union*. Oxford: Oxford University Press, 144–60.

Larsson, A. (2002). 'The New Open Method of Co-ordination: A Sustainable Way between a Fragmented Europe and a European Supra State?' Lecture delivered at Uppsala University, March 4.

Lewis, J. (1992). 'Gender and the Development of Welfare Regimes'. *Journal of European Social Policy*, 2/3: 159–73.

—— (1997). 'Gender and Welfare Regimes: Further Thoughts'. *Social Politics*, 4: 160–77.

Meyer, B. D. and Holtz-Eakin, D. (eds) (2001). *Making Work Pay: The Earned Income Tax Credit and Its Impact on America's Families*. New York: Russell Sage Foundation.

Nicolaidis, K. and Howse, R. (eds) (2001). *The Federal Vision: Legitimacy and Levels of Governance in the United States and the European Union*. Oxford: Oxford University Press.

OECD (1994). *OECD Jobs Study*. Paris: OECD.

ÖSB/INBAS (2001). 'Evaluation of Peer Review Programme on Active Labour Market Policy 2000–2001'. Report prepared for the European Commission (DG EMPL), Brussels, October.

PECK, J. (2001). *Workfare States*. New York: Guilford Press.

PIERSON, P. (1995). 'The Creeping Nationalization of Income Transfers in the United States, 1935–94', in S. Leibfried and P. Pierson (eds), *European Social Policy: Between Fragmentation and Integration*. Washington, DC: The Brookings Institution, 301–28.

PIORE, M. J. and SABEL, C. F. (1984). *The Second Industrial Divide: Possibilities for Prosperity*. New York: Basic Books.

POCHET, P. (2002). 'La lutte contre la pauvreté et l'exclusion sociale et la méthode ouverte de coordination', *Revue belge de sécurite sociale*, no. 1, 159-76.

REGINI, M. (1997). 'Still Engaging in Corporatism? Recent Italian Experience in Comparative Perspective'. *European Journal of Industrial Relations*, 3/3: 259–79.

RHODES, M. (2001). 'The Political Economy of Social Pacts: 'Comparative Corporatism' and European Welfare Reform', in P. Pierson (ed.), *The New Politics of the Welfare State*. Oxford: Oxford University Press, 165–97.

RODRIGUES, M. J. (forthcoming). 'The Open Method of Coordination as a New Governance Tool'. *Journal Europa Europe (Fondazione Istituto Gramsci, Rome)*.

ROMANO, C. (2002). 'La Méthode Ouverte de Coordination: Un nouveau mode de gouvernance?' Report prepared for the Task Force on the Future of Europe, Brussels: European Commission, April.

SABEL, C. F. (2001). 'A Quiet Revolution of Democratic Governance: Towards Democratic Experimentalism', in OECD (ed.), *Governance in the 21st Century*. Paris: OECD, 121–48.

——, FUNG, A., and KARKKAINEN, B. (2000). *Beyond Backyard Environmentalism*. Boston: Beacon Press.

——and O'DONNELL, R. (2001). 'Democratic Experimentalism: What to Do about Wicked Problems after Whitehall', in OECD (ed.), *Devolution and Globalisation: Implications for Local Decision-Makers*. Paris: OECD.

SCHARPF, F. (2001a). 'Employment and the Welfare State: A Continental Dilemma', in B. Ebbinghaus and P. Manow (eds), *Comparing Welfare Capitalism: Social Policy and Political Economy in Europe, Japan and the US*. London: Routledge, 270–83.

——(2001b). 'European Governance: Common Concerns vs the Challenge of Diversity' in C. Joerges, Y. Méry, and J. H. H. Weiler (eds), 'Mountain or Molehill? A Critical Appraisal of the White Paper on Governance', *Jean Monnet Working Paper* no. 6. Robert Schuman Centre for Advanced Studies, European University Institute, Florence/the Joan Monnet Program, Harvard Law School and NYU School of Law, 1–12.

——(2001c). 'Notes toward a Theory of Multilevel Governing in Europe'. *Scandinavian Political Studies*, 21/1: 1–26.

——(2002). 'The European Social Model: Coping with the Challenge of Diversity'. Working paper 02/8, Cologne: Max Planck Institute for the Study of Societies.

SCHARPF, F. W. and SCHMIDT, V. A. (eds) (2000). *Welfare and Work in the Open Economy, Vol. I: From Vulnerability to Competitiveness*. Oxford: Oxford University Press.

SIEBERT, H. (1997). 'Labor Market Rigidities: At the Root of Unemployment in Europe'. *Journal of Economic Perspectives*, 11/3: 37–54.

SOSKICE, D. (1993). 'Social Skills from Mass Higher Education: Rethinking the Company-Based Initial Training Paradigm'. *Oxford Review of Economic Policy*, 9/3: 101–13.

——(1999). 'Divergent Production Regimes: Coordinated and Uncoordinated Market Economies in the 1980s and 1990s', in H. Kitschelt, P. Lange, G. Marks and J. D. Stephens (eds), *Continuity and Change in Contemporary Capitalism*. Cambridge: Cambridge University Press, 101–34.

STRAWN, J., GREENBERG, M., and SAVNER, S. (2001). 'Improving Employment Outcomes under TANF', in R. M. Blank and R. Haskins (eds), *The New World of Welfare*. Washington DC: Brookings Institution Press, 223–44.

STREECK, W. (2001). 'High Equality, Low Activity: The Contribution of the Social Welfare System to the Stability of the German Collective Bargaining Regime', *EUI Working Papers* RSC No. 2001/06. Florence: European University Institute, Robert Schuman Center.

SUNDHOLM, M. (2001). 'The Open Method of Co-ordination: The Linux of European Integration?' Master's Thesis, Bruges: College of Europe, Department of Political and Administrative Studies.

VANDENBROUCKE, F. (2001). 'Open Co-ordination on Pensions and the Future of Europe's Social Model'. Closing address to the conference on Towards a New Architecture for Social Protection in Europe? Brussels, October 19–20.

VISSER, J. and HEMERIJCK, A. (2001). 'Learning and Mimicking: How European Welfare States Reform'. Unpublished paper University of Leiden/University of Amsterdam.

WALKER, R. (1998). 'The Americanization of British Welfare: A Case Study of Policy Transfer'. *Focus: Journal of the Institute for Poverty Research of the University of Wisconsin-Madison*, 19/3: 32–40.

White Paper on EU Governance Working Group 4a (2001). 'Involving Experts in the Process of National Policy Convergence'. Brussels: European Commission, June, http://europa.eu.int/comm/governance/areas/group8/report_en.pdf.

WINCOTT, D. (2001). 'Reassessing the Social Foundations of Welfare (State) Regimes'. *New Political Economy*, 6/3: 409–25.

—— (forthcoming). 'Beyond Social Regulation? Social Policy at Lisbon: New Instruments or a New Agenda?' *Public Administration*.

ZEITLIN, J. (2000). 'Introduction: Americanization and Its Limits: Reworking US Technology and Management in Post-War Europe and Japan', in J. Zeitlin and G. Herrigel (eds), *Americanization and Its Limits: Reworking US Technology and Management in Post-War Europe and Japan*. Oxford: Oxford University Press, 1–50.

Part I

Experimenting with the Work–Welfare Nexus: The European Union

2

New Governance, Employment Policy, and the European Social Model

DAVID M. TRUBEK AND JAMES S. MOSHER

2.1. Introduction

Recent actions by the European Union, especially in employment and social policies, reveal an increased use of alternative approaches to governance that are more accepting of diversity and encourage semi-voluntary forms of coordination (Scott and Trubek 2002). This occurs under the traditional Community legislative method, as many recent directives tend to be relatively open and flexible. But the move from top–down, uniform rules to more flexible and participatory approaches can best be seen in areas like the European Employment Strategy (EES), also known as the Luxembourg process, which departs radically from traditional regulatory approaches.

The European Union has endorsed the EES and similar new governance arrangements and dubbed them 'the open method of coordination'. They combine broad participation in policy making, coordination of multiple levels of government, use of information and benchmarking, recognition of the need for diversity, and structured but unsanctioned guidance from the Commission and Council (Mosher 2000; de la Porte 2000a,b; de la Porte, Pochet, and Room 2001; Hodson and Maher 2001; Zeitlin 2001). Because this new type of governance does not rely primarily on top–down command and control-type regulation backed by sanctions, its use has been described as a move from 'hard law' to 'soft law' (Snyder 1994; Abbott and Snidal 2000).

The use of the Open Method of Coordination (OMC) to deal with social policy in general and employment in particular is controversial. Where some see a creative breakthrough that will solve problems heretofore considered intractable, others see another threat to Europe's generous social policies. For the optimists, the EES is not only a methodological breakthrough for the Union, but also an innovation with superior capacity to solve the many social problems Europe faces (Gerstenberg and Sabel 2000; Vandenbroucke 2001).

Others, however, fear that by moving away from efforts to mandate uniform social and employment standards, the Union might contribute to the gradual erosion of Europe's commitment to a distinctive social model (Degryse and Pochet 2000). For the pessimists, the move to soft law is at best a waste of time, and at worst a smokescreen behind which the welfare state might be dismantled.

This chapter examines the EES as an alternative form of governance in the European Union. We ask why the European Union adopted this novel approach, describe its operation, and make an assessment of its impact on national policymaking, its capacity to promote learning and innovation, and its potential impact on the future of European social policy.

2.2. Origins: The Crisis in European Social Policy

The EES emerged from a crisis that came to a head in the mid-1990s. Welfare states were under acute strain, and joblessness had risen dramatically. Defenders of generous social policies in Europe knew that action was needed both to preserve a commitment to expansive benefits, relative wage and income equality, and coordinated bargaining by organized interest groups where they existed and to spread these features where they were missing. This three-fold commitment has been described as the 'European Social Model'. Although the term underplays the diversity among West European states (Esping-Andersen 1990), it is used in official and academic circles and represents a desire to maintain protection in those countries that have advanced welfare states and expand it in those that do not. Reformers who recognized that something needed to be done to sustain and diffuse the 'European Social Model' faced two challenges. The first was the number and magnitude of the tasks they faced: existing unemployment strategies were inadequate, and significant changes in social policy would be needed in most Member States. The second was the scope of the problem and the limits of existing governance methods: it was one thing to recognize unemployment as a common problem demanding a Europe-wide response; it was another to find an appropriate Union level mechanism in the face of substantial resistance to 'Europeanizing' employment policy.

2.2.1. *The Magnitude of the Tasks to be Undertaken*

By the mid-1990s, many Member States faced high levels of unemployment and/or low levels of employment participation as well as the need to restructure labor markets and welfare systems to take account of internal changes and external shocks (Esping-Andersen 1996). These challenges coincided with a paradigm shift in thinking about progressive social policies as Europeans began to realize that the welfare state itself could contribute in some cases to the unemployment problem and that increasing the employment rate was necessary in many places to sustain generous benefits. Two issues helped force this shift. First, in many countries efforts to deal with unemployment by expansion of income maintenance programs and early retirement had led to relatively low levels of workforce participation, thus weakening the fiscal base for the welfare state. Second, methods used to finance welfare state expansion had made it harder to create low-wage jobs and make work pay. Flat-rate social charges to pay for generous benefits deterred low skill employment, and the interaction of benefit and tax systems created employment and poverty traps (e.g. Coron and Palier 2002). Policy-makers began to move away from an exclusive focus on keeping unemployment rates low and started paying more attention to increasing the percentage of the potential workforce actually employed. This drew attention to the low *employment rates* in many continental Member States where low labor-force participation was part of a social equilibrium that secured lower unemployment rates and maintained substantial wage equality while subsidizing inactivity and keeping women at home. However, these low employment rates became increasingly unacceptable as more women desired to work, the welfare without work strategy became discredited, and budget problems developed because of high social expenditures and lowered tax revenues.

For neo-liberals, the solution was simple: problems could be solved, and budgets made more sustainable, by radically cutting back on social protection systems. But this solution was unacceptable to many governments, and in the 1990s several Member States looked for ways to solve employment problems while preserving the European Social Model. That meant finding ways to increase the overall level of employment, not just reduce the number of job-seekers who could not find work. They had to recalibrate welfare state and employment policies to focus on employment rates, be sensitive to the impact of social policy on employment and poverty, and adapt to changes in demography, society, and productive organization. At the same time, they also had to deal with potential external shocks and races to the bottom brought about by the creation of the single market and globalization. All these challenges had to be met in a period of slow economic growth when most countries faced severe budget constraints in the run-up to Economic and Monetary Union (EMU) and in a political environment in which opponents of generous social provision were proposing to dismantle protections and reduce benefits.

2.2.2. *The Limits of European Union Competence and Capacity*

Faced with tasks of this magnitude, and recognizing the Europe-wide nature of the problem, many looked toward the European level as the best place from which to mount an attack on unemployment and a defense of Member State social policies. For some, the solution lay in a strong centralized regime that would reproduce the main elements of the more generous national social models at the European level. Throughout the late 1980s and early 1990s, there were efforts to move in this direction. This strong version of 'Social Europe' was a widely held dream that goes back well into the 1970s. But this vision had never materialized. Despite efforts by the Delors Commission to put social policy and the preservation of the European Social Model into the center of EU policymaking, the actual results were modest; while progress had been made in a few areas of social policy, the Union's role in the social field remained limited (Rhodes 1995). The Social Protocol of the Maastricht Treaty did expand authority for some regulatory forays into industrial relations and social policy, but European competence was carefully circumscribed.

An EU-level solution would not be easy as the Union lacked competence and capacity for such a daunting task. The Member States had always been reluctant to give the Union even limited authority over social policy and industrial relations (Streeck 1995). Moreover, the push for enhanced Europeanization in social policy came just when there was a growing anti-Brussels backlash in many countries and substantial resistance to expanding the European Union's competence in *all* areas. This backlash, which led to the development of the subsidiarity doctrine and threatened the Maastricht Treaty itself, meant that it was difficult for the Union to expand its competence anywhere, let alone in a field so sensitive to national concerns as social policy.

But competence was not the only barrier. The nature of the problems to be faced, the great diversity of policies and practices within Europe, and the deep embeddedness of social policy in unique national institutions made it impossible to craft uniform policies for all of Europe. Added to that, the problems often cut across traditional administrative boundaries and required cooperation among local, regional and national authorities. It is hard for national governments to cope with such 'wicked problems' (Sabel 2000). It would be harder still for the Union, with its limited resources, distance from local government, and circumscribed competence, to tackle such issues on its own.

2.2.3. *Emergence of a Strategy in the 1990s*

The EES developed in the late 1990s as a way for the Union to deal with these daunting tasks in the face of the obvious limits of traditional methods for action at the Union level (Goetschy 1999; Cameron 2001; Kenner 1999). It consisted of a 'soft law' governance mechanism to link the European-level to the national and local levels in policy areas not previously touched by EU policy and a strategy that embodied the new paradigm shift in employment policy. Several interrelated factors contributed to the EES's passage at the Amsterdam Intergovernmental Conference (IGC) in 1997. First, by the late 1990s, the already long-standing employment crisis worsened, and critics began to argue more forcefully that there was a link between European economic integration and layoffs. Second, deft lobbying and maneuvering by the Commission subtly put pressure on the Member States to use the European Union to respond to the crisis. Third, under German pressure, the Member States agreed to sign the Stability and Growth Pact. Some leaders believed that this move could further alienate the public from the European Union unless counterbalanced by action on the jobs front. This dovetailed with the need to respond to increasing criticism that the European Union was not relevant to ordinary citizens. Finally, by the time of the IGC, three new Member States more favorable to EU action on employment (Sweden, Austria, and Finland) had joined the Union and center–left governments had come to power in several of the major Member States (Italy, the United Kingdom, and France). The new French Socialist Prime Minister, Lionel Jospin, was particularly vocal in demanding that the EU focus on employment creation to counterbalance the effects of EMU.

Yet, while all these forces were moving the Union towards some action, many Member States continued to remain reluctant to transfer real policy-making competence to the EU-level. Facing a political impasse, the Member States forged a careful political compromise. The solution was to adapt the multilateral surveillance process developed for EMU to employment policy-making.[1] This process was set up to monitor Member State economic policies

---

[1] The Maastricht treaty set convergence criteria that needed to be met before the Euro could be adopted and before Member States could join. The three main convergence criteria were: (a) a government deficit to GDP (Gross Domestic Product) ratio of no more than 3%, (b) a general government debt to GDP ratio of no more than 60% (or sustained improvement towards this level), and (c) inflation no greater than 1.5% above the average of the three best performing countries. On the one hand, the convergence criteria were relatively straightforward once the relevant statistics were properly computed. A minimum number of states needed to satisfy the criteria before EMU could go forward, and whether a Member State could join depended on whether that Member State met the criteria. However, to meet the criteria, states would need to pursue economic policies at the national level that would gradually lead their economies to satisfy the criteria. It would have been possible to leave to the Member States the entire responsibility for satisfying the convergence criteria. Who met the criteria and who did not, accounting tricks not withstanding, would have been clear. States could have been left on their own to carry out whichever policies they chose and to decide when to implement them to meet the criteria, without any further EU supervision. Instead of this hands-off approach, the more intrusive multilateral surveillance process was established.

and ensure economic convergence in the run-up to monetary union. Member States were required to submit national plans for convergence. The Commission and the other Member States vetted these plans. Peer review and recommendations for corrective action provided an additional push to Member States to pursue the difficult and politically controversial policies that would be necessary. By the time of the Amsterdam IGC, this system was a proven success and offered a model that could be adapted to deal with employment policy. The European Union had already begun to play a modest role in coordinating employment policy in the Essen process (Goetschy 1999; Cameron 2001). By using some of the methods developed for EMU to shape employment policy at EU level, it seemed possible to accommodate pressures for increased action at the EU level with contradictory pressure against expanding EU competence. The result was the Employment Chapter of the Amsterdam Treaty that formally created the EES.

EU leaders did not wait for the ratification of the Amsterdam Treaty to implement the Employment Chapter. In November 1997, the European Council, meeting in Luxembourg and acting by consensus, launched the process envisioned by the Employment Chapter.

In Luxembourg, there was a heated debate on the scope of the guidelines. The Commission proposed a set of guidelines that was more comprehensive and detailed than most Member States were willing to accept. The Council used their power to reject or modify many elements in the guidelines. In the end, the European Council approved 19 guidelines organized into four pillars: *Employability*-policies to make unemployment systems more active and increase the skills of workers; *Entrepreneurship and Job Creation*-policies to encourage new, smaller and more innovative businesses and make tax systems more employment friendly; *Adaptability*-policies to increase the flexibility of workers and work organization arrangements; and *Equal Opportunity*-policies to promote gender equality. Each pillar contained 3–7 guidelines. More recently, 'horizontal objectives' have been added to promote a coherent overall strategy.

2.3. The EES: Process and Strategy

In this section, we describe the overall process and outline key features of the actual strategy the EU has adopted to improve employment performance. Important characteristics of the process are its iterative and multi-level procedures. As a strategy, the EES is focused on the supply-side and supplements other EU and national policies that have a significant impact on employment.

2.3.1. *An Iterative Multi-level, Multi-actor Process*

The implementation of the European Employment Strategy is outlined in Fig. 2.1 and involves several steps (Biagi 2000; Bercusson 2000).[2] In discussions with the Council of Ministers, Member States, the relevant social actors, such as unions and employer's organizations, and academics, the Commission develops general ideas about the best employment strategy for EU Member States to pursue. These are detailed in annual guidelines proposed by the Commission and modified and approved by the Council of Ministers. Each year Member States draw up National Action Plans (NAPs) outlining their response to the guidelines and progress in the prior period. Then the Commission and Council review Member State actions, give recommendations, and plan for a new set of guidelines. An Employment Committee with two members appointed by each Member State and two by the Commission contributes comments on the guidelines, the Joint Employment Report and the recommendations and monitors Member State progress.

The EES is a 'soft law' governance mechanism because there are no 'hard' sanctions to ensure adherence by the Member States to the guidelines. Compliance rests on the assurances made by the Member States to follow the guidelines, supported by multi-lateral surveillance of Member State activities, the possible effect of what some see as 'naming and shaming' mechanisms, the iterative elements of the process, and its capacity to shape the discourse of debate. In theory, the process can shape the discourse by defining the nature of the debate, providing a focal point for views to converge on, shaping the factual knowledge base used in the debate, and managing the diffusion of knowledge (Jacobsson, forthcoming). Some think that the 'softness' of the mechanism makes it more likely that Member States will make commitments to the strategy and submit to EU level coordination in these sensitive policy areas. And it is suggested by some that a 'soft law' mechanism is a superior way to coordinate diverse domestic systems that cannot be steered with overly rigid instruments as well as the best way to create an environment conducive to crossnational policy learning.

The process, if fully implemented, would have several positive features. Because it is iterative and conducted annually, progress can be closely monitored, new ideas introduced, and goals gradually ratcheted up. It should engage many levels of government and involve social actors as well as public

---

[2] Some of the steps we describe are explicitly specified in EU documents. To complement these explicit features we describe other steps that are implicit in the process. In addition, there were proposals in early 2002 to change the timing of the process so that it would be more closely coordinated with the process of developing the Broad Economic Policy Guidelines. Under these proposals, the guidelines would come out in July and the rest of the process would be adjusted accordingly.

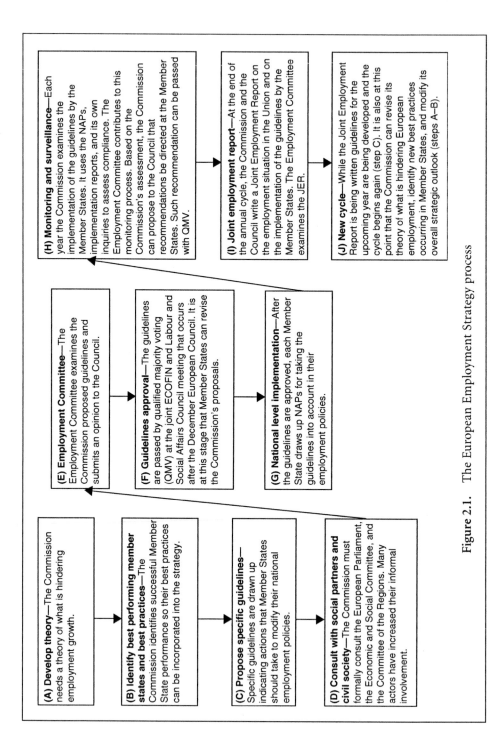

(A) Develop theory—The Commission needs a theory of what is hindering employment growth.

(B) Identify best performing member states and best practices—The Commission identifies successful Member State performance so their best practices can be incorporated into the strategy.

(C) Propose specific guidelines—Specific guidelines are drawn up indicating actions that Member States should take to modify their national employment policies.

(D) Consult with social partners and civil society—The Commission must formally consult the European Parliament, the Economic and Social Committee, and the Committee of the Regions. Many actors have increased their informal involvement.

(E) Employment Committee—The Employment Committee examines the Commission proposed guidelines and submits an opinion to the Council.

(F) Guidelines approval—The guidelines are passed by qualified majority voting (QMV) at the joint ECOFIN and Labour and Social Affairs Council meeting that occurs after the December European Council. It is at this stage that Member States can revise the Commission's proposals.

(G) National level implementation—After the guidelines are approved, each Member State draws up NAPs for taking the guidelines into account in their employment policies.

(H) Monitoring and surveillance—Each year the Commission examines the implementation of the guidelines by the Member States. It uses the NAPs, implementation reports, and its own inquiries to assess compliance. The Employment Committee contributes to this monitoring process. Based on the Commission's assessment, the Commission can propose to the Council that recommendations be directed at the Member States. Such recommendation can be passed with QMV.

(I) Joint employment report—At the end of the annual cycle, the Commission and Council write a Joint Employment Report on the employment situation in the Union and on the implementation of the guidelines by the Member States. The Employment Committee examines the JER.

(J) New cycle—While the Joint Employment Report is being written guidelines for the upcoming year are being developed and the cycle begins again (step C). It is also at this point that the Commission can revise its theory of what is hindering European employment, identify new best practices occurring in Member States, and modify its overall strategic outlook (steps A–B).

Figure 2.1. The European Employment Strategy process

officials. Many levels and units of government should cooperate to produce the NAPs, and the social partners should have opportunities to participate. The annual review process involves discussion between Member State and Commission officials and creates contacts among officials and social partners from different Member States, thus fostering a transnational policy network or 'epistemic community'.

2.3.2. *A Partial Strategy and a Political Compromise*

The EES does not embrace all policies that affect employment. Important areas such as monetary, fiscal, and wage policy that critically affect growth and job creation in the European Union are outside the scope of the process. At the EU level, these are addressed in the Broad Economic Policy Guidelines, the Cologne Process Macroeconomic Dialogue, and/or by the European Central Bank (ECB). As a result, the EES has had to develop largely as a supply-side strategy focusing on altering structural impediments to employment. Nonetheless, the strategy does touch on a much larger number of areas than has ever been addressed at the EU level through traditional social policy regulation. It could be said that the EES gives up the legal force of traditional regulations in order to allow the European Union to deal with some core areas of social policy that were hitherto solely reserved to the Member States.

The overall goal of the strategy is to maintain generous European welfare states by reforming them. The Commission wrote in the preparatory documents for the extraordinary Luxembourg Employment Summit that 'meeting the challenge of insufficient growth and intolerable unemployment *requires a profound modernization* of Europe's economy and its social system for the twenty-first century *without giving away the basic principles of solidarity* which should remain the trademark of Europe' (European Commission 1997—emphasis supplied).

To do that, the guidelines seek to accomplish the following:

(a) Higher Employment Participation—Because of the aging of its population and the threat to pension systems, Europe needs to have a higher proportion of its working-age population working.
(b) More Active Unemployment Systems—Passive unemployment systems allow skills to deteriorate, fail to encourage workers to actively seek work, and do not supply the skills the workers need to find work.
(c) More Skills—Accelerating technological change means that workers need greater skills at the outset and the ability to develop new skills throughout life.
(d) More Employment Intensive Growth—Europe lags behind in the provision of services, which provide employment intensive growth.

(e) Fewer Obstacles to Low Skilled Work—Tax systems, especially high, flat-rate social charges discourage low skilled workers from working and impede employers from hiring them.

(f) Flexibility with Security—The model of a male worker working full-time on a normal work week for one company his entire life must be replaced by a model that allows companies more flexibility in terms of working time, envisions greater heterogeneity in the types of workers (men, women, full-time, and part-time), and supports workers who will shift companies and careers much more often. This new flexibility must be fostered while providing new mechanisms for providing security to workers.

(g) Smaller Companies and Entrepreneurship—The most dynamic areas of the economy are small and medium-sized enterprises, and innovation will be driven by entrepreneurial companies.

(h) Gender Equality—In order to increase employment participation by women and provide equal opportunity, the disadvantages that women face in the labor market must be addressed.

In addition to the individual strategy elements embedded in specific guidelines, the more recent 'horizontal objectives' specify a set of overarching goals that include: (1) specific overall employment rate targets and separate ones for women and older workers in 2005 and 2010; (2) the promotion of quality of work; (3) the promotion of lifelong learning; (4) further incorporation of the social partners into the process; (5) translation of the guidelines into action by the Member States in a balanced and integrated manner; and (6) developing better common indicators to gauge progress.

While the EES rejects radical deregulatory approaches, it bears traces of a compromise between more traditional Social Democratic views and 'Blairite' ideas of a 'Third Way'. It avoids neo-liberal proposals for a radical reduction in income maintenance programs. The stress on working, flexibility, and the role of entrepreneurship in creating jobs embodies the Third Way emphasis on overcoming dependency and shows acceptance of the need to promote risk-taking and adapt social protection to businesses' need for flexibility (Kenner 1999). Nonetheless, the guidelines foresee an important role for the state and for the social partners: they presume that the core of the welfare state will remain in force and do not envision major changes in the organization of industrial relations.

2.4. The Impact of the EES on Member State Policy

Although the EES operates at EU level, its goal is to reduce unemployment by affecting policies and programs at the national level. To assess its effectiveness, one must ask two questions: has the EES played a role in changing national policies, and have the changed policies reduced unemployment and raised the employment rate? Neither question is easy to answer. Where changes in policy can be found, there are always multiple factors at work, including domestic forces and other external influences. And tracing the effect of any policy on macro-variables like employment and unemployment is a tricky business.

Data to answer these questions is hard to come by, but an important resource for evaluation of the EES's impact is the five-year review of the EES process completed in 2002 that includes 'national impact evaluation studies' carried out by the Member States and an 'aggregate assessment of labour market performance at EU level' written by the Commission. In preliminary drafts of its five-year review, the Commission was generally encouraged, albeit with important reservations. It argued that:

[T]he general perception is that the EES strengthened the national policy framework. The annual review and monitoring mechanism, based on indicators, has stimulated Member States to confirm their political commitment in the form of targets. . .It could be concluded that, over the years, the EES triggered a shift in approach from curative thinking towards longer-term thinking.

On the key question of direct impact of the EES on changing national policies, the Commission was clearly guarded, saying:

A number of national reports stress the main employment policy features were already in place prior to the Luxembourg Summit, and that therefore the contribution of the EES to policy formation was limited.

But the Commission did point to some positive examples of EES influence, especially France and Greece.

If we look at impact studies done by individual Member States, we find a wide range of reported effects. At the extremes some countries, like the Netherlands, report little impact because they had already adopted many elements of the strategy while others, like Italy, report little impact because the guidelines do not fit their labor market. The Netherlands had adopted many aspects of the EES strategy before the first guidelines were written, and Dutch employment and unemployment levels were already improving when the EES started. Thus the Netherlands report suggests that the EES had no major effect on its employment policy. It does, however, acknowledge some changes as a result of the EES: these include implementing a preventative policy for medium-term unemployed adults; increasing emphasis on lifetime learning; and improving statistical indicators and monitoring (Zijl *et al.* 2002).

The Italian case makes for a strong contrast. Italy has high unemployment and low employment levels. Its policies fall far short of those called for in the guidelines, and it would benefit tremendously from more effective employment policies. While the report acknowledges that the EES has helped stimulate reform in Italy, it makes a broad attack on the appropriateness for Italy of the specific strategy embodied in the EES, contending that

The EES, while highlighting the need for an organized strategy to support employment and the importance of policy mainstreaming, has simply given particular emphasis to certain concrete guidelines which were not very suited to the often fundamental nature of the Italian structural problems, with respect to the actual labour market. (Italy 2002: 7)

The Italian report questions whether the EES is sufficiently flexible to accommodate very different national contexts and suggests a need for more emphasis on results and respect for subsidiarity. The report says that the guidelines are designed for very different conditions than those Italy faces. This reaction suggests a preference by Italian officials for more neo-liberal measures and more subsidiarity in the EES process.

The French five-year assessment is very different. The Dutch say they like the strategy but reject the idea that they adopted it because of EES, while the Italians question the strategy and thus the wisdom of following the guidelines at all. The French, on the other hand, not only applaud the approach and report that EES has had a substantial impact on French policy and institutional structures; they also claim it has led to real employment gains (France 2002). The French evaluation report argues:

French employment policies are not, in general, the same as they were before the Luxembourg process. To one degree or another, the framework for policy making, the content of policies, methods of implementation, and the role of different actors, especially the social partners, were modified. (France 2002: 4-authors' translation)

The French report states that the EES has reshaped the policy-making process and led to numerous specific policy reforms. It shows how the EES has impacted French policymaking. The guidelines and recommendations have both made a difference. Annual revision of the NAPs has created pressure for greater coherence in employment policy. Indicators have made it easier to monitor performance, and the alignment of the Structural Funds with the EES helped reshape priorities, especially at regional level. The report indicates that France has learned from the good practices of others, citing what was learned from the Finnish program for 'active ageing'.

The report goes on to note several changes in orientation and organization that can be traced to the EES. Thus, France believes that the EES has helped it shift from a short-term to a long-term perspective on employment, give greater emphasis to active and preventive policies, and begin to focus on the employment rate, not just the unemployment rate. At the same time, EES has helped bring about greater cooperation among the various ministries that deal with the employment problem, promoted mainstreaming of gender and social exclusion policies, and reinforced tendencies to devolve employment policy to regional levels. Finally, EES has expanded the social dialogue in France by adding new topics to the traditional labor relations agenda. All this, the report concludes, has led to substantial policy changes. These include expansion of activation policies, introduction of a preventive approach, more employment-friendly tax systems, more incentives for job creation in the service sector, better integration of employment and education policies, and simplification of rules and procedures affecting job creation by smaller enterprises.

What is apparent is that the impact of the EES on Member State policy choice varies significantly across countries. Some countries made few changes either because that was all that was required based on their advanced starting point or because many of the changes required were deemed inappropriate in their context. Other countries made many more changes. The extent of impact also varies significantly across policy areas covered by the guidelines. We see much more change under the guidelines that require a shift to a preventative unemployment policy and an increase in the use of active unemployment policies than we do in those that call for taxation systems to be more employment friendly. The explanation lies both in the structure of the guidelines and the politics of policy change. The guidelines on preventative employment policies and activation are specific, they include quantitative indicators, and there is less political opposition to these reforms. On the other hand, the tax reform guidelines are much more general, it is easier to make it appear as if some change has occurred even if not motivated by the EES, and mandates for tax changes by the European Union often generate sharp political resistance by Member States. A general conclusion to draw is that an uneven impact on Member State policymaking across countries and policy areas seems to be a key characteristic of the EES process.

The most difficult question of all is whether, to the extent the EES is followed, it has helped lower the unemployment rate and increase levels of employment participation? The Commission's five-year review suggests that progress has been made during the past five years, noting that recent economic growth in the European Union has been far more employment intensive in the 1990s than it was in the 1970s and 1980s. But these effects cannot yet be directly traced to the EES. In addition, there is controversy about the direct impact of specific aspects of the strategy, such as its emphasis on activation, which may turn out to be less effective than proponents had hoped.

2.5. Does the EES Promote Policy Learning?

One of the strongest claims made for the EES, in contrast to more traditional forms of governance, is that it will promote policy learning (Ferrara,

Hemerijck and Rhodes 2001; Esping-Andersen *et al.* 2001). If the EES is a better way to generate new ideas for how to deal with the employment problem and diffuse those ideas from one part of Europe to another, it would clearly be an important addition to the European Union's tool kit. There is an important literature promoting the view that governance systems that promote learning can be preferable to traditional regulatory approaches (Sabel 2000; Dorf and Sabel 1998; Teague 2001). If the EES's adoption of a 'soft law' approach facilitates learning that might not otherwise occur, it would constitute a strong argument both for continuing this system and for employing its methods in other policy domains (Scharpf 2001).

To be sure, the architects of the EES have never placed great stress on the learning dimension. Both the Commission and the European Council have put more emphasis on the EES as a tool for policy convergence. The design for the five-year assessment process did not directly mention learning as a factor to be considered and the Commission's first communication summarizing results of the assessment described the EES as 'management by objectives', suggesting a very different vision than one that stresses bottom-up learning processes. (European Commission 2002). But both Council and Commission have from time to time expressed hopes that the system will produce learning. And in a recent statement, Juhani Lönnroth, Deputy Director-General of Employment and Social Affairs in charge of the EES, emphasized convergence of outcomes over policy convergence and put more stress on learning mechanisms such as benchmarking (Lönnroth 2000).

To assess this feature of the EES, we think it useful to identify three types of learning. Following Peter Hall (1993) we distinguish among learning that (1) fine-tunes existing policy instruments; (2) keeps goals intact but modifies instruments; and (3) leads to a change of the goals themselves (see also Zijl *et al.*, 2002). To see if the EES has promoted learning, and of what type, we employ three methods: we look at the process itself to see if it contains learning-producing mechanisms; we look at evidence of change within the strategy, and we review the only available study of EES as a learning mechanism.

2.5.1. *Assessment of Policy Learning in Process*

The EES contains many features that could promote policy learning. The literature identifies a number of governance mechanisms that promote learning and innovation (Sabel 1994; Easterby-Smith *et al.* 2000). These include mechanisms that destabilize existing understandings, bring together people with diverse viewpoints in settings that require sustained deliberation about problem-solving; facilitate erosion of boundaries between both policy domains and stakeholders; reconfigure policy networks; encourage decentralized experimentation; produce information on innovation; require sharing of good practice[3] and experimental results; encourage actors to compare results with those of the best performers in any area; and oblige actors collectively to redefine objectives and policies.

The EES contains all these elements to one degree or another. The guidelines and the underlying strategy they reflect do, to varying degrees, challenge national policies in many countries and thus should destabilize prior understandings. The process is designed to create ongoing policy dialogues engaging diverse groups and crossing boundaries within government, between government and social partners, among actors from different countries, and between localities, national governments, and Union-level actors and institutions. For example, representatives of the Member States and the Commission meet regularly in the Employment Committee discussing employment policy and dealing with issues specifically assigned to them by the Commission and the Member States such as improving quantitative indicators. An *Ad Hoc* Working Group of the Employment Committee meets more intensively than the Employment Committee to deal with selected issues. All the forms of dialogue are repeated on an annual basis and so should encourage continued deliberation.

Member States provide detailed information on their unemployment-reduction efforts, share good practices, and comment on each other's annual plans. There are benchmarking mechanisms that encourage Member States to measure their performance against that of the best performers in the Union and the world. Through peer review and exchange of good practices, each Member State directly confronts the plans and experiences of others, thus acquiring benchmarks against which they can measure their own performance. The Commission and the Council regularly review the national plans and provide comments and recommendations: these are often based on comparisons with the best performers and create additional benchmarks for each Member State.

Moreover, the EES process is iterative and iteration fosters deliberation. The guidelines can be and are changed from time to time so that new information and ideas can be incorporated. Since changes in the guidelines involve discussions with Member States and Social Partners, it sets in motion deliberations that may themselves bring new ideas and information to light. The process brings together actors from different parts of many national governments and social partners from various levels who interact with the Commission; in this way it could promote the further development of a policy community examining employment issues that links multiple levels of governance.

---

[3] The Commission has shifted from exclusively using the term 'best practice' and now commonly uses the term 'good practice'.

The existence of such learning-promoting mechanisms suggests that the EES has real potential. But the learning will not occur unless these mechanisms are used, and used effectively. A preliminary glance suggests that the EES has yet to realize the full potential of the learning mechanisms it has embraced. Look, for example, at the obligation placed on Member States to share good practices. Beginning with the second annual cycle of NAPs, Member States have been required to present examples of good practice. But this dimension of the strategy is not particularly robust. While a few practices are highlighted in the Joint Employment Report, the primary method for practice exchange is in review of the NAPs of other nations: these are circulated to all the Member States. Yet, the section on good practices appears only in an appendix at the end of the reports, usually is only 2–3 pages in length, and normally provides only a few examples. After the first few years of the process, the Commission has begun to supplement good practice reporting in the NAPs with peer review conferences on good practices in individual Member States. By the fifth year of the EES process, a large number of these conferences were being held. The five-year assessments report some instances in which these exchanges had positive results, but participants differ in their evaluation of their value and it is too early to reach a final judgment on this aspect of the EES.

Similar concerns can be raised about the mutual surveillance ('Cambridge review') process, another learning method that on its face seems very promising. Each year, Member States present their NAPs to all the others and are required to comment on each other's plans. But less than an hour is allocated for the entire session on each National Plan, including a presentation by the Member State, comment by two other states, and discussion. It is hard to imagine that so truncated a session could produce an in-depth assessment or offer very much useful feedback.

2.5.2. *Evidence of Change*

A second way to measure learning is to observe changes in policy over time and see if these changes can be attributed to new understandings brought about by learning-promoting mechanisms. If we look at the guidelines themselves, we see significant change taking place at least in part due to the learning-promoting mechanisms. While the Commission has been reluctant to make radical changes in the guidelines for fear of creating confusion, there were important shifts between the 1998 and the 2001 guidelines. Some of these changes can be seen as an effort to refine the original guidelines in light of experience, the first level of learning, while others really introduce new objectives and set new targets, the second level of learning. In both cases, it appears that some of the changes came about because exchange of information and deliberation within the EES process brought new ideas to the fore. One could even argue that the addition of targets for increasing the employment rate significantly represents a degree of 'third level' learning as Member States came to see how central this goal was to their overall objectives.

Of course, whether learning occurs at the national or local level is the crucial test. But comprehensive information about learning induced by the EES at these levels is not available. The Commission did not make an examination of EES-promoted learning an explicit part of the five-year national evaluation studies—a clear sign that the Commission does not always place learning at the center of its thinking about the EES even if this may be its most important feature. However, the Dutch in their report did recognize the policy-learning potential of the process and made it an important and explicit part of its review. The Dutch report indicates that disentangling learning induced by the EES from the many other sources of learning is difficult. For example, ideas embodied in the EES have been discussed by the relevant actors in the Netherlands, but these ideas are also present in other sources. The report does indicate that the Netherlands is taking more of a comprehensive approach to employment policy and that the EES has played a significant role in this change. This represents the second type of more comprehensive learning.

From this analysis it seems clear that the EES includes significant learning-promoting mechanisms; these mechanisms are working to some degree, although limited primarily to the first two levels of policy learning; and the learning that results is affecting policy development at the Union level and at least to a modest degree at the national-level. But there are obstacles to the EES developing into an effective learning instrument. The number of domestic policy-makers involved in the EES process is limited in many member states. Some Member States treat the NAPs as a bureaucratic reporting task, not an opportunity for policy reflection (Jacobsson 2002). While the process does produce a large amount of information allowing for cross-national comparison, it is not clear how often this information is being used.

While there has been a modest level of learning so far, it may be that the EES is only now reaching the stage of 'learning take-off'. For instance, the national evaluation studies and the EU-level transversal studies that were completed in 2002 represent a dialogue with a diverse set of options and conclusions about both the structure of the process and the contents of the strategy. This might lead to important future policy learning and policy change, especially if the Commission were to pay more attention to this aspect of the EES.

2.6. Overall Assessment: Creating New Governance
Mechanisms and Developing a European Social Model

In this section, we ask two basic questions: how successful has the EES been in constructing a new form of governance, and to what degree is it likely to contribute to efforts to develop a European Social Model based on generous social benefits?

2.6.1. *Assessing a New Governance Mechanism*

The EES embraces five major governance objectives: promote learning; enhance coordination among levels of government; integrate separate policy domains; enhance participation; and promote convergence while allowing diversity. We have already analyzed the first goal—promote learning—in Section 2.5 above. Here we comment on the others:

(a) *Coordinate actions of multiple levels of government.* Effective labor-market reform, and other aspects of a successful employment strategy, must be implemented at local and national levels, which in turn must be aligned with European-level programs and policies. Thus, an effective strategy should include ways to engage multiple levels of government in a common enterprise.

The very existence of the EES, with its national plans and Europe-wide guidelines, is evidence that efforts are being made to integrate the several levels. Seen as one of many approaches to multi-level integration, EES has several cardinal features. First, most of the policies must be carried out at the national or regional level: there is relatively little the EU organs themselves can do directly to reduce unemployment. The exception is the modest use of structural funds to support the EES. Second, the European Union's primary role in the system is to construct the broad strategy, develop specific guidelines, monitor performance, and call for periodic adjustments. To the extent that institutional or legal reform is needed, and money must be spent, these are to be done largely at the national or even the regional level. And the European Union is especially eager to encourage action at the (sub-national) regional level because this is the level at which the most innovative activity seems to take place.

It is clear that the EES has created a formal mechanism to coordinate the local, national, and Union levels. The issue is how effective this coordination is in practice. We know it is far from perfect: some Member States have failed to respond to Union-led efforts to change national policies and there is concern that regional and local governments have not been adequately integrated into the process. But we have also seen that some change is occurring at all levels, thus suggesting that the new machinery offers promise.

(b) *Cut across policy domains.* A major feature of the employment problem, like many other social issues, is that it involves several policy domains and cuts across institutional boundaries. For example, to create more jobs, it is necessary both to foster entrepreneurship and upgrade workers' skills. And these efforts should be coordinated. But, traditionally, enterprise promotion and worker training have been handled by different agencies and operated independently. And as the guidelines themselves demonstrate, there are many other areas where boundary-crossing efforts are needed.

Even a casual look at the guidelines and the NAPs shows that the EES has successfully identified a number of important areas where agency and policy domain boundaries must be crossed, and set forth policies that require cooperation of several agencies at the national level. These include such key areas as:

- *jobs and taxes*: an obstacle to creating jobs in many countries are the high social costs employers must pay but changing this situation requires action both by labor and finance ministries;
- *equal opportunity for men and women*: this goal requires an increase in child care services (Social Affairs); changes in tax systems that penalize women's participation in the labor force (Finance); and introduction of more flexible forms of employment arrangements (Labor; social partners).

But are they cooperating? Evidence is mixed. In 2000, the Commission expressed concern about the degree of real cooperation (European Commission 2000: 89). By 2002, things were looking up. In the five-year assessments, France and other Member States report substantial improvement in inter-ministerial co-operation, and the Commission review indicates that the EES has had an influence on such policy fields as social exclusion, education and training, fiscal policy and family policy. But these effects are not uniform across the 15 Member States.

(c) *Enhance participation and ensure functional representation.* Since the development and effective implementation of successful policies will require the co-operation of, and action by, employers and worker representatives, and since policies will require public input and public support at the national level, any successful employment strategy-making process needs to ensure broad participation of the public and effective representation of the social partners.

Initially, this was a problem in the operation of the EES. There is evidence that in the early years there was little participation by the social partners in the shaping of the guidelines and the NAPs.[4] Recently, however, some efforts

---

[4] The EES anticipates two types of participation by the social partners. The first is participation at the EU and national levels in writing the guidelines, EU reports, and the NAPs. The second is participation in implementing the guidelines on work reorganization. The Commission has attempted to increase participation of both types and in both areas has been only moderately successful.

have been made to ensure broader and more effective participation at the European level. At the national level, some unions report favorably on their participation in the process of writing the NAPs, but many still complain of having only very minimal input (ETUC 2001). At present, the EES still remains heavily driven by a bureaucratic core in the Commission and the national labor ministries.

(d) *Encourage partial convergence while accommodating diversity.* Although all EU Member States share some common problems, the extent of the problems varies from state to state. Because the legal rules and institutional structures in industrial relations and social policy of the 15 Member States are extremely varied yet deeply embedded, any effort to demand uniformity would be unrealistic. Nonetheless, the Commission and the European Council have made clear that the EES is designed to produce *convergence* at least in some areas. But what is sought at least so far is *partial* convergence on a *partial* strategy. Moreover, to the extent that the EES does seek convergence, it is generally a convergence of outcomes, not of policies. Many of the guidelines set targets for results and let the Member States choose the best means to reach those results. Finally, the Strategy is designed more to encourage Member States to change than to force them to do so and, while the Council does issue recommendations from time to time, there are no hard sanctions for failure to follow the guidelines. Nonetheless, the Commission's five-year review found clear evidence of some convergence. Member States that had already adopted the EES's active labor market principles continued down that path while other countries began to move in the same direction (European Commission 2002). The Commission noted that peer review of good practices and recommendations have contributed to the convergence process.

2.6.2. *The EES, the Politics of the Welfare State, and the Future of a Generous European Social Model*

The final question to look at is the potential effect of the EES on the debate over the future of the European Social Model. Views range from calls to deregulate labor markets and roll back benefit systems to demands that existing generous social systems be maintained largely intact. In between lie those who support generous protections but recognize the need for some change. Modest reformers of this type accept the need to reallocate funds to serve previously excluded groups, rethink strategies to increase employment, find ways to accommodate new types of work and workers, combine security with flexibility, and recalibrate benefits to avoid fiscal crises (Levy 1999). Their agenda overlaps with the strategy of the EES. The issue is: to what degree will the presence of the EES help the efforts of the modest reformers in political struggles over the future of the welfare state?

This question will largely be decided at the national level. Despite some Europeanization in social policy, most of the final decisions on the future of the welfare state will be taken by national governments. So what are the prospects that this mechanism will have a significant impact on the outcome of national debates?

The EES cannot significantly affect the balance of power in a given Member State. True, Member States make some tentative commitments to a modest reform agenda by accepting the guidelines, but it is unlikely this would deter a powerful right-wing government intent on rolling back the welfare state. In other political configurations, however, ideas and strategies developed at the European level through the EES process can help bring about significant change in national laws, policies, and budgetary allocations. In the easiest case, the EES may point to strategies that improve conditions for everyone and thus can gain very widespread support. But the EES could also have an effect in cases where there are some divisions on welfare state issues. Thus, in a country where political support for the welfare state is strong, but supporters are split between those who accept the need for recalibration and those who oppose any change whatsoever, the EES can strengthen the hand of the moderate reformers. Similarly, in situations where the dominant political actors accept the need for some reform, the EES can help shape the strategies that are selected. Finally, the EES could be used by unions, NGOs, and other national-level actors as support for reform measures they favor.

Where the EES is more likely to have impact is in cases where there is support for the welfare state and the political choices are between the *status quo* and modest 'recalibration'. The EES encourages states to redirect existing resources to women, the unemployed, and other groups previously not well served. It promotes efforts to preserve the fiscal base needed for a generous welfare system by encouraging policies that will increase the percentage of working age adults who are in the workforce and paying into the system, rather than out of it. It encourages efforts to get more people in the workforce by upgrading skills across the board but with special emphasis on new entrants, the unemployed and those in low skill jobs. While all of these measures have substantial support, they will also meet resistance from those who are afraid that any change is likely to lead to more radical cuts, as well as those who may lose from a redirection of welfare state services and resources. In such situations, the EES can provide domestic leaders and other domestic political actors in favor of moderate reform with arguments for the necessity of change as well as show that other countries have successfully made these changes without having the whole system unravel.[5]

The EES can be especially effective if it were to lead to more efficient ways to use existing resources or provide guidance to people who accept reform but are unsure of how to proceed. Policy learning might produce win–win situations in which some can benefit at no cost to others, or where gains are so large that modest cost increases or losses to some can be accepted. And ideas contained in the EES can channel reform efforts when there is genuine doubt as to how best to accomplish reform goals and reformers are uncertain how to proceed.

2.7. Conclusion

The establishment of the European Employment Strategy with its novel governance arrangements may represent the beginning of a substantial shift in both European social policymaking and in EU governance. It has been touted as a 'third way' in EU governance to be used when harmonization is unworkable but mutual recognition and the resulting regulatory competition may have unwelcome consequences (Mosher 2000; Larsson 2000; Ferrara, Hemerijck, and Rhodes 2001). At the Lisbon Summit the European Council recognized the EES as an important governance innovation and indicated that in the future similar 'open methods of coordination' would be used in several domains of social policy and other areas as well (Portuguese Presidency 2000; de la Porte, 2002). The EU's new White Paper on Governance recognizes the importance of the open method, albeit with some reservations.

While the OMC remains controversial, and its operation still not fully understood, it seems clear that the European Union will continue to employ this method for the governance of social policy. Our study of the EES, which is the oldest and most developed of the OMCs now in operation, suggests that the OMC has potential in certain areas of policy making but that its potential has not yet been fully realized. Further work is needed to determine the conditions most appropriate for open coordination, the reforms needed to make the method most effective, and the relative importance of 'soft' methods like OMC and more traditional, 'harder' forms of EU-level regulation.

The OMC is an appropriate tool to use in situations when common problems exist across Europe but conditions make uniform policies impossible

---

[5] For an example of the EES dovetailing with domestic moderate reform efforts, note how its emphasis on increasing the employment rate of older workers reinforces the controversial arguments in favor of reducing early retirement in the 'Plein emploi' report to the French government on employment policy by Jean Pisani-Ferry (2000).

and there is great uncertainty concerning the best way to deal with problems. In such situations, a learning-producing system that engages multiple levels, promotes dialogue, cuts across traditional boundaries, and fosters local experimentation could produce better results than directives or other binding and more or less uniform solutions. We have seen that the EES has some of these features. But for the EES fully to perform in this way, it will be necessary to improve its learning-producing capacities, increase effective participation, and ensure more real buy-in by all Member States.

A final question is the relationship between soft law processes like the EES and any future 'hard law' initiatives in social policy at the EU level. Some believe that to preserve the European Social Model it is necessary to have specific standards for social protection enshrined in EU law. Others think that it would be better to create broad but mandatory principles at European Union level but give the Member States discretion in how they satisfy these principles. In the first case the OMC would seem a doubtful route to take; in the second it would have to be combined with hard law mechanisms like framework directives or even enforceable social rights (Scharpf 2001; Sciarra 2000). Either way, it would be important to delimit the scope of soft law mech-anisms so they do not preclude hard legislation when that is needed.

To assess this set of issues, one would need a more robust theory of this relationship than we have today. The EES was not adopted after a careful study of all alternative paths; it was chosen as a pragmatic accommodation to limited competence, regulatory impasse, and a lack of workable uniform solutions. While we understand the concerns of those who fear 'soft law' might drive out hard law, our study suggests that the process may have positive features that could make it a superior approach in many cases. Therefore, until we develop a more comprehensive theory of governance that embraces both hard and soft options, see if the flaws in the EES process can be ironed out, know more about the nature of the employment problem, and better understand the effects of the EES, it would be premature to draw bright lines around this promising experiment.

References

Abbott, K. W., and Snidal, D. (2000). 'Hard and Soft Law in International Governance'. *International Organization*, 54/3: 421–56.

Bercusson, B. (2000). 'The European Employment Strategy and the EC Institutional Structure of Social and Labour Law'. Presented at the conference on Legal Dimensions of the European Employment Strategy, SALTSA/Swedish National Institute for Working Life, Brussels, October 9–10, 2000.

BIAGI, M. (2000). 'The Impact of the European Employment Strategy on the Role of Labour Law and Industrial Relations'. *The International Journal of Comparative Labour Law and Industrial Relations*, 16/2: 155–73.

CAMERON, D. (2001). 'The Europeanization of Employment Policy: Creating a New Mode of Governance in the EU'. Prepared for Presentation at the European University Institute, March 2001.

CORON, G. and PALIER, B. (2002). 'Changes in the Means of Financing Social Expenditure in France Since 1945', in C. de la Porte and P. Pochet (eds). *Building Social Europe through the Open Method of Co-ordination*. Brussels: PIE Peter Lang.

DE LA PORTE, C. (2000a). 'The Novelty of the Place of Social Protection in the European Agenda in 1999 through "Soft Law"'. Presented at the workshop on New Governance Process in the EU, July 12, 2000, Brussels.

—— (2000b). 'The Instruments of "New Governance" for Analyses and Policy-making in the EU'. Manuscript.

—— (2002). 'Is the Open Method of Co-ordination Appropriate for Organizing Activities at European Level in Sensitive Policy Areas?' *European Law Journal* 8/1: 38–58.

——, POCHET, P., and ROOM, G. (2001). 'Social Benchmarking, Policy-Making and the Instruments of New Governance in the EU'. Manuscript.

DEGRYSE, C. and POCHET, P. (2000). 'The Likely Impact of the IGC on European Social Policy'. *IGC Info, Observatoire Social Européen Electronic Newsletter on the Intergovernmental Conference*. 3 (November 2000).

DORF, M. C. and SABEL, C. F. (1998). 'A Constitution of Democratic Experimentalism'. *Columbia Law Review*, 98/2: 267–473.

EASTERBY-SMITH, M., CROSCAN, M., and NICOLINI, D. (2000). 'Organisational Learning: Debates Past, Present and Future'. *Journal of Management Studies*, 37/6: 783–96.

ESPING-ANDERSEN, G. (1990). *The Three Worlds of Welfare Capitalism*. Princeton, New Jersey: Princeton University Press.

—— (1996). 'After the Golden Age? Welfare State Dilemmas in a Global Economy', in Gosta Esping-Andersen (ed.), *Welfare States in Transition: National Adaptations in Global Economies*. Sage Publications.

——, GALLIE, D., HEMERIJCK, A., and MYLES, J. (2001). 'A New Welfare Architecture for Europe?' A Report submitted to the Belgian Presidency of the European Union.

ETUC (European Trade Union Congress). (2001). 'Luxembourg Process: ETUC Employment "Fiches"'. Manuscript.

European Commission. (1997). *An Employment Agenda for the Year 2000: Issues and Policies*. www.europa.eu.int/comm/employment_social/summit/en/papers/emploi2.htm.

—— (2000). *Joint Employment Report 2000, Part I*.

—— (2002). *Taking Stock of Five Years of the European Employment Strategy*. Brussels, July 17, 2002. COM (2002) 416 Final.

FERRERA, M., HEMERIJCK, A., and RHODES, M. (2001). *The Future of Social Europe: Recasting Work and Welfare in the New Economy*. Oxford: Oxford University Press.

FRANCE. (2002). *Evaluation de la strategie europenne pour l'emploi*. http://www.europa.eu.int/comm/employment_social/news/2002/may/eval_en.html

GERSTENBERG, O. and SABEL, C. F. (2000). '*Directly-Deliberative Polyarchy: An Institutional Ideal for Europe?*', in C. Joerges and R. Dehousse (eds). *Good Governance in Europe's Integrated Market*. Oxford: Oxford University Press, 289–341.

GOETSCHY, J. (1999). 'The European Employment Strategy: Genesis and Development'. *European Journal of Industrial Relations*, 5/2: 117–37.

HALL, P. (1993). 'Policy Paradigms, Social Learning, and the State: The Case of Economic Policymaking in Britain'. *Comparative Politics*, 25/3: 275–96.

HODSON, D. and MAHER, I. (2001). 'The Open Method as a New Mode of Governance: The Case of Soft Economic Policy Coordination'. *Journal of Common Market Studies*, 39/4: 719–46.

ITALY. (2002). *Impact Evaluation of the European Employment Strategy: FINAL REPORT (Draft)*. http://www.europa.eu.int/comm/employment_social/news/2002/may/eval_en.html

JACOBSSON, K. (2002). 'The Open Method of Coordination at Work: The Swedish Case', Paper Presented to the OSE-SALTSA-EU Center Conference on 'The OMC: An Effective and Legitimate Instrument for EU Governance?' Brussels, 16–17, June.

—— (forthcoming). 'Soft Regulation and the Subtle Transformation of States: The Case of EU Employment Policy', in B. Jacobsson and K. Sahlin-Andersson (eds). *Transnational Regulation and the Transformation of States*.

KENNER, J. (1999). 'The EC Employment Title and the "Third Way": Making Soft Law Work?' *The International Journal of Comparative Labour Law and Industrial Relations*, 15/1: 33–60.

LARSSON, A. (2000). 'The European Employment Strategy: a New Field of Research'. Presented at European Society of the London School of Economics, Monday, January 17, 2000.

LEVY, J. (1999). 'Vice into Virtue? Progressive Politics and Welfare Reform in Continental Europe'. *Politics and Society*, 27/2: 239–73.

LÖNNROTH, J. (2000). 'The European Employment Strategy, a Model of Open Co-ordination: and the Role of the Social Partners'. Presented at the Conference on Legal Dimensions of the European Employment Strategy', SALTSA/Swedish National Institute for Working Life, Brussels, October 9–10, 2000.

MOSHER, J. (2000). 'Open Method of Coordination: Functional and Political Origins'. *ECSA Review*, 13/3: 6–7.

PISANI-FERRY, J. (2000). *Plein emploi*. Paris: La Documentation française. http://www.ladocfrancaise.gouv.fr/fic_pdf/30a.pdf

PORTUGUESE PRESIDENCY. (2000). 'Presidency Conclusions'. Lisbon European Council, March 23 and 24, 2000.

RHODES, M. (1995). 'A Regulatory Conundrum: Industrial Relations and the Social Dimension', in S. Leibfried and P. Pierson (eds). *European Social Policy: Between Fragmentation and Integration*. Washington DC: Brookings Institution.

—— (1998). 'Globalization, Labour Markets and Welfare States: A Future of "Competitive Corporatism?"', in M. Rhodes and Y. Meny (eds). *The Future of European Welfare: A New Social Contract?* London: Macmillan.

SABEL, C. (1994). 'Learning by Monitoring: The Institutions of Economic Development' in Smelser & Swedberg (eds), *The Handbook of Economic Sociology*. Princeton: Princeton University Press.

SABEL, C. (2000). 'A Quiet Revolution of Democratic Governance: Towards Democratic Experimentalism'. Presented at the EXPO 2000, OECD Forum on the Future, Conference on 21st Century Goverance, Hannover, Germany, March 25 and 26, 2000.

SCHARPF, F. W. (2001). 'European Governance: Common Concerns versus The Challenge of Diversity'. *Jean Monnet Working Paper* 07/01. NYU School of Law.

SCIARRA, S. (2000). 'Integration through Coordination: the Employment Title in the Amsterdam Treaty'. *The Columbia Journal of European Law*, 6: 209–29.

SCOTT, J. and DAVID M. T. (2002). 'Mind the Gap: Law and New Approaches to Governance in the European Union'. *European Law Journal*, 8/1: 1–18.

SNYDER, F. (1994). 'Soft Law and Institutional Practice in the European Community'. in S. Martin (ed.). *The Construction of Europe: Essays in Honour of Emile Noël*. Dordrecht: Kluwer Academic Publishers.

STREECK, W. (1995). 'From Market-Making to State-Building: Reflections on the Political Economy of European Social Policy'. in S. Leibfried and P. Pierson (eds). *European Social Policy: Between Fragmentation and Integration*. Washington DC: Brookings Institution.

TEAGUE, P. (2001). 'Deliberative Goverance and EU Social Policy'. *European Journal of Industrial Relations*, 7/1: 7–26.

VANDENBROUCKE, F. (2001). 'Open Co-ordination on Pensions and the Future of Europe's Social Model'. Closing address at the Conference 'Towards a New Architecture for Social Protection in Europe? A Broader Perspective of Pension Policies,' October 19–20, 2001.

ZEITLIN, J. (2001). 'Constructing Social Europe: Social Dialogue, Subsidiarity, and Open Coordination'. Comment Presented to the European Conference 'Pour une politique européene des capacités: Un cadre de travail entre chercheurs et acteurs du dialogue social européen'. Sponsored by the European Commission, DG for Employment and Social Affairs. Brussels, January 12–13.

ZIJL, M., VAN DER MEER, M., VAN SETERS, J., VISSER, J., and KEUZENKAMP, H. A. (2002). 'Peer Pressure and Policy Learning', in M. Zijl, M. van der Meer, J. van Seters, J. Visser, and H. A. Keuzenkamp. *Dutch Experiences with the European Employment Strategy*. Amsterdam: The Netherlands EES National Impact Evaluation Study.

3

The European Employment Strategy, Multi-level Governance, and Policy Coordination: Past, Present and Future

JANINE GOETSCHY

Formalized by the Amsterdam Treaty (1997), the idea of the European Employment Strategy (EES) had already been initiated by the Delors White Paper on *Growth, Competitiveness and Employment* (1993) and had been made operational on a pragmatic basis by the Essen procedure after the European Council in December 1994. Following Amsterdam, the EES was put into practice before the official implementation of the Treaty on the basis of the employment guidelines formulated at the special Luxembourg summit (November 1997).

Since then the EES has been reaching what can be called its 'cruising speed'. The Lisbon European Council (March 2000) gave the EES a new impetus by formulating a ten-year strategy to reach a 70 percent employment rate and to achieve better articulation between employment and other policy fields, including macroeconomics, structural economic reforms, social protection, education and training, and implementation of new technologies. Since Lisbon, the EES has also been referred to as 'the open method of coordination', as it represents a new regulatory method for constructing 'Social Europe', which is designed to complement the existing instruments at the EU level, such as legislation, European collective agreements and the social dialogue, structural funds, support programs, the integration processes of different policy fields, and analysis and research. In the first half of 2002, five years after its conception, a comprehensive evaluation of the EES's merits and shortcomings was carried out at both the EU and national levels.

This chapter will examine the antecedents of the EES, describe its functioning and achievements, analyze its current strengths and weaknesses, and reflect upon its future development by examining potential links with other EU regulatory tools (legislative and contractual), other policy fields, and national social pacts.

3.1. The Antecedents of the EES

The emergence in the 1990s of a European strategy for coordinating national employment policies needs to be understood within a dual context: (a) the history of EU social, economic, and monetary integration; and (b) national employment policy experiences over the preceding two decades.

3.1.1. *A Classical Imbalance: Shortcomings of Social Europe in the Context of Accelerated Economic Integration*

First, the EES should be analyzed within the history of European economic integration, which accelerated in the 1990s with the advent of Economic and Monetary Union (EMU). Supported by the Member States, this acceleration considerably altered the national employment policy context, making traditional job-creation policies obsolete in three ways:

1. It was no longer possible to foster employment by means of competitive devaluation and adjustment of national interest rates because EMU entailed an increasingly centralized monetary policy for the EU;
2. EMU and the adoption of the Stability Pact (1997) prohibited large public deficits and hence attempts to combat unemployment by means of public-sector job creation;
3. Community competition law began to weigh upon employment by increasingly limiting certain types of state aid to undertakings in specific sectors and by granting or withholding permission for mergers and takeovers by major industrial or financial groups.

The range of policy options, particularly in the macroeconomic field, available to the Member States in the fight against unemployment was thereby restricted. This development compounded the fact that the Member States had largely abandoned the pursuit of Keynesian demand-side policies since the 1980s. At the same time, the new arrangements for macroeconomic policy coordination put in place at the European level in the early 1990s, that is, the convergence criteria laid down in the Maastricht Treaty, proved insufficient.

While some of the traditional national macroeconomic policy instruments used to promote and safeguard employment were disappearing, the progress towards completion of the internal market and the pressure of globalization continued to accelerate the restructuring of companies and sectors and to exacerbate regional inequalities, leading at least temporarily to new imbalances in the labor market. Against this background in the 1990s all EU Member States emphasized structural policies as a way of dealing with unemployment and underemployment—out of a sense of realism but also for more ideological reasons (Gold, Cressey, and Gill 2000).

In the mid-1990s, it therefore became clear that employment measures had to be taken if the EMU project, or at least the planned timetable, were not to be put at risk. One must recall here the public pessimism of the early and mid-1990s about the implications of EMU for employment, public services and company relocation. The Renault Vilvoorde affair in particular touched off a crisis that prompted various employment-related actions (Hyman 2001). Finally, in 1997 elections in France and the United Kingdom isolated Germany in its rejection of an employment title in the EU Treaty. These factors, combined with fairly poor progress in other areas of Treaty reform, made the Employment Title a unifying and popular project which was easy to 'sell' to European citizens. Curiously enough, the Employment Title in the Amsterdam treaty was adopted at a time when Member States were already experiencing very different levels of national employment performance.[1]

Second, the EES should also be set within the history of Social Europe, which experienced setbacks during the 1990s in both the legislative and contractual routes to regulation. After the fairly active legislative period of the early 1990s, following the EU Social Charter (1989) and the Commission's Social Action Plan (1990), legislative progress was slowing down under the next EC Social Action Plan (1995). The latter's philosophy was, on the one hand, to rely increasingly on voluntarist practices rather than directives and, on the other, to improve implementation of existing EU legislative measures at the national level (Goetschy and Pochet 1997).

It became increasingly clear that despite the broadened scope of EU competences in the Maastricht Social Agreement, the newly opened possibilities were not actively taken advantage of either by Member States through legislation, or by the EU social partners through contractual routes. Fewer directives were adopted than in earlier periods and only four European collective agreements were reached, under the threat of legislation by the European Commission and the Council. These unsatisfactory results stemmed partly from the ambivalence of the Maastricht Treaty itself, which enlarged the EU's social competences on the one side while prescribing respect for the principle of subsidiarity on the other (Falkner 1998).

During the Intergovernmental Conference (IGC) prior to the Amsterdam Treaty, it appeared that the scope of EU competences could hardly be further extended in a classical manner and moving subjects from unanimity to qualified majority voting rule proved equally difficult. Paradoxically, despite those

---

[1] A more detailed presentation of the EES's origin and development can be found in Goetschy (1999) as well as in Chapter 2 by Trubek and Mosher in the present volume.

difficulties, Member States were pushed by national public opinion to develop some convergent solutions at the EU level in respect to their most urgent social priorities, such as the fight against unemployment, and later, social exclusion, pensions, and social security reform. Attention was thus focused on two alternative options for EU action: on the one hand, what Streeck (1996) called 'neo-voluntarism' (including, among other things, exchange of good practices) and on the other, on the coordination of national policies around commonly defined Community guidelines. In this context, procedures such as the EES could present advantages for both the Member States and the European Union itself by contributing to the construction of supranational coordination (Wessels 1997).

3.1.2. *Member States' Experience of National Employment Policies before the Amsterdam Treaty*

By the mid-1990s, Member States themselves had learned major lessons regarding the performance of their own national employment policies pursued since the early 1980s. After two decades of unemployment and the introduction of a wide array of employment measures, Member States had acquired vast experience and understanding of the likely factors contributing to improvement in the employment situation. Indeed, both the problems and the solutions adopted had varied a great deal throughout the EU countries. Between 1977 and 1997, certain countries such as Denmark, Ireland, the Netherlands, Portugal, and the United Kingdom had managed to reduce successfully their fairly high unemployment rates, whereas in other countries, such as France, Germany, Spain, Italy, Belgium, and Greece unemployment remained persistently high and reforms blocked by institutional 'stickiness'. Still others, like Austria and Luxembourg, managed to keep their unemployment levels low throughout the period. Several lessons were learned from the comparative assessment of Member States employment performances.

First, it appears clear that the most successful countries were those which combined in a coordinated strategy appropriate macroeconomic policies, structural labor-market reforms and employment measures, often implemented by means of a social pact (Fitoussi and Passet 2000; Pisani-Ferry 2001; Traxter, Blaschke, and Kittel 2000).

Second, concerning structural labor-market reforms, none of the traditional variables taken on their own (hiring and firing rules, duration of employment contracts, centralization/decentralization of collective bargaining, wage rigidity/flexibility, working time rigidity/flexibility, work sharing, proportion of public employment, duration and levels of unemployment benefits, minimal social benefits, spending on active measures, and so on) explained by themselves the employment performance of a given country. The relationship of each of these variables with employment levels has been subject to bitter ideological and political debates over the last 20 years and been at the heart of the yearly OECD employment reports. The evidence shows that to bear fruit structural reforms have to be carried out in a coherent way and need to make use of a variety of devices. Moreover, no automatic and linear relationships between some of these variables and employment levels could be identified.

Third, a striking feature of the evolution of Member States' employment policies is their growing internal diversification over time, especially during the last decade. It has been observed that employment policies and measures taken in a single country have been borrowing more and more from very different ideological sources—thus neo-liberal employment measures (reduction of indirect labor costs, numerous employment flexibility measures, and so on) are employed alongside traditionally more social-democratic devices, such as work sharing, reduction of working hours, part-time work and targeted training measures. Given years of experience and probably also due to mimetic effects among Member States, employment policies appear now to be less closely connected to a strictly defined ideological stance. In France, for example, where the reduction of indirect labor costs was traditionally promoted by the Right, it has become a routinely employed tool that further gained in importance under the Left government throughout the 1990s.

Fourth, national employment policies have entered a 'reflexive' stage where they can benefit from national assessment and evaluation exercises. Indeed, understanding of the impact of each employment measure in terms of the number of jobs created, their quality and relative cost had seriously improved over the decade before the EES, making it possible to compare their effectiveness. The relevant statistical and methodological tools have been improving too, although there remains significant variation among Member States in this respect. In addition, countries with social pacts (Ireland, Denmark, the Netherlands, Portugal, Spain, and Italy) and those who attempted but failed to negotiate social pacts (Belgium and Germany), as well as others such as France have become increasingly aware of the benefits to be drawn from interrelating policy fields at both national and EU levels (macroeconomic, social protection, employment, fiscal policies, and so on). Understanding of the 'negative externalities' arising from insufficient coordination between policy fields has also been increasing. All this knowledge accumulated over the preceding two decades about the performance of national employment policies and the virtuous effects of policy coordination served in turn as a fertile source of substantive content and policy instruments for the EES.

3.2. The Employment Title of the Amsterdam Treaty: Major Characteristics and Achievements

3.2.1. *The Employment Title of the Amsterdam Treaty*

The EES process as designed by the Amsterdam Treaty is the following. Each year, following the Commission's proposal, the Council (Social Affairs and Ecofin) adopts common European employment guidelines by a qualified majority vote. Afterwards they have to be translated into national employment policies on which each Member State reports to the Commission and the Council in their yearly 'National Action Plans' (NAPs). An annual joint evaluation by the Commission and the Council then takes place, on the basis of which the Council can issue recommendations to the Member States. Such recommendations to individual states which are deemed not to have followed the guidelines have no binding effect but could nevertheless be politically powerful. The Employment Committee participates in the EES as an advisory body. Although the Employment Title was not very explicit on the point, subsequent EU summits insisted that national governments be expected to engage trade unions and employer associations at various levels in both developing and implementing their NAPs. Three elements characterize the Employment Title in the Treaty: it is based on the previous experience of the Essen procedure (1994) establishing a multilateral monitoring procedure for national employment policies; the procedural approach of the EES was inspired by the convergence process in the macroeconomic field set up in the Maastricht Treaty (1992); and it is the national level which remains primarily responsible for employment policies and achievements, though employment is considered an issue of common concern for both the national and the Community level. The fact that employment is a 'shared competence' between the Community and national levels is consistent with the principle of subsidiarity and clearly shows that the EES represents an effort to promote greater convergence of national employment policies while at the same time respecting national diversity.

Since the Luxembourg summit of 1997, the annual European employment guidelines have been organized under four pillars:

(a) improving employability: aimed at improving the access of the unemployed to the labor market, it focuses on the development of a 'preventive approach' to avoiding long-term unemployment and on the implementation of 'activation policies';

(b) developing entrepreneurship: making it easier to start and run a new business and to hire people in it by reducing administrative constraints and rendering taxation more employment-friendly;

(c) encouraging adaptability both for employees and businesses: this entails modernization of work organization and other forms of adaptability in enterprises;

(d) strengthening equal opportunity policies; this involves a gender mainstreaming approach for all four pillars, reducing the gender gap, reconciling work and family life, and facilitating re-integration into the labor market.

About 20 such EU guidelines are formulated each year with only a few of them corresponding to quantified targets.

3.2.2. *Assessment of the EES's Operation and Results*

What do the various assessments of the EES carried out by the four successive EU Joint Employment Reports teach us? Although all Member States have fulfilled their obligation to deliver a national plan each year, numerous shortcomings but also improvements were emphasized by the successive EU Joint Employment Reports (1998, 1999, 2000, 2001).

Their main conclusions about the overall operation of the EES were the following:

1. The main focus of most NAPs is on 'employability', followed by the 'entrepreneurship' pillar. The implementation of the four pillars' provisions is uneven, which is especially true for the 'adaptability' and 'gender equality' pillars.

2. Most plans often consist of a mere list of discrete initiatives that Member States already had in stock, lacking in overall integration and coherence among the four different pillars. The need for a more coherent approach has become a 'horizontal' objective of the 2001 guidelines.

3. Under many guidelines with no quantified objectives, or where target setting is left to individual Member States, policy progress is slow and less visible, which makes the assessment of the guidelines' impact difficult.

4. The lack of definition and precision about the resources allocated to various measures, the timetable for implementation and the statistical tools used render the evaluation even more difficult.

5. Most Member States lack a coordinated strategy or structure for creating synergy between the various ministries involved in the EES [many countries have separate ministries dealing with finance, the economy, small and medium-size enterprises (SMEs), employment, social protection, education and training, and so on].

6. As for the new employment rate targets fixed in Lisbon in March 2000 (70 percent on average and 60 percent for women by 2010) and the intermediate rates fixed at Stockholm in March 2001 (67 percent on average and 57 percent for women by 2005), it is mainly those countries that are already above or close to the planned objectives which have set their own national targets as required (Denmark, Sweden, the Netherlands, the United Kingdom, Finland, and Portugal).

7. As for regional employment policies, the key role of the European Social Fund (ESF) in the EES is recognized in the NAPs, but that of the other structural funds is not made sufficiently explicit by the Member States (at the EU level, 195 billion euros of structural funds over the coming six years are the financial tools to support the attainment of employment objectives. Of this amount some 70 billion euros are allocated to human resources through the ESF).

8. Regional employment disparities within certain EU countries remain wide, especially in Italy, Spain, Germany, and Belgium (in the latter two countries they have been increasing).

When looking at each pillar separately, the following lessons can be drawn:

1. *Employability.* Unlike in the past, there is clear progress in the implementation of active and preventive policies, which is largely accounted for by the common EU quantitative targets. Fourteen Member States are already meeting the 20 percent target for the unemployed in active measures (the United Kingdom is not ready in that respect). More worryingly, however, it is likely that five Member States will not manage to meet the 2002 deadline for reaching the two so-called quantitative targets of reducing youth and long-term unemployment (the objective was to offer a new start to each individual in such situations) due to insufficient measures taken (Germany, Italy, Greece, and Belgium) or missing statistical tools for evaluation (the Netherlands). The review of tax-benefit systems to encourage activation policies lacks follow-up and the link between tax systems and social/unemployment benefits systems is infrequently made (except for Belgium, France, the Netherlands, and the United Kingdom). Altogether, the relevant reforms rely more on tax-friendly policies than on changes in unemployment and disability benefits. Only half of the Member States have introduced global strategies for promoting education and lifelong learning as required (Denmark, the Netherlands, Finland, Sweden, the United Kingdom, France, and Germany), while very little has been achieved in terms of the recent objective to prolong working life among persons aged between 55 and 64.

2. *Entrepreneurship.* A wide array of measures has been taken over the five years to reduce red tape, legal and administrative burdens hampering the creation of SMEs and, more recently, to fight undeclared work (11 countries committed themselves in that respect) as well as to favor local development and the social economy. But progress in reducing the tax burden on labor (indirect labor costs) has remained too slow and concerns essentially low-wage and low-skill work (taxes on labor remain high within the European Union at 40.6 percent). The successive joint reports deplore the lack of more coherent strategies for the enterpreneurship pillar and stress the difficulty of launching a real entrepreneurship culture within the European Union.

3. *Adaptability.* If progress has been registered on the questions of more flexible working time arrangements and more flexible forms of employment contract (part-time, fixed-term, and temporary), there is much less evidence of improvement in the NAPs on issues related to the modernization of work organization within enterprises. New management techniques, revision of hierarchical structures, team work, participative decision-making processes, and other similar items are not adequately covered in the NAPs, which might partly be due to lack of ministerial insight on these organizational matters. In addition, too little attention is still paid in the NAPs to quality of work and employment, which is understandable, since the framing of guidelines and indicators on those issues has only begun recently.

4. *Equal opportunities for men and women.* Beside representing a separate pillar, the aim of these EU guidelines has been to develop gender main-streaming across the three other pillars. Despite some significant progress in trying to reduce inequalities between men and women (as regards unemployment, employment rates, occupational segregation, wages, and reconciliation of work and family life), the measures taken vary greatly among Member States. Three areas are insufficiently addressed: continuing wage differentials between men and women which stagnate at around 14 percent (19 percent in the private sector and 10 percent in the public sector); lack of childcare facilities (especially in Italy, Spain, Austria, Germany, and the Netherlands) which hampers the growth of women's employment; while virtually no initiatives were mentioned to enhance women's role in decision-making.

3.2.2.1. *Role of the Social Partners*

Both in the elaboration and implementation phases, the social partners have been insufficiently involved in the process of producing NAPs, which often remained a purely governmental issue. But an improvement is recorded in social partners' involvement in the elaboration of the NAPs: eight countries have set up tripartite structures for that purpose (Germany, Sweden, Ireland, Belgium, Greece, Italy, Portugal, and Spain). Although consultations over the NAPs generally took place only at the central level, it was not always the top officials on each side who were involved. This contrasts with the experience in negotiating social pacts at the national level, where top representatives of the union and employers' organizations are invariably the protagonists (Foden 1999). On the whole, the consultation process over NAPs does not seem to have generated new initiatives from the social partners or new national strategies towards unemployment.

As to social partners' role in implementing the 'adaptability pillar', they took numerous initiatives over the years with respect to flexicurity agreements (essentially in the form of collective agreements at various levels whereby flexible working time arrangements are traded off for employment retention and creation) and health and safety at work. As to flexible forms of work (part-time, fixed-term contracts, and interim), virtually all Member States have by now introduced legal or negotiated framework rules. However the overall visibility of social partners' joint activities remains blurred (especially concerning work organization reforms) and all the more difficult to assess due to its interconnection with national social pacts. National social partners could have improved the visibility of their activities by submitting a progress report on work organization reforms undertaken at plant level, as was required by the Commission in the 2001 Employment Guidelines (guideline 13), but they failed to do so (Lönnroth 2000).

When looking at the contribution of EU social partners to the EES, negotiations on employment issues at the EU level have led to fairly poor results: at the cross-sectoral level, four agreements were reached on parental leave (February 1995), part-time work (June 1997), on fixed-term contracts (January 1999) and on telework (July 2002), but negotiations on temporary work failed; in October 2001 inter-sectoral negotiations on teleworking began, but soon ran into difficulties. At the sectoral level several Euro-agreements related to employment issues (working time and teleworking) were more successfully settled (in telecommunications, commerce, civil aviation, agriculture, construction, and leather industries), but the prospects of their actual implementation remain uncertain.

The evaluation of how effectively the annual European guidelines have been implemented in Member States through a comparative analysis of the NAPs—as in the Joint Reports—essentially tells us about national employment policy changes that have occurred. Such assessments help us to reflect upon the extent of Europeanization of national employment policies and to assess how far the EES leads to greater convergence on the one hand and preserves the diversity of national policies on the other.[2] But the Europeanization of national employment policies proves to be a much more complex issue, as it is always difficult, especially in the case of non-binding EU-level decisions, to distinguish between the measures that Member States would have taken anyhow and those taken under the pressure of the EES. Besides the vast array of new national employment measures to which it gave rise, the impact of the EES could also be assessed on the basis of the improved performance of employment figures it induced (lower unemployment rates, and higher employment rates). Here we encounter another difficulty. It is not easy to

---

[2] For recent discussions of the Europeanization of national policies, see Schmidt (2001), Radaelli (2000), Börzel and Risse (2000), Knill and Lehmkuhl (1999).

evaluate what share of the increase in employment is due to structural labor-market reforms such as those associated with the EES and how much of it is due to economic growth (itself influenced by the world economic situation, national macroeconomic policies, the European Central Bank(ECBs)'s monetary policy, and so on). This uncertain issue has given rise to sharp debates and divergent views among both researchers and policy-makers within the European Union over the past 20 years. So, it is for the moment very difficult to determine the respective share of labor-market reforms and growth in explaining the improved employment situation within the European Union over the past three years (1998–2001).

But before studying the impact of the EES on national employment policies, it is necessary to develop a better understanding of the potential strengths and weaknesses of these policies.[3]

3.3. Strengths and Weaknesses of the EES: from Theory to Practice

3.3.1. *The Strengths of the EES*

The strengths of the EES derive from the iterative nature of the process which allows employment issues to be tackled in a medium-term perspective as well as from the use of a multi-step procedure involving targets, deadlines, and evaluations.

1. As an iterative process between EU and national levels that closely articulates intergovernmental and supranational logics while combining Community competence with subsidiarity, the EES presents a number of advantages.

(a) It enhances Member States' political commitment to EU decision-making on employment matters: the EES provides the Member States with a planned sequence of meetings, new statistical tools and procedures, as well as a longer term perspective, which puts them in a better position to define, accept and implement EU guidelines. Moreover, the iterative structure of the EES, with its jointly defined guidelines and incremental adjustments of national policies, encourages the commitment of Member States as they can gradually adjust to the process. In addition, as their commitment to the process grows, an interdependence of understanding and interests among Member States will also strengthen, justifying in turn further development of the EES.

(b) The EES should lead to decisions which are better adjusted to the national diversity of institutions and employment policies. Three factors

---

[3] This discussion expands arguments previously presented in Goetschy (1999, 2000).

necessitate respect for national diversity in building Social Europe: the implementation of the subsidiarity principle prescribed by the Maastricht Treaty (1992), the growing divergence of employment situations within the EU over the past decade (Visser 2001; Ferrara, Hemerijck, and Rhodes 2000), and the increased heterogeneity of Members States' situation which will result from EU enlargement (Pollert 1999). The EES contains five elements favoring respect for national diversity. The annual guidelines generally define overall objectives to be met, whereas concrete means for implementation are left to individual Member States. Moreover, on several issues, Member States are encouraged to set up their own national targets. The EU assessment is carried out on the basis of the relative progress made by each country compared to its point of departure. The absence of legal sanctions in case of non-compliance creates significant room for maneuver in national implementation of the EU guidelines. Finally, Member States are aware that employment remains primarily a national issue, which legitimizes in their eyes the continuing diversity in institutional arrangements and outcomes. This respect for national diversity reflects the implicit acceptance of path-dependency and the fact that each country has its own national social protection, industrial relations, and employment policy systems, which are 'deeply embedded in the institutions, values and established practices of specific societies' (Scharpf 1999).

(c) As a result of this iterative process, decisions are expected to become more *realistic* and less prone to 'would-be-policy'. First, the 'back and forth' process increases the likelihood of decisions being actually taken, whereas earlier regulatory mechanisms (legislative and contractual) could not often be activated in a timely manner and thus remained elements of a 'would-be policy'. Indeed, one must recall that the enhancement of EU competences and expansion of qualified majority voting introduced by the Maastricht Social Agreement (1992) represented new opportunities which the Member States and social partners have not used as actively as could have been expected. Second, Member States' deeper and more frequent involvement in the rule-making process itself should yield decisions with a more realistic content, better fitted to diverse national situations and cognizant of potential implementation difficulties.

(d) The EES is now a subject of EU 'high politics' (Hoffmann 1966) involving a variety of economic, social and political actors at multiple levels from the supranational through the national to the regional, which should increase both the input legitimacy of EU decisions (more actors involved) and their output legitimacy (better employment performance) (Scharpf 1999; Marks *et al.* 1996; Teague 2001). The EES represents an interplay among different levels of governance, though the dominant actors remain the European Commission, the acting EU Presidency, the EU Social Affairs Council (with its Employment

Committee), and the Member States (essentially national governments and their employment and social affairs ministries, although several countries have set up inter-ministerial coordination structures). At the same time, multi-level governance implies an enabling of lower levels and opening of new fora, which also requires new coordination functions, currently performed by the European Commission and the acting EU Presidency. Following the Lisbon Summit (March 2000), multi-level governance in reference to the EES means not only actions at various levels involving a multiplicity of actors, but also better coordination of the EU employment guidelines with other policy fields. Apart from employment, the Open Method of Coordination (OMC) is also being applied to other policy fields, such as structural economic reforms, innovation and the knowledge society, combating social exclusion, education and lifelong learning, and modernization of social security systems (including pensions and health care). Moreover, a better articulation and coordination of economic and social policy fields at the European level was proposed to avoid 'negative externalities'. As of today, the EES multi-level governance process has yet not reached its full potential and retains a predominantly elitist character, with government officials playing a central role.

(e) The iterative EES process also leads to a change of content and priorities in the EU agenda and to an enlargement of its competences in a way which can be 'acceptable' to Member States. The open method of coordination at the heart of the EES finally gives a chance for the real national social priorities (employment, social exclusion, and social protection) to figure on the EU agenda. Previously, EU social policy initiatives were often linked (either directly or indirectly) to the creation of the internal market, to facilitate its functioning or correct some of its negative social consequences. The principal issues addressed by Social Europe tended to lie outside the core of national social policies so as not to upset Member States by encroaching upon their national sovereignty. By contrast, the EES deals with issues that are central to all Member States, their employment policies, labor markets and industrial relations systems. The severity of the unemployment problem in the 1990s encouraged acceptance of the idea that social measures taken at the Community level must include issues crucial for the Member States' national policies. The OMC served as the institutional and procedural solution for addressing national social priorities at the EU level while preserving national diversity. In the case of employment issues the Treaty envisaged a shared competence. The OMC was designed to deal with issues such as social protection which fall within the Union's competence but are subject to unanimous vote and often do not lead to EU legislation because of their contentious character. It can also be a useful procedure for dealing with issues that lie outside the legal competence conferred by the Treaty. Just as the

Maastricht social agreement sought to bring the regulation of social affairs at the EU level 'in line' with those operating in national industrial relations systems by promoting European collective bargaining and framework agreements, so can the EES introduced by the Amsterdam Treaty be viewed as an effort to ensure that unemployment, as the most urgent national issue, should also be the first addressed at the EU level. This development was later reinforced by the Lisbon summit, which advocated the use of OMC in other policy fields.

(f) The iterative process of the EES implies further convergence of national social and employment policies while at the same time respecting national diversity. But these two elements are subject to an implicit and permanent tension. Indeed, the EES contains important 'vectors' favoring convergence (externalization of constraints; common EU guidelines; comparative evaluations in the joint report; recommendations; peer review; recurrent annual procedure; and common long-term EU employment perspectives), as well as numerous 'vectors' mentioned earlier which ensure respect for national diversity. On the one hand, the EES contributes to enhancing the ongoing Europeanization and convergence of certain elements of national employment policies, as shown in the NAPs and the Joint Employment Report. However, on the other hand, through the EES process of evaluation and comparison, Member States become increasingly aware of the respective strengths and weaknesses of their national labor markets and employment policies, which in turn supports new institutional arrangements, such as national social pacts and the mobilization of national assets in the context of globalization.

(g) The iterative process and multi-level governance approach create a real opportunity for an encompassing learning process to take place. It appears that the EES contributes to the emergence of an 'epistemic community' (Haas 1992) at the EU level, where experts and social and political actors share similar cognitive and normative orientations towards the key objectives and issues for employment reforms. The development of such an epistemic community relies on and at the same time engenders confidence-building, learning processes and favors convergence processes among Member States. A longer time span for acting collectively, appropriate procedural tools and multi-level governance indeed help to link more tightly the preferences and outcomes of supranational organizations, social partners and the Member States. A mutual socialization process—subject to a multiplier effect due to multi-level governance (more actors, more fora, and more policy fields)—should thus develop, as a result of which actors adjust their respective value systems. While a gradual Europeanization of national views should occur, the supranational institutions for their part are expected to pay greater attention to national diversity. Such a process does not prevent Member States from maintaining a clear view of their national interests. On the contrary, through

comparison with the other countries, it helps them sharpen their own positions and views.[4]

2. The aim of the EES is to integrate Member States' policies with
Community-level guidelines in a medium-term, multi-year perspective,
whereby incremental results will transcend short-term political gains and
help solve progressively the more fundamental problems of unemployment
within the European Union. One can say that the EES is a way to 'depoliticize'
the unemployment problem from its immediate national contingencies and
to address it in a longer-term perspective. Implicit in this orientation (as with
EMU and its convergence criteria) is the belief that politicians need to be
detached from their immediate national constraints and political contingencies. The fact that the EES was designed to be an enduring process means also
that the nature of transactions between Member States is different from that
which applies in the case of the adoption of directives. In the latter instance,
the diplomatic mode of interaction—where utilities are exchanged, involving
trade-offs among a variety of issues, and where short-term political conjunc-
tures are often decisive tends to prevail. This is less true of the EES, whose legal
Treaty base reinforces its enduring character (unlike other OMC social policy
fields such as social exclusion or pensions).

Beyond being an annually recurring process, now set into a 10-year perspective by the Lisbon summit, the EES has drawn stability from the fact that the
annual European guidelines and recommendations remained fairly consistent over time. The content of the EES, as we have seen, was organized around
four pillars, which were expected to remain in place at least for the first five
years. Altogether about twenty guidelines were adopted under these four
pillars. Though some changes occurred each year, on the whole the EU
employment guidelines remained fairly stable. Member States and the
Commission were keen to avoid a proliferation of new guidelines each year.
The major change took place in the 2001 guidelines, where new themes
were introduced relating to education and lifelong learning, to tackling
discriminatory aspects of the labor-market and reinforcing their link with
social exclusion, to combating emerging bottlenecks, to fighting undeclared
work, enhancing active labor-market policies, promoting good jobs and

---

[4] Interestingly enough, rather than 'rationalist institutionalist' explanations, it is 'sociological
institutionalist' approaches whereby Europeanization and domestic change take place through
socialization and learning processes (Börzel and Risse 2000) which are privileged for the moment
by academics studying the national impact of the EES and other OMC processes operating in fields
such as social exclusion and pensions (de la Porte and Pochet 2002; Trubek and Mosher 2002;
Jacobsson and Schmid 2002; Keller 2000).

encouraging higher employment rates among older workers through support for active aging. Among the innovations in the proposed guidelines for 2002, new issues such as quality of work, labor mobility within the European Union, gender wage inequalities, and intermediate employment targets (settled at the Stockholm summit in spring 2001) are addressed. Beside the relative stability of the EU employment guidelines, one can observe a similar consistency as regards EU recommendations addressed to Member States which did not change much from year to year: the third set of recommendations proposed for 2002 looks very similar to those for 2000 and 2001 (see Goetschy 2001*a*, 2001*b*, 2002).

A final and crucial element for the stability of the EES lies in the fact that the Commission plays a major role in the process. Indeed, the Commission carries out an important initiative and coordination function: it proposes guidelines and future themes for debate through its COM papers, assesses the content of the NAPs against the guidelines, monitors their actual implementation, assesses how far they address the problems and needs of each country, verifies that national social partners have been involved, accelerates the adoption of common statistical instruments and policy-evaluation methods, proposes recommendations concerning Member States' inadequate implementation, identifies 'best practices', and monitors peer review meetings between a cluster of Member States in order to disseminate these practices. By defining problems, solutions, and interpretations, the Commission structures the behavior of the multiplicity of actors, channels conflicts, organizes alliance-building, and socializes the actors to share its definition of issues and objectives (Greenwood 1997). In its guidance role, it will be crucial for the Commission to maintain the momentum of the EES over the long-term and to introduce new incentives each year so as to prevent the process from becoming a mere bureaucratic and symbolic exercise. Further, the Commission needs to be diplomatic in its management of the process. It must exercise firm control, but must not irritate Member States by ongoing harassment or undermine their own voluntary political engagement. Here too a learning process takes place: whereas the monitoring of the 2000 Recommendations to the Member States had caused certain annoyance among some of them, the monitoring procedure for the 2001 Recommendations has changed and proved to be more diplomatic. Faced with a great diversity of national interests, the Commission directs the show, as it manages the agenda, has intimate knowledge of the institutional and procedural complexities of the European Union and is able to represent the history and memory of Community proposals against the background of circulating Union presidencies and the changing political identities of Member States.

3. The method of the EES itself is also intended to serve as a catalyst for improving the effectiveness of national employment policies and for promoting convergence on the basis of common EU targets. This is to be achieved in several ways:

(a) By establishing external constraints over national policy. This method of 'externalizing constraints' within a specified timetable succeeded in the case of EMU, where national finances and economic performance were subjected to the discipline of the convergence criteria. It facilitates the implementation of difficult or unpopular employment reforms, as national politicians can shift the political blame onto the EU shoulders. Unlike the EMU convergence criteria, however, the employment guidelines are less binding, but the multi-level governance aspects are also much more pronounced, with the EES inducing an interpenetration of actors' decisions at various levels and relying much more on mutual learning-processes.

(b) By making national policies more transparent, putting them to the test of comparison and submitting them to examination by a range of national and EU institutions and social actors. This mutual control of national employment policies creates pressure on Member States to improve the efficiency and performances of their national employment policies. This approach also legitimizes the search for greater effectiveness of the Community's own policies such as the structural funds.

(c) By contributing to the development of a monitoring and evaluation culture both at EU and national level through modern public management tools and procedures such as the establishment of targets, deadlines, common statistical tools, benchmarking, best practices, and peer review (Tronti 1999; Hoffmann 2001; Mosher 2000).[5] But these tools and procedures are neither neutral nor innocent. They are intended to promote common frames of reference; shape national political and social actors' representations, discourse, strategies, and interests; and disseminate practices based on shared EU policy paradigms (such as activation, flexicurity, adaptability, and so on). These EU policy paradigms are aimed both at modernizing national labor markets in

---

[5] A set of 28 indicators across four policy domains as well as 7 more general economic background indicators (based on an earlier communication by the Commission [COM (2000) 594 final, 27 September 2000]) were annexed to the Stockholm synthesis report which concern: employment indicators (7), innovation and research indicators (7), economic reform indicators (7), social cohesion indicators (7). The employment indicators are: the employment rate; the female employment rate; employment growth rate; the employment rate of older workers; the unemployment rate; the tax rate on low wage earners; lifelong learning (adult participation in education and training). The social cohesion indicators include: the distribution rate; the poverty rate before and after social transfers; persistence of poverty rate; jobless households; regional cohesion; early school-leavers not in further education and training; and long-term unemployment.

the context of globalization and increased international competition, and at preserving certain features of the European Social Model, such as sustainability of social protection, by encouraging high employment rates, social inclusion through work, and more effective and less costly employment policies.

3.3.2. *Weaknesses of the EES*

But the EES also has some serious weaknesses.

1. The lack of real sanctions, which contrasts sharply with the stability pact monitoring process. Further, the EES provides only soft law measures to address employment issues. In the face of such criticisms, however, several lawyers have insisted on the fact that although some soft law measures have no binding force, they are not without legal significance (Kenner 1995; Biagi 2000). Indeed, the European Court of Justice can use soft law measures, such as EU recommendations and resolutions, for instance as aids for interpretation 'when national provisions are vague or uncertain, or indeed non-existent, in order to ensure conformity with other binding Community laws and the objectives of the EC Treaty', so that soft law can exert indirect legal effects (Kenner 1995, 1999). Further, certain political scientists who believe in the virtues of voluntarism reckon that it is precisely the lack of real sanctions which induces Member States to adopt employment guidelines which they would not otherwise accept. But if the lack of real sanctions can indeed facilitate the adoption of employment guidelines by providing Member States with a broader margin for maneuver, it renders their actual implementation more difficult. This is why a tough monitoring and follow-up system is then required on behalf of the Commission to compensate for the weak legal density of the guidelines. Others assert that with a soft law approach 'the use of legally binding measures which antagonize national governments or sectoral interests is avoided until the policy areas become "softened up"' (Cram 1997). This implies that the OMC would only represent a transitional phase facilitating the subsequent adoption of harder legal measures.

2. Another frequently evoked weakness of the EES has to do with the subordination of EU employment guidelines to monetary and economic guidelines (i.e. the Broad Economic Policy Guidelines and the Stability Pact). The Cologne process (June 1999) and especially the new commitments of the Lisbon summit (March 2000) have attempted to change this dependence by establishing a new balance between economic and social objectives for European integration and mainstreaming employment issues in all other EU

policies. To create mutually reinforcing objectives in both economic and social policies will require real political will on the part of the Member States and the European Council, which is far from easy as the preparation and rather mixed achievements of the Stockholm and Barcelona summits (March 2001 and 2002 respectively) showed.

3. The scarcity of EU financial resources for facilitating the development of an active European employment policy is yet another weakness. The fact that Social Europe has traditionally been subject to regulatory rather than redistributive mechanisms was stressed by Majone (1996). If the EES falls short of a real redistributive function—although through the structural funds it relies more on EU financial means than the traditional legal measures did—its aim is nevertheless to guarantee more equity across the European Union, so that citizens could benefit from improved performance of national employment policies. As the structural funds themselves constitute an area of multi-level governance, they could serve as an example from which the EES could learn and benefit (Jacobsson and Ekengren 2000).

4. Another fundamental criticism of the content of the EES concerns *the quality of jobs created*. The urgency of finding solutions to unemployment and increasing employment levels does not justify overlooking the nature of the jobs created. Assigning priority to the quantitative reduction of unemployment may accelerate the development of forms of employment, such as involuntary part-time work, badly paid and insecure jobs, and workfare schemes, which lack adequate social protection and recognition. Such work lacks social dignity and fails to achieve its purpose of social integration of the individual. In addition, encouraging work of this kind tends to exacerbate inequality between the sexes. The Commission and Member States quickly appreciated the strength of such criticism and have hence proposed to emphasize not only quantitative job creation, but also job quality (general working conditions, health and safety, wage levels, equality between men and women, a balance between flexibility and security and between work and family life, and the nature of industrial relations). The employment guidelines for 2001, the EU Social Agenda adopted at Nice (December 2000) and the conclusions of the Stockholm summit (March 2001) underscore the priority to be given to 'better jobs and not only more jobs'. The Commission has issued a communication in June 2001 on job quality where it proposes an EU strategy for long-term investment in high-quality jobs and living standards. It proposes to introduce regular reviews of the quality of jobs created by Member States based on a set of common indicators and benchmarking exercises. The tension between employment performances to be achieved and a growing awareness of the necessity to create quality jobs has become more acute in 2000 and 2001. At the same time as the

Lisbon summit initiated the race for enhancing employment rates within the European Union (with intermediary objectives set in March 2001), an elaborate strategy is being designed to improve the quality of jobs.

5. The complexity of the multi-level governance process of the EES itself, coupled with the existence of several other coordination processes, constitutes a serious problem of governability. Beyond the various eponymous processes initiated at successive EU summits, Luxembourg (1997: convergence of labor market policies), Cardiff (1998: convergence of economic structural policies), Cologne (1999: coordination of macroeconomic policy, wages, and employment), Lisbon (2000: interlinkages of policies; new policy fields subject to the OMC), there exist three other arenas of economic coordination (the Broad Economic Policy Guidelines for macroeconomic coordination, the surveillance procedure for implementing the Stability Pact, and the Eurogroup for coordinating fiscal policies) and two other coordination processes in the social protection field (the one on social exclusion is ahead of the one on pensions). All these processes have indeed different constitutional and institutional status. They are marked to varying degrees by 'inter-governmentalism' and the 'Community method'. Some of them are only nascent and their functioning still remains fairly imprecise. The EES, and more broadly speaking the OMC, were introduced to improve the democratic legitimacy of EU's decisions by bringing the Member States, as well as the social partners, back in and by giving greater consideration to the diversity of national situations. But including a broader range of interests and actors means greater complexity in compromises to be struck and creates some difficulty for democratic transparency. Moreover, whereas the EU rests upon two types of legitimacy (the one emanating from Member States, the other exerted through the European Parliament), the former type has clearly been favored to the detriment of the latter. The European Parliament's role, which remains rather minor in various OMC processes, will have to be more clearly defined in the future, if greater democratic legitimacy is to be achieved. In turn, this may render those processes even more complex. It remains to be seen though, to what extent the European Parliament is really interested in having a greater say in policies with weak legal density, an issue which is far from clear for the moment. Such complexity might decrease over time with unfolding learning processes and a gradual establishment of an EU epistemic community. But it will be more difficult to alleviate the criticism of the elitist drift resulting from such complex processes.

6. A more ideological criticism of the EES has emanated from some macroeconomists, who claim that to improve employment performance one needs foremost to secure faster economic growth, to improve the coordination of national macroeconomic policies, and to relax the ECB's overly restrictive monetary policy, whereas structural labor-market reforms contribute

little to job creation. In the same way as it is difficult to evaluate what proportion of unemployment is due to structural rigidities and how much to insufficient demand and economic growth, it is indeed difficult to assess the EES's contribution to the improving employment situation in the European Union between 1998 and 2001 in comparison to that of stronger economic growth. Many specialists assert, though in a fairly sibylline way, that a combination of both stronger economic growth and further labor-market reforms is necessary to improve employment.

7. The last criticism, or rather question addresses future developments. What incentives will Member States have to maintain the momentum of the EES given the heterogeneity of national employment performance within the European Union, particularly since the most severe remaining problems in this field might in fact be country-specific? It is clear that the EES process is a costly and a cumbersome task for national administrations and as time goes by the Member States will want to see the real gains from such EU cooperation. The gloomy economic prospects and decreasing economic growth rates announced for 2001 and 2002 and their consequences for employment might on the contrary give a new boost to the *raison d'être* of the EES for those countries whose employment performance has until now been more adequate.

3.4. The Future of the EES: Conditions for its Satisfactory Operation

Three types of problems need to be overcome to improve the future operation of the EES.

3.4.1. *Better Articulation with Other Community Regulatory Instruments*

The OMC should not be regarded as an alternative which would allow the Member States to place social issues on the back burner and perhaps jeopardize established Community regulations. Instead, it should be seen as a means to develop Social Europe in areas where no Community powers yet exist or in contested areas where Community action has been blocked due to the unanimity rule, but where the Member States are concerned to achieve policy convergence in a more flexible mode. The OMC inspires many fears among those who wish to advance Social Europe because they see it as a threat to the instrument of legislation. And yet this fear relates not so much to employment—a field in which the OMC is not really contested—as to its possible application in other fields in the future. There are fears of an insidious slide from legislative regulation (hard law) to regulation by means of the OMC (soft law) even within the domains where Community powers do exist.

Some also fear that the very existence of the OMC will inhibit ambitious reforms of the Treaty in the social sphere: in other words, that the Community powers will not be extended to new areas and that those currently requiring unanimity will not be transferred to 'qualified majority voting'. The extremely slim social policy reforms included in the Nice Treaty lend themselves to such an interpretation and thereby reinforce the skeptics' fears about the OMC. It is essential that the OMC should not turn into a new mode of regulation intended to compete with and displace more binding forms.

The best way to alleviate these concerns is to link the OMC closely to other instruments of Community action. It would be helpful if the EES were to be associated with the other methods rather than operating in isolation. Some of its components could, for example, be addressed by means of directives and thus link up, where the legal foundations of the Treaty so permit, with the Community legislative method (Bercusson 2000). Further directives on employment matters could reinforce particular results of the Luxembourg process. Of course, the legislative channel is an option only insofar as the Commission manages to find a legal basis in the Treaty, although in the past it has demonstrated considerable imagination in this respect. As the Commission requires a legal basis for action, it is true that such an approach could come into play at present only in isolated areas covered by the EES. In the longer term, however, might it not be possible for a future IGC to introduce new institutional linkages between the OMC and the legislative method by reforming the relevant provisions of the Treaty?

Similarly, the OMC, or more specifically the EES, could be linked up more closely with the collective agreement approach to European social regulation. The European Council has called for greater involvement of the social partners at all levels in both the preparation of the guidelines and the drafting of the NAPs, as well as in their implementation. The 2001 guidelines conferred an important role on the social partners, especially in relation to the adaptability of businesses and employees (pillar 3), inviting them to negotiate and implement, agreements on the modernization and organization of work at all appropriate levels. It would also be desirable to link the content of the EES guidelines more closely to the existing Community-level social dialogue. Further, the European social partner organizations (inter-sectoral and sectoral dialogue) might themselves propose and produce one or more employment guidelines which could then be formally adopted by the Council. The recent sectoral agreement on telework in telecommunications (February 7, 2001), for instance, gives some hints about possible ways to link the EES and the social dialogue. Such a closer articulation between different regulatory tools would, as a consequence, strengthen the coordinating function of the Commission.

3.4.2. *How Should the EES be Linked to National Social Pacts?*

If there is a genuine will to achieve convergence of the goals and results of the national employment policies and to make the EES into a first rather than a second-order instrument, this strategy should not operate in isolation from the national social pacts. It is important to create a better nexus between the content of the EES and the 'employment' components of national social pacts. Obviously, the social partners, both European and national, have a strategic role in implementing this task. Though the employment guidelines do indeed refer to national bargaining in relation to questions of employability, adaptability, education and training, and equal opportunities, it has to be acknowledged that in practice the links between the internal dynamic of national social pacts and the sometimes quite formalistic preparation of the NAPs have proved rather weak. Moreover, it has frequently appeared to be the case that, whereas the national social pacts of the 1990s (Italy, Portugal, Spain, Ireland, the Netherlands, Finland, and Denmark) produced innovative and imaginative initiatives (Ebbinghaus and Hassel 2000), the implementation of the employment guidelines has led to no such strong impetus.

To establish links between the NAPs and national social pacts is no straightforward matter because the EES is based upon two rather contradictory rationales (Rhodes 2001). Whereas the EES aims to achieve better European convergence of national employment policies, national social pacts generally seek to exploit local advantages in order to improve the competitive position of the domestic economy in the overall European or global arena. Several authors have deplored the downward spiral characteristic of such pacts (Streeck 1999), whereas the aim of the EES is, precisely, to stem this potential race to the bottom by defining convergent goals among Member States on employability, entrepreneurship, adaptability of businesses and individuals, and equal opportunity between the sexes. The general idea of the EES is indeed to promote high employment rates and a reduction of unemployment, but not at any price. This means that unemployment has to be reduced and the employment rate raised while preserving quality jobs (as regards contractual terms, working conditions, skills, pay levels, social protection, and so on), not undercutting the financing of social protection systems, avoiding tax competition between countries and so forth. This tension between European coordination in the EES and the NAPs and cross-national competition in the social pacts is not necessarily harmful in itself, insofar as the latter refrain from exporting 'negative externalities' to the other Member States, whereas the former seeks to remedy some of their existing consequences. Indeed, let us recall that the Community employment guidelines are not confined to the labor market *stricto sensu* but also cover significant aspects of social protection, education, taxation, pay, and regional exclusion, seeking to achieve some policy convergence in these areas. Beyond the EES which focuses above all on structural labor-market reforms, other forms of European macroeconomic convergence currently being developed (see Section 3.4.3, below) may also contribute to curbing this downward spiral which is suspiciously present in national social pacts of a competitive type.

3.4.3. *More Effective EU Coordination Processes between Various Policy Fields*

The decision was taken at the Lisbon Summit (March 2000) to reestablish full employment as the European Union's major social and employment policy objective. In this context, the European Council stressed the need to meet a double challenge: to continue reducing the rate of unemployment on the one hand, and to raise the employment rate on the other.[6] The conditions for a return to full employment in Europe rest simultaneously upon structural reforms such as those envisaged by the EES, appropriate macroeconomic policies at both national and European levels, and upon better EU coordination among various policy fields as advocated by the Lisbon Summit. The introduction of an annual spring summit was intended to give political impetus to a coordinated policy mix (macroeconomic, innovation, education, employment, social exclusion, social protection, and taxation) aimed at achieving full employment, and to set precise goals and timetables for implementation of these policies.

Solutions to unemployment are to be sought in a dynamic approach to an economic and labor-market situation that is in a state of constant change. A new balance has to be found between stability in efforts to reduce unemployment and the need for flexible responses in the future. The combination of macroeconomic policy and structural reform which underlie the employment success recorded in the last few years in some European countries are not to be perceived as constituting 'the right answers once and for all'.[7] Structural labor-market reforms are politically more difficult to implement than economic reforms insofar as they require adjustment of established institutional and legal frameworks and acquired social rights. It is for this reason that structural reforms, if they are to succeed, must be conceived over the long-term and on the basis of stable strategic guidelines understood by all those involved and must be subject to concerted action among a large range of different actors (European institutions, monetary authorities, member state governments, and national and European social partners) (Fitoussi and Passet 2000).

[6] For a recent discussion in the French context of how a return to full employment could be defined, see Pisani-Ferry (2000).

[7] For French debates about the relative weight to be placed on job-intensive vs. productivity-raising growth strategies in the pursuit of full employment, see Pisani-Ferry (2000).

To achieve full employment, two types of European policy coordination are required, which are still far from sufficiently developed: coordination between monetary policy and national budgetary policies on the one hand; and coordination between monetary policy, structural employment, and wage policies on the other. On the European institutional front, the coordination procedures and arrangements required to pursue such policies already exist, even if they appear to be too numerous. But it is necessary to redesign more clearly and coherently the overarching institutional framework for such coordination and the respective roles of the various institutions responsible for its implementation.

3.5. Perspectives and Conclusions

Seen as a process or mode of governance, the EES has been rather well received and has even inspired other EU policies in fields such as social exclusion, innovation policy, economic reform, education and lifelong learning, as well as to a lesser extent in social protection.[8] It appears to be a useful tool in policy spheres which are not yet subject to classical EU competence. Moreover, the principles of modern public policy-making which the EES entails (targets, deadlines, benchmarking, peer pressure, and evaluation and recommendations) have also been adopted in policies and processes outside the direct ambit envisaged by the Lisbon summit.[9] It remains clear, however, that the OMC will be applied very differently in each of these fields: their legal, institutional and procedural bases, the degree of ambitions of their respective objectives, and the importance of their results will vary a great deal.

But the OMC has also been subjected to harsh criticism. To meet the serious challenge of such criticism as discussed above, a three-fold strategy is essential.

1. It must be clearly specified that use of the OMC should be reserved to policy areas where Community competence is absent or where agreement is very difficult to reach under the Community method. It should be made clear as a general rule, that the OMC should not be used instead of the traditional Community method.
2. The political momentum for broadening the scope of the EU fields of competence during IGC preparing Treaty reforms should not be lost due to the existence of the OMC.

---

[8] Cf. the conclusions of the Lisbon summit.

[9] Two examples. First, the Commission has made a range of propositions in a recent communication on 'The reinforcement of the coordination of economic policies within the Euro zone' (7 February 2001) aiming to apply some sort of OMC to the functioning of the Eurogroup. A second case where the OMC has inspired new developments can be found in the EU sectoral social dialogue (e.g. see, the European agreement on telework adopted on 7 February 2001 by the sectoral social dialogue committee in telecommunications).

3. Whenever the OMC is used, it remains crucial to articulate the OMC closely with the two other major EU regulatory methods—legislative and contractual.

Apart from jeopardizing the Community method, it was also feared that the OMC might lead to a certain form of intergovernmentalism, by reducing the role of the Commission and the European Parliament, while increasing that of the Member States, the specialized EU ministerial councils (social, economic and financial affairs, and education), and the European Council. But the experience of the EES shows that this need not happen, since the Commission managed to preserve an important initiatory and coordinative role for itself in the process by closely articulating Community and intergovernmental logics. This was facilitated by the Treaty base of the EES on the one hand, and by the complexity of the multi-level governance process, on the other.

At this stage, assessments of the EES's quantitative and qualitative impacts on national employment policies and performances must remain cautious. The process is still recent and it is quite difficult to separate the effects of the EU guidelines from those induced by purely national policies and macro-economic growth more generally.

It is clear, especially after the Lisbon summit, that the major objective of the EES is to regain full employment by reducing unemployment and in particular by raising the employment rate. To do so the employment guidelines are seeking—through the four pillars (employability, entrepreneurship, adaptability, and gender equality)—to promote new labor-market policy paradigms such as activation for the unemployed, taking more account of the diversity of individual situations with special attention to long-term unemployment and social exclusion. In particular, they advocate increasing the employment rate of women and elderly workers, enhanced 'flexicurity' for wage earners (e.g. guarantees of social security benefits and training opportunities for workers frequently changing their employment status, thereby encouraging the development of so-called 'transitional labor markets' (Schmid 1995), trying to avoid situations of 'mismatch', and developing appropriate education and lifelong learning policies. Heading toward full employment is both a social and an economic choice: social as it is the best way to fight social exclusion, to improve the quality of jobs, to finance social protection and pensions, and thus secure their sustainability; and economic insofar as it generates income and favors innovation and risk-taking. However, the debates remains open and controversial about what full employment really means and how to reach it, that is, which is the best policy mix between macroeconomic, structural, and labor-market reforms (Pisani-Ferry 2000).

The Lisbon summit (2000) has provided an integrated EU strategy calling for parallel action across a range of interconnected areas to develop virtuous circles over a 10-year period between various policy fields, that is, creating more and better jobs, adopting appropriate broad economic guidelines, speeding up economic reforms, promoting innovation and the knowledge society, and strengthening social cohesion. Such an integrated approach is supposed to enhance the chances for full employment. This could represent a sort of meta-framework with a broader time perspective which might help to offset 'beggar-my-neighbor' competitive national social pacts and avoid negative externalities. However, vigilance and renewed political commitment seem essential to sustain the Lisbon momentum without betraying its original intentions.

Finally, more general questions will have to be asked: to what extent are the EU employment guidelines able to reshape the triangle of preferences of each nation state relative to its employment levels, its desired degree of social justice and its tax policy preferences? (Scharpf 1999). The increasing interconnection of policy fields and better understanding of their reciprocal links (between employment, macroeconomic policy, social protection, training and education, innovation, and so on), the multiplicity of actors involved in the various EU coordination policies (monetary authorities, EU institutions, governments, local authorities, and social partners) and the multiplicity of discussion/negotiation fora and coordination procedures (Broad Economic Policy Guidelines, the Luxembourg process, the Cologne process, the Cardiff process, the Lisbon approach, and so on) open up different sorts of perspectives. Which guidance levels will become more important and determinant than others? Will the traditional spearhead function assumed by the European Commission in the monitoring of Social Europe's policies remain important in such coordination processes? Will the OMC become the dominant regulatory method within the European Union or will an avant-garde of Member States instead be tempted to pursue 'closer cooperation' in the social field?

References

BERCUSSON, B. (2000). 'The European Employment Strategy and the EC Institutional Structure of Social and Labour Law'. SALTSA-Arbetslivsinstitutet Seminar, October 9–10, 2000, Brussels.

BIAGI, M. (2000), 'The Impact of European Employment Strategy on the Role of Labour Law and Industrial Relations'. *The International Journal of Comparative Labour Law and Industrial Relations*, 16/2: 155–73.

BÖRZEL, T. and RISSE, T. (2000). 'When Europe Hits Home: Europeanization and Domestic Change'. *European Integration online Papers (EioP)*, 4/15. Available at: http://eiop.or.at/eiop/texte/2000-015a.htm

Commission of the European Communities (2000, 2001). *Joint Employment Report 2000*. Brussels: The European Commission.

—— (2000, 2001). *Proposal for a Council Decision on Guidelines for Member States' Employment Policies for the Year 2001*. Brussels: The European Commission.

—— (2000, 2001). *Recommendation for a Council Recommendation on the Implementation of Member States' Employment Policies*. Brussels: The European Commission.

—— (2002). *Taking Stock of Five Years of the European Employment Strategy.* COM 416 (final), July 17.

Council of the European Union (2000). 'The Ongoing Experience of the Open Method of Coordination', Presidency Note, June 13.

CRAM, L. (1997). *Policy-Making in the European Union; Conceptual Lenses and the Integration Process,* London: Routledge.

DE LA PORTE, C. and POCHET, P. (2002). *Building Social Europe through the Open Method of Co-ordination.* Brussels: PIE-Peter Lang.

—— (2002). 'Is The Open Method Of Coordination Appropriate for Organising Activities at European Level in Sensitive Policy Areas?'. *European Law Journal,* 8/1: 38–58.

EBBINGHAUS, B. and HASSEL, A. (2000). 'From Means to Ends: Linking Wage Moderation and Social Policy Reform', in G. Fajertag and P. Pochet (eds), *Social Pacts in Europe: New Dynamics.* Brussels: ETUI-OSE.

FAJERTAG, G. and POCHET, P. (2000). *Social Pacts in Europe: New Dynamics.* Brussels: ETUI-OSE.

FALKNER, G. (1998). *EU Social Policy in the 1990s: Towards a Corporatist Policy Community.* London: Routledge.

FERRERA, M., HEMERIJCK., A., and RHODES, M. (2000). *The Future of Social Europe. Recasting Work and Welfare in the New Economy.* Oeiras: Celta Editore.

FITOUSSI, J. P. and PASSET, O. (2000). 'Réformes structurelles et politiques macroéconomiques: les enseignements des "modèles" de pays', in *Réduction du chômage: les réussites en Europe,* rapport du conseil d'analyse économique, n. 23, Paris: La documentation française.

FODEN, D. (1999). 'The Role of Social Partners in the European Employment Strategy'. *Transfer,* 5/4: 215–45.

GOETSCHY, J. and POCHET, P. (1997). 'The Treaty of Amsterdam: a New Approach to Economic and Social Affairs?'. *Transfer,* 3/3: 607–22.

GOETSCHY, J. (1999). 'The European Employment Strategy: Genesis and Development', in *European Journal of Industrial Relations,* 5/2: 117–37.

—— (2000). 'The European Employment Strategy: Strengths and Weaknesses'. *European Community Studies Association Review,* 13/3: 4–6.

—— (2001a). 'The Future of the European Employment Strategy', in U. Mückenberger (ed.), *Manifesto Social Europe.* Brussels: ETUI, 150–76.

—— (2001b). 'The European Employment Strategy from Amsterdam to Stockholm: has it reached it cruising speed yet?'. *Industrial Relations Journal,* 32/5: 401–18.

—— (2002). 'A Transition Year for Employment in Europe: EU Governance and National Diversity under Scrutiny', *Industrial Relations Journal,* 33/5.

GOLD, M., CRESSEY, P., and GILL, C. (2000). 'Employment, Employment, Employment: Is Europe Working?'. *Industrial Relations Journal,* 31/4: 275–91.

GREENWOOD, J. (1997). *Representing Interests in the EU.* London: Macmillan.

HAAS, P. (1992). 'Special Issue on Epistemic Communities'. *International Organization,* 46/1: 187–224.

HOFFMANN, S. (1966). 'Obstinate or Obsolete? The Fate of the Nation State and The Case of Western Europe'. *Daedalus,* 95: 862–915.

HOFFMANN, R. (2001). 'Strengthening Social Europe via Benchmarking', in U. Mückenberger (ed.), *Social Manifesto Europe,* Brussels: ETUI, 129–50.

HYMAN, R. (2001). 'A la recherche de la mobilisation perdue', in Comité de rédaction (ed.), *40 ans de sociologie du travail,* Elsevier.

KENNER, J. (1995). 'EC Labour Law: The Softly, Softly Approach'. *The International Journal of Comparative Labour Law and Industrial Relations,* 14: 307–27.

—— (1999). 'The EC Employment Title and the Third Way: Making Soft Law Work?'. *The International Journal of Comparative Labour Law and Industrial Relations,* 15/1: 33–60.

KNILL, C. and LEHMKUHL, D. (1999). 'How Europe Matters: Different Mechanisms of Europeanization'. *European Integration online Papers (EIoP)*, 3/7. Available at http:// eiop.or.at/eiop/texte/1998-007a.htm

JACOBSSON, K. and EKENGREN, M. (2000). 'Explaining the Constitutionalization of EU Governance: the Case of the European Employment Cooperation'. Working Paper No. 8, Score, Stockholm.

—— and SCHMID, G. (2002). 'Real Integration or Just Adaptation? On the Implementation of the NAPs for Employment', in C. de la Porte and P. Pochet (eds), *Building Social Europe through the Open Method of Coordination*. Brussels: PIE-Peter Lang.

KELLER, B. (2000). 'The New European Employment Policy Or: Is the Glass Half Full of Half Empty?' in R. Hoffman *et al.* (eds), *Transnational Industrial Relations In Europe*, Düsseldorf: Hans Böcker Foundation.

LÖNNROTH, J. (2000). 'The European Employment Strategy: a Model for Open Coordination and the Role of the Social Partners'. SALTSA-Arbetslivsinstitutet Seminar, October 9–10, 2000, Brussels.

MAJONE, G. (1996). *Regulating Europe*. London: Routledge.

MARKS, G., SCHARPF, F., SCHMITTER, PH., and STREECK, W. (eds) (1996). *Governance in the European Union*. London: Sage.

MOSHER, J. (2000). 'Open Method of Coordination: Functional and Political Origin?'. *ECSA Review*, 13/3: 6–7.

PISANI-FERRY, J. (2000). *Plein emploi*. Paris: La documentation française.

RADAELLI, C. (2000). 'Whither Europeanization? Concept Stretching and Substantive Change', *EIOP*, 4/8. Available at http://eiop.or.at/eiop/texte/2000-008a.htm

RHODES, M. (2001). 'The Political Economy of Social Pacts: Competitive Corporatism and European Welfare Regime', in P. Pierson (ed.), *The New Politics of the Welfare State*. Oxford: Oxford University Press, 165–96.

SCHARPF, F. (1999). *Governing in Europe: Effective and Democratic?* Oxford: Oxford University Press.

SCHMID, G. (1995). 'Is Full Employment Still Possible? Transitional Labour Markets as a New Strategy of Labour Market Policies'. *Economic and Industrial Democracy*, 16: 429–56.

SCHMIDT, V. (2001). 'Europeanization and the Mechanics of Economic Policy Adjustment'. *EIOP*, 5/6. Available at http://eiop.or.at/eiop/texte/2001-006a.htm

STREECK, W. (1996). 'Neo-Voluntarism: A New European Social Policy Regime?', in G. Marks, F. Scharpf, P. Schmitter, and W. Streeck (eds), *Governance in the EU*. London: Sage, 64–94.

—— (1999). 'Competitive Solidarity: Rethinking the "European Social Model" '. Paper presented at the 11th Annual Meeting of the Society for the Advancement of Socio-Economics, June 8–11, 1999, Madison, Wisconsin.

TEAGUE, P. (2001). 'Deliberative Governance and EU Social Policy'. *European Journal of Industrial Relations*, 7/1: 7–26.

TRAXLER, F., BLASCHKE, S., and KITTEL, B. (2000). *National Labor Relations in Internationalized Markets*. Oxford: OUP.

TRONTI, L. (1999). 'Benchmarking Employment Performances and Labour Market Policies', *Transfer*, 5/4: 552–62.

TRUBEK, D. and MOSHER, J. (2003). 'EU Governance, Employment Policy and the European Social Model'. This volume.

VISSER, J. (2001). 'From "Keynesianism" to the "Third Way": Labour Relations and Social Policy in Postwar Western Europe'. *Economic and Industrial Democracy*, 21/4: 421–57.

WESSELS, W. (1997). 'An Ever Closer Fusion: A Dynamic Macropolitical View on Integration Processes'. *Journal of Common Market Studies*, 35/2: 267–99.

4

Recalibrating Europe's Welfare Regimes

MAURIZIO FERRERA AND ANTON HEMERIJCK

4.1. From Growth to Limits to Recalibration

In a well-known series of volumes on European welfare states published in the mid-1980s, Peter Flora coined the metaphor of 'growth to limits' (Flora 1986). This notion contained an institutional diagnosis of the social policy predicament which afflicted the Old Continent: the ambitious programs introduced during the *trente glorieuses* had come to (quasi–full) maturation and were therefore reaching their maximum extension in terms of coverage and generosity. While the realization of the 'golden' commitments of the past meant invaluable material advances for large masses of the population, growth to limits was causing a number of worrying budgetary and institutional strains: mounting public debts and deficits, the accrual of 'automatic' entitlements often treated as property rights, a gradual loss of overall policy flexibility, and so on (Ferrera 1998*a*).

In the decade that followed Flora's work, the situation became gradually worse. The growth-to-limits syndrome combined with other endogenous and exogenous transformations (rapid ageing, the shift to service employment, swift changes in the structure of households and their relation to paid employment, the rising pressures of globalization, and European economic and monetary integration) to create a climate of 'permanent austerity' (Pierson 2001*a*), which is very likely to accompany mature welfare states for many decades to come. As suggested by Taylor Gooby, a 'silver age' of social policy development is now clearly dawning, in which 'citizen welfare remains a major objective …, but is tempered by concerns about international competitiveness and cost-constraint' (Taylor Gooby 2002: 3). As underlined *ad abundantiam* by this new debate, permanent austerity has not only made the *status quo* less sustainable and institutional reform more urgent, but also seems to require a sort of quantum leap in terms of adaptability. European welfare states must not only re-adapt to the new context, they must become structurally more adaptable to environmental change. Since the mid-1990s, this process of re-adaptation has taken off in all EU countries and the main purpose of this chapter is precisely that of highlighting the resulting trends and potential outcomes. But first, we would like to reflect a bit further on appropriate metaphors. How can we conceptualize this process of re-adaptation? What terms can best capture the multifaceted and multi-dimensional dynamics of social policy change in contemporary Europe?

The early debates on the welfare state crisis tended to take a rather biased and restrictive view, interpreting change primarily in negative terms (both descriptively and normatively), that is, as steps backwards from the golden age, assuming a sort of linear trajectory of evolution. But we know that trajectories of change are seldom linear. It is certainly legitimate and useful to speak of *cuts* and *retrenchment*: traditional benefits have indeed been reduced or even eliminated in certain sectors and in certain countries. But a lot of other things have been taking place—often in those very sectors and countries. In order to escape from the traps of terminological (and at times ideological) reductionism, recent debates have suggested various more neutral metaphors to describe ongoing changes: *modernization* (a term launched by the European Commission) (EC 1997), *recasting* (a term coined for a broad research Forum organized at the European University Institute in Florence in 1998–99) (Ferrera and Rhodes 2000), or *restructuring*. This latter term has been aptly discussed by Pierson (2001*a*), who has further articulated it on a number of dimensions: *re-commodification* (which has to do with changes that restrict alternatives to labor-market participation, either by tightening eligibility or by cutting benefits), *cost-containment* (referring to changes primarily motivated by the urgency of reducing debts and deficits) and *recalibration* (involving both *rationalization*, i.e. modifications of existing programs in line with new ideas about how to achieve established goals and *updating*, i.e. specific initiatives in response to newly recognized social needs).

In a recent volume written with Martin Rhodes, we have ourselves discussed the metaphor of recalibration,[1] which we find useful for both descriptive and prescriptive purposes. In our understanding, this metaphor is meant to suggest an act of institutional reconfiguration and re-balancing characterized by:

1. The presence of a set of constraints conditioning policy choices and developments, stemming from the interaction between new external pressures and domestic challenges;

---

[1] Cf. Ferrera, Hemerijck, and Rhodes (2000). This volume was the result of a project promoted by the Portuguese Presidency of the European Union during the first semester of 2000. As acknowledged by Pierson, the term 'recalibration' was originally suggested by Jonathan Zeitlin during the final seminar of the European Forum on 'Recasting European Welfare States', EUI, Florence, 18 June 1999. We are grateful to Jonathan for having broken this path of reflection for us.

2. the interdependence between additions (or upgradings) and subtractions in the social policy menu, as a consequence of such constraints; and
3. A deliberate shift of weight and emphasis among the various instruments and objectives of social policy, in the wake of complex dynamics of social and institutional learning.

Thus defined, recalibration can be further articulated on a number of sub-dimensions. We have proposed four distinct sub-dimensions: functional, distributive, normative and politico-institutional recalibration.

Functional recalibration has to do with the social risks around which welfare provision has developed over time. It involves acts of re-balancing both *within* and *across* the established functions of social protection. It denotes shifts from passive compensation to secured activation (e.g. in the field of employment or disability policy), but especially the containment of old age protection and pension insurance, on the one hand, and the promotion of new benefits and services for the risks (old and new) which are typical of other phases of the life cycle (e.g. dependency, training, child and elderly care, poverty, and exclusion).

The predicament of ageing is a formidable challenge for today's welfare states. Retirement costs will rise significantly in the first quarter of the twenty-first century. Small changes in the age of retirement, fertility, and immigration can potentially alter the magnitudes, but the direction is clear: there is pressing need to rewrite the contract between the generations.

Population ageing also pushes the issues of gender equality and gender equity to the forefront of the reform agenda. Women's revolutionary role-change in the labor-market is arguably the leading dynamic behind functional recalibration. It is the driving force of service employment growth, new household forms and new gender relations. The financial viability of the welfare state in the twenty-first century depends critically on the revenues generated by high (in many countries, hopefully higher) levels of women's labor-force participation. On the other hand, however, the viabilty of European welfare states also relies on women's willingness to reproduce the next generation and have children. This double bind poses a major challenge. The decline in fertility levels that generates population ageing is connected in complex ways to women's labor-force participation. Although dual-earner families are increasingly becoming the new norm, women continue to bear most of the burden of reproducing and caring for both the next generation and the older generation. Recent evidence indicates that fertility and participation can indeed go together (Castles 2001; Orloff 2001). The key to activating such a virtuous circle lies primarily in the promotion of greater gender equality and equity. On the one hand, achieving gender equality requires policies and incentives that lead to a reallocation of caring work within families (i.e. between men and women) and between families and the public sector. On the other hand, gender equity requires acknowledgement and compensation for persistent gender differences in the allocation of such work.

Regarding new social risks, a problem that deserves much greater policy attention is child poverty—which, together with lone motherhood, is on the rise in many of the EU countries. Child poverty, unlike poverty among the aged, has long-term negative consequences as it often translates into less education and inferior cognitive skills, with the likely effect of low pay and high vulnerability to unemployment in the 'new economy' (Esping-Andersen *et al.* 2002).

Functional recalibration, it needs to be emphasized, takes place against the background of intensified international integration in both product and capital markets. The internationalization of capital markets largely prohibits the liberal use of fiscal and monetary policy for employment growth and social protection. More intense international competition in product markets is driving up productivity and skill requirements, which tends to limit or reduce employment opportunities in exposed sectors, especially for low-skill groups. Most likely, employment losses in the exposed sectors can only be compensated by employment gains in the sheltered service sectors (Scharpf 2000). If labor markets continue to widen wage and skill inequalities, this could lead to a new polarization between households and classes. Re-integration policies require much more attention to skill development than under current remedial labor-market policy programs.

Distributive recalibration has to do with social groups. As underlined, again, by a rich debate, the European social model is characterized to a large extent by a syndrome of labor-market segmentation and the insider/outsider cleavage. In many countries there is evidence of an over-accumulation of insurance benefits on the side of 'guaranteed' workers, with quasi-tenured jobs (often two or more of these jobs per household), alongside inadequate (if not total) lack of protection for those employed in the outer, weaker sectors of the labor market. The emerging skill-based cleavages associated with the new economy are accelerating and reinforcing this dynamic. In certain countries, marked distributive inequalities are evident not only between insiders and outsiders, but also among the insiders themselves, that is, between different categories of the insured. Many of these transfers have lost their original rationale and have become a source of growing inequity. Thus, distributive recalibration denotes reform acts more or less explicitly aimed at rebalancing public protection not across risks, but across social clienteles.

Distributive recalibration clearly has a generational component too. The predicament of ageing, if unresolved, could provoke a 'generational clash'— with pension expenditures originated by the increasing number of elderly crowding out resources for the younger generations. How to distribute the costs and benefits as countries make the transition to ageing societies? Should the costs of ageing fall on contributors and their dependents, on retirees, or should they be shared in some proportion by both groups? The good news about such dilemmas is that increased longevity, improved health status of older workers, rising educational and literacy levels among younger cohorts make later and more flexible retirement increasingly feasible.[2]

Normative recalibration has to do with symbols, norms, values, and discourses. The postwar welfare states were founded on the normative goal of protecting the vulnerable—the aged, the sick, the unemployed—from poverty and from social and political marginalization. On this front too an 'incongruence' can be noted in the contemporary European welfare state: the 'goodness of fit' between the broad value premises that inspired its construction and the policies we now observe in practice has been gradually eroding through time, largely as a consequence of institutional inertia. In many countries, lively debates have taken place on the need to rethink the 'moral foundations' of existing arrangements. Normative recalibration therefore denotes symbolic initiatives and new discourses addressing the functional and distributive dilemmas of the *status quo* and the future directions of policy (Schmidt 2000). The current normative debate within Europe's recalibrating welfare state is no longer exclusively centered on issues of distributive justice and income maintainance, but increasingly also on work-related values and aspirations, the spirit of entrepreneurship and the learning society, the division of labor between men and women in and outside the family. These developments are in large part the result of the increased orientation of women towards labor-market participation. This in turn reflects higher levels of education, the greater salience of values of economic independence, and the spreading conviction that labor-market participation is a demonstration of gender equality. Survey research reveals quite clearly that today both men and women wish to partake in regular employment, not merely in order to earn a living, but also for reasons of social status, prestige, security, companionship, and engagement in collective action (Gallie and Paugum 2000; Hemerijck 2001). With double-earner households increasingly becoming the new norm however, this may create greater family instability and perhaps also provoke an undesirable low-fertility equilibrium. Despite women's new life histories—the driving force of service employment growth—social policy programs in many European welfare states remain encapsulated in the breadwinner model designed in the postwar decades. The challenge of normative recalibration lies in the need to elaborate new symbolic frameworks and discourses capable of recasting the reform agenda as a 'win–win' project, convincingly justifiable in terms of its underlying value premises.

---

[2] For an articulated and innovative discussion of the dilemmas of pension reforms cf. Esping-Andersen *et al.* (2002).

The elaboration of such a new framework is particularly urgent in the field of old age policy. The demographic predicament calls for a normative benchmark for reforming pension systems in a fair and orderly way. This should center on norms of intergenerational equity and intragenerational justice. Intergenerational equity implies that the transition costs associated with population aging be proportionately shared by both the young and old. The principle of intragenerational justice touches on the Rawlsian benchmark, suggesting that any change of the *status quo* should turn to the advantage (or the least disadvantage) of the worst off within both the working and the retired population (Esping-Andersen *et al.* 2002).

Finally *politico-institutional* recalibration has to do with the levels and actors that are or should be involved in the governance of social protection. As the very words suggest, one of the most distinctive elements of the European welfare *state* has been its public nature: the responsibility for ensuring social solidarity and cohesion lies with the government—ultimately the national (i.e. central) government. Public funds, public schemes and public bureaucracies have traditionally been the main pillars of the welfare edifice. Various developments have challenged this institutional paradigm in recent years—a challenge often summarized in descriptive and normative arguments about the emergence of new forms of 'governance' of social protection. On the one hand, many countries (especially the larger ones) have been experimenting with decentralization of competences to sub-national (regional and local) governments in response to numerous pressures—from increased international competition to fiscal overload at the state-national level. In many respects, sub-national policy arenas provide the best context for fostering both competitiveness and social solidarity, through innovative institutional solutions and organizational arrangements. On the other hand, the European Union has been gradually emerging as an autonomous supranational level of social regulation and to some extent redistribution (through the structural funds), thus creating a complex system of multi-level interactions that has changed national welfare states from fully sovereign to semi-sovereign entities (Leibfreid and Pierson 2000; Ferrera 2001). The first type of changes denoted by the politico-institutional dimension of recalibration are thus reforms that re-configure the division of labor between levels of government in the provision of welfare and the promotion of employment.

But there is a second aspect that is also important on this front, involving the actors of social policy making in the new system of governance. A rich literature has discussed in recent years the potential merits of social dialogues and 'pacts' at all institutional levels and the desirability of widening the scope of negotiation and 'coordination' among actors (Rhodes 2001). Thus with politico-institutional recalibration we aim to capture not only steps towards a more articulated *multi-level* governance of Europe's social policies, but also

steps towards a wider (but still coordinated) *multi-actor* and network governance, hopefully open to the voice of 'outsiders' and capable of encouraging
'other-regarding' stances on the part of established interest associations.

In the rest of this chapter, we will survey the 'recalibration agenda' of the
four 'Social Europes',[3] highlighting not only the main problems and challenges, but also a few emblematic reforms, that in our view constitute 'intelligent' examples of recalibrative progress.

4.2. Trajectories of Change in the Four Social Europes

As shown by Table 4.1, the levels of social protection expenditure and of total
taxation display wide variations across the EU countries, with the Nordic and
Continental countries at the top of the league and Anglo-Saxon and Southern
Europe at the bottom. The Nordic countries are by far the most generous
welfare states in Europe. But the price that Scandinavian citizens have to pay
for this generous system of social protection is a high level of taxation. The
Continental countries occupy an intermediate position, closely followed by the
Southern European countries, with the Anglo-Saxon countries at the bottom
of the league with low overall levels of taxation.

Table 4.2 offers some information on the internal composition of social
spending, depicting the situation as it was in the mid-1990s, that is, the
period in which the momentum of the Maastricht process—in the wider
context of socio-economic transformations summarized above—awakened
most governments to the urgency of reform.

The Scandinavian welfare states offer a wide range of high-quality public
social services. In this respect, the Scandinavian welfare state is an important
employer, especially for women in the social-service sector. The Nordic countries spend almost twice as much on family and children services as average continental and Anglo-Saxon countries, and three times as much as some Southern
European countries. The data in Table 4.2 also show that Scandinavian welfare
states devote more financial resources to active labor-market policies and training programs, with Sweden and Denmark again in a leading position. But the
Continental welfare states are catching up, with the Netherlands, France,
Belgium, and Germany all spending more on active labor-market policies than
Finland. Ireland is far more enthusiastic about active labor-market policies
than the United Kingdom. The Southern countries, trailing behind the

---

[3] We use here a fourfold typology of European welfare states originally suggested by Ferrera
(1998*b*) and mainly based on four dimensions: the principles of eligibility; the structure of benefits;
the methods of financing; and organisational arrangements.

Table 4.1.   Social protection expenditure and total taxation in the
four Social Europes

	Social protection expenditure as (% of GDP, 1998)[1]	Total taxation as (% of GDP, 1997)[2]
Sweden	33.3	53.3
Denmark	30.0	52.2
Finland	27.2	47.3
United Kingdom	26.8	35.3
Ireland	16.1	34.8
France	30.5	46.1
Germany	29.3	37.5 (1996)
Netherlands	28.5	43.3
Austria	28.4	44.4
Belgium	27.5	46.5
Luxembourg	24.1	46.0
Italy	25.2	45.0
Greece	24.5	40.6
Portugal	23.4	34.5
Spain	21.6	35.3
EU 15	27.7	42.8

Sources:
1. Eurostat, *Social Protection in Europe* (2000).
2. OECD, *Revenue Statistics* (2000).

Continental welfare states, once again bring up the rear. One area in which the Southern welfare states stand out is that of old age and survivors' benefits; social security systems in Mediterranean Europe can be considered 'pension heavy'. Italy is exemplary in this respect, spending 13.6 percent of its GDP (1995) on pensions, the highest figure in the European Union. The other Southern European countries spend about half of their social budget on pensions.

Finally, Table 4.3 gives an idea of the labor-market situation of the EU member states as of 1999, in terms of employment and unemployment—with some relevant breakdowns. With respect to overall levels of employment, female employment, public employment, and unemployment indicators, the Nordic countries, Denmark, Finland, and Sweden outperform the Anglo-Saxon and Continental models of welfare. The Anglo-Saxon countries, Ireland and the United Kingdom have favorable levels of employment with relatively low rates of public employment and exceptionally low rates of female

Table 4.2.   Social expenditure on selected functions (% of GDP, 1995)

	Pensions	Education	Family and elderly services	Active labor-market policy[a]	Labor-market training[a]	Social exclusion[b]
Denmark	5.6	6.5	5.28	1.89	1.07	1.5
Sweden	9.0	6.6	5.10	2.01	0.48	1.1
Finland	9.1	6.6	3.10	1.23	0.41	0.7
United Kingdom	7.6	4.6	1.16	0.42	0.09	0.3
Ireland	4.6	4.7	0.60	1.66	0.21	0.4
Austria	13.4	4.5	0.85	0.44	0.15	0.3
Belgium	10.3	5.0	0.28	1.29	0.29	0.7
Germany	10.9	4.5	1.36	1.27	0.34	0.6
France	12.2	5.8	1.14	1.37	0.35	0.5
Netherlands	7.8	4.6	1.03	1.76	0.22	0.7
Luxembourg	10.4	4.3	0.91	0.30	0.01	0.4
Italy	13.6	4.5	0.30	1.08	0.01	0.0
Spain	9.2	4.8	0.35	0.72	0.21	0.1
Portugal	7.7	5.4	0.53	0.87	0.28	0.1
Greece	10.1	3.7	—	0.35	0.06	—
EU 15	9.4	5.1	1.57	1.2	0.27	0.5

Source: OECD, *Social Expenditure Database* (2001).

[a]1998 or latest year available.

[b]*Source*: Eurostat, *Social Protection in Europe* (1997) (there may be a slight overlap with the other categories of expenditure).

employment in Ireland. The Continental countries offer a mixed picture, with above average employment performance in Austria, Germany, and the Netherlands. Low levels of employment are evident, especially amongst women and elderly workers, in Mediterranean countries like Greece, Italy, and Spain, with Portugal as the exception.

To some extent, variations across countries reflect 'developmental' differences (i.e. differences in the timing of previous reforms and in the degree of program maturation, as well as in aggregate levels and speed of economic and social well-being). But such variations are also quite clearly the result of specific (and largely 'deliberate') politico-institutional configurations. The 'recalibration agenda' that had emerged or was emerging in each of the four clusters of countries around the mid-1990s was thus heavily influenced by these configurations. Let us now briefly survey each cluster.

Table 4.3. Employment performance in the European Union (1999)

	Employment rate[a]	Unemployment rate[b]	Long-term unemployment[c]	Female employment rate	Youth unemployment rate[d]	Participation rate, men aged 15–64
Austria	68.2	3.7	1.2	59.7	2.9	76.7
Belgium	58.9	9	5.5	50.2	8.4	67.5
Denmark	76.5	5.2	1	71.6	7.1	81.2
Finland	67.5	10.2	2.3	64.7	10.9	70.3
France	60.4	11.3	4.4	53.5	8.2	67.5
Germany	64.8	8.7	4.5	57.1	4.6	72.4
Greece	55	11.7	6.5	40.4	12.4	70.2
Ireland	62.5	5.7		51.4	4.2	73.5
Italy	52.5	11.3	6.9	38.1	12.4	67.1
Luxembourg	61.6	2.3		48.7	2.2	48.7
Netherlands	70.9	3.3	1.4	61.3	4.8	80.4
Portugal	67.4	4.5	1.9	59.6	4.3	75.6
Spain	52.3	15.9	7.4	37.3	12.4	67.8
Sweden	70.6	7.2	2.1	69	6.1	72.1
United Kingdom	70.6	6.1	1.8	63.9	8.8	77.2
EU 15	62.1	9.2	4.3	52.6	8.4	71.6

Notes: [a] Total employment/population 15–64 years; [b] Standardized ratio; [c] Long-term unemployed (12 months and over) as % of labor force; [d] % of population 15–24.

Source: *Employment in Europe 2000*, European Commission, 2000.

4.2.1. *Nordic Europe*

In the Nordic countries, as is well known, social protection is a citizen's right, coverage is fully universal and everybody is entitled to the same 'basic amounts' (quite high by international standards) in the face of social risks—even though the gainfully-employed get additional benefits through mandatory occupational schemes. Besides generous income maintenance benefits, the Nordic systems offer a wide array of public social services and active labor-market programs, which sustain high participation rates for both men and women. Public employment is also very extensive. General taxation plays a dominant (though not exclusive) role in the financing of the welfare state: taxation and spending levels are high by international standards—especially in Sweden. Public assistance plays a rather circumscribed, residual and supplementary role. The various functions of social protection are highly integrated and the provision of benefits and services is mainly under the responsibility of (central and local) public authorities. The only sector that remains substantially outside this integrated organizational framework is unemployment insurance, which is not formally compulsory and is directly managed by the trade unions.

The strong emphasis on social services not only provides employment opportunities for highly-trained professionals but also a large number of decently paid jobs for persons with modest levels of formal education and training. High levels of female employment go hand-in-hand with the large numbers of (often low-skilled) public sector jobs. Especially in Sweden, active labor-market policies have, until the recession of the 1990s, helped to retrain redundant industrial workers for alternative jobs. The downside of the Scandinavian model has been a growing political resistance to extremely high tax rates, and since the early 1990s the need for fiscal retrenchment increased in the wake of the process of European integration. Swedish-style public sector job growth and active labor policies are seriously constrained by stringent budgetary compatibilities. Both Sweden and Denmark have begun to reduce public-sector employment.

Thanks to their institutional solidity and coherence, the Nordic systems have long been regarded (and to a large extent still are) as the quasi-ideal type of welfare state. As shown by Table 4.2, the architecture of Nordic welfare seems already well 'calibrated' for responding to the new risks and needs associated with ageing societies and the transition to the 'new economy'. The presence of basic income guarantees is a safeguard not only against poverty and exclusion, but also against the penalties deriving from spells out of work and broken or 'composite' careers. The availability of a wide array of services allows Nordic welfare systems to respond more effectively to the caring needs of families and to socialize their costs (including the cost of children). Moreover, high rates of labor-market participation attenuate the financial strains on pension systems. As the table shows, the Scandinavian countries also invest highly in labor-market training (a crucial policy for more knowledge-intensive economies) and their education expenditure ratios are by far the highest in Europe. Thus in the Nordic context our metaphor of 'recalibration' finds a relatively smaller scope of application than in other contexts for either diagnostic or prescriptive purposes.

Yet, the exogenous and endogenous challenges mentioned in the introduction have also been at work in this area of Europe, generating two main problems: a cost problem and a jobs problem. Throughout the 1990s the Nordic countries have been grappling with the pressures to contain the high and constantly increasing costs of their generous programs, on the one hand, and the pressure to re-organize their labor markets, on the other, especially with a view to generating greater demand for private employment. Given the high popular support for the welfare state (rooted in the *volkhemmet* culture and tradition: the welfare state is the house of the people) the reform agenda has been shaped by a pragmatic, problem-solving approach mainly centered around the issue of cost-containment, with no 'grand controversy' over alternative views and scenarios (Kuhnle 2000*a,b*; Eitrheim and Kuhnle 2000). The principles of universalism have not been significantly questioned, even if this meant 'across the board' cuts in replacement rates (e.g. in sickness benefits) or transfer payments (e.g. family allowances in Sweden: a sort of universalism in reverse gear). But significant steps have been taken towards the 'Bismarckian

tradition' in the field of pensions: the link between contributions and benefits has been significantly strengthened in both Sweden and Finland, with a
view to containing the relative weight of this sector (i.e. re-calibrating it, according to our metaphor) within overall social protection in the years to come.
Besides cost-containment, a second important *leitmotiv* of the Scandinavian
reform agenda in the 1990s has been 'activation', that is, the modification of social
security programs in a direction which gives actual and potential beneficiaries
incentives to find gainful employment. This trend can also be interpreted in
terms of recalibration: functional (from passive compensation of the risk of
unemployment to the active promotion of employability), distributive (more
investment in youth training to ease the transition from education to work and
to prevent occupational segregation) and normative (a stronger emphasis on
'productivism' and the work ethic).

The country which has gone farthest down the activation road is Denmark
(Goul Andersen 2000; Kautto *et al.* 1999). Starting in 1994 the Danish government introduced a series of reforms that have significantly changed the
institutional profile and functional logic of its labor-market policy (Benner
and Vad 2000). Eligibility for cash benefits was tightened, especially in terms
of duration: the maximum period of eligibility was gradually reduced from
nine to four years between 1994 and 1999. Individual action plans to ease
occupational re-integration were introduced, especially for the young unemployed. A wide array of 'activating' instruments were deployed: information
and counseling, subsidized employment in both the public and private sector, various kinds of training and educational initiatives, forms of job rota-
tion combined with an expansion of leave possibilities for employed workers
and so on. In order to implement this new strategy, the organizational framework of Danish labor-market policy was broadly decentralized, with the
establishment of 14 regional councils composed of representatives of the
social partners and local authorities, whose objective is not only to tailor
active measures to regional labor-market conditions, but also to foster
stronger links between enterprises, educational institutions, social services,
and employment centers, as well as encourage cooperative behavior by all
stakeholders. Following again our metaphor, in the Danish case we could
speak of an explicit strategy of politico-institutional recalibration in the field
of labor-market governance. This articulated activation offensive has
produced positive results: Danish unemployment fell from 8.1 percent in
1994 to 5.6 percent in 1999, while the employment rate rose from 72.4 percent
to 76.5 percent in the same years. Together with the Netherlands,
Denmark stands out as a 'path breaker' of welfare state recalibration in many
respects.

In terms of distributive recalibration, fundamental changes were introduced
in the Swedish pension system. In 1999, Sweden switched its pay-as-you-go

public pension systems from defined-benefit schemes to 'notional' defined-contribution schemes. In a notional defined-contribution model, each insured employee's contributions are recorded in an individual account that will earn interest, typically at a rate tied to the growth of wages—either the rate of increase in the average wage or the rate of increase in total wages. At retirement, the balance in the account is converted into a life annuity based on estimates of the cohort's expected life-span (Schludi 2001). Since Sweden continues to finance pensions according to pay-as-you-go principles, however, its defined-contribution scheme is 'notional' in the sense that contribution credits (rather than financial assets) are accumulated in the workers' individual accounts. When a worker retires, the balance of the individual account will be converted into a stream of monthly pension payments using a 'transformation coefficient' that depends on the worker's age at retirement and the cohort-specific life expectancy at that age (OECD 2001). The applicable life expectancy will be based on the previous five-years' unisex mortality table. The 1999 reform has made Sweden's pension system approximately actuarially neutral. It also introduced a small funded defined-contribution component into the system. In terms of distributive effect, the new Swedish pension system will operate on the basis of fixed relative position (FRP) principles, stipulating a balance between contributions and benefits which holds constant the ratio of per capita earnings of those in the working population (net of contributions) to the ratio of earnings per capita (net of taxes) of retirees (Esping-Andersen *et al.* 2002). As the shift from defined-benefits to a notional defined-contribution format involved steps into the unknown, Swedish policy-makers put much effort into carefully forging a farsighted consensus. First, a broad political consensus between the social democratic and bourgeois parties was achieved. Subsequently, this political agreement was brought to the social partners. The deep recession in the first half of the 1990s strengthened a common understanding across the political spectrum over the need for fiscal sustainability of the Swedish welfare state, including the pension system.

Despite efforts on the activation and pension front, according to many observers a lot of unsolved problems remain in the labor markets of the Nordic countries (especially those of Sweden and Finland). The major problem seems to be how to promote the growth of private service employment, hampered by a wage structure that reflects the overarching importance of egalitarian principles. And if it is true (to use Esping-Andersen's imagery) that *Homo Socialdemocraticus* is still very reluctant to relax these principles, then normative recalibration is perhaps the crucial front (or better: a precondition) for further policy adaptations in the regimes of this area.

4.2.2. *Anglo-Saxon Europe*

The second 'Social Europe' comprises two countries: the United Kingdom and Ireland—even though the latter has been distancing itself in many respects from the United Kingdom in recent years. Generally speaking, in these two countries the coverage of social protection is highly inclusive, though not fully universal (except for health care): non-active adults and the employed earning less than a certain threshold have no access to National Insurance benefits. These benefits—which are flat rate—are moreover much more modest than in Scandinavia. Conversely, the range of social assistance and means-tested benefits is much more extensive. Health care and social services are financed through general taxation, but contributions play an important role in the financing of cash benefits. Tax and expenditure levels have remained relatively low (at least compared to Scandinavia and Continental Europe), and the same is true for public sector employment. As in Scandinavia, the organizational framework of the welfare state is highly integrated (including unemployment insurance) and entirely managed by the public administration: the social partners are only marginally involved in policy making or management.

The United Kingdom is considered as the closest European approximation to the 'liberal' regime typical of North America and the Antipodes, characterized by modest levels of protection, tough 'commodification' incentives, and a predilection for targeted provision—with all its adverse effects. This view is partly exaggerated: in fact, aggregate social spending in the United Kingdom is around the EU average, the NHS is a solid institution catering to the needs of the whole population, the range of benefits offered (if not their level, in many cases) is wide and well-articulated by comparative standards. But unemployment benefits are modest and of short duration, taxes are relatively low, wage dispersion is high, labor markets are weakly regulated, the legal minimum wage is low, and social assistance is not generally available. Also the so-called 'tax-wedge'—that is, the difference between labor costs for employers and disposable incomes of workers—is fairly low in the UK. This makes the institutional logic of the British welfare states indeed distinct from that of the other 'Social Europes': this logic has generated specific outcomes and problems over time and thus shaped a specific reform agenda.

In contrast to the Scandinavian model, welfare-state financing and private-sector service employment do not appear to be particularly problematic in the Anglo-Saxon countries. But the Anglo-Saxon welfare states lack support for highly competitive, export-oriented, high-quality specialization in production based on co-operative industrial relations and a well-trained labor force. As a result, there is little investment in training in the low and medium bands of the labor-market's skills spectrum. Since the lean Anglo-Saxon welfare states provide only meager levels of social protection, low qualifications go hand in hand with poverty and social exclusion.

The strategy of recalibration under the Conservative governments of the 1980s and 1990s may be described as one of intensifying labor-market deregulation and income polarization between households. The flat-rate nature of 'Beveridgean' benefits and their coverage loopholes (based on earnings thresholds) allowed the Thatcher and Major governments during the 1980s and 1990s to promote a creeping residualization of social protection and an expansion of low-pay, low-skill jobs (Rhodes 2000). Institutionally supported by the majoritarian Westminister model of democracy, the Conservative governments were able to speed up labor-market deregulation and social security retrenchment. The real value of benefits was allowed to erode, while the middle classes were encouraged to 'opt out' towards non-public forms of insurance (e.g. in pensions: cf. below) and targeted, means-tested benefits started to soar—despite the tightening of eligibility rules inspired by the new 'workfare' philosophy. These developments have had a number of significant consequences: the erosion of universal provision (as well as the market-oriented re-organization of health and social services) has contributed to an early defusal of the cost problem; radical labor-market deregulation has fostered an expansion of private employment; but inequality and poverty levels have also markedly increased—partly in the wake of the perverse effects created by means-testing itself. The creation of a stricter benefit regime served the goals of cost-containment by reducing the number of claimants.

As a consequence of the Conservative recalibration agenda, the nature of British employment and the distribution of earnings have changed considerably. On the one hand, there has been a sharp decline in 'Fordist' jobs in manufacturing and other non-service sectors in the middle range of the earnings distribution. On the other hand, the increase in employment has been concentrated in sectors like banking, finance, and business services where earnings are relatively high and in hotels, catering, and other services where pay is low. Meanwhile, earnings at the upper end of the spectrum have grown relative to those at the bottom. The result has been a rapid polarization of incomes and a process of labor-market segmentation (Rhodes 2000).

A new ingredient of the United Kingdom effort at functional recalibration since the 1980s has been the introduction of wage subsidies to supplement low-paid groups. For the Anglo-Saxon welfare states (including the United States), where guaranteed minimum income arrangements at subsistence level are generally not available and unemployment benefits are low and of short duration, individual tax credits and social services to support workers and their families who work for wages below the poverty line are very popular

(Drèze and Sneesseens 1997). In-work benefits seem a straightforward solution as they increase the difference between incomes in- and out-of-work, especially if wages and benefits are low. The relative merits of labor-cost subsidies and wage supplements depend upon the reaction of supply and demand to such incentives. In general, where labor supply is inelastic in relation to demand, tax credits for employees will be more effective in raising earned income and expanding supply, while subsidies are more effective in increasing demand for labor and thus employment by reducing costs for employers. Under the prevailing welfare regimes, two hazards need to be circumvented. These are the 'poverty trap' and the 'inactivity trap'. The poverty trap refers to a situation where benefits are cut when people increase their disposable income. The lack of a financial incentive for the unemployed to seek work is an important cause of long-term unemployment in the United Kingdom. The inactivity trap, which prevails in Continental welfare regimes (see below), refers to the high level of benefits relative to the earning capacities of low-skilled workers. While tax credits can help to overcome inactivity traps, they can also potentially create new poverty traps for low-paid groups in subsidized jobs at the bottom end of the labor-market.

The strong dualistic tendencies in economy and society, inherited from the Conservatives, posed especially serious ideological and normative problems for New Labour. The Blair government has embarked upon a broad strategy of functional recalibration resting on the following elements: fine-tuning benefit rules to neutralize the various 'traps' created by old and new welfare-to-work schemes, fighting poverty and social exclusion through an increase in minimum wage and income guarantees, tax reforms and the introduction of new targeted programs (Clasen 2001).

The most distinctive feature in New Labour's strategy of functional recalibration is its strong reliance on work and employability in tackling poverty, disadvantage, and social exclusion. New Labour's 'welfare-to-work' strategy combines a prescriptive, job-search enhancement labor-market policy with in-work benefits to help 'make work pay'. In 1997 the Blair government introduced the *New Deal* program, aimed at moving youngsters in particular from benefits into employment by a mixture of incentives for skill enhancement and job-search compulsion. A personal advisor, assigned to any new entrant, draws up individual 'action plans' to ensure that placement, job search assistance, and training opportunities are targeted to individual needs. Sanctions for failing to take up an appropriate job or training offer are strengthened, and (renewed) access to benefits is made more difficult. Since 1999, three other New Deals have been introduced to cater for the special needs of the long-term unemployed, lone parents, and disabled workers (Clasen 2001).

New Deal activation programs rely heavily on tax credits, which gained in importance under New Labour's policy strategy to 'make work pay'. Most important in this respect has been the introduction of the Working Families Tax Credit (WFTC) in 1998, aimed at guaranteeing any family with a full-time worker a relatively generous minimum income. As the WFTC is run through the tax system, the stigma of applying for a benefit is avoided, while the direct link with wages clearly reveals the advantage of work over welfare (Glyn and Wood 2001).

Reconciling work and family life is slowly becoming an important agenda in New Labour's strategy of functional recalibration. The WFTC already features additional subsidies to cover childcare expenses. The National Childcare Strategy combines the establishment of nursery places in many neighborhoods with subsidies for pre- and post-school child care to promote measures that enable parents to balance paid work with the needs of their children. Childcare expenses are tax-deductible for lone parents and there is a means-tested benefit for childcare costs (Clasen 2001).

In an overall assessment of the policies adopted by New Labour, as compared to the Conservative recalibration agenda, Jochen Clasen concludes, on a positive note, that the overall scope of New Labour's 'welfare-to-work' strategy, including special programs for lone parents and disabled workers, is much wider than Conservative workfare policies. Moreover New Labor's policy repertoire is far more coherent in the sense that there is a much better 'fit' between employability measures and more passive wage subsidy measures to support the overriding goal of 'making work pay'. More critically, Clasen finds that the creation of temporary jobs, which play a large role in activation strategies in Scandinavian countries, remains underdeveloped. What is more, the 'Third Way' 'welfare-to-work' strategy is not underpinned by generous income transfers programs, as is the case many mature Continental welfare states. Finally, and this in sharp contrast to 'Third Way' rhetoric of 'learning and education as the key to prosperity', the relative significance of vocation training, skill enhancement and upward mobility is rather limited. The emphasis on 'sticks' rather than 'carrots', implies that for those who remain for whatever reasons outside the reach of employment through employability measures and tax credits, poverty remains a persistent threat (Clasen 2001).

Coming to distributive recalibration, New Labour's agenda is highly targeted on those in need. The introduction of a national minimum wage in 1999 was central to the New Labour agenda of distributive recalibration. Although the introduction of the minimum wage is fairly recent, it is already possible to evaluate some of its consequences. It appears that two million employees have already benefited from the new provision within the first year from implementation. Two-thirds of this group are comprised of part-time working women. There is even a growing acceptance of the value of a statutory minimum wage, both on the part of employers and the trade unions, but also—surprisingly—on the part of the Conservative opposition. The Blair government has also taken steps to reverse the dramatic decline in coverage rates and benefits of occupational pensions in the United Kingdom, by introducing a 'stakeholder pension'. Several characteristics of the British pension system increase the low-income risk for older people. Eligibility for the flat-rate basic pension is not based on residence but on wage-related contributions. Persons who earn less than the minimum ceiling—mostly women—are excluded from the system altogether. When the Conservative governments curtailed the public supplementary pension scheme, the middle classes were given incentives to 'opt out' and take out private occupational pension insurance. Although this served to consolidate public finances, the reforms also triggered massive increases in poverty and inequality among the aged. As women are the least covered by other private pension arrangements, their risk of falling into poverty in old age is the greatest. Moreover, with the shift towards price indexation, an increasing number of pensioners in the United Kingdom were receiving means-tested income support and supplementary benefits such as housing allowance. To address this problem, the Blair government introduced a minimum income guarantee for pensioners in 1999, which is higher than the basic state pension and is indexed to earnings (OECD 2001). The new stakeholder pension is partially designed to cater for people in insecure employment, supported by the minimum income guarantee. All employers are obliged to provide workers access to this benefit unless they already offer an occupational pension plan with immediate vesting or pay contributions into a personal plan for the worker.

Institutionally, and this should come as no surprise, the Blair government has deliberately shied away from corporatist exchanges with the social partners over broad social and economic policy-making issues (Crouch 2001). Instead, New Labour's approach to institutional recalibration is to keep intervention and regulatory burdens to a minimum in a well-functioning deregulated labor market. With respect to skill formation, the Blair government stresses the responsibility of individuals and favors business in the delivery of training, education, and human resource management in the 'knowledge-based economy'.

Turning finally to the dimension of normative recalibration, New Labour has set out a long-term strategy aimed at tackling poverty and social exclusion, under the heading 'Opportunity for All'. In 1999 the Blair government made a high-profile commitment to eradicating child poverty in 20 years and halving it in 10 years. The central feature of 'Third Way' egalitarianism is its strong reliance on work and policies designed to encourage individuals to increase their earning potential by participating in paid employment. Ideologically, the 'Third Way' largely rejects pursuit of greater equality through interventionist policies of income redistribution on moral grounds. New Labour seems to accept greater inequality if this is necessary for raising standards at the bottom. The result of this combination of fighting poverty, while tolerating greater inequality is overtly meritocratic (Glyn and Wood 2001). New Deal measures reflect a new approach to poverty which focuses more on the absolute, not the relative, position of the least advantaged, couched in terms of a 'new contract' between citizens and the state. It is government's obligation to provide opportunities for claimants to become more 'proactive', matched by the duty of benefit claimants to accept training, work, or education offers. New Labour's recalibration agenda boils down to a radical redefinition of the goals and functions of the welfare state. Rather than provide a generous safety net for the unemployed, New Labour sees the state's role as enabling their re-entry into the labor market, which is seen as the basic sphere of social integration.

But will the 'Third Way' succeed in reducing poverty and inequality while preserving the competitiveness of the UK economy in the context of the self-imposed constraint not to raise the (relatively low) tax burden? The main political challenge for a strategy of 'modernization' is that of overcoming not the vested interests of entrenched welfare constituencies but the resistance of the general public to paying higher taxes, regardless of their oft-recounted willingness to do so in opinion polls (Rhodes 2000). So far, the Blair government has tried so solve this dilemma 'by stealth', that is, by finding indirect and invisible ways of spending and taxing. It remains to be seen whether this strategy will continue to be politically feasible and—more importantly—whether it will prove adequate for the tasks at stake.

Ireland followed a distinctly different path of welfare state recalibration than Britain, as it moved closer to the continental European pattern (see Section 4.2.3). Two dimensions stand out: institutional recalibration with respect to wage bargaining and normative recalibration with respect to social cohesion and poverty alleviation. At first, the Irish imitated the British response of decentralized wage bargaining and radical labor-market deregulation in the later 1970s and early 1980s. After this failed to bring down unemployment which reached 18 percent in 1987, the Irish abandoned the decentralized, market-led approach to collective bargaining in favor of a more coordinated approach in the early 1990s. Beginning with the 'National Recovery' accord, which ran from 1987 to 1991, Ireland embarked on a whole series of tripartite accords: the 'Economic and Social Progress' agreement (1991–4), the 'Competitiveness and Work' accord (1994–7), and finally, the 'Partnership 2000' agreement (1997–2000) (Hardiman 2000). By way of an institutionalized commitment to consultation between employers, trade unions, farmers, and the voluntary sectors, the social partners agreed on a long-term strategy of wage moderation in exchange for tax-cuts and keeping inflation under control. This strategy of competitive corporatism bore fruit: Ireland's rates of output and employment growth are the highest in the European Union and its fiscal balance today is structurally healthy. Since the mid-1990s Ireland has experienced remarkable levels of economic growth and a dramatic decline in unemployment.

Relative income poverty has not decreased over this period, principally because transfers per recipient, although rising significantly in real terms, have lagged behind the exceptionally large increases in average incomes. This has meant that while the numbers relying on transfers have fallen as unemployment declined, more of those remaining reliant on them are below relative income lines. In these—admittedly unusual—circumstances, such indicators taken on their own fail to register change despite what would be widely seen as genuine improvements in the circumstances of the poor. The Irish method and measures combining both relative income lines and other deprivation indicators show a marked decline in poverty from 1994 (Nolan, Connell, and Whelan 2000; Atkinson *et al.* 2001). This progress induced Irish policy-makers to revise their original poverty reduction target to make it more ambitious, which illustrates the strong commitment to normative but also distributive recalibration in Ireland today. Of European countries Irish policy-makers have experimented the most with new forms of cooperation and partnerships, including in some cases the socially excluded alongside the traditional social partners. The 'Sharing in Progress' program in the National Anti-Poverty Strategy (based on a target to bring down long-term poverty in the population from about 15 per cent to less than 10 per cent with a long-term target of 5 per cent) stands out in terms of its strong partnership commitment at various levels of decision-making and implementation.

4.2.3. *Continental Europe*

This family includes Germany, France, the Benelux countries, Austria, and (outside the European Union) Switzerland. Here the Bismarckian tradition, normatively supported by traditional (single breadwinner) family values, centered on the link between work position (and/or family status) and social entitlements is still highly visible both in the field of income maintenance and in the health sector. Only the Netherlands and Switzerland have hybridized tradition by introducing some universal schemes (basic pensions in both countries; health care for 'catastrophic' risks in the Netherlands). Benefit formulas (proportional to earnings) and financing (through social security contributions) largely reflect insurance logics—even if not in a strict actuarial sense—often with different rules for different professional groups. Replacement rates are generous, benefit duration is very long (in some cases virtually unlimited) and coverage is highly inclusive (although organizationally fragmented): thus spending and taxing levels are high. The occupation-oriented approach manifests itself also in the institutional structure of Bismarckian welfare states. Trade unions and employers' associations actively participate in governing the insurance schemes, maintaining some marginal autonomy vis-à-vis public officials—especially in the health field. The majority of the population is covered by social insurance, through individual or derived rights. Insurance obligations come into effect automatically at the beginning of a paid job—though in Germany and Austria a minimum earning threshold is required. Whoever slips through the insurance net in these countries can fall back on a network of fairly substantial social assistance benefits.

The Continental type of welfare state is often regarded as a villain in comparative debates: not only because of its costs, but above all because of some inherent perversities, aptly captured by the metaphors of 'frozen Fordism' (Esping-Andersen 1996) and 'inactivity trap' (Hemerijck and Manow 2001). The root of the Continental syndrome lies in the combination of four distinct institutional elements: the generosity and long duration of insurance-based income replacement benefits; the mainly 'passive' or compensatory nature of such benefits; their contributory financing; and high minimum wages. Honoring generous insurance entitlements (especially those of maturing pension systems) has required the maintenance of high contributory rates on the wages of standard workers—in the presence of highly protective labor laws. This has in turn produced at least three adverse consequences in the labor market. It has discouraged firms from continuing to offer traditional 'Fordist' employment, accentuating those labor-shedding inclinations already connected with globalization and post-industrialism. It has created pressures for subsidized early exit from the labor market, rather than encouraging part-time work, so as to ease processes of productive restructuring. Finally, the Continental regime has severely hampered the expansion of private service employment, because of its high wage floors, while leaving little room for expanding public service employment (due to the fiscal overload). The ensuing unemployment problems have been met by further expanding passive schemes of income maintenance (unemployment, sickness, disability, and early retirement schemes), in turn requiring further increases in social charges. This self-reinforcing negative spiral has had a particularly heavy impact on low-skilled workers, the young and women. Historically characterized by low levels of female participation, the Continental systems, with their high rates of single-income households, have not been effective in promoting arrangements allowing women to combine work and family (especially child rearing) responsibilities, resulting in an emerging 'bad' equilibrium between low female employment (and high unemployment) and low fertility—with all the ensuing fiscal consequences. The conventional emphasis on 'passive' income transfers, coupled with strong job guarantees for male breadwinners becomes problematic when marital instability grows and conventional one-earner households decline.

With their highly regulated labor markets, the Continental regimes are confronted by low employment levels (both in the private and the public sector), high levels of benefit dependency, as well as high long-term and—in the case of Belgium and France—youth unemployment. The explanation largely lies in the 'Bismarckian' design of their social security systems. As a large share—over 80 percent in France and over 70 percent in Germany—of their welfare budgets is financed through payroll taxes, this creates a large wedge between the net wage received by the worker and the gross wage paid by the employer. At the lower end of the labor market, however, where the net wage of the worker cannot fall below the level defined by social assistance, the total burden must be assumed by the employer (Scharpf 2001). In other words, as a direct consequence of social policy design, many workers are not sufficiently productive to earn the cost of their labor back for their employers. The productivity threshold thus turns into an 'unemployment trap' for job-seekers with low levels of marketable skills. As a consequence, employment disappears, especially in those sectors where productivity increases stagnate and the prices of goods and services cannot be raised significantly. This frustrates job growth in the labor-intensive private service sector. The welfare states of continental (but also southern: see Section 4.2.4.) Europe have been unable to compensate for the undersupply of private sector jobs in labor-intensive services through the provision of social services in the public sector. In fact fiscal capacity is often limited due to a narrow tax base, on the one side, and costly pension commitments on the other side.

This Continental syndrome has generated a complex reform agenda centered on various elements: containing the expansionary dynamics of social insurance; rationalizing the structure of social spending by trimming pensions and 'passive' benefits, improving and updating family policy, introducing 'active' incentives in all the various short-term cash benefits; reforming labor-market norms to overcome the insider/outsider cleavage; reducing the incidence of social charges, also via broad financial restructuring; and so on. Significant steps in all these directions have been taken in all the countries of this group during the 1990s. But the road to adjustment has proved quite turbulent from a social and political viewpoint: unfreezing the Fordist *status quo* and neutralizing its inactivity traps will definitely require additional efforts in the future. The functional need to 'defrost' the Continental welfare state is compounded by the central role of the social partners in the administration of Bismarckian social insurance systems. Especially the trade unions are able to mobilize strong opposition against functional recalibration by defending the interests of insiders as both beneficiaries and professional administrators of the current division of labor (Palier 2000).

Notwithstanding the formidable functional, distributive, and institutional barriers to recalibrating the Continental welfare states, we nevertheless observe signals of policy change. In the wake of the European Employment Strategy (EES), at both the cognitive and normative levels, today there exists a virtual consensus that expanding employment levels among women (and perhaps also older workers) is a *sine qua non* for long-term sustainability. As a result of this shared diagnosis, most Continental welfare states have substantially increased spending on active labor-market policy in recent years, thereby emphasizing the activation content of social insurance instead of exclusively relying on passive transfers. Higher pressures on the unemployed to accept suitable job offers or participate in education have strengthened activation programs. Moreover, fighting social exclusion has become a central priority for many governments. Under the stimulus of the new 'inclusion process' launched by the European Union in 2001,[4] all the countries of this area have embarked upon an integrated approach to social exclusion, to be implemented through specific mechanisms of policy coordination and issue linkage across relevant policy areas. Most Continental welfare states remain half-hearted in introducing woman- and child-friendly policies of affordable access to day care, paid maternity and parental leave, a more equal division of household tasks between men and women, and finally, reasonably generous provisions for work absence when children are ill. But there is a clear realization across continental Europe that services, especially for small children and for the aged, are becoming an urgent priority.

Since the early 1990s, most Continental welfare states have taken steps to reduce the volume of beneficiaries moving towards early exit. Actions included abolishing the labor-market conditions provisions which took into account diminished labor-market opportunities of partially disabled persons, tightening administrative controls, and reducing benefit replacement rates in social insurance programs. In the Netherlands, sickness and disability

---

[4] Based on the 'open method of coordination', the inclusion process invites the Member States to submit a NAP every other year to promote the 'Nice objectives' (to facilitate employment and access to resources, rights, goods and services; to prevent the risk of exclusion; to help the most vulnerable; to mobilise all stakeholders). The Naps/incl. are subject to peer review, monitoring and evaluation by both the Commission and the Council. The first Naps/incl. were submitted by all 15 Member States in June 2001 (Ferrera, Matsaganis, and Sacchi 2002).

benefits have been made more costly to employers. Germany has tried to encourage beneficiaries to return to work with targeted training and employment policies, including the provision of subsidized jobs for older workers. The result of these policy initiatives in the area of social protection has been a general trend toward later withdrawal from the labor market (OECD 2001). The Netherlands has gone the furthest in resolving the continental pathology of 'welfare without work' by embracing a new policy agenda centered around jobs rather than benefits and transfers. The Dutch miracle was based on a long-term strategy of organized wage restraint, restriction of access to (and curtailing heavy misuse of) disability pensions and sickness insurance, and promotion of part-time work (Visser and Hemerijck 1997; Hemerijck and Visser 2001). The Dutch experience with long-term wage restraint suggests that its employment effects have been the strongest in domestic services that were previously priced out of the regular labor market. Thus, there is solid evidence for the view that responsive wage moderation would also be beneficial to the larger and less-exposed Continental economies of Germany and France. What is more, to the extent that wage developments in the private and public-sector are coupled, responsive pay settlements can lower the public-sector wage bill, curtail the costs of social security, and broaden the revenue bases of the welfare state (Ebbinghaus and Hassel 2000). Finally, there is some empirical evidence, also from Denmark and Ireland, that responsive income policy cooperation allows for a smoother interplay among income, monetary, and fiscal policy, thus stimulating economic growth while keeping inflation low. Attempts at orchestrating organized wage restraint have been tried in other Continental welfare states, thus far with little success. In the first half of the 1990s, the Belgian social partners failed to reach agreement. In 1996, the government imposed a wage norm, based on developments in Belgium's main trading partners, the Netherlands, Germany, and France. In 1998, a 'Central Agreement' was reached voluntarily. While the German 'Alliance for Jobs' of 1995–6 under Kohl broke down, the 'Alliance for Jobs, Training, and Competitiveness' of 1999 under Schroeder is fragile but not dead (Manow and Seils 2000). Finally, Jospin also launched an attempt to promote national social dialogue in 1997, but with little success.

In the Netherlands, female labor-force participation has increased rapidly, doubling since the early 1970s. The massive entry of Dutch women into the labor market is inherently related to the changing status of part-time work. Today 68.8 percent of all female workers are employed on a part-time basis in the Netherlands (Visser and Hemerijck 1997). Dutch employers essentially recruit part-time workers to strengthen organizational flexibility, not to pursue low-price competition, as in the United Kingdom. In many Dutch households, the low pay increases resulting from long-term wage restraint were in a way compensated (or even overcompensated) for by additional family income coming from women's growing job opportunities.

Dutch labor developments have increased the pressure for policy measures allowing working parents, especially women, to combine child rearing and participation in the labor market. The 1995 flexicurity agreements between the social partners established a win–win relation between flexible employment afforded by safeguarding social security and the legal position of part-time workers and temporary workers in exchange for a slight loosening of legislation concerning the dismissal of (full-time) employees. The 2000 Working Hours Act now gives part-timers an explicit right to equal treatment in all areas negotiated by the social partners, such as wages, basic social security, training and education, subsidized care provision, holiday pay, and second tier pensions. As a result, earnings differences between full-time and part-time jobs have narrowed to 7 percent. The new 2002 Work and Care bill will provide for short-term paid care leave and paid adoption leave. The Dutch experience thus renders a telling example of how through a concerted effort of labor-market desegmentation (a term coined by Jonathan Zeitlin) problems of labor-market dualism and gender marginalization can be avoided in a Continental welfare regime (Hemerijck and Schludi 2000).

Continental policies to increase demand for low-skilled workers have typically aimed at exempting employers hiring low-skilled workers from social contributions. For Belgium, France, and the Netherlands, it indeed makes sense to use regressive employment subsidies to create a low-wage job-intensive service sector. In these countries with relatively high minimum wages and high gross labor costs, there is a considerable potential for an expansion of low-skilled jobs in services like wholesale and retail trade, personal services, personal and public safety, house improvements, environmental protection, tourism, and cultural recreation. Targeted wage subsidies could permit a scenario of 'labor-cheapening' and job growth, without an American-style surge in poverty and inequality. This could open up a wide range of additional, economically viable employment opportunities at the lower end of the labor market. In-work benefits for low-income households now also begin to play a role in the Netherlands and Belgium. As employment subsidies are likely to increase labor demand, Fritz Scharpf believes that, when successful, subsidies could pay for themselves in terms of reduced outlays for full-time unemployment compensation. The overall advantage is that job-creation and hiring-decisions remain in the hands of private firms in the regular economy. Notwithstanding the favorable verdict on employment subsidies in Continental welfare states, they are not without problems. As many Continental programs are targeted on unemployed people who have been out of work between one and three years, employers are tempted to substitute the long-term unemployed for the short-term unemployed, or delay hiring until the subsidy can be collected. Also, it is important to emphasise that a policy of lowering social security contributions for employers hiring low-skilled workers could harm workers and employers' incentives to upgrade skills. This creates the danger that the employment subsidies could lock low-skilled workers in a secondary low-wage economy from which they cannot escape. Hereby, a 'skill trap' would replace the 'inactivity trap'. To be sure, in a graduated scheme, modeled on a negative income tax, there remains a clear incentive to seek better education and a better job.

Activation programs based on individual guidance and training opportunities, primarily targeted on youngsters and low-skill groups, have gained in importance in all Continental welfare states over the past decades. Many of the recent policy reforms pursued in Continental welfare regimes, highlighted above, have triggered important processes of institutional recalibration, that is, a reconfiguration of the involvement of the social partners and the division of labor between public and private actors and levels of governance in the provision of welfare and promotion of employment. At the interface of the public and the private sector, the proliferation of supply-side approaches to labor-market policy, providing for one-to-one counseling, has come hand-in-hand with a demonopolization and regionalization of public employment services, for instance in Belgium (Cantillion and De Lathouwer 2001). In the Netherlands, the privatization of public employment services and liberalization of the rules and regulation governing private temporary employment agencies, has extended the use of market-type mechanisms, such as contracting out, and organizational reforms, including, among other things, separating purchasers and providers. Private re-integration services and health and safety at work services are growing in a fair number of Continental welfare states. In terms of regulation, these developments share in a shift away from 'heavy' legislated or rule-governed labor-market regulation and employment policy to 'lighter' forms of decentralized coordination, including the social partners, private actors, and third-party groups.

Another form of institutional recalibration concerns a shift in the financing of the welfare state. Steps in this direction have been taken in France, whereby the bulk of health-care expenditures and the RMI ('minimum insertion income'), introduced in 1988, have been moved from social insurance contributions to general taxation, as a means to reduce payroll taxes and to increase the leverage of the state over social policy. In France, Parliament is now obliged to vote every year on the social security budget. With the institutionalization of a parliamentary vote, government is now regularly able to plan adaptation measures, especially with respect to cost-containment, instead of having to negotiate its interventions with the social partners (Palier 2000). This signals a shift from insurance to welfare.

Pension reform in Continental welfare states, especially in the pay-as-you-go systems of Belgium, France, and Germany makes for especially cumbersome exercises in distributive recalibration. Groundbreaking pension reforms, like the ones enacted in Italy in 1995 (see Section 4.2.4) and Sweden in 1999 (see Section 4.2.2), have thus far proved difficult to pursue in the Continental welfare regime. A dominant approach to improving sustainability of Continental pension systems has been the rise in contribution rates, especially in Germany and the Netherlands. In Austria, the reference period has been extended as part of an all-encompassing package of pension reforms. Changes to indexation rules for pensions have been enacted across the board in Continental Europe. Austria and Germany have moved from gross to net wage indexation. France has shifted from wage to price indexation. A fair number of Continental welfare states, notably the Netherlands, France, and most recently Belgium, have started building up advance-funded reserves within existing pay-as-you-go public pensions. Such funds can be used to maintain adequate pension provision when the baby-boom generation retires, while for now putting fiscal policy, and thereby the growth potential of the economy, on a sounder footing (Esping-Andersen *et al.* 2002). Among Continental welfare states, Germany has gone furthest with reforms to encourage savings in private occupational pensions through the use of direct transfers and tax advantages. Moreover, German policy-makers are planning to support contributions to supplementary pension schemes for low-income earners through state subsidies. But while wage earners are encouraged to pay up to 4 percent of their income into this additional pillar, German pension policy-makers have failed in their attempt to make supplementary old age provision compulsory, as in the Netherlands (Schludi 2001). Another weakness of the German pension policy reform—compared to successful efforts in Austria—is that no efforts have been made to harmonize civil servants' pensions with the general scheme. Also in France similar proposals for system integration were blocked by trade unions. The absence of cooperation and consensus among mainstream parties and the social partners in France can be considered to be an important cause for the lack of progress in reforming the French pension system (Bonoli and Palier 1997; Levy 2000).

Among Continental welfare states, in contrast to Scandinavian countries, thus far little progress has been made to support actively the employability of older workers by way of an active job policy for older workers (Guillemard 1999). Nonetheless, Austria, Belgium, France, and Germany now add pension credits in terms of contribution years to the insurance records of parents who raise children, in order to mitigate the negative effects of interrupted careers. In 1994, Dutch policy makers also introduced splitting rights for occupational pensions in the event of divorce or the dissolution of the marriage during retirement. Germany introduced several options for partial retirement in the 1990s for workers over the age of 55. In Belgium employees of a certain age can opt to reduce their hours of work progressively until they reach retirement age in exchange for a partial pension. Tax credits have been introduced in Belgium and the Netherlands to make it more attractive for older people to work.

Pressed by EU gender equality law, finally, Continental countries, like Austria, Belgium, and Germany, have now equalized the legal retirement ages of men and women, or are in the process of doing so. While France still holds a retirement age of sixty, in most other countries the legal retirement age is now 65.

4.2.4. *Southern Europe*

The last family of European welfare states comprises Italy, Spain, Portugal, and Greece. The degree of social protection maturity is different in these four countries: historically, the Italian system took off much earlier than the other three, and this is reflected in higher spending and taxation levels (cf. Table 4.1). But the South European welfare states display a number of common institutional traits, which set them somewhat apart from the Continental cluster (Ferrera 1996; Guillen and Alvarez 2001; Petmesidou 1996). They share a mixed orientation in terms of coverage: they are clearly Bismarckian in the field of income transfers (with generous pension formulas) and Beveridgean in the field of health care, having established universal national health services (fully realized, however, only in Italy and Spain). The safety net underneath social insurance is not very developed in these countries and occupational funds and the social partners play a prominent role in income maintenance policy, but less so in health care, which is largely decentralized—especially in Italy and Spain. Social charges are widely used (causing some of the 'traps' typical of Continental Europe), but general taxation is gradually replacing contributions as a source of financing for health and social services (again, in Italy and Spain the process has been completed). The family is still highly important in Southern Europe and largely acts as a welfare 'broker' for its members—with peculiarly adverse implications for women's position (Saraceno 1994; Trifiletti 1999).

Although the South European welfare states suffer from many of the problems of the Continental cluster, their structural crisis during the 1990s was characterized by specific traits. The reasons are basically geo-evolutionary. As mentioned, in Spain, Portugal, Greece, and (to a lesser extent) Italy the welfare state developed with a later timing and had to cope with more diverse socio-economic environments. In these four countries social protection thus entered the age of 'permanent austerity' in a state of institutional and financial underdevelopment and laden with internal imbalances, of both a functional and a distributive nature. Their social transfer systems displayed an institutional bias in favor of old age protection, to the detriment of other life-course risks (and typically of the needs linked to family formation, family expansion and more generally 'care' needs: cf. Table 4.2). From a distributive viewpoint, Southern welfare was in turn characterized by peaks of generosity (at least in terms of legal formulas) for certain occupational groups ('core' industrial employees and civil servants) and gaps of protection for certain others (e.g. irregular workers, workers located in small enterprises, workless households in general). 'Insiders' and 'outsiders' were separated by a sharp divide in terms of guarantees and opportunities—in some cases with a middling group of semi-peripheral workers bouncing between the inside and the outside (Moreno 2000; Perez Diaz and Rodriguez 1994). The black economy was very extended in these countries, posing serious efficiency and equity problems. Public services were rather unevenly distributed and in some cases insufficient and/or inefficient. It must be noted that the 'calibration' problems of Southern Europe were aggravated by pronounced territorial disparities—with the south of the South displaying a situation of cumulative disadvantage.

The most natural and politically simplest way out of this syndrome would have been to complete the developmental parabola, gradually ironing out the internal imbalances with more institutional and quantitative growth. But this option was ruled out in the early 1990s by exogenous constraints (especially Economic and Monetary Union, EMU). South European countries were thus forced to tread on the politically perilous grounds of internal restructuring: less generous benefits for insiders in order to cut down debts and deficits and—to the extent that budgetary constraints allowed—in order to finance new benefits and services for the outsiders. Southern Europe is definitely the geo-social context for which the metaphor of recalibration seems most appropriate. To a large extent this is also the context where this metaphor has served as an explicit reference point for policy reform: both *per se* and in connection with the wider goal of 'catching up' with the other Member States—perceived, precisely, as possessing a more balanced and solid array of social programs (Guillen, Alvarez, and Adao e Silva 2001; Guillen and Matsaganis 2000). The discourse that accompanied the reform process in the four countries was rooted in this goal, and its implicit (and at times explicit) reference to value judgments can be considered as an emblematic (and observable) example of 'normative recalibration'.

Given the starting points, promoting the recalibration of Southern welfare has not been an easy operation. The inherent difficulty of this operation has been aggravated not only by EMU's forced march and the increasing winds of 'globalization' but also by a particularly adverse demography. South European populations (especially those of Italy and Spain) are ageing at one of the fastest speeds in the world (Castles 2001). Yet, despite such difficulties a rather ambitious agenda has been pursued in the four countries during the last decade, centered on the following ingredients: attenuation of generous guarantees for historically privileged occupational groups, accompanied by an improvement of minimum or 'social' benefits; introduction and consolidation of the so-called safety net, especially through means-tested minimum income schemes; the expansion and amelioration of family benefits and social services—with explicit attention to gender equality and equity issues; measures against the black economy and tax evasion; the reform of labor-market legislation with a view to promoting desegmentation and modification of unemployment insurance benefits. Another distinctive element of South European recalibration has been politico-institutional: additional competences have been assigned to regions and local governments (especially in the fields of health and social services and especially in Spain and Italy) and novel concertative approaches have been experimented with (at the national, but also subnational levels: e.g. territorial pacts), promoting the involvement of social actors in the process of policy formulation and the formation of mixed partnerships in processes of policy implementation.

Italy can be regarded as an almost emblematic case of multi-dimensional recalibration since the early 1990s (Ferrera and Gualmini 2000). Functionally, this country strove to halt the expansion of its hypertrophic pension system, with a view to 'restoring to health' its battered public budget in the new post-Maastricht framework and to make room at the same time for some upgrading in the underdeveloped areas of family policy and social assistance. Pensions were reformed in 1992 and then again in 1995 and 1997. The so-called Dini reform of 1995 completely changed the pension formula, linking it closely to contributions in a quasi-actuarial fashion—not too distant from the Swedish formula described above. Between 1998 and 2000 family benefits were improved and a broad reform of social services and assistance was passed by the Amato government, establishing an 'integrated system of social services and interventions' and introducing—among other things—a minimum income guarantee against extreme poverty.[5]

From a distributive point of view, the reforms of the 1990s worked in the direction of leveling off social rights and obligations (e.g. contributory rates) across the various occupational groups. Within the pension system, for example,

---

[5] The new scheme is called *reddito minimo d'inserimento*-RMI (minimum insertion income) and is largely modeled on the French RMI analog. The Italian scheme was introduced in 1998 as a pilot experiment in a number of local municipalities and was subsequently extended to a larger sample in 2000. By the year 2003 the Italian Parliament is expected to decide on the eventual generalization of the RMI throughout the whole national territory.

the privilege enjoyed by civil servants to retire after only 20 years of service regardless of age (which had created a mass of 'baby pensioners' since the 1960s) was phased out by the 1995 and 1997 reforms; on the other hand, pension rights were accorded to atypical workers, and lower pensions were repeatedly upgraded—most recently through the 2002 budget law passed by the new Berlusconi government. Outside the field of pensions, some traditional gaps in social coverage were eventually filled (e.g. the introduction of means-tested maternity benefits for uninsured mothers, accompanied by a thorough-going reform of parental leave), and new schemes were created for poor households (e.g. a means-tested allowance for families with three children or more, as well as the experimentation with the RMI). Despite the efforts of the subsequent *Ulivo* governments (1996–2001), little progress was made in deseg-menting the Italian labor market: the rigid labor norms protecting the employed were only marginally relaxed and the baroque system of 'social shock absorbers' (i.e. the panoply of wage guarantee and unemployment compensation schemes) was not reformed. But in the winter of 2001 the Berlusconi government asked Parliament for a broad mandate to proceed on both fronts.

The reforms of the 1990s have sculptured a new organizational profile to the Italian welfare state—especially in the fields of health care, active labor market policies, social services and assistance. Between 1997 and 2001 substantial powers were transferred from the central government to the regions (and from these to municipalities). While creating numerous problems of implementation and giving rise to new risks of inter-territorial inequities, this process of quasi-federalization of important sectors of Italy's social protection system constitutes a far-reaching experiment in politico-institutional recalibration. In the spheres of active labor-market policies and social assistance, such recalibration implies not only a movement from the national to the sub-national levels of governments, but also the establishment of direct links between the sub-national levels and the European Union's coordinated strategies on employment and social inclusion.

Finally, this sequence of reforms was accompanied by the appearance of a novel discourse on the current state and future prospects of the Italian social protection system. This new discourse contained an articulated diagnosis of the traditional imbalances of the *status quo* and put forward a range of possible courses of remedial action, explicitly building on various notions of 'social equity', 'inter-generational justice', 'gender equality', 'productive efficiency', 'economic compatibilities', 'subsidiarity' (vertical and horizontal), and so on. The ideas that the Italian welfare state ought to give 'more to children, less to fathers' (Rossi 1997), that it should be aimed less at 'indemnifying' than at 'promoting' people's opportunities, and that more autonomy should be given to the local level became the object of a dense calendar of public discussions and events (from TV shows to party congresses). Measured against an historical background of harsh ideological confrontations between opposing visions of the world ('communism' vs 'capitalism'), the new argumentative climate of the late 1990s can be undoubtedly taken as a clear indicator of a significant normative recalibration, that is, a process of collective redefinition of the nature and role of Italy's *stato sociale* in a changed economic context— especially in the wake of European integration.

European integration also played a prominent role in prompting recalibrating reforms in the Iberian countries (Guillen, Alvarez, and Adao e Silva 2001). In their effort to join EMU by 1998, both Portugal and Spain engaged in restrictive pension reforms, in 1993 and 1997 respectively. Like Italy, however, they also proceeded during the 1990s to improve minimum benefits: in the fields of pensions, of family allowances, and of the basic safety net. As regards the latter, in Spain all the regions introduced their own RMI schemes, embarking on a path originally opened by the Basque country in 1989. Portugal introduced in turn a pilot national minimum income scheme in 1996, which was generalized in 1997.

Again like Italy, Spain witnessed in the 1990s a thoroughgoing process of decentralization of competencies in health care and social services from the central government to the regions. But the major challenge that this country had to confront during that decade was labor-market reform, in order to reduce the remarkably high levels of unemployment. Several measures were introduced with this objective in mind by the Socialist government up to 1996 and by the Conservatives thereafter: the introduction of flexible forms of contract, the rationalization of unemployment benefits, new programs and incentives to reconcile family responsibility and work (and thus gender equality), various activation measures, and a broad reform of employment services. Compared to Italy, Spain has made more progress in terms of labor-market desegmentation: in 1997 and again in 2001 labor laws were changed, relaxing the protection of 'core' employees and improving both the social security rights of irregular/temporary workers and their opportunities to access the regular labor market. As a result of these policies, Spain's employment performance has undoubtedly improved. At the same time, while Spain's unemployment rate has fallen from 24 percent in 1994 to 13 percent in 2001, it still the highest in the European Union.

In contrast to Spain (and many other European countries) Portugal's employment performance appears remarkably good. As shown by Table 4.3, in 1999 this country registered one of the highest employment rates in the European Union (including a surprisingly high female employment rate of 59 percent) and an unemployment rate of only 4.5 percent. While the superior employment performance of the Portuguese labor market in the European context is connected with certain characteristics of this country's economic structure and political history,[6] its low unemployment rates during the 1990s are instead linked to specific policy choices—especially with the advent of the new Socialist government in 1995. The modernization of social protection was a prime objective of the new government, which placed particular emphasis on active labor-market measures and, more generally, social inclusion policy (Cabral Villaverde 1999; Guillen, Alvarez, and Adao e Silva 2001). Unemployment insurance was broadly reformed, occupational training and insertion programs were expanded and specific incentives were deployed in order to promote a 'social market for employment', based on insertion enterprises and local initiatives targeted on the most vulnerable groups of workers. In 1996, an innovative 'social pact for solidarity' was signed between the government and the associations of municipalities, charities, and mutualities, with a view to mobilizing local potentials for employment creation. With its explicit reference—in official policy statements and public debates—to the principles of solidarity, social inclusion, but also to the fight against fraud and abuses on the one hand (especially in the field of sick pay) and to the need to rationalize pension protection, on the other, the Portuguese reforms of the 1990s can be interpreted as an interesting case of normative redefinition of the tasks and priorities of this country's social policy.

While Italy and the Iberian countries have clearly taken significant steps forward in recalibrating their welfare systems, Greece has definitely lagged behind (Guillen and Mastaganis 2000; Matsaganis 2000). The 1990s did witness in this country some movement towards reform in many sectors and a gradual re-orientation of the overall discourse on social policy, reflecting the new EU guidelines and recommendations. But the pace of institutional innovation has been very slow (especially as regards the reform of an internally polarized and financially unsustainable pension system) and most of the items on the Greek-specific recalibration agenda still remain to be implemented.

4.3. Conclusion

Europe's welfare regimes are in varying need of reform. Intensified international competition, ageing populations, de-industrialization, changing gender

---

[6] As a consequence of the colonial wars, which kept large numbers of men away from home serving as soldiers, Portuguese women were already used to participating in the labor market in the 1960s and 1970s. In the mid-1970s, at the time of the collapse of the authoritarian regime, the female employment rate was 48.2% (EU average = 44.5%; Spain = 31.5%; Italy = 30.7%; Greece = 33.6%). Female employment was (and still largely is) concentrated in agriculture (which absorbed in 1999 more than 15% of total female employment), traditional industrial sectors (e.g. textiles, often resorting to forms of subcontracted home work) and domestic services (data taken from EC 1999).

roles in labor markets and households, and the introduction of new technologies, place severe strains on welfare-state programs designed for a previous era. Since the late 1970s, all the developed welfare states of the European Union have been recalibrating the basic functional, normative, distributive and institutional underpinnings upon which they were based. In the 1970s, against the background of the emerging problem of stagflation, policy adjustment primarily revolved around macroeconomic management and wage bargaining to counter spiraling cost-push inflation and demand-gap increases in unemployment. After the mid-1980s, policy attention and action shifted towards issues of economic competitiveness. In the area of employment policy, there was a decisive shift towards supply-side measures. Alongside labor-market deregulation initiatives, many welfare states tried to contain the rise in open unemployment through strategies of labor-supply reduction via early-retirement and disability pensions (Ebbinghaus 2000). The destabilizing consequences of large-scale subsidization of early retirement and other forms of paid inactivity were only perceived as major policy problems when the European Monetary Union set limits to deficit and debt financing. As a consequence, politicians became more willing to adopt measures of cost-containment, often in conjunction with the introduction of more proactive functional labor-market policies, supported by new values of work, family, gender relation, distributive fairness, and social integration.

We live in a world of path-dependent solutions, and radical change in Europe's welfare states is institutionally ruled out (Esping-Andersen *et al.* 2002). Common internal and external challenges manifest themselves in terms of divergent problem loads from one welfare state to the next. The predicament of effective welfare reform today is not so much to design, in the abstract, a completely new welfare architecture, but rather, as we argue in this chapter, to *recalibrate* prevailing social and economic policy profiles, including their basic cognitive and normative underpinnings, to make them more responsive to regime-specific vulnerabilities. It is important to emphasize that path-dependency is about historical contingency: no more, no less. In other words, welfare state futures are not foreordained. In this chapter we highlight, in contrast to the diagnosis of Europe as 'sclerotic', the dynamic of welfare reform. The basic character of welfare recalibration we see as a form of institutionally-bounded policy innovation. Most of the policy changes in areas of wage bargaining, social protection, social services, and pensions have worked themselves out through policy experimentation. As traditional employment and social policies ran into severe problems of sustainability, because they were built on political, economic, demographic, and household conditions that no longer obtained, this triggered a progressive dynamic of *renovation* and *re-casting* current policy legacies and institutional structures so as to achieve a better 'fit' with prevailing societal challenges, new value orientations and pressing economic constraints. The precise policy mixes that have ensued from these ventures have been critically shaped not only by path-dependent policy legacies and institutional structures of decision-making, but especially by policy makers' capacity for *innovation*, intelligently recalibrating the institutional constraints and resources, and normative and cognitive orientations at their disposal (Crouch 2001).

Many reform efforts across Europe were couched in terms of the idea of 'social protection as a productive factor', the recognition that social justice can be made to contribute to economic efficiency and progress. Institutionally, moreover, it is again generally accepted, except perhaps for different reasons in France and the United Kingdom, that a productive balance between economic and social policy is best achieved through a dialogue among multiple actors, including the social partners, also at the level of the European Union. Practices of social partnership, with 'trust' as a constitutive element, moreover, encourage a problem-solving style of policy-making, giving collective actors the necessary social capital to overcome sectionalist interests.

The constraints of EMU and the Stability and Growth Pact on public spending and deficit financing seem to have had a remarkably positive effect on the resurgence of social pacts between national government and the social partners, allowing for various market and social policy reforms that encourage welfare sustainability (see also Rhodes, Chapter 5 this volume). Apparently, the shift to hard currency effectively brought the social partners closer together (Fajertag and Pochet 2000). These new types of social pacts were initiated in the Netherlands in the early 1980s, followed by Denmark, Ireland in the late 1980s, and Finland in the early 1990s. Also in Italy, Portugal, and Spain a number of social pacts were reached throughout the 1990s. The political feasibility of pension reforms is even more dependent on the institutional capacities of different political systems to orchestrate a consensus among major political parties and/or between the government and the social partners, especially the trade unions (Schludi 2001). The shifts from a defined-benefit to a defined-contribution format in Sweden and Italy were enacted through a careful and farsighted orchestration of consensus, whereby politicians and social interests committed each other to look beyond the political cycle and narrow institutional self-interest. Also in other South European countries, pension reform initiatives were part and parcel of encompassing 'package deals' with the trade unions, whereby union consent for cuts in pension benefits for the 'better off' were 'traded' for enhancements in the positions of the lower income earners. In short, social-democratic supporters of the welfare state, back in power during the 1990s and faced with the fiscal strain of EMU, realized that sustaining core tenets of the European social model(s) required significant adjustments, especially in Continental and Southern welfare regimes, resulting in a new willingness to experiment. But not in France: the absence of cooperation among mainstream French parties and the social partners can be considered an important cause of the lack of progress in reforming the French pension system (Levy 2000).

Another common thread that runs through the majority of experiences in recalibrating European welfare states is the normative emphasis on gainful employment as the principal channel to achieve effective citizenship. The new vocabulary of 'employability', 'lifelong learning', 'activation', 'insertion', 'make work pay', and 'welfare-to-work', signals a general shift in ideas. This shift was accompanied by a change in the balance from demand-driven macroeconomic management towards an even greater emphasis on supply-side labor-market measures. The new policy objective is no longer to keep overt unemployment down by channeling (less productive) workers into social security programs, but rather to maximize the rate of employment as the single most important policy goal of any sustainable welfare state. In terms of functional recalibration, this implies more immediate linkages between the policy areas of employment policy and social security.

Activation, targeted employment subsidies, concerted efforts at labor-market de-segmentation and experiments with regional pacts, constitute important steps towards expanding labor-market participation, which in turn—when successful—not only serve to broaden the revenue basis of the welfare state, but also reinforce its legitimacy in terms of the prevailing norms of economic independence, self-respect and social integration through gainful employment. Although paid employment offers the best safeguard against poverty and social exclusion, not everyone is employable. There is a danger of 'unactivatable' citizens ending up in a carousel, rotating between unemployment and activation. For these disadvantaged groups, policy-makers have to settle for basic income support plus less ambitious, but nevertheless costly, measures of social activation so as to prevent further marginalization and social exclusion, in support of 'social policy as a cohesive factor' (Vandenbroucke 1999).

Beyond important supply-side activation measures, of key importance has been the rediscovery of public social services with respect to childcare, maternity and parental leave arrangements. The Scandinavian countries offer mothers the widest array of choices; mothers can take leave from the labor market for the purpose of caring for their children or they can remain in the labor market, both full-time and part-time, while relying on high-quality professional care services. This suggests that the Continental and Anglo-Saxon welfare states should make the best of their backward position by simply emulating Scandinavian 'best practices'. But it should be remembered that the Swedish success in expanding female employment on a mass scale in the

1970s was based on a Keynesian full-employment strategy when governments were still in a position to do so. Under the shadow of EMU and the Stability and Growth Pact and the ongoing fear of tax competition, the Scandinavian policy response of the 1970s is no longer available. The 'second best' of the Dutch sequence of policy change is more instructive for most other Continental welfare states. Initially, female employment increases were achieved by way of enhancing employment conditions for relatively short-hour part-time jobs. Once part-time work has contributed to a dramatic increase in female employment, additional growth will have to be sought through improvements in the area of childcare. The shift towards longer-hour part-time jobs, under conditions of favorable economic growth, puts pressure on the government and private employers jointly to increase and subsidize the expansion of childcare facilities, as the demand for these services rises with the increasing employment rate for women. As a consequence, the Netherlands has the highest incidence of employer-based childcare provision, often subsidized by state, in the European Union (OECD 2001).

Domestic efforts at welfare recalibration, portrayed in this chapter, mark distinctive, and sometimes already successful responses to the massive external and internal policy challenges. Country-specific trajectories, we believe, are not really guided by some grand design or carefully thought out master plan, from which successful policy responses then ensued. The European trajectories of recalibration are paved with many contingencies, major recessions, multiple policy failures and regime-specific pathologies, severe coordination and implementation deficits between national and increasingly European tiers of governance (see Chapters 2 and 3 of this volume), and important changes in the balance of political and economic power. Institutionally-bounded recalibration and innovation in the welfare state required hard-won changes, interrupted policy experiments, and both fast and slow learning processes.

Since the mid-1970s macroeconomic instability stimulated a learning process whereby eventually the hard-currency EMU was established. The strengthened imperatives of monetary integration put severe pressure on different systems of industrial relations, leading to multiple reconfigurations in wage-bargaining systems. New bargaining procedures, in turn, encouraged a further search for new forms of active labor-market policies and activating social security provisions. Against the background of the rise of the service sector and the feminization of the labor market, a significant reorientation towards policy support for double-earning families then took place. Last but not least, new steps were taken towards making pension systems fair and sustainable in the face of population aging. Politically, most of these 'sequentially related' stages of bounded policy innovation across different areas of social and economic regulation were outcomes of lengthy processes of re-negotiation between various political coalitions, often in concertation with the social partners (Hemerijck and Schludi 2000).

The successes achieved through domestic policy innovation in turn shaped the employment and social policy agenda of the European Union. Although the principal site for welfare reform and policy innovation remains the nation-state, today domestic reform efforts are severely constrained (EMU) and increasingly shaped (EES and the other new processes of open coordination) by supranational regulation and policy initiatives. While domestic policy-makers are correctly wary of surrendering any authority to the European Union, for reasons of effective problem-solving, there is nonetheless a case to be made for greater co-ordination at the European level. Persistently high levels of unemployment in the run-up towards EMU, despite innovative national reform efforts, raised the stakes for common European employment and social inclusion strategies. In the second half of the 1990s, also in the wake of a significant change in the balance political power to the center-left across the Member States, a number of important breakthroughs led to new policy solutions trying to reconcile the goals of economic efficiency and social equity. Countries such as the Netherlands, Denmark, Ireland, and to some extent also Portugal have pioneered this new path: but, in many important respects, welfare recalibration is now clearly under way in all European countries, including the larger ones.

References

ATKINSON, A., CANTILLON, B., MARLIER, E., and NOLAN, B. (2002). *Social Indicators: The EU and Social Inclusion.* Oxford: Oxford University Press.

AUER, P. (2000). *Employment Revival in Europe—Labor Market Success in Austria, Denmark, Ireland, and the Netherlands.* Geneva: International Labor Office.

BENNER, M. and BUNDGAARD VAD, T. (2000). 'Sweden and Denmark: Defending the Welfare State', in F. Scharpf and V. Schmidt (eds), *Welfare and Work in the Open Economy. Diverse Responses to Common Challenges,* Vol. 2. Oxford: Oxford University Press, 399–466.

CABRAL VILLAVERDE, M. (1999). 'Unemployment and the Political Economy of the Portuguese Labor Market', in N. Bermeo (ed.), *Unemployment in Southern Europe—Coping with the Consequences,* special issue of *Southern European Politics and Society,* 4/3: 222–38.

CANTILLON, B. and LATHOUWER, L. DE (2001). 'Report on Belgium'. Paper presented at the Conference on Welfare Systems and the Management of the Economic Risk of Unemployment. Florence: European University Institute, December 10–11.

CASTLES, F. (2001). 'The Future of the Welfare State: Crisis Myths and Crisis Realities'. Paper presented at the RC19 Annual Conference. Oviedo: Oviedo University, September 6–9.

CLASEN, J. (2001). 'Managing the Economic Risk of Unemployment in the UK'. Paper presented at the Conference on Welfare Systems and the Management of the Economic Risk of Unemployment. Florence: European University Institute, December 10–11.

CROUCH, C. (2001). 'Welfare State Regimes and Industrial Relations Systems: The Questionable Role of Path-dependency Theory', in B. Ebbinghaus and P. Manow (eds), *Comparing Welfare Capitalism: Social Policy and Political Economy in Europe, Japan, and the USA*. London: Routledge, 105–24.

DALY, M. (2000). 'A Fine Balance: Women's Labor Market Participation in International Comparison', in F. Scharpf and V. Schmidt (eds), *Welfare and Work in the Open Economy. Diverse Responses to Common Challenges*, Vol. 2. Oxford: Oxford University Press, 467–509.

DRÈZE, J. H. and SNEESSEENS, H. (1997). 'Technological Development, Competition from Low Wage Economies and Low-Skilled Unemployment', in D. J. Snower and G. de la Dehesa (eds), *Unemployment Policy: Government Options for the Labour Market*. Cambridge: Cambridge University Press, 250–82.

EBBINGHAUS, B. (2000). 'Any Way Out of "Exit from Work"? Reversing the Entrenched Pathways of Early Retirement', in F. Scharpf and V. Schmidt (eds), *Welfare and Work in the Open Economy. Diverse Responses to Common Challenges*, Vol. 2. Oxford: Oxford University Press, 511–53.

—— and HASSEL, A. (2000). 'Striking Deals: Concertation in the Reform of Continental European Welfare States'. *Journal of European Public Policy*, 7/1: 44–62.

EBBINGHAUS, B. and MANOW, P. (eds) (2001). Comparing Welfare Capitalism: Social Policy and Political Economy in Europe, Japan, and the USA. London: Routledge.

EITRHEIM, P. and KUHNLE, S. (2000). 'Nordic Welfare States in the 1990s: Institutional Stability, Signs of Divergence', in S. Kuhnle (ed.), *Survival of the European Welfare State*. London: Routledge, 39–57.

ESPING-ANDERSEN, G. (1990). *The Three Worlds of Welfare Capitalism*. Cambridge: Polity Press.

—— (ed.) (1996). *Welfare States in Transition*. London: Sage.

—— (1999). *Social Foundations of Post-industrial Economies*. Oxford: Oxford University Press.

—— with GALLIE, D., HEMERIJCK, A., and MYLES, J. (2002). *Why We Need a New Welfare State*. Oxford: Oxford University Press.

European Commission (EC) (1997). *Modernizing and Improving Social Protection*. Brussels: EC (COM 102/97).

European Commission (EC) (1999). *Employment in Europe*. Brussels: EC.

FAJERTAG, G. and POCHET, P. (eds) (2000). *Social Pacts in Europe—New Dynamics*. Brussels: ETUI.

FERRERA, M. (1996). 'The Southern Model of Welfare in Social Europe'. *Journal of European Social Policy*, 6/1: 17–37.

—— (1998a). *Le trappole del welfare*. Bologna: Il Mulino.

—— (1998b). 'The Four "Social Europes": Between Universalisms and Selectivity', in M. Rhodes and Y. Mény (eds), *The Future of European Welfare: a New Social Contract?* London: Macmillan, 79–96.

—— (2001). 'European Integration and National Social Sovereignty: Changing Boundaries, New Structuring?' Working Paper No. 2.87. University of California at Berkeley: Center for German and European Studies.

—— and GUALMINI, E. (2000). 'Italy: Rescue from Without?', in F. Scharpf and V. Schmidt (eds), *Welfare and Work in the Open Economy. Diverse Responses to Common Challenges*, Vol. 2. Oxford: Oxford University Press, 351–97.

——, HEMERIJCK, A., and RHODES, M. (2000). *The Future of Social Europe*. Oeiras: Celta Editora.

——, MATSAGANIS, M., and SACCHI, S. (2002). 'Open Coordination against Poverty: the New EU "Social Inclusion Process"'. *Journal of European Social Policy*, 12/3: 227–39.

—— and RHODES M. (eds) (2000). *Recasting European Welfare States*. London: Frank Cass.

FLORA, P. (ed.) (1986). *Growth to Limits. The West European Welfare States Since World War II*. Berlin/New York: De Gruyter.

GALLIE D. and PAUGAM, S. (eds) (2000). *Welfare Regimes and the Experience of Unemployment in Europe*. Oxford: Oxford University Press.

GLYN, A. and WOOD, S. (2001). 'New Labour's Economic Policy', in A. Glyn (ed.), *Social Democracy in Neoliberal Times. The Left and Economic Policy since 1980*. Oxford: Oxford University Press, 200–22.

GUILLEMARD, A. M. (2000). *Aging and the Welfare State Crisis*. London: Associated University Press.

GUILLEN, A. M. and ALVAREZ, S. (2001). 'Globalization and the Southern Welfare States', in R. Sykes, P. Prior, and B. Palier (eds), *Globalization and European Welfare States*. London: Macmillan, 103–26.

——and MATSAGANIS, M. (2000). 'Testing the Social Dumping Hypothesis in Southern Europe'. *Journal of European Social Policy*, 7/2: 120–45.

——, ALVAREZ, S., and ADAO E SILVA, P. (2001). *Redesigning the Spanish and Portuguese Welfare States: the Impact of Accession into the European Union*. Working paper, Harvard (MA): Center for European Studies, Harvard University.

GOUL ANDERSEN, J. (2000). 'Welfare Crisis and Beyond: Danish Welfare Policies in the 1980s and 1990s', in S. Kuhnle (ed.), *Survival of the European Welfare State*. London: Routledge, 69–87.

HARDIMAN, N. (2000). 'The Political Economy of Growth: Economic Governance and Political Innovation in Ireland. Paper presented at Society for the Advancement of Socio-Economics. London: (SASE), July 7–9.

HEMERIJCK, A. (2001). 'Prospects for Effective Social Citizenship in an Age of Structural Inactivity', in C. Crouch, K. Eder, and D. Tambini (eds), *Citizenship, Markets, and the State*. Oxford: Oxford University Press, 134–71.

——and SCHLUDI, M. (2000). 'Sequences of Policy Failures and Effective Policy Responses', in F. Scharpf and V. Schmidt (eds), *Welfare and Work in the Open Economy: From Vulnerability to Competitiveness*, Vol. 1. Oxford: Oxford University Press, 125–228.

——and MANOW, P. (2001). 'The Experience of Negotiated Reforms in the Dutch and German Welfare States', in B. Ebbinghaus and P. Manow (eds), *Comparing Welfare Capitalism: Social Policy and Political Economy in Europe, Japan, and the USA*. London: Routledge, 217–39.

——and VISSER, J. (2001). 'Learning and Mimicking: How European Welfare States Reform'. Unpublished paper.

KAUTTO, M., FRITZELL, J., and HVINDEN, B. (eds) (1999). *Nordic Social Policy: Changing Welfare States*. London: Routledge.

KUHNLE, S. (ed.) (2000a). *Survival of the European Welfare State*. London: Routledge.

——(2000b). 'The Scandinavian Welfare State in the 1990s: Challenged, but Viable', in M. Ferrera and M. Rhodes (eds), *Recasting European Welfare States*. London: Frank Cass, 209–28.

MEIBFREID, S. and PIERSON, P. (2000). 'Social Policy', in H. Wallace and W. Wallace (eds), *Policy Making in the European Union*, 4th edn. Oxford: Oxford University Press, 267–92.

LEVY, J. D. (2000). 'France: Directing Adjustment?', in F. Scharpf and V. Schmidt (eds), *Welfare and Work in the Open Economy. Diverse Responses to Common Challenges*, Vol. 2. Oxford: Oxford University Press, 308–50.

MANOW, P. and SEILS, E. (2000). 'Adjusting Badly: The German Welfare State, Structural Change and the Open Economy', in F. Scharpf and V. Schmidt (eds), *Welfare and Work in the Open Economy. Diverse Responses to Common Challenges*, Vol. 2. Oxford: Oxford University Press, 264–307.

MATSAGANIS, M. (2000). 'Social Assistance in Southern Europe: the Case of Greece Revisited'. *Journal of European Social Policy*, 10/1: 68–80.

MORENO, L. (2000). 'The Spanish Developments of the Southern Welfare State', in S. Kuhnle (ed.), *Survival of the European Welfare State*. London: Routledge, 146–65.

NOLAN, B., O'CONNELL, P. J., and WHELAN, C. T. (2000). *Bust to Boom: The Irish Experience of Growth and Inequality*. Dublin: Institute of Public Administration.

OECD (1998). *Employment Outlook*. Paris: OECD.

OECD (2001). *Ageing and Income: Financial Resources and Retirement in 9 OECD Countries.* Paris: OECD.

ORLOFF, A. S. (2001). 'Gender Equality, Welfare and Employment: Cross-national Patterns of politics and Policy'. Paper presented at the RC19 Annual Conference. Oviedo: Oviedo University, September 6–9.

PALIER, B. (2000). ' "Defrosting" the French Welfare State', in M. Ferrera and M. Rhodes (eds), *Recasting European Welfare States.* London: Frank Cass, 113–35.

PEREZ DIAZ, V. and RODRIGUEZ, J. (1994). 'Inertial Choices: Spanish Human Resources Policies and Practices'. Analistas Socio-Politicos Research Paper 2b. Madrid.

PIERSON, P. (2001*a*). 'Coping with Permanent Austerity: Welfare State Restructuring in Affluent Democracies', in P. Pierson (ed.), *The New Politics of the Welfare State.* Oxford: Oxford University Press, 410–56.

PIERSON, P. (ed.) (2001*b*). *The New Politics of the Welfare State.* Oxford: Oxford University Press.

PETMESIDOU, M. (1996). 'Social Protection in Southern Europe: Trends and Problems'. *Journal of Area Studies*, 9: 95–125.

RHODES, M. (2000). 'Desperately Seeking a Solution: Social Democracy, Thatcherism and the "Third Way" in British Welfare', in M. Ferrera and M. Rhodes (eds), *Recasting European Welfare States.* London: Frank Cass, 161–85.

—— (2001). 'The Political Economy of Social Pacts: "Competitive Corporatism" and European Welfare Reforms', in P. Pierson (ed.), *The New Politics of the Welfare State.* Oxford: Oxford University Press, 165–94.

ROSSI, N. (1997). *Più ai figli, meno ai padri.* Bologna: Il Mulino.

SARACENO, C. (1994). 'The Ambivalent Familism of the Italian Welfare State'. *Social Politics*, 1: 60–82.

SCHARPF, F. W. (2000). 'Economic Changes, Vulnerabilities and Institutional Capabilities', in F. Scharpf and V. Schmidt (eds), *Welfare and Work in the Open Economy. From Vulnerability to Competitiveness,* Vol. 1. Oxford: Oxford University Press, 21–124.

—— (2001). 'Employment and the Welfare State: A Continental Dilemma', in B. Ebbinghaus and P. Manow (eds), *Comparing Welfare Capitalism: Social Policy and Political Economy in Europe, Japan, and the USA.* London: Routledge, 270–87.

—— and SCHMIDT, V. (eds) (2000*a*). *Welfare and Work in the Open Economy. From Vulnerability to Competitiveness,* Vol. 1. Oxford: Oxford University Press.

—— (eds) (2000*b*). *Welfare and Work in the Open Economy. Diverse Responses to Common Challenges,* Vol. 2. Oxford: Oxford University Press.

SCHLUDI, M. (2001). 'The Politics of Pensions in European Social Insurance Countries'. MPIfG Discussion Paper 01/11. Cologne: Max Planck Institute for the Study of Societies.

SCHMIDT, V. (2000). 'Values and Discourse in the Politics of Adjustment', in F. Scharpf and V. Schmidt (eds), *Welfare and Work in the Open Economy. Diverse Responses to Common Challenges,* Vol. 2. Oxford: Oxford University Press, 229–309.

TAYLOR GOOBY, P. (2002). 'The Silver Age of the Welfare State. Perspectives on Resilience'. Forthcoming in *Journal of Social Policy*, 31/4, October.

TRIFILETTI, R. (1999). 'Southern European Welfare Regimes and the Worsening Position of Women'. *Journal of European Social Policy*, 9/1: 49–64.

VANDENBROUCKE, F. (1999). 'The Active Welfare State: A European Ambition'. Den Uyl Lecture. Amsterdam, December 13.

VISSER, J. and HEMERIJCK, A. (1997). *'A Dutch Miracle': Job Growth, Welfare Reform and Corporatism in the Netherlands.* Amsterdam: Amsterdam University Press.

5

National 'Pacts' and EU Governance in Social Policy and the Labor Market

MARTIN RHODES

5.1. Introduction

Recent developments in EU-level social and labor market policy and politics have stimulated much speculation about more general issues of European governance. These include the emerging form of the multi-level EU polity, the capacity of Europe to defend the core policies and beliefs of its so-called 'social model', and the on-going transformation of national decision-making systems. Gradually there has been a shift away from an earlier concern with the dangers of a 'race-to-the-bottom' in social and labor standards, toward a view that, given the right kind of pan-European regulatory system, Economic and Monetary Union (EMU), the single market and 'globalization' might have much less dramatic consequences than often feared for Europe's social and economic fabric.

Other chapters in this volume focus on the contributions made to a new European system of social policy and labor market regulation by the European Union's employment strategy, the search for new, positive-sum trade-offs in European welfare reform, and policy implementation via local social partnerships and employment pacts. This chapter considers how *national* forms of socio-economic governance have changed over the last decade, how they have contributed toward EMU qualification on the part of its Member States, and how—EMU now achieved—they will evolve in the future. How, having assisted in debt and deficit reduction, as well as price stability and wage moderation, will these systems adjust to the reality of EMU, in which the 'convergence imperative' has given way to the demands of a new 'stability culture'?

Innovations in national governance systems, spanning wages and the labor market, the adjustment of social protection systems, and general budgetary policy have not only critically facilitated the process of EMU convergence and qualification, but have also helped lay the ground for subsequent developments at higher levels of EU policy co-ordination. Although much analysis of globalization and Europeanization has speculated about the erosion, or 'hollowing out' of the state, as a source of authority, guarantor of social and territorial cohesion, and locus for distributive politics, national systems of governance remain the key pillars for pan-EU social and economic policy making. If EMU is to function effectively, if it is not to be undermined by inflation and budget deficits, and if—as is hoped—there truly is to be a process of welfare and labor market reform steered and shaped by new linkages between EU decision-making forums and Member States, then the results of earlier innovations, especially in systems of negotiation and bargaining, must also be sustained.

Nevertheless, it would be over-optimistic to expect that national incomes policies and systems of social concertation can provide a stable, solid, and unproblematic link between EU initiatives and national policy domains. This view, in which social conflict is absorbed or neutralized by consensual mechanisms of deliberation and learning, is as inadequate as one in which, under the pressures of EMU and increased product market competition, a process of 'Anglo-American' convergence is engineered among Europe's varieties of continental capitalism (Teague 2001). Reality is likely to be much less uniform: conflict over both the substantive and procedural components of policy-making may well be rechannelled but will certainly not disappear. It is also likely to involve the reconfiguration of bargaining systems themselves into more complex, multi-level forms. But since the levels of bargaining are also the objects of contestation, a future of 'punctuated' rather than stable equilibria can be forecast.

In the following I argue that macroeconomic management and social and labor market policy making under EMU will indeed provide significant functional incentives for sustaining or creating consensus-seeking arrangements in its member countries. I also argue, however, that the recent experience of national incomes policy agreements and broader social pacts reveals other, destabilizing pressures. These operate in favor of a decentralization and fragmentation of such systems, requiring a complex process of reconfiguration to sustain their governability. Rather than reaching a stable equilibrium, national systems of governance in social policy and the labor market will require constant re-negotiation as functional imperatives and political pressures interact, and sometimes collide.

This interpretation is neither optimistic nor pessimistic about the possibilities of deliberative or negotiated governance under EMU. Rather it should be seen as a realistic assessment of the changing set of constraints and opportunities for concertation at various levels in national systems. Attempts to innovate in EU governance, either via new bargaining structures (the cross-border co-ordination of collective bargaining), new legislative intervention (the promotion of firm-level concertation through the new EU information and consultation Directive), and the proliferation of 'new instruments' (including National Action Plans, or NAPs, and the much discussed 'Open Method of Co-ordination') will inevitably feed into these systems with unpredictable, rather than convergence-generating, effect.

Section 5.2 considers contemporary trends in concertation and the transition from wage bargaining to social pacts in the 1990s. Section 5.3 analyzes processes of social conflict and system management, wage bargaining, and the negotiation of welfare and labor market reform in greater detail, focusing on four national cases. Section 5.4 confronts the functional demands for coordinated forms of governance in the Euro-zone with current trends in incomes policies and social policy concertation. The potential for a European contribution to alleviating the strains in these systems is also considered. Section 5.5 concludes by discussing five future scenarios for national systems of socio-economic governance.

5.2. System Governance under EMU: From Wage Bargaining to 'Social Pacts'

What are the most important changes to systems of socio-economic governance over the last decade or so? Many forecasts for the 1990s by social scientists and members of neo-liberal policy circles involved a decentralization and fragmentation of wage bargaining across Europe, with adverse consequences for welfare more generally as competition generated a 'race-to-the bottom' in social and labor standards (Gros and Hefeker 1999). In fact, despite the usual skirmishing between employers and unions, there has been remarkable stability in patterns of wage bargaining, and little evidence for a competitive downgrading of social protection systems.

At a general level we can explain this by the presence of both centralizing and decentralizing forces in domestic economies. New mechanisms for social conflict management have developed as a result of both a new external constraint (the Maastricht convergence criteria) and the resolution of what we can term 'flexibility struggles' in the Member States. For in addition to its impact on budgetary policy, the realization of EMU has placed new pressures on wage–cost competition by making competitive devaluation impossible. Meanwhile, employers in all systems are searching for greater company and plant-level flexibility in three areas: internal (or functional) flexibility in the work place; external (or numerical) flexibility vis-à-vis the wider labor market; and greater pay flexibility at local levels. At the level of the individual firm, new forms of what

Sisson (2001) calls 'integrative' as opposed to adversarial bargaining have emerged in many industrial relations systems, as employers seek both to minimize costs and promote the co-operation and commitment of the work force.

But employers have also been reluctant to dismantle systems of wage co-ordination where unions retain bargaining power. For even if high levels of unemployment have reduced this power, achieving reforms in the labor market and wider welfare system in most countries has proven much easier with the unions on side. Furthermore, cost competitiveness and monetary stability—as well as 'credibility' with financial markets—have required a means of preventing wage drift and the emergence of new inflationary pressures. This has focused the attention of governments on revitalizing incomes policies, a critical component of most new national bargains. Of course, the potential for conflict among these contradictory pressures is considerable—as will be explained below. But under the EMU convergence constraint even those countries least likely to achieve an incomes policy deal (or achieve deficit reductions, linked in part to public sector pay restraint) were able to qualify.

In order to understand the evolution of national governance systems, one can usefully begin by distinguishing four main ideal-types of wage co-ordination (derived from Traxler 1999, 2000; Schulten and Stueckler 2000):

(1) *inter-associational co-ordination*, or centralized collective bargaining by national peak organizations (Belgium, Finland, and Ireland have stronger forms of such co-ordination, while Germany has a non-binding central recommendation);

(2) *intra-associational co-ordination* by peak employer and union organizations of their affiliates (Denmark, Finland, Germany, Ireland, Netherlands, Spain, and Sweden, with a weaker form of peak-level information exchange in Germany);

(3) *pattern bargaining*, that is, co-ordination by a sectoral trend-setter (evident in Austria, Denmark, Finland, Germany, the Netherlands, and Norway), where either a large sector—for example, metalworking—or large individual firms play this role;

(4) *state-imposed co-ordination* via legal pay indexation or a reference point in a statutory minimum wage (set by national-legal agreements as in Belgium and Greece or by law as in the Netherlands, Portugal, Spain, and the United Kingdom).

Across the EU countries the major changes in recent years have been in Sweden (a big shift from inter-sectoral to sectoral bargaining in the early 1990s); in the Netherlands (a simultaneous decentralization and centralization, depending on the sector); and in Spain (where company agreements have declined in favor of sectoral settlements). The United Kingdom is an outlier in its radical shift from sectoral to company bargaining. But the general tendency during the EMU convergence years has been for a reinforcement of commitments to existing structures, with several novel—although far from stable or fully institutionalized—trends.

The first is the linking of incomes policies to broader social bargains. Denmark, Finland, Germany, Greece, Ireland, Italy, Norway, and Portugal have all either attempted or achieved national tripartite deals, some of which (Ireland, Portugal, Italy, and Finland) have assumed the form of on-going, quasi-institutionalized pacts. Meanwhile others (Belgium, the Netherlands, and Sweden) have relied more on cross-sectoral bipartite agreements, though in the Dutch case linked to the negotiation of general welfare reforms. Concertation is driven by the involvement of social partners in social insurance management in many countries, as well as the existence of complex policy interactions, due to the impact of non-labor costs on competitiveness, links between social benefits and salaries, and the problem of high reservation wages (Hassel and Ebbinghaus 2000).

The southern countries have also relied greatly on tripartite or bipartite solutions to bring inflation rates into line with the Maastricht criteria, and have made considerable changes to the articulation of bargaining levels. In those countries where the preconditions for such deals were weak, a broadening of bargaining from wages to adjacent areas of welfare reform helped strengthen and legitimize the bargain. This form of 'generalized political exchange' has also allowed a number of innovations in both productivity and distributive bargains (discussed below), which might not otherwise have been achieved.

A second general trend has been the result of innovation in the relationship between levels of bargaining. In many systems there have been simultaneous processes of centralization and decentralization: while the macro-level has retained important steering functions, there has been a gradual devolution of many issues to the company level. The spread of 'pacts for employment and competitiveness' (or PECs) seems to be strengthening partnership in the work place, especially in the Netherlands and Germany, where they now concern between 5 and 10 percent (and maybe more) of private sector firms (Pedersini 2000). New reforms to company consultation systems in Germany will reinforce such developments, as will the implementation of the European Union's new Directive on national information and consultation where, as in Ireland, company-level partnership remains weak.

A recent assessment (Sisson 2001) notes that such deals have mostly been employer-driven. But it also contrasts such deals with US-style concession bargaining where there is rarely an effective 'quid pro quo'. Freyssinet and Seifert (2001: 625) argue that company-level PECs represent a kind of exchange agreement, in which unions make concessions in the areas of pay and working time and employers offer employment or investment guarantees. PECs may be isolated individual measures, can be integrated components of national employment strategies, or may be linked to the efforts of the social partners to engage in 'organized decentralization' in their search for a new division of labor between levels of collective bargaining.

A third trend concerns cross-national bargaining. Some of the incomes policy deals mentioned above (Belgium, Denmark, and Norway) have sought to co-ordinate wage increases with those in other countries in an attempt to preserve levels of competitiveness. But there have also been two attempts—both beginning in 1998, and both with the German IG Metall as prime mover—to coordinate *across* borders. In the Doorn Agreement, Germany and the Benelux countries have sought to co-ordinate productivity-linked deals in metalworking in order to prevent competitive under-cutting by one country or another. Meanwhile in direct response to EMU, the European Metalworkers' Federation (EMF) has introduced guidance for collective bargaining across the sector, which tries to promote wage deals linking compensation for local inflation rates with productivity growth (Gollbach and Schulten 2000).

Although limited, for some observers these developments herald the emergence of a *European* industrial relations system. As a procedural norm for a mass of separate bargains, the EMF initiative could in theory create the basis for a Europe-wide wage consensus and strategy, providing some of the wage flexibility and local adaptability sought by employers while also preventing downward competition among bargaining units (Traxler 1999; Crouch 2002). With this goal in mind, the European Trade Union Confederation (ETUC) is seeking to generalize the EMF initiative.

It is tempting to suggest, then, that during the 1990s industrial relations no longer revolved around the dichotomy of centralization or decentralization, and that the first steps were being put in place to prevent competitive bidding across borders. Within national systems, the extent to which the social partners managed to combine decentralized bargaining autonomy with macroeconomic considerations in wage setting was increasingly important. This is because, in principle, agreements in two-level systems allow sectoral bargainers to strike decentralized deals over productivity, training, and job opportunities for less productive workers within the framework of a longer-term commitment to macroeconomic stability. If structures can be developed involving high levels of trust, not only between the social partners at the national level, but even more so between sectoral negotiators and central leadership, then the sustainability of these systems is also increased. They can then be extended to parallel deals in areas where labor market and broader social security issues overlap. Indeed, this has been the logic and aspiration behind many of Europe's social pacts in recent years.

But as discussed below, there are numerous problems in achieving such a strategy—including critically the organizational architecture of the system.

The articulation between employers and unions (horizontal co-ordination) and between various levels of the bargaining system (vertical co-ordination) has already been problematic in many countries. Experience shows that the twin pressures for a centralization of wage setting and a decentralization of productivity and manpower issues can be contained in certain junctures. But when circumstances change, these same pressures may also begin to unravel these fragile social compromises.

The equilibria between the national and lower levels are frequently threatened by the determination of employers in many countries to push for further decentralization. This has adverse knock-on effects for the organization of the labor movement, with the danger that union confederations are weakened in favor of sectoral unions, and sectoral agreements hollowed out in favor of company agreements or 'escape clauses'. Equally, although they may be integrated into a vertically coordinated strategy of bargained adjustment, PECs may also destabilize the system. If the devolution of the substance and procedures of collective bargaining also transfers the locus of organizational strength downwards, then the traditional balance of power between unions and employers may well also be undermined.

There are further problems in sustaining explicit national 'pacts' in weakly institutionalized systems of concertation. In certain countries, attempts to combine incomes policy with agreements on labor market and welfare reform have assisted and legitimized a process of broader political exchange. But while functional for the EMU convergence period, none of these pacts are conflict free. As discussed below, there seems to be a threshold beyond which the utility of general political exchange declines and a complex reconfiguration of bargains and their levels of negotiation becomes necessary.

5.3. Social Pacts in Principle and Practice: Negotiating Welfare Reform and Labor Market Flexibility

One of the distinctive features of recent social pacts has been the attempt to cover both productivity and broader distributional issues, sometimes in the same high-profile bargain or in more limited agreements between governments, employers, and unions. In a recent study (Rhodes 2001) I argued that in ideal-typical form, a social pact could begin successfully to bridge welfare, employment, and competitiveness issues and tackle many of the problems afflicting certain continental European economies. Especially manifest in the south, these include 'insider–outsider' disparities, both in terms of benefit entitlements and employment opportunities; low levels of female labor market participation; inadequate training and employment mismatches; and large regional concentrations of unemployment (see also Ferrera and Rhodes 2000).

On the *distributional* side, the following initiatives might be (and have been) elaborated: a national incomes policy with sufficient flexibility to prevent less productive workers from being priced out of employment; a relaxation of high levels of security for full-time core employees, in return for greater protection for temporary and part-time workers; a redesign of social security systems to improve the entitlements of female and part-time or temporary workers and; a parallel redesign of social security systems to promote labor market participation, while also innovating in education and training systems.

On the *productivity* side of the bargain, the principal innovations might include a shift away from legislated or rule-governed to negotiated labor market regulation; the development of a decentralized component within the national wage bargaining system that allows productivity-linked pay deals; concerted adjustment in companies in response to new demands from markets or technologies; a shift away from adversarial industrial relations toward a more consensual model; and a joint implementation of training mechanisms and priorities.

We can hypothesize (see Rhodes 2001) that the most successful such pacts would entail a balanced set of both distributional and productivity innovations. But such innovations—creating 'augmented pacts' (see Casey and Gold 2000)—will also entail changes to the architecture of governance. On the distributional side, they require the development of what we can call, after Treu (1992), 'qualitative integration', in which, horizontally, a large number of policy areas are linked together. They may also require a greater degree of 'quantitative' integration, that is, an increase in the number of actors involved. On the productivity side, they require innovation along a vertical dimension of 'qualitative integration'; for if a process of 'organized decentralization' is to be successful, the links between the national, sectoral, and local levels of bargaining must also be improved (see Molina and Rhodes 2002). Distinguishing between their distributional and productivity components, and also considering their capacity for 'system integration', we can assess both the degree of innovation in systems of concertation and their level of governability.

Prior to discussing these issues at a general level, the experience of four countries—the Netherlands, Ireland, Italy, and Portugal—will be considered. Other national examples would be equally pertinent. Other countries (e.g. Denmark and Norway) have also engaged in enhanced forms of concertation to facilitate economic adjustment without, however, committing to a specific, high profile pact (Dølvik and Martin 2000; Lind 2000). Others still have attempted but failed to achieve a national 'Pact for Employment' (Germany) or 'Alliance for Growth' (Sweden) due to the configuration of their systems, and primarily the strength of sectoral organizations (Hassel 2001; Stephens 2000). The experiences of France and Spain are also interesting for government attempts to encourage concertation and overcome strong traditions of adversarial industrial relations (Palier 2000; Pérez 2000).

The four cases that follow are chosen first because of their attempts to put in place an iterative process of 'pacting' as the basis for parallel labor market and social security reforms; second because of their experience in seeking equitable trade-offs between social justice and competitiveness; and third because of the problems in sustaining their system governability and reconciling distributive with productivity-oriented policies. Together they help illustrate some of the more general problems afflicting Europe's complex 'negotiating systems'.

5.3.1. *The Netherlands*

The Dutch have gone further than most in seeking to innovate across these areas of policy. On the distributional side of the bargain, concertation has been the prerequisite for innovation in 'flexicurity' and labor market de-segmentation. Recent reforms have reduced the differences between high levels of security for full-time core workers and lower levels of protection for peripheral temporary and part-time workers. Promoting part-time work and boosting employment flexibility subsequently paved the way for a virtual paradigm shift in Dutch labor market regulation with the adoption of the 1999 'flexicurity' law which innovated in tax and social security to facilitate 'secured' part-time work.

Distributional considerations have also led to the inclusion in policy deliberation and collective agreements of those marginalized from the labor market, including the long-term unemployed, the disabled, and ethnic groups. But a major weakness of the Dutch system remains its dependence on disability benefits as a cushion for unemployment and the use of subsidized employment programs to compensate for the lack of unskilled jobs at prevailing wages. On the productivity side, since 1993 and the beginning of the 'New Course' agreement, Dutch unions and employers have exchanged wage moderation for working time reduction, leading to shorter working hours, an expansion of leave arrangements, and the guarantee of income stability throughout the year (Visser and Hemerijck 1997).

As for system architecture, the social partners have retained their role in reintegrating unemployed and disabled people into the labor market following a January 2000 compromise agreement. This was preceded by several years of dispute after the 1997 Social Insurance Organization Act shifted the governance of social security from bipartite Industrial Insurance Boards (run by the social partners) to a tripartite national public authority and their implementation to private organizations. Regarding vertical integration, the Netherlands has achieved a high degree of co-ordination between levels of bargaining in its ordered and sophisticated version of 'organized decentralization' (Huiskamp and van Riemsdijk 2001). Hemerijck, Van der Meer, and Visser (2000) demonstrate the clear impact that national agreements have on sectoral and firm-level accords in areas such as training, performance-related pay, job expansion, and flexible working hours.

Yet numerous strains have appeared throughout the system which, together, threaten its integration, governability, and capacity to achieve a broad range of objectives. Tighter labor markets, and the new militancy of small groups that are overtaking traditional unions in certain sectors, have driven up wage demands. Wage hikes above the norm undermined the central agreement of December 2000, which limited wage increases in exchange for expanded training and education facilities for employees. In response, unions have called for new representativeness criteria, arguing that only unions of a certain size should be able to negotiate dispensation from coverage by sectorally agreed deals. Employers support this stance to the extent that they are opposed to bargaining anarchy and free riding on collective agreements.

Nevertheless, employers are also pushing for greater pay flexibility at the level of individual firms, while the role of works councils is becoming increasingly important in setting the terms and conditions of employment. As a result, sector-wide agreements are beginning to fragment. Unions are finding it increasingly hard to recruit members in private-sector services, or to defend their position in the public sector where pay and conditions are lagging behind. Overall, the ability of unions to exert control in the system is being diminished—one factor stimulating debate on whether it is better for them to retreat to their core tasks of pay bargaining and defense of their members, leaving broader distributive policies to the state (Hemerijck, Van der Meer, and Visser 2000: 274).

5.3.2. *Ireland*

In Ireland, the social partners hammered out their first tripartite response to the crisis in public finances in 1987 in the form of the Programme for National Recovery (1987–90). Subsequent agreements renewing and extending that accord have been linked to a centralization of wage bargaining and a growing willingness to address tax, education, health, and social welfare issues via central negotiation (O'Donnell 1998). The emphasis of all four agreements to date has been on macroeconomic stability, greater equity in the tax system, and enhanced social justice. Specific innovations include inflation-proof benefits and improved labor legislation covering part-time work, employment equality, and unfair dismissal.

In the process, Ireland has experienced a remarkable transformation of its industrial relations system. While retaining its voluntarist character, it has made a transition from one strongly resembling the British adversarial system, to one with strong corporatist elements, capable of delivering low inflation (from 1987 to 1996, wage drift was limited to fewer than 5 percent of companies), a high rate of economic growth and innovation in social security, taxation, and labor market policy.

Productivity aims have been explicitly combined with a broad distributive agenda—one that integrates not just a wide range of policies under concertation but also an extended group of actors. 'Partnership 2000' (1996–97), which included a National Anti-Poverty Strategy, was negotiated with a number of partners, including the Irish National Organisation of the Unemployed and other groups addressing problems of social exclusion. In March 2000, the social partners endorsed a new tripartite national agreement—the Programme for Prosperity and Fairness (PPF)—which provided for pay increases of at least 15 percent over 33 months and also innovated in taxation, equality, and social inclusion policies. Special emphasis in the April 2000 Social Welfare Bill was given to improving the position of the low paid. Productivity and distributional elements seem to have been effectively combined.

In reality, there have been many difficulties in realizing objectives on both sides of the bargain—as well as severe organizational strains. The main problems are the lack of flexibility in the national incomes policy; the lack of progress with equity issues; and the failure of partnership to take root in the majority of firms.

On wage flexibility, inflation in 2000 of 5.25 percent wiped out the nationally agreed pay increase of 5.5 percent, while strikes in support of pay claims above the norm threatened social partnership with collapse. The accord came back from the brink with additional pay increases agreed between social partners for 2001 and 2002, bolstered by tax and welfare provisions in the 2001 budget. With economic slowdown in 2001–2, the accord is again under strain with a growing number of employers trying to curb labor costs and increase profits by invoking the PPF's 'inability to pay' clause. To prevent future collapse, a recent report from ESRI (the Irish Economic and Social Research Institute) advocates a shift to a 'contingency-based contract' that would take the form of an 'additional wage term'. Rather than setting a fixed wage increase, the total wage increase 'could be divided between a fixed term and a more flexible term that is made contingent on a range of *ex-post* outcomes in the economy over a range of variables. These variables could encompass factors such as changes in prices, exchange rates and productivity' (Dobbins 2002). This would not deal with the thorny issue of pay relativities, however, which, as elsewhere, is a major destabilizing element in Ireland's incomes policy.

As for productivity, a fragmented industrial structure, with a large number of small firms alongside multinationals that command particular sectors, makes it difficult to reach consensus on a national strategy of industrial partnership. The absence of statutory representation in firms means that 'organized decentralization' along the lines of the Dutch system is impossible, with unilateral decision-making dominating in most companies (Roche 1998; Roche and Geary 2000). A National Centre for Partnership and Performance was established in 2001 to address this issue. As for the distributive side of the bargain, there has been a widening of the relative income gap between rich and poor: the number below the relative poverty line of half-average income increased from 17.4 to 20 percent between 1994 and 1998. Despite some attention to social inclusion policies in PPF 2000, there was no clear commitment to improving welfare benefits in line with average earnings, nor to markedly improving childcare provisions as requested by voluntary and community groups.

5.3.3. *Italy*

In Italy—characterized by extensive industrial relations strife until the 1980s—social pacts since 1993 not only contributed to the fulfillment of EMU entry conditions by taking inflation out of the labor market, but also included agreements on negotiated flexibility and job security. The major step on the broader welfare front was the agreement signed between the unions and the government on pension reform in May 1995 (the employers abstained). The bargain was put to referendum in the workplaces by the unions where it obtained a hard-won but significant majority backing. This consensus was achieved at the expense of a more radical reform: it retained the previous pension system for elderly workers and introduced, whether partially or in full, a more rigorous system for their junior counterparts. But it also avoided protracted industrial dislocation, and prevented adverse consequences for other aspects of the pact, despite the fact that the incomes policy has favored an increase in company profits at a time of reductions in employees' purchasing power.

In terms of system architecture, in July 1993, the *scala mobile* system of wage indexation was abolished and a far-reaching reform of incomes policy and collective bargaining was achieved. Henceforth, biannual tripartite incomes policy and collective agreements were to set macroeconomic guidelines and establish a framework for wage formation. Sectoral agreements were to be signed at the national level on wages (valid for two years) and conditions of employment (valid for four); and enterprise level agreements were to be concluded for four years and negotiated by workers' representatives. The latter innovation created a new form and level of representation within the firm—*Rappresentanza sindacale unitaria*—in which two-thirds of representatives were to be elected by the entire work force (and not just union members as before) and one-third appointed by representative unions. This emphasis on the associational basis of the agreement has played an important part in consolidating the Italian social pact, forging an important link between the workplace and higher levels of union organization (Regini and Regalia 1997).

The thorniest issue in Italy has been the negotiation of employment flexibility—arguably an area of reform that spans both productivity and distributional arenas. In 1997, the Treu package on labor market reform was adopted, which legalized temporary work agencies (as well as fixed-term and part-time work contracts) and simultaneously sought to protect or to improve the rights and entitlements of such workers. In addition, improvements were adopted in training programs, giving firms a strong voice in course design and organization. In the process, Italian unions appeared to be moving away from their strong defense of rigid labor market regulation at all costs to a policy of more flexible bargaining practices, perhaps better able to resolve the threat of deskilling and growing employment segmentation.

The so-called 'Christmas Pact' of 1998 simultaneously expanded both the ambitions of concertation and the number of organizations involved, including actors from local and regional governments. It also sought to reinforce the architecture of the system, with agreement on the two-level wage bargaining system. This was designed to prevent a further fragmentation of wage formation and marginalize small, unrepresentative breakaway organizations, while also extending concertation to a wider range of social and economic issues. But all the evidence shows that, following the failure to fully implement the 1998 pact, Italian concertation had hit a period of major uncertainty well before Silvio Berlusconi's center-right government came to power in 2001, with its commitment to force through new legislation against the wishes of the unions.

A major problem—also characteristic of other Southern countries such as Spain—derives from the difficulty of gaining union agreement to less rigid legal controls on dismissals when the so-called 'social shock absorbers' (training, reintegration policies, passive and active unemployment benefits) are also under-developed. This, plus the symbolism of the Italian Workers Statute, explains the fierce union opposition to the Berlusconi government's proposed reform to its Article 18 which allows the courts to reinstate employees who are fired 'without just cause'.

5.3.4. *Portugal*

Before the mid-1980s, attempts at incomes policy and concertation in Portugal were unsuccessful due to the absence of an adequate institutional architecture. Particularly problematic—as in the Italian case—was the absence of strong authority on the part of the unions and the need for a strengthened role for the state, making it a more reliable and consistent bargaining partner (Rocha Pimentel 1983). Also as in Italy, it was the commitment to eventual EMU membership after 1990 that led to an emphasis on an anti-inflation, lower public debt strategy. At the same time there developed a broad consensus on the need for a new distributional coalition linked to the country's aspiration for full EMU membership.

Reflecting this consensus—and regardless of the continuing fragility of the unions (Stoleroff 2001)—there have been five tripartite pacts since 1987 (the last signed in 1996) on wage formation and social and employment policy. The agreements have been wide-ranging, covering pay rise ceilings, levels of minimum wages, regulations on the organization of work (rest, overtime, and shift work), the termination of employment, and the regulation of working hours. Under the 1996 agreement, income tax for the low paid has been reduced and a more favorable tax regime applied to a range of health and education benefits and old age pensions (Campos Lima and Naumann 2000).

However, as in the other cases, there have been serious strains, leading to the slow demise of the pact over 1996–99 and the rejection by both unions and employers of further concertation in 1998. That year the government introduced legislation on part-time work that differed from commitments made in the social pact, while both unions and employers had been critical of their relationship with parliament in matters requiring legislation. When social dialogue was finally renewed under government initiative in January 2000, none of the social partners were interested in a new, over-arching pact. Instead, they accepted a separation of employment, social security, health and safety, and incomes policy into separate 'meso-bargains', with the latter left solely to collective bargaining. But they have also continued to dispute the institutional changes introduced since the January 2000 relaunch. A new Basic Law on Social Security in July 2000 provided for increased involvement of the social partners in the management of the system, but participation in a new Social Security Council has been criticized as an empty formality.

Nonetheless, these changes helped produce a new and significant social security reform agreement in November 2001, in which a new pensions' calculation formula (establishing whole career contributions) was accepted as a means of securing the system's continued viability. Two parallel agreements (one on health and safety, the other on employment and training) were signed in February 2001. These create a network of shared responsibilities through joint bodies in which the role of the state remains central. These innovations are regarded as important in institutionalizing the social dialogue and in providing a more flexible alternative to a central social pact (and for the first time bringing the CGTP union on board). A more flexible reconfiguration seems to have saved the system from breakdown. However, the arrival in power in early 2002 of a new coalition comprising the center-right Social Democrats (PSD) and conservative Popular Party (PP) may herald a difficult future for concertation.

The lower levels of the system reveal in any case a severe lack of vertical integration. A report by Portugal's Employment and Vocational Training Observatory (OEFP) in 2000 revealed that though the 1996–9 tripartite pact had improved national concertation and the passage into law of numerous social and labor agreements, the predominant sectoral level of bargaining had failed to address the key issues of employment, qualifications, work organization, and vocational training (Cristovam 2000). As elsewhere, unions are trying to promote changes to collective bargaining that allow a better articulation between levels, with some decentralization to the firm which is highly under-developed. For now, the collective bargaining system remains fragmented and chaotic, with overlapping agreements in sectors and companies due to the absence of representativeness criteria and inadequate mediation and arbitration.

5.4. Pacts under Pressure: Organizational and Policy Challenges

What conclusions can be drawn from these cases? In all four the social partners and governments have been compelled to concert in a number of inter-related areas. In none of them has there been a complete repudiation of the value of concertation by one or more principal partner (although in Italy that stage may now have been reached). This is not to say that the employers or all union confederations have always signed up for every deal elaborated under these pacts. They have not: in numerous instances, one or the other partner has abstained, knowing that the deal would in any case go through and proceed to implementation. Such 'face-saving' tactics have given these pacts considerable flexibility and avoided outright vetoes.

So far at least, the partners have been bound together by a common concern to enhance the governability of their systems in the face of numerous challenges, some internal (unemployment, strains in social security systems), others external (perceptions of enhanced competitive pressure, the convergence criteria for EMU). Underpinning that relationship has been the persistence of the politics of exchange, confounding expectations that corporatist concertation would become impossible in the post-Fordist, post-Keynesian era. The currency of that exchange has certainly been changed (some would say 'debased'), for income moderation is no longer purchased by an expansion of the social wage, as under classical Keynesian concertation.

Rather, collaboration in incomes policy is secured by consultation and participation in social policy and labor market reform, as well as negotiation of changes in the industrial relations system and the broader framework of socio-economic governance (Molina and Rhodes 2002).

Nevertheless, all four cases also reveal significant strains in which the functional imperatives of continued concertation (the need for price and wages stability under EMU, the tackling of social security and budget deficits) hit up against the often divergent interests of the partners to the bargain. Despite their apparent success, all of these systems find themselves in a state of uneasy equilibrium.

What happens next? One view would argue that globalization and EMU's Stability and Growth Pact will disrupt the difficult compromises underpinning these bargains. In this scenario, there will be increasing polarization between winners and losers—'competitive solidarity' to use Streeck's (1999) term—and external pressures will begin to unravel Europe's existing regulatory structures. As discussed below, there is some evidence for the first if not the second of these claims: until now there has been little sign of regulatory arbitrage or 'social dumping' on the part of firms (Traxler and Woitech 2000). The critical issues relate rather to the internal operation of EMU and the sustainability of national consensus-creating mechanisms. If under the new European employment (and broader welfare) strategies the latter are to bear the load of mediating between supranational initiatives and lower level implementation, and if the relationship between stability-oriented monetary policy, budgetary policies, and wage policy is also to be secured, then much depends on the strengthening of national incomes policies and broader systems of socio-economic governance.

So far, tripartite or bipartite bargains in social policy and the labor market have been underpinned by: (1) the powerful external constraints of EMU convergence (2) strong state involvement in backing up pacts (3) the tolerance of social partners for each other's aims and (4) the weakness of one of the partners to this bargain—the unions—in a period of slack labor markets. Under post-EMU entry conditions, the external constraint remains, in terms of the 3 percent deficit requirement and the pressures for preserving wage moderation. European nations remain faced with the difficult choices and trade-offs that they have always had to deal with; but EMU will now discipline the form and substance of those trade-offs, ensuring that the large budgetary imbalances of the past are not repeated (see Rhodes 2002). Strong state involvement in securing low levels of inflation will also continue, and statutory incomes restraint will replace consensus-based incomes policies when they fail.

Against this background, the problems for national social pacts lie in the following areas, stemming from the nature of the bargains, the articulation of levels in complex governance systems, contradictions between broader flexibility and social protection reforms and the contested nature of outcomes.

A major problem is sustaining broader, or 'augmented' social pacts of the type agreed to explicitly in the Irish and Dutch cases, or implicitly as in Portugal and Italy, will stem from problem 'overload'. A shift from 'linkage strength' (cementing the bargain by linking policy initiatives and broadening deals) to 'linkage stress' occurs when the danger of failure in one part of the bargain (most obviously the incomes policy pillar) puts everything else at risk. Overload problems have clearly caused strains and near collapse in social pacts in the Netherlands, Italy, Portugal, and Ireland. The Italian 'Christmas Pact' of 1998 is clearly a case of a pact becoming more ambitious in its aims, scope, and representative base at a time when essentials of the earlier bargain were already in question.

In its attempt to 'augment' its social pact, Ireland has also experienced strains in linking the traditional social partners with representatives of other groups, including the anti-poverty lobby and third sector organizations, and this had led the unions (and government representatives) to question the value of such strategies. In late 2000, the whole deal was threatened by a major incomes policy dispute that was only just resolved by stressing the 'linkage strength' of the whole bargain and the costs of dissolution. There, as in the Dutch case, the social partners have advocated a return to their more traditional roles as pay bargainers, with a further decentralization of productivity-linked issues to firms. The end of the 'rush for EMU' qualification period may also make collaboration in health and pensions reform less compelling.

If 'augmented bargains' spanning adjacent policy domains are harder to achieve, then linking social partners with other groups will also be more difficult. Ambitious attempts to reduce 'insider–outsider' divides in employment opportunities and protection will be the first casualty of such failure. Resolving flexibility problems where high levels of labor market protection compensate for the absence of decent income support or retraining (e.g. Italy, Spain, and Greece) requires complex policy trade-offs. The slowness or failure in implementing better unemployment benefits and training systems has hardened positions on hiring and firing costs and regulations in Italy, and produced a breakdown of bargaining, and the imposition of new laws by the state, in Spain.

A third problem concerns the nature of earnings outcomes and the distributive consequences of EMU-linked wage bargaining. As discussed above, there has been a significant trend toward wage moderation in the European Union over the last decade, and this is reflected in a strong trend of declining nominal wage growth as well as average below-productivity-growth increases in real wages (Schulten and Stueckler 2000). Incomes policy deals across

Europe are now being put in jeopardy by several interrelated problems. Although employment has fallen in many countries, it still remains high across the European Union (with strong regional concentrations) and wage concessions and higher profit margins have not been accompanied by a corresponding increase in investment. Along with the increase in atypical forms of employment in many countries, this is destabilizing relations between unions and employers and among the unions themselves.

A contributing problem may stem from the increasing use of variable pay. Although this has apparently not led to a decline in sectoral collective bargaining (indeed, many sectoral agreements provide scope for just such company deviations) there is a major question of its impact on solidarity and the role of sectoral and national unions in defending this principle. Although in some pacts and some reforms distributive and productivity issues have been effectively linked, there is a growing problem of equity in most cases. One of the key problems of the Irish pact, for example, is the evidence that income dispersion continues to increase and that not all have benefited equally from more than a decade of concertation (Ó Riain and O'Connell 2000). As argued by Pontusson, Rueda, and Way (2002), increasing wage inequality can have important consequences for the welfare state, potentially undermining support for universal programs and encouraging greater reliance on means-testing.

A fourth (and related) problem concerns the levels of negotiation and internal cohesion of the participating organizations (Waddington 2001). All of the pacts discussed above have experienced difficulties in sustaining co-ordination, both horizontally (between national peak associations) and vertically (between subsidiary levels of employers' and union organization). As already argued, the very weakness of certain systems has produced efforts to develop new co-ordinating capacity, strengthening links between levels of organization and introducing new rules on the division of labor between collective bargaining levels. This has been particularly successful in countries such as Spain and Italy where unions are still relatively strong but collective bargaining systems chaotic and unstructured. Nevertheless, that capacity for co-ordination remains subject to numerous pressures.

Containing the devolution of bargaining to company level on pay and employment conditions (in some cases within PECs) is just one challenge facing these systems. Another is the decline in union membership, which, though slow in many countries, seems likely to continue in line with the changing structure of employment. In recent years, the only countries to sustain membership or see it increase have been those that use the Ghent system in which unions manage unemployment schemes, as in Sweden, Denmark, Finland, and Belgium. Others (the remaining EU countries) have seen membership decline in the 1980s and 1990s (Blaschke 2000). While it is usually supposed that those systems with statutory employee representation will secure higher union membership rates, Blaschke's evidence indicates that their recruiting advantage is not thereby enhanced.

Although the evidence is uncertain, this suggests that there may be even fewer incentives for workers to join unions if a decentralization of key pay and employment matters is accompanied by, or coincides with stronger forms of company-level representation. In numerous countries, the shift of influence from union confederations to sectoral unions—especially the 'pace setters' in national wage bargaining rounds—and from sectoral unions to workplace collective bargaining, is having serious consequences for higher levels of the labor movement. As argued by Waddington (2001: 450), 'the roles undertaken by confederations will be subject to extensive reform if they are to contribute to the restoration of articulated trade union structure and activity'.

As for sectoral unions, the opposite may be true. Le Queux and Fajertag (2001) expect EMU to strengthen their importance, arguing that this level has a core function in monitoring numerous 'social pacts', and that the continued success of organized decentralization depends on bargaining co-ordination provided by the sector or industry. Regarding wage bargaining under EMU, Iversen (1999), Traxler (1999), and Crouch (2002) all recognize the critical role of these unions in ensuring the minimum procedural co-ordination objectives required in relations with the independent European Central Bank.

But this functional requirement may not prevent the diminution or transformation of the role of sectoral unions. Even if they remain strong, there are growing doubts that they can sustain traditions of solidaristic wage formation. Either the loss of power by sectoral unions or their strengthening as 'pace setters' can have adverse consequences for social solidarity. In Finland, decentralization has tended to reduce sectoral bargains to framework agreements, while in Norway, sectoral co-ordination has been strengthened; but in both cases, the role of pace setting unions in wage bargaining makes it difficult also to cater to the needs of low pay sectors. In many countries (including Austria—a 'classical' corporatist country) decentralization is increasingly limiting the capacity of unions to monitor (and influence) developments on the shop floor. For Sisson (2001: 611–12), the critical issue is whether or not the substantive as well as procedural content of agreements at higher levels can be sustained or strengthened. For if regulation at the higher level becomes increasingly 'soft', then there is danger of fragmentation and disintegration of the industrial relations system.

A fifth and potentially very important development is 'the return of politics' with the arrival in power of liberal and conservative parties in several European countries. This follows a long period in which the dependence of corporatist concertation on Left governments had apparently been replaced by a new pragmatism in both macroeconomic management and micro-policy reform, making newer forms of corporatism 'rather neutral to government composition' (Traxler *et al.* 2001: 302). In reality, the ideological truce may only have been temporary.

The new coalition in Austria from February 2000 between the conservative People's Party (ÖVP) and the right-wing Freedom Party (FPÖ) has broken with the country's strong corporatist tradition, introducing unilaterally a series of pensions and social security reforms. There has been a bitter dispute over government imposed reform of the organization of the public social insurance system to the benefit of the FPÖ-affiliated FA union. In Italy, there was an initial truce after the election of the Berlusconi government in April 2001, during which a framework accord was signed on collective agreements in the public sector, in conformity with the 1993 tripartite incomes policy pact. But in early 2002, the government broke with consensus and embarked on a unilateral reform of Article 18 of the Workers Statute, which guarantees protection against 'unjust dismissal'. In November 2001, a Liberal/Conservative coalition won the Danish general election, leading to the abolition of the closed shop and antagonism toward, but as yet no outright attack on, the labor movement. In Denmark there are significant pressures on the government to keep a strong bargaining system alive, since the social partners had only recently reached a so-called 'climate agreement' on pay moderation. In March 2002, a center-right Social Democrat (PSD) and conservative Popular Party (PP) coalition gained power in Portugal. The new PSD Prime Minister Durao Barroso has vowed to confront the vested interests he accuses of blocking reforms in health, justice, and social security and to implement drastic cuts in corporate taxation. This bodes ill for the future of concertation in that country.

Quite apart from their common embrace of neo-liberal policy initiatives, the parties of these new governments share a distance from the cozy corporatist relations that have linked social democratic, and in some countries Christian democratic parties to the main union confederations. It is unlikely that they will fully abandon concertation in favor of a continental version of Thatcherism; governing in coalition makes this difficult if not impossible. But their presence in power will contribute to a further shift in the balance of power toward employers, and diminish the power of the 'shadow' of intervention of the state in encouraging concertation.

Sixth, and finally, European-level developments may, in theory, contribute to consensus. Numerous initiatives are being undertaken to sponsor a European sphere of industrial relations and social policy reform. These include cross-border bargaining, the Luxembourg process and NAPs, the emergence of the 'Open Method of Coordination' as a consensual instrument of EU policy intervention, and the recent EU Directive on national information and consultation rules. Under these conditions, one might expect a supranational strengthening of national concertation systems. So far, however, there is little evidence that the Luxembourg process has significantly contributed positively to national bargains where they are already weak or non-existent.

The NAPs have only contributed to genuine consultation in countries with economy-wide bargains and agreements (Finland, Ireland, and the Netherlands) or experience of tripartite bargaining (Austria, Denmark, Luxembourg). And even in some of those cases, a recent assessment of the 2001 NAPs reveals disappointing results. In Finland, and especially Ireland, the unions have been highly critical of the lack of serious social partner involvement in drawing up the plans, while in the Netherlands the employers have shown little interest in the NAP (ETUC 2001). Elsewhere (France and Greece) and in countries where social pacts or concertation have been recently put in place (Spain and Italy), there were only formal (and rather empty) forms of consultation with the social partners (Léonard 2001). In France, however, there was a significant improvement in social partner involvement between the 2000 and 2001 NAP, in conformity with efforts made by the Jospin government to promote concertation, a process linked to the creation in 1998 of a Committee for Social Dialogue on European and International Issues.

If the NAPs reveal the tendency for European initiatives to be subsumed by national circumstances—setting firm limits to Europeanization of industrial relations (Keller and Bansbach 2001)—so too will the translation into effect of the EU directive on national information and consultation. This will be applicable to firms with at least 20–50 workers (the choice is given to the Member States) with implementation in accordance with national law and industrial relations practice. But given its focus on company-level concertation, and the proviso that Member States may entrust management and labor to define information and consultation arrangements through negotiation (which may differ from those set out in the Directive) it may well simply reinforce the decentralization of substantive bargaining to firms.

As for European wage co-ordination, there is still a tendency for the literature to polarize between advocates of European centralization or co-ordination and those supporting a regionally based system that would improve the local responsiveness of national wage bargains (e.g. Gros and Hefeker 1999). Hassel and Hoffman (2000) support Traxler (1999) in arguing for a third alternative: a European co-ordination structure for a productivity plus inflation wage strategy. If this worked it would simultaneously counter the trend for real incomes to decline while also preventing competitive wage bidding by sectoral unions across borders. But once again this depends on a viable system of co-ordination across multiple and complex levels; and a continued decentralization of productivity and wage bargaining to companies may well prove a more likely alternative. If this is also accompanied by a fragmentation of collective bargaining institutions, then wage pressures could become less governable, with the possibility of inflationary and deflationary pressures at work simultaneously in different EU regions, undermining the manageability of the Euro economy (see Kittel 2000).

As Dølvik (2000) argues, the best-case solution would be one in which emerging forms of cross-national pattern-bargaining at the sectoral level (as promoted by the EMF) would be combined with a national cross-sectoral co-ordination, via centralized concertation or industrial pattern-bargaining. This would be functionally compatible with the macroeconomic requirements of EMU by 'conditioning (upstream) national participation in European co-ordination and transposing (downstream) European margins and parameters into national systems in accordance with different national and sectoral conditions' (Dølvik 2000: 45–6). The workability of this system may not be affected by the fact that key unions only cover a limited share of workers, that initiatives in cross-border bargaining are extremely limited to date, or even that the bargaining governability of different countries varies enormously. Traxler *et al.* (2001: 302ff) argue that decentralized, non-hierarchical co-ordination across systems can be based on the participation of a limited number of economic bargaining units. Nevertheless, it is hard to see how the stability of such a system would be enhanced by the current trend for unions in most countries to weaken, and for decentralized, company-level bargaining to increase.

5.5. Future Scenarios for European Social Pacts

At the very least, the trends identified above suggest that we are witnessing the emergence of a highly uneven and differentiated system of industrial relations in Europe. This will combine many different forms of co-ordination and pattern bargaining, alongside the further decentralization of much of the substance of collective bargaining to individual firms (Sisson and Marginson 2000). In this scenario, forecasts that such unevenness will seriously undermine the macro-management of the Euro-economy gain some credence. De Grauwe and Skudelny (1999) argue that differences in social conflicts and bureaucratic inefficiency lead to different effects on economic growth after the same terms of trade shock, thereby compounding the 'sub-optimum' currency union character of EMU. The southern states are expected to suffer more from a negative shock than their northern neighbors, mainly because of their weaker bureaucracies, problems in managing a coherent fiscal policy, and poor capacities for conflict resolution. This danger might provide sufficient incentive for a re-regulation of these systems. But as revealed in the analysis of Italy and Portugal above, that process of reform has so far been slow, uneven, and prone to breakdown.

Others are even more pessimistic. Streeck (1999) argues that EMU is likely to produce a degeneration of traditional mechanisms of wage solidarity in favor of 'competitive solidarity', while Martin (1998: 20) forecasts a 'deflationary vicious circle of labor cost dumping, or competitive internal depreciations'. In this scenario, 'competitive corporatism' becomes less a mechanism for the consensual adjustment of industrial relations and social policies (see Rhodes 1998, 2001), than one in which the fragmentation of wage bargaining is intimately linked to the (un)sustainability of distinct national welfare systems (Schulten 2002). At worst, argues Martin, EMU would then turn out to be part and parcel of the neo-liberal project of eliminating the obstacles to labor-market flexibility posed by union and social policy institutions.

More optimistically, Marginson and Sisson (2002) suggest that 'rather than the two extremes of social union versus a completely deregulated free-for-all', a multi-level system of industrial relations is emerging in Europe with both convergent and divergent features. Conforming to much of the analysis above, they forecast a future of complexity, uncertainty, and instability with policy makers and social actors seeking to influence directions to their own advantage. This is an analysis in which many different national scenarios are possible, to which complexity developments at the cross-border sectoral, and inter-professional EU levels will contribute. While complexity would appear to be unavoidable, there are still a distinctly limited number of futures open to national systems. As the strong functional requirements of EMU (price and wage stability) are mediated by national institutional structures, one can posit a number of developmental dynamics based on recent experiences of concertation.[1]

1. *Back from the Brink.*   In this scenario, the pacting process (whether in 'augmented' or more limited incomes policy form) is pushed to the brink of collapse by the strains described above. But the participants are aware of the possible consequences of failure, and go the extra mile to reach a new agreement. This occurred in Ireland in 2000 and, less dramatically, in Denmark in 1998. In Ireland a series of proposals have been made for retaining a central incomes agreement while also making it more flexible to sector-specific

---

[1] I am grateful to Jonathan Zeitlin for suggesting this line of analysis.

demands and the macroeconomic cycle. A future reconfiguration of the system seems much more likely than its abandonment. In Denmark in 1998, the social partners peered into the abyss but pulled back at the point where the traditional bargaining system seemed threatened. They then signed a 'climate agreement', renewing pay bargaining co-ordination among the confederations, assisted by co-operation with the state in a new tripartite forum established by the government for this purpose (Lind 2000). In early 2000, new four-year collective agreements were signed covering most of the private sector, providing a new basis for the further 'coordinated decentralization' of collective bargaining.

2. *Into the Abyss.*   In this scenario, whatever the parties' ostensible preferences, they do not or cannot reach a satisfactory compromise and the pacting process breaks down. But the functional problems remain of ensuring compatibility between the outcomes of national wage bargaining and the macroeconomic constraints of EMU. This tension can be resolved (at least provisionally) in two ways:

(a) through statutory wage restraint imposed by governments where this is legally and politically possible (as in Belgium);
(b) through the further decentralization of collective bargaining and de-unionization in the face of rising unemployment and intense cost pressures on individual companies (as in the UK even without EMU membership). Forecasts of an 'Americanization' of the European labor market would thereby be confirmed.

Thus far, the only danger of a total repudiation of concertation occurring is in Italy; yet in that country, and elsewhere, the level of disruption to political and economic stability caused by social conflict in these circumstances (especially under 2b) is likely to produce a third scenario, resurrection.

3. *Resurrection.*   In this scenario, the collapse of a pact serves as a learning experience for the parties concerned. The latter discover that whatever the downsides, a renewal of concertation is preferable to the conflicts and other associated costs of unilateral action. Something of this sort may well happen in Italy over the next couple of years, as well as in other countries where liberal parties in power are tempted to break with bargained, incremental processes of reform. The problem with resurrection is that, as the UK case reveals, once certain levels of bargaining capacity are diminished, and institutional practices disembedded, they are then extremely difficult to rebuild. The role of the state will therefore prove essential in creating new mechanisms of concertation and mediation. An evolution along these lines has occurred in Sweden, following more than a decade of decentralization in wage bargaining. In 1998 the social partners failed to agree to their own 'pact for growth' and new rules for bargaining (Stephens 2000). But due to competitive pressure from surrounding

EU countries for more orderly wage bargaining, the government stepped in. In 1999 it established a new Mediation Authority to help resolve labor conflicts and develop a more satisfactory system of pay determination. In reality, this amounts to less than a resurrection of the Swedish past than movement in the direction of the co-ordinated Danish and Norwegian bargaining systems from which cross-border lessons have been drawn.

4. *Reconfiguration.* This is a variant of the preceding scenario, in which the revival of national social pacts after a period of breakdown results in the construction of a more complex, articulated, and flexible architecture linked, perhaps to European-level developments. This will involve some combination of the following: (a) cross-national sectoral and company wage co-ordination; (b) national framework agreements; and (c) increased scope for regional differentiation. Countries might also move toward this kind of articulated multi-level co-ordination architecture by incremental steps within scenario 1. As in the case of scenario 3, a learning process, which may include lessons from other countries, plus perhaps some input from the European Union under the 'Open Method of Co-ordination', is likely to be important. The difficulty lies in achieving horizontal co-ordination while also sustaining some order in the process of vertical decentralization. If authority at the higher levels of the system becomes increasingly 'soft', this will have important consequences for union (and in some cases employer) organizations and their capacity for system monitoring and control. If that authority and control is diminished, then they will become less useful partners for governments seeking to steer the system. In the worst-case scenario, such reconfiguration could degenerate, via gradual erosion, into scenario 2 (Hyman 2001).

5. *Pre-emptive Adjustment.* In this case (the most likely scenario for European countries), the collapse of the pact is avoided by rendering it more flexible (or in some cases, more rigid), via mutual agreement. The Portuguese, Spanish, Dutch, and Danish cases all reveal the search for new flexibility via the creation of a new division of labor between national, sectoral, and local levels, and in particular by placing social policy and incomes policy in distinct spheres of bargaining. In Portugal in 1998, there was mutual agreement on the part of all partners not to conclude a national pact to follow that of 1996–99, but rather to elaborate separate agreements on discrete issues. Three such agreements have now been signed. In Spain, the political problems in producing an explicit national pact led to a framework agreement (the 1994 'Toledo Pact') which has subsequently generated a series of separate agreements, including a major pensions system reform in 1996. The degree of flexibility possible in such a framework was revealed in 2001 when, despite a collapse in negotiations on employment flexibility (and subsequent unilateral legislative action by the government), two significant agreements

in other areas of policy were achieved. First, a new pensions reform was agreed via tripartite negotiations, and second, a reference wage level was agreed to for the first time since 1984, coupled to a new procedure for co-ordinating collective bargaining on pay and other issues (including employment, training, and equal opportunities) between central and lower levels.

In all of these scenarios, politics and the scope for political exchange remain central in determining how 'functional necessities' are translated into actual policies and processes. Critical to our understanding of the evolution of these systems is the way in which political exchange between the major actors in the system is institutionalized via hierarchical networks and modes of integration along horizontal and vertical dimensions. Of major importance in these increasingly complex bargaining systems will be the linkages and mechanisms that connect the macro-, meso- and micro-levels of socio-economic governance and adjustment (Molina and Rhodes 2002). There has been a tendency to construe post-Keynesian forms of corporatism as a distinct mode of network-based governance 'beyond hierarchy and market' (Traxler *et al.* 2001: 301), in which the weak foundations of governability are substituted by the external straightjacket of tough monetary policy. But in itself a hard currency regime is insufficient for explaining the nature or survival of these pacts.

This is especially so since, as revealed in the four national case studies analyzed above, conflicts between productivity and distributional aims generate instability and can threaten system governability unless both hierarchy and integration—linking levels of bargaining and involving strong commitments (and exchange) between social partners and the state—are sustained. The future of such experiments in governance is uncertain. In some cases, commitment to the bargain and to a constant renewal of its substance and processes will continue to generate routine and institutional solidity. In other cases, the reverse will occur as the process of exchange is exhausted and there is an erosion of hierarchy and levels of authority. What is clear, however, is that the new external environment of EMU will continue to promote such experimentation in national systems and the creation of new linkages between national and supranational spheres of policy-making and influence. Amidst the complexity many now forecast for the future of socio-economic governance in Europe, systems of negotiated governance will remain essential for domestic and European political and economic stability.

References

BLASCHKE, S. (2000). 'Union Density and European Integration: Diverging Convergence'. *European Journal of Industrial Relations*, 6/2: 217–36.

CAMPOS LIMA, M. and NAUMANN, R. (2000). 'Social Pacts in Portugal: From Comprehensive Policy Programmes to the Negotiation of Concrete Industrial Relations Reforms?' in G. Fajertag and P. Pochet (eds), *Social Pacts in Europe: New Dynamics*. Brussels: European Trade Union Institute/Observatoire Social Européen, 321–42.

CASEY, B. and GOLD, M. (2000). *Social Partnership and Economic Performance: The Case of Europe*. Northampton, MA: Edward Elgar.

CRISTOVAM, M. L. (2000). 'Portugal: New Ways Forward for Collective Bargaining?' *EIRO on-line*, November.

CROUCH, C. (2002). 'The Euro and Labour Market and Wage Policies', in K. Dyson (ed.), *European States and the Euro: Europeanization, Variation and Convergence*. Oxford: Oxford University Press, 278–304.

DE GRAUWE, P. and SKUDELNY, F. (1999). 'Social Conflict and Growth in Euroland', *Centre for Economic Policy Research Discussion Paper* No. 2186. London: CEPR.

DOBBINS, T. (2002). 'Ireland: ESRI Report Calls for More Flexible Model of Centralized Wage Bargaining'. *EIRO on-line*, February.

DØLVIK, J. E. (2000). 'Economic and Monetary Union: Implications for Industrial Bargaining in Europe', *ETUI Paper*, DWP 2000.01.04.

DØLVIK, J. E. and MARTIN, A. (2000). 'A Spanner in the Works and Oil on Troubled Waters: The Divergent Fates of Social Pacts in Sweden and Norway', in G. Fajertag and Ph. Pochet (eds) *Social Pacts in Europe: New Dynamics*. Brussels: European Trade Union Institute/Observatoire Social Européen, 279–319.

ELVANDER, N. (2002). 'The New Swedish Regime for Collective Bargaining and Conflict Resolution: A Comparative Perspective'. *European Journal of Industrial Relations*, 8/2: 197–216.

ETUC (2001). *Luxembourg Process: ETUC Employment 'Fiches' (June 2001)*. Brussels: ETUC.

FERRERA, M. and RHODES, M. (2000). 'Building a Sustainable Welfare State'. *West European Politics*, 23/2: 257–82.

FREYSSINET, J. and SEIFERT, H. (2001). 'Pacts for Employment and Competitiveness in Europe'. *Transfer*, 4: 616–28.

GOLLBACH, J. and SCHULTEN, S. (2000). 'Cross-border Collective Bargaining Networks in Europe'. *European Journal of Industrial Relations*, 6/2: 161–79.

GROS, D. and HEFEKER, C. (1999). 'Labour Costs and Wage Policy within EMU'. European Commission, Directorate-General for Research, *Economic Affairs Series Working Paper*, ECON 111 EN, March.

HASSEL, A. and HOFFMANN, R. (2000). 'National Alliances for Jobs and Prospects for a European Employment Pact'. *ETUI Paper*, DWP 2000.01.01 (E).

HASSEL, A. and EBBINGHAUS, B. (2000). 'Concerted Reforms: Linking Wage Formation and Social Policy in Europe'. Paper Presented at the 12th International Conference of Europeanists. Chicago, March 30–April 1.

HASSELL, A. (2001). 'The Problem of Political Exchange in Complex Governance Systems: The Case of Germany's Alliance for Jobs'. *European Journal of Industrial Relations*, 7/3: 307–26.

HEMERIJCK, A., VAN DER MEER, M., and VISSER, J. (2000). 'Innovation through Co-ordination: Two Decades of Social Pacts in the Netherlands', in G. Fajertag and P. Pochet (eds), *Social Pacts in Europe: New Dynamics*. Brussels: European Trade Union Institute/Observatoire Social Européen, 257–78.

HUISKAMP, R. and VAN RIEMSDIJK, M. (2001). 'Competitive Consensus: Bargaining on Employment and Competitiveness in the Netherlands'. *Transfer*, 4: 682–95.

HYMAN, R. (2001). 'The Europeanisation—or the Erosion—of Industrial Relations'. *Industrial Relations Journal*, 32/4: 280–94.

IVERSEN, T. (1999). *Contested Economic Institutions: The Politics of Macroeconomics and Wage Bargaining in Advanced Democracies*. Cambridge: Cambridge University Press.

KELLER, B. and BANSBACH, M. (2001). 'Social Dialogues: Tranquil Past, Troubled Present and Uncertain Future'. *Industrial Relations Journal*, 32/5: 419–34.

KITTEL, B. (2000). 'Trade Union Bargaining Horizons in Comparative Perspective: The Effects of Encompassing Organization, Unemployment and the Monetary Regime on Wage-Pushfulness'. *European Journal of Industrial Relations*, 6/2: 181–202.

LÉONARD, E. (2001). 'Industrial Relations and the Regulation of Employment in Europe'. *European Journal of Industrial Relations*, 7/1: 27–47.

LE QUEUX, S. and FAJERTAG, G. (2001). 'Towards Europeanization of Collective Bargaining: Insights from the European Chemical Industry'. *European Journal of Industrial Relations*, 7/2: 117–36.

LIND, J. (2000). 'Recent Issues on the Social Pact in Denmark', in G. Fajertag and P. Pochet (eds), *Social Pacts in Europe: New Dynamics*. Brussels: European Trade Union Institute/Observatoire Social Européen, 135–59.

MARGINSON, P. and SISSON, K. (2002). 'EMU and Industrial Relations: A Case of Convergence and Divergence?' Paper Presented at the JCMS 40th Anniversary Conference. Florence 12–13 April.

MARTIN, A. (1998). 'EMU and Wage Bargaining: The Americanization of the European Labor Market?' Paper Prepared for the 11th International Conference of Europeanists. Baltimore, MD. February 26–28.

MOLINA, M. and RHODES, M. (2002). 'Corporatism: The Past, Present and Future of a Concept'. *Annual Review of Political Science*, 5: 305–31.

O'DONNELL, R. (1998). 'Social Partnership in Ireland: Principles and Interpretations', in R. O'Donnell and J. Larragy (eds), *Negotiated Economic and Social Governance and European Integration*. Brussels: European Commission, Directorate-General, Science, Research and Development, 84–106.

Ó RIAIN, S. and O'CONNELL, P. J. (2000). 'The Role of the State in Growth and Welfare', in B. Nolan, P. J. O'Connell, and C. T. Whelan, (eds), *Bust to Boom? The Irish Experience of Growth and Inequality*. Dublin: Institute of Public Administration, 310–39.

PALIER, B. (2000). 'The Necessity to Negotiate Welfare Reforms in Bismarckian Social Protection Systems: The French Case', Paper Presented at the IPSA World Congress, Quebec City, 1–5 August.

PEDERSINI, R. (2000). 'Pacts for Employment and Competitiveness'. *EIRO on-line*, March.

PÉREZ, S. (2000). 'Social Pacts in Spain', in G. Fajertag and Ph. Pochet (eds), *Social Pacts in Europe: New Dynamics*. Brussels: European Trade Union Institute/Observatoire Social Européen, 343–64.

PONTUSSON, J., RUEDA, D., and WAY, C. R. (2002). 'Comparative Political Economy of Wage Distribution: The Role of Partisanship and Labour Market Institutions'. *British Journal of Political Science*, 32/2: 281–308.

REGINI, M. and REGALIA, I. (1997). 'Employers, Unions and the State: The Resurgence of Concertation in Italy?' *West European Politics*, 25/1: 210–30.

RHODES, M. (1998). 'Globalisation, Labour Markets and Welfare States: A Future of "Competitive Corporatism"?' in M. Rhodes and Y. Mény (eds), *The Future of European Welfare: A New Social Contract?* London: Macmillan, 178–203.

RHODES, M. (2001). 'The Political Economy of Social Pacts: Competitive Corporatism and European Welfare Reform', in P. Pierson (ed.), *The New Politics of the Welfare State*. Oxford: Oxford University Press, 165–94.

RHODES, M. (2002). 'Why EMU is—or May Be—Good for European Welfare States', in K. Dyson (ed.), *European States and the Euro: Europeanization, Variation and Convergence.* Oxford: Oxford University Press, 305–34.

ROCHA PIMENTEL, J. M. (1993). 'Concertação social e política de rendimentos em Portugal: Experiência recente e perspectivas para a década de 80'. *Economia,* 17/2: 357–94.

ROCHE, W. K. (1998). 'Between Regime Fragmentation and Realignment: Irish Industrial Relations in the 1990s'. *Industrial Relations Journal,* 29/2: 113–25.

ROCHE, W. K. and GEARY, J. F. (2000). ' "Collaborative Production" and the Irish Boom: Work Organization, Partnership and Direct Involvement in Irish Workplaces'. *The Economic and Social Review,* 31/1: 1–36.

SCHULTEN, S. (2002). 'A European Solidaristic Wage Policy'. *European Journal of Industrial Relations,* 8/2: 173–96.

SCHULTEN T. and STUECKLER, A. (2000). 'Wage Policy and EMU'. Wirtschafts- und Sozialwissenschaftskiches Institut in der Hans-Boeckler-Stiftung & European Foundation for the Improvement of Living and Working Conditions, July.

SISSON, K. (2001). 'Pacts for Employment and Competitiveness—an Opportunity to Reflect on the Role and Practice of Collective Bargaining'. *Transfer,* 4: 601–15.

SISSON, K. and MARGINSON, P. (2000). 'Co-ordinated Bargaining: A Process for our Times?' *University of Warwick Industrial Relations Research Unit Working Paper* 14/00.

STEPHENS, J. (2000). 'Is Swedish Corporatism Dead? Thoughts on its Supposed Demise in the Light of the Abortive 'Alliance for Growth' in 1998', Paper Presented at the 12th International Conference of Europeanists, Chicago, March 30–April 1.

STOLEROFF, A. (2001). 'Unemployment and Trade Union Strength in Portugal', in N. Bermeo (ed.), *Unemployment in the New Europe.* Cambridge: Cambridge University Press, 173–202.

STREECK, W. (1999). 'Competitive Solidarity: Rethinking the "European Social Model" ', *Working Paper* No. 99/11. Max Planck Institut für Gesellschaftsforschung.

TEAGUE, P. (2001). 'Deliberative Governance and EU Social Policy'. *European Journal of Industrial Relations,* 7/1: 7–26.

TRAXLER, F. (1999). 'Wage-Setting Institutions and EMU', in G. Huemer, M. Mesch, and F. Traxler (eds), *The Role of Employers Associations and Trade Unions in EMU: Institutional Requirements for European Economic Policies.* Aldershot: Ashgate, 115–35.

TRAXLER, F. (2000). 'National Pacts and Wage Regulation in Europe: A Comparative Analysis', in G. Fajertag and P. Pochet (eds), *Social Pacts in Europe: New Dynamics.* Brussels: European Trade Union Institute/Observatoire Social Européen, 401–17.

TRAXLER, F. and WOITECH, B. (2000). 'Transnational Investment and National Labour Market regimes: A Case of "Regime Shopping"?' *European Journal of Industrial Relations,* 6/2: 141–59.

TRAXLER, F., BLASCHKE, S., and KITTEL, B. (2001). *National Labour Relations in Internationalised Markets: A Comparative Study of Institutions, Change and Performance.* Oxford: Oxford University Press.

TREU, T. (1992). *Participation in Public Policy Making: The Role of Trade Unions and Employers' Associations.* Berlin: De Gruyter.

VISSER, J. and HEMERIJCK, A. (1997). *'A Dutch Miracle': Job Growth, Welfare Reform and Corporatism in the Netherlands.* Amsterdam: Amsterdam University Press.

WADDINGTON, J. (2001). 'Articulating Trade Union Organisation for the New Europe'. *Industrial Relations Journal,* 32/5: 449–63.

6

Decentralizing Employment Protection in Europe: Territorial Pacts and Beyond

IDA REGALIA

6.1. Introduction

A recent OECD report has shown that over the last two decades the EU countries have reacted differently to the employment challenge and the related need to reform national labor market institutions (OECD 1999). For example, since the mid-1980s employment protection regulation relative to temporary workers has been relaxed in Italy, but tightened, after a period of relaxation, in France and Spain. And in Germany, too, a prolonged process of relaxing the rules has been interrupted in the late 1990s by proposals to reverse the trend. From this perspective, the popular assumption of a convergence among the strategies adopted by governments faced by similar problems appears not to be confirmed (Esping-Andersen and Regini 2000).

A widespread trend over the past 10–15 years, which accelerated considerably in the second half of the 1990s, instead concerns employment and labor-market policies. I refer to the tendency to decentralize the design and implementation of these policies and programs from the center to sub-national levels of governance (regions, provinces, municipalities) according to a logic which gives priority to their territorial dimension.

There are certainly considerable differences among countries in this regard. But it is not these differences that I intend to discuss here. Instead, I point out that this trend toward decentralization is the outcome of various processes, not necessarily interconnected, now ongoing in production and the economy, at the level of government policies and of those of the European Union.

As regards production, these processes result from the development of a post-Fordist economy which has dismantled the consolidated, predictable, and relatively linear model of the occupational structure, and the substantial stability and uniformity of the employment relationship, which long characterized the labor market. A first and immediate consequence has been increasing pressure for the local-level management of demand for, but also the supply of, labor which has grown much more differentiated, specific and complex.

At the level of government policy, these processes are consequent on the devolution of a wide variety of competencies to sub-national administrative and political levels, at a time when centralized regulation seems much less able than previously to handle the increasingly diversified needs of the economy and society, has ever fewer resources for expenditure to sustain the economy, and is confronted by the increasing mobility of factors of production and the proliferation of transnational authorities, which blur its boundaries and weaken its functions.

At the European level, they are the consequences of increasing intervention in the social sphere, and particularly in the area of employment policies (especially since the Treaty of Amsterdam in 1997), which tends to create new opportunities for regional and local institutions, both by providing incentives for development (structural funds) and by providing guidelines for local-level action inspired by principles of social partnership.

From various points of view, the decentralization of employment protection in the labor market is not dissimilar to the decentralization of collective bargaining in industrial relations that has occurred in all the European countries since the 1980s (Regini 1995; Traxler 1996; Ferner and Hyman 1998). If anything, the latter has come about somewhat earlier than the former. As Wolfgang Streeck (1991) pointed out some time ago, these two aspects—the centralized bargaining on wages and terms of employment and the development of a centralized, universalistic and egalitarian system of labor protection— long constituted the cornerstones for what, despite the many differences among countries, could be called the 'European model' of industrial relations. As in the case of bargaining, therefore, so the decentralization of policies of labor-market governance and employment can be viewed as a breakdown of, or a distancing from, that model.[1]

In effect, not only differences of level in the implementation of policies and initiatives (and therefore differences in the types and numbers of actors involved, and in the complexity of the procedures adopted) lie behind the decentralization of measures for labor-market intervention. There are also

---

[1] Likewise, the parallel movement in the opposite direction of collective bargaining and employment protection may constitute the basis for a new 'European model' of labor regulation, especially if it is characterized by organized, rather than disorganized, decentralization (Traxler 1996).

differences among the goals that these measures are intended to pursue, and differences in the manner through which they are supposed to be achieved.

As to goals, decentralization is functional for the implementation of active labor market policies based on the delivery of quality employment services, and to a lesser extent on the provision of incentives. But its prime purpose is to generate fine-gauge measures targeted on specific and difficult problems which would be impossible to deal with from the center and which spring from the new characteristics of highly differentiated and segmented labor markets.

But this affects the style of action to adopt, given that the characteristics of tailor-made active policies targeted on specific problems do not lend themselves to bureaucratic-administrative management. Rather, they require the mobilization and involvement of all relevant actors, and the consensus-based coordination of initiatives. It is for this reason that the new tendencies are generally interpreted as moves towards local or territorial concertation, which typically assumes the form of a 'pact' among the actors concerned.

Local-level pacts on issues of economic development and employment creation first arose during the second half of the 1990s in many European countries. They were the outcome of endogenous dynamics and/or programs promoted on an experimental basis by the European Commission. However, the decentralization of employment protection and labor market governance involves more than such pacts. The latter are probably the most visible to the external observer, because they are more institutionalized and publicized; but other types of initiative are coming to the fore. They are doing so more covertly and therefore require closer attention for their observation and discussion.

In a study some years ago (Regalia 1998), I drew up a list of possible forms of interaction and local-level initiatives between labor-market and industrial relations actors, namely:

- pressures applied by the social partners separately on local/regional governments and institutions;
- coalitions between the social partners (in the form of agreements or pacts, but also of stable arenas in which positions are aligned) to exert pressure on local/ regional governments and institutions;
- tripartite contacts and agreements within particular policy-making processes;
- the more or less stable inclusion of interest representatives within bipartite or tripartite committees set up by the public authorities to implement public policies at the regional level or to perform an advisory or consultative role towards regional governments and institutions (in the fields of vocational training or labor market regulation);
- the promotion of joint private–public initiatives and institutions (like agencies or foundations) for the development of particular programs or to provide public support for private initiatives;

- direct intervention by the regional government in the sphere of labor relations to mediate conflicts which have not been resolved collectively, or to regulate the behavior of the industrial relations actors;
- the provision of resources (or incentives) by the regional government to influence the behavior of industrial relations actors.

There is consequently a wide range of possible local initiatives to promote concerted action. Drawing on the results of a recent Europe-wide survey coordinated by the author (Regalia 2000, 2001),[2] this chapter examines the features, outcomes, and possible future development of these initiatives, beginning with a general overview of territorial pacts for employment. In the absence of systematic data, and given the fluid and changeable nature of the phenomenon, only qualitative treatment will be possible. But first some clarification of what is meant by 'employment protection' will be necessary.

6.2. Employment Protection: Against What, How?

The term 'employment protection' implies that there are risks against which workers should be shielded. What these risks are—or better, which ones are possible or convenient to counteract, and how to do so—varies in time and according to numerous circumstances.

In general, the concern is to avert or reduce the risk that the earning capacity of workers (and their families) will be reduced. But more specifically, for a long time the principal objective was to avert the risk of unemployment (especially of male heads of households). As already mentioned, in the European countries coverage against these risks was traditionally provided mainly by the welfare state and by the rules laid down in collective agreements, based in both cases on the standard model of employment (Supiot 1999).

---

[2] Cf. the research project '*Local Level Concertation: The Possible Role of the Social Partners and Local Level Institutions in Regulating the New Forms of Employment and Work*' (LOCLEVCONC). The project, which was carried out between January 1999 and February 2001, formed part of the Fourth Program of Targeted Socio-Economic Research promoted by the Directorate-General for Research of the European Community. It involved research groups from the five largest European countries: Ires Multiregionale coordinated by Ires Lombardia in Italy; Fondation Nationale des Sciences Politiques-CERAT in Grenoble, France, coordinator Olivier Mériaux; ISO Institut in Saarbrücken, Germany, coordinators Hermann Kotthoff and Hans G. Grewer; Universitat Autónoma de Barcelona (Grup d'estudis Sociologics sobre la Vida Quotidiana i el Treball) in Spain, coordinator Andreu Lope; University of Warwick Industrial Relations Research Unit (IRRU) in the United Kingdom, coordinator Paul Marginson. The research concerned the use of new or 'atypical' forms of employment and work now developing widely and increasingly subject to political debate. The specific aim was to study the different ways in which joint or concerted regulation at local level addresses the use of such non-standard forms of employment, based neither solely on market regulation nor on law or contractual provisions established at national level in each country or by the European Union. LOCLEVCONC Working Papers and reports are available at the web-site of Ires Lombardia (www.ireslombardia.it).

Employment protection was therefore long understood as protection against the risk of unemployment. And for much of the 1990s, the concerns and policies of the EU Member States and the European Commission were still centered on the quantitative reduction of unemployment—evaluated principally in terms of reduction in aggregate unemployment rates (Reyneri 1999). At the policy-making level, this gave rise mainly to programs designed to foster entry into the labor market and permanence within it. At the administrative and policy-implementing level, it led to an emphasis on increasing and reforming (where necessary, as in Italy) employment services.

More recently, however, the profound changes that have taken place in demand by firms (for greater labor 'flexibility' and broad recourse to non-standard or 'atypical' forms of employment and to workers on different types of contract) and in supply (increased female supply, increased supply of weaker segments of the labor market, rising educational levels with the consequent change in expectations), as well as the difficulties in matching the two that have accompanied the upturn in employment apparent in the countries of the European Union since 1998–9, have highlighted a tendency toward an objective reduction in levels of employment security.

Beyond the risk of unemployment, workers—especially 'atypical' workers—may be faced with uncertainty over whether they will continue to earn an adequate income and whether it will be paid regularly; over their lack of protection in the case of illness, accident, maternity, disability, and old age; over the risk that they may be unable to develop and update their skills adequately, or that they will not be able to use the skills acquired in different work contexts; over the fact that they have no career prospects and are unable to gain access to sufficient know-how and resources (e.g. software); or over the risk of suffering discrimination or being unable to compete on equal terms and conditions with workers on different contracts, or being unable to have their interests properly represented.

These risks can be grouped under three main headings:

(a) the risks of future unemployment and job insecurity;
(b) the risks of limitations on human capital development;
(c) the risks of reduced rights and entitlements, including the risk of under-representation.

The more one believes that employment protection should be extended to cover a broader range of risks, the further one moves away from the logic of predominantly quantitative and aggregate employment policies toward more qualitative approaches focused on specific needs and problems, and the more it becomes necessary to decentralize initiatives to the local level.

Yet, this does not mean solely the decentralization of the design and implementation of active labor policies to be delivered by employment service centers.

It also requires the involvement of a wider range of local actors and the development of new forms of intervention.

On the basis of the data collected by the aforementioned research on forms that regulation of new forms of employment and work may assume, the initiatives observed range among:

- regional/territorial pacts, or concerted multilateral initiatives;
- bilateral agreements/contracts between local institutions and agencies providing services (temporary labor, job placement, training, and business services);
- agreements among firms and employers;
- territorial (local) collective agreements;
- bilateral agreements between public institutions and firms;
- forms of self-organization by workers;
- collective agreements signed by organizations representing non-standard employees;
- company-level formal/informal agreements.

The feature shared by these various forms is a search for solutions and approaches agreed upon by the main local actors, rather than reliance on authoritarian fiat from above.

I shall now discuss these various initiatives, beginning with the most complex and perhaps most ambitious: territorial pacts.

6.3. The Experience of Territorial Pacts

In the second half of the 1990s, the majority of European countries experimented with territorial concertation (or pacts) based on formal agreements among local authorities, social partners, and other important local actors aimed at promoting economic development and employment creation. In a very broad sense, partnerships between public and private actors for the promotion of local development had already been present for some time in many of European countries. The novel feature in this case was the creation of more stable coalitions or partnerships and the reaching of agreements or pacts among a multiplicity of local actors.

The 'pact' label covers a relatively wide variety of experiences. Firstly there are those which enjoy European recognition. Territorial pacts for employment were promoted by the European Commission under the European Pact for Employment of 1996, aimed at coordinating local initiatives and creating more suitable conditions for the efficient use of structural funds.[3] By the year 2000, 90 such pacts had been constituted. Formally, in order to obtain

---

[3] On the position of the European Commission, see the *Employment in Europe 2000* Report, which also provides a number of different examples.

European endorsement they must be the outcome of an agreement by the broadest possible network of local public and private partners, independent of external influences, and each of equal status within the network. Moreover, projects and initiatives must be innovative and characterized by a bottom-up approach. The obtaining of European recognition for pacts enhances the visibility of local initiatives, increases their importance, and improves their chances of receiving financing.

Territorial pacts as innovative forms of decentralized social dialogue, or of concertation and the joint and consensual planning of local initiatives for economic and occupational development, had already developed autonomously in the Southern regions of Italy in the early 1990s, when policies for extraordinary intervention in the *Mezzogiorno* were discontinued. They were initially conceived by the CNEL (Consiglio Nazionale dell'Economia e del Lavoro[4]), which actively supported them as self-sustaining development projects to foster the growth of local leaders able to mobilize all indigenous resources for bottom-up development and break with the tradition of 'development without autonomy' typical of the country's most backward regions (Trigilia 1992). Their promoters at CNEL envisaged these first territorial pacts as a 'process of negotiation among actors who freely negotiate their participation in projects of common interest, filling the vacuum left by the retreat of policy from the economic arena' (CNEL 1994). The initial success of these pacts, which was often attributed to the attraction of being freely able to 'forge a pact' from the bottom up according to a logic which gave primacy to local social practices over state-political ones, was indubitably also due to the interest of entrepreneurs in the possible new sources of financing for their activities then taking shape. The formal recognition of the pacts by the government through legislation in 1995 which granted them financial support, engendered a sudden increase in the number of applications and spread such initiatives to every part of the country. This led to reforms in 1996 and 1997, as well as to the introduction of other instruments (e.g. area agreements) in order better to allocate resources and differentiate solutions according to needs at the local level. In this process, during which the criteria for the eligibility of projects for financing were established, guidance and control by the central government once again became crucial (Bolocan Goldstein, Pasqui, and Perulli 2000; Barbera 2001). On April 30, 2000, some 61 pacts were

---

[4] In Italy, the Consiglio Nazionale dell'Economia e del Lavoro is a tripartite body created by the Constitution which comprises representatives of the social partners and the government: a sort of parliament of economic interests. But its role has often been somewhat marginal. Beyond engaging in research, debate and documentation of collective bargaining and industrial relations, the CNEL has sought to promote new initiatives in the field of local development, supporting the project for territorial pacts.

approved (41 in the south), of which 10 were to be financed by the European Union (8 in the south), for a total of around 1350 entrepreneurial initiatives funded by around 3900 billion lire of public money and projected to create more than 60,000 jobs. A further 200-odd pacts at various stages of maturation throughout the country should be added to the 61 already formalized (Cersosimo 2000).

But there were other initiatives in multilateral concertation at the local level. As in Italy—although not necessarily with the same degree of formal recognition—territorial pacts for employment beyond those recognized by the European Union were widespread in Spain, for example, especially in Catalonia, where all the main cities formulated their own pacts (Lope *et al.* 2001); or in Germany (e.g. the 'Saar Joint Initiative' promoted at the Land level in opposition to the macroeconomic policies of the federal government at the end of the 1980s; or conversely the recent regional or local pacts for employment promoted by the Federal government) (Grewer 2001).

Beyond those just mentioned, in Italy local pacts arose with distinctive features or ones that were substantially extraneous to the national, or European, legislation. The best known and most controversial case was the 'Milan Employment Pact' of February 2000 targeted on the work entry of non-EU immigrants, the disabled and the long-term unemployed and promoted by the city council with the participation of the social partners and civil society associations, but opposed by the largest trade union, the CGIL, which strongly disagreed with the proposed use of temporary contracts in derogation from the rules established by national collective agreements (Bolocan Goldstein 2000). Another, very different case is that of the local concertation scheme introduced at the end of the 1980s in an area to the north of Milan— the 'Consorzio Area Alto Milanese' (CAAM)—which over time became a model of active policies for employment. Or again, in the United Kingdom, projects for the local implementation of government activation programs, like the 'New Deal for Young People', may take the form of concerted multilateral action, or, more specifically, 'Joint Venture Partnerships' comprising public agencies, voluntary organizations and social partners (Marginson, McIlroy, and Gilman 2001).

Notwithstanding the numerous differences among the organizational models adopted and among the specific goals pursued, all these experiences share the following features:

- in terms of their logic of action, the use of stable partnerships between public and private actors at the local level, in which the former constantly interact with the latter. From the perspective of the public authorities (Urbani 2000; Bobbio 2000), this amounts to the transformation of action by administrative measures into action by negotiated agreements;

- in terms of the general goals pursued, twofold territorial development and employment growth, according to a vision where the two aspects are mutually reinforcing;[5]
- in terms of the range of action, the structuring of pacts as frameworks for numerous projects with multiple aims (e.g. the European pacts of Albertville in Rhône-Alpes, France, or the Birmingham-Solihull-Black Country Territorial Employment Pact, United Kingdom, or the Vallès Occidental Employment Pact in Catalonia, Spain, cover 18 types of initiative, variously structured into a smaller number of thematic pillars. The other types of pacts are no less broad);
- in terms of participants, the strongly inclusive nature of these initiatives, which tend to involve all the local organized actors (which may number in their dozens) (Cersosimo 2000);
- in terms of incentives for participation, the predominant supply (at least in the initial stages) of club goods, that is, incentives which can be obtained by excluding non-participants.

Unlike the other solutions described below, as has been pointed out elsewhere (Barbera 2001: 7), in these cases the alternative is not between participation and non-participation, but between two modes of participating: doing so by 'maximizing the payoffs from present cooperation, giving rise to costless concertation intended only to obtain funding, and thereby creating distributive–collusive pacts; or by balancing the payoffs from present cooperation with those from future cooperation, paying the costs of concertation and increasing the locally available social resources, thereby giving rise to integrative–distributive pacts'.

These observations enable us to frame the problem of evaluating the results more satisfactorily. Judgements on the matter are almost unanimously critical and rather pessimistic. At most there is talk of 'empty containers', of labels attached to already existing programs. Given the complexity and heterogeneity of projects, moreover, it is very difficult to draw overall conclusions.

The majority of comments on territorial pacts in Italy, whether of European type or endogenous origin (cf. Mirabelli 2000 on pacts in Calabria; *Qui Nord-Ovest* 2000 on pacts in Piedmont; Bolocan Goldstein 2000 on the Milan Pact), as well as in France (Mériaux and Duclos 2001), Germany (Grewer 2001) and Catalonia (Lope *et al.* 2001), tend to emphasize their inconclusiveness. Complex and detailed projects are devised but achieve results disproportionate to the huge initial investments made in planning and social engineering, and more attention is paid to the logic of concertation than to the problems to be dealt with. The explanations for this are often couched in terms of 'cultural limitations', or 'an excess of institutionalization', or the 'inefficiency of

---

[5] This and the next goal, however, are less appropriate to initiatives involving specific intervention in the labor market like the 'New Deal for Young People'.

the bureaucracy' that should attend to the selection, approval, and implementation of initiatives.

These explanations, however, are unsatisfactorily generic and allusive. Assessment can be more precise if we bear in mind that (i) a pact essentially defines a structured space for interaction which is broad and heterogeneous in scope because it is not established *a priori* and is conditioned only by agreement among the largest possible number of actors on local-level goals of employment promotion and growth: a kind of pre-equipped policy arena where numerous programs may coexist, and which is relatively cheap to use because it is already organized; and (ii) the costs of participation are low and therefore encourage very extensive participation as long as this gives rise to eminently distributive–collusive coalitions intended to maximize the immediate advantages of cooperation (access to the financial resources available): for participation to give rise to integrative–distributive coalitions, it is necessary for the actors involved to sustain greater costs of participation, which is by no means certain that they will see as convenient and in their interest.

The first of these two points tells us that assessment of outcomes must consider individual programs (as well as or instead of the overall design); the second that it is not so much the structural characteristics of pacts as the conditions of participation in them that should be examined.

Some of the cases studied by the LocLevConc Project are illuminating in this regard. One of the most interesting of them forms part of the Birmingham–Solihull–Black Country Territorial Employment Pact, in the United Kingdom. This initiative concerns the development of a not-for-profit employment agency designed to support local people in obtaining jobs at Birmingham International Airport and the National Exhibition Centre (NEC)—two of the largest employers in the area. As Paul Marginson and colleagues report (Marginson, McIlroy, and Gilman 2001: 9–10):

The agency—called Jobs Junction—began operating in August 2000. [It] is targeted mainly on the residents of North Solihull, which has higher levels of unemployment and lower levels of schooling, labor market participation and self-employment than the rest of the area. Whilst the Birmingham International Airport and the National Exhibition Centre (NEC) are themselves poised for employment growth and help stimulate growth in other firms in the surrounding area, the key problem for residents in North Solihull is accessing these jobs. The employment agency was set up by the NEC, Airport and the public Training and Enterprise Council (TEC) as a way of tackling two related issues. The first was the NEC's and airport's demand for temporary employees: to be able to manage peaks and troughs whilst employing trained and trustworthy individuals. The second problem was that whilst the TEC wanted to help unemployed people into the labor market, the social security system works against them taking temporary work. Therefore measures to make temporary working easier to take up, by removing penalties in terms of loss of benefit entitlement, would assist claimants to take temporary work. This in turn would enable them to keep in touch with the labor market, thereby increasing their chances of securing permanent employment. It is envisaged that the Jobs Junction employment agency should be able to fund itself as a not-for-profit organization. The agency is targeted on local people who are unemployed, or are returning to work, especially lone parents. It will also target those individuals requiring training and guidance before they can enter or re-enter the world of work.... Employment agency workers will typically be employed on fixed-term six or 12-month contracts. They will be paid a standard hourly rate of pay based on annualized hours. Therefore, even when workers are assigned irregular placements, their monthly wage will remain unchanged. The agency, in recognizing the problems faced by local residents in accessing jobs, is also addressing transport problems as well as other barriers such as lack of training. The employment agency offers the airport and the NEC the potential to match variations in staffing needs whilst having a pool of trained workers on hand. Whilst costs are reduced compared to sourcing staff from a commercial agency, it appears that the enhanced recruitment procedure, offering regular temporary workers through the employment agency is the key issue. For employees, it is a way to make jobs available to people disadvantaged in the local economy and improve their long-term employability, without jeopardizing their short-term social security situation. This innovative program, involving local, social partners with the aim of improving the social wealth and health of a community, is an important example of the way employers' needs can be addressed and resources accessed to target people who are economically and socially excluded.

Note that in this case the project preceded the territorial pact; but it was easier to realize because it was supported by the mobilization of resources—both economic and symbolic—facilitated by the pact, which therefore efficaciously performs the function of a structured space for interaction among the participants and of a facilitator of change. On the other hand, it is because there already existed the prerequisite of a project to implement, and therefore an interest in cooperation, among the actors involved—in other terms, an embryonic endowment of social capital—that from the outset the logic of the pact may prove to be not simply distributive–collusive in character. But it should be emphasized that the project was still in its initial stages when the survey was carried out.

Another significant example is provided by the territorial pact of eastern Veneto. In this area, which, represents a weak economic enclave within prosperous northeastern Italy, the creation in 1993 (after the collapse of the previous power structure following the Tangentopoli bribery scandal) of a coordination body among the municipal administrations—the *Conferenza dei Sindaci* (or Mayors' Conference)—provided an opportunity to plan local development autonomously, differentiating it from the rest of the region. The territorial pact, signed in 1997, after strong trade-union pressure on all the local actors, provided the template for development policies. It has since been integrated with other agreements like the employment and social solidarity pacts. Presently being finalized are a training pact, a security pact and an agriculture pact. The territorial pact outlines infrastructural interventions and employment targets, with an investment of 117 billion lire aimed at creating 1800 new jobs, whereas the employment pact and the social solidarity pact seek to foster flexibility of employment and work within a network of institutions capable of maintaining social cohesion. The employment pact encourages the use of fixed-term contracts as an instrument to create and consolidate new jobs supported and regulated by an agency for intervention in the local labor market. Flexibility is incentivized selectively, with priority being given to time-flexibility schemes which help create stable employment (annualized hours, part-time work, and raising the maximum age for apprenticeships). This is implemented through the submission of projects on an *ad hoc* basis and their joint examination by the social partners. The trade unions are granted the right of active involvement in implementation of the new programs, especially as regards working time and the organization of work, in exchange for their commitment to wage restraint. Furthermore, in order to encourage the extension of the tourist season, the social partners have proposed to the Ministry of Labor that seasonal tourist areas should qualify for social-security tax exemption in off-peak periods. The results in economic and employment terms have been more than encouraging. Most of the investments initially foreseen have been, or are in the process of being, implemented; a further 80 projects have been added, for a total investment of around 260 billion lire, in order to create an environment favorable to industrial relocation. On the other hand, the agency for local employment has not been instituted; there have been no central government schemes to promote employment in areas of seasonal tourism; and the concerted monitoring of employment growth resulting from the new investments has only come about in one case. Better results have been achieved with the pact for social solidarity. In order to support female employment, crèches have been opened in municipalities without such facilities located close to the new industrial zones; and childcare services and services for the elderly have been introduced. Finally, the integration of non-EU immigrants has been favored by a quota system of public housing, and by cheap credit for firms which purchase rental accommodation for their employees (Bortolotti and Giaccone 2001: 6–7). Once again evident are the characteristics of pacts as catalysts, and as ways to structure a field accessible to subsequent actions by local actors; but on the other hand, the differing levels of success achieved by initiatives are due to the varying economic convenience—even in a setting of dense social relations—of cooperating in a non-collusive manner.

Similar considerations apply to the EU-supported pact of Vallès Occidental in Catalonia (Lope *et al.* 2001), which is distinguished by its wide range and number of initiatives providing space for multiple participants. Especially noteworthy in this case is the experimental action of a task force created to promote contractual flexibility negotiated at the company level. Company pacts on the use of temporary forms of employment, so that firms' flexibility needs can be combined with worker protection in the best way possible, are viewed by its promoters—the unions and the local authorities—as an innovative complement to the active labor policies pursued through other initiatives envisaged by the pact. By contrast, less inventiveness is shown by another Catalan territorial pact of endogenous origin: that of Mataró. Significantly, in this case, beyond a lesser endowment of financial resources, the area has a much more restricted previous tradition of local-level social dialogue (Lope *et al.* 2001). In other words, local actors have not yet developed a habit of interacting within consolidated social networks. And this lesser endowment with micro-social resources probably renders the limited investments that have been made even less productive.

Finally, in the case of the Milan employment pact, its disappointing results are probably due to the absence of one of the minimum prerequisites for success: its ability to include all the important local actors. In this case, the absence of the largest union—which regarded the costs of participating in the pact as excessive[6]—seems to have discouraged the potential beneficiaries of the proposed measures (incentives for the use of temporary contracts for the fixed-term hiring of disadvantaged workers retrained at the expense of the local institutions, and derogations from national collective agreements)—that is, companies—probably worried about the future risks of an organized opposition in a far from economically depressed context like Milan.

Overall, therefore, these cases show the great potential, but also the intrinsic fragility, of territorial pacts.

6.4. A Plurality of Experimental Solutions

I have already pointed out that the solution of territorial/regional pacts, or at any rate of concerted multilateral initiatives, does not exhaust the range of experimentation with the decentralization of employment protection in

---

[6] The CGIL withdrew from the coalition on the grounds that the mechanisms proposed for the facilitated hiring of temporary workers by firms did not provide sufficient protection for the former, and that precedents were thus created for the de-legitimization of the rules established by the social partners themselves in national collective agreements.

Europe—although in many cases it is the solution that prepares the terrain for the development of other initiatives.

As suggested by studies dealing particularly with the regulation of the new or non-standard forms of employment and work, other kinds of employment protection can be provided by bilateral agreements/contracts between local institutions and agencies providing labor-market services; agreements among firms, among employers; territorial collective agreements; bilateral agreements between public institutions and firms; self-organization by non-standard workers; collective agreements signed by an organization representing non-standard employees; as well as company-level formal/informal agreements.

6.4.1. *Bilateral Agreements Between Institutions and Agencies or Firms*

The use of bilateral agreements/contracts between local institutions and agencies providing labor market services may occur in the context of broader territorial concerted multilateral initiatives, as shown by the aforementioned case of the Airport-NEC not-for-profit Temporary Employment Agency within the Birmingham–Solihull Territorial Employment Pact. But it may also constitute an initiative in its own right.

An innovative case in Germany is the joint venture in Saarland between municipal and regional authorities and the German affiliate of a Dutch private employment agency specialized in finding jobs for the hard-to-place unemployed (Grewer 2001). This case arises within a highly structured system of labor market intervention affording close protection for the unemployed, as in Germany, where costs have risen steeply (especially since reunification) but space for autonomous expenditure and experimentation has also recently increased. The joint venture was set up on an experimental basis in order to reduce the deficit in the municipality's budget for assistance to the long-term unemployed. It has achieved notable success as regards labor-market reintegration, at least on fixed-term contracts, of former recipients of social welfare benefits, and perhaps even more so as regards cost cutting. It has therefore been extended and re-confirmed, becoming a key factor in renewal of traditional bureaucratic procedures. Another example, which is similar in many respects although still in the initial stages, is provided by certain preliminary agreements between municipal administrations and a not-for-profit temporary employment agency (Obiettivo Lavoro) in Italy, whose aim is to find placements for workers receiving redundancy benefit after being laid off by companies in crisis (Ballarino *et al.* 2001). In both cases, the use of an agency has made more satisfactory results possible without reducing the level of worker protection.

Forms of bilateral agreements and cooperation between public institutions and firms may also figure among the actions envisaged by wider territorial concerted multilateral initiatives, as exemplified by direct agreements with companies in which worker representation has not yet been introduced: as in the case of the initiatives envisaged by the already-mentioned Vallès Occidental Employment Pact (Lope *et al.* 2001), where the local institutions have undertaken to provide services or incentives (e.g. services for personnel recruitment, or tailor-made training courses) in exchange for a pledge by companies to create jobs. But it may also develop independently.

In effect, this is a form of cooperation quite common in industrial districts and areas of diffused small-firm production (Pyke and Sengenberger 1992; Cooke and Morgan 1998; Crouch *et al.* 2001). An interesting case is the Coventry Clothing Resource Centre in West Midlands (Marginson *et al.* 2001). Through this initiative, local public institutions stimulate innovation and greater competitiveness—which small firms would find difficult to achieve on their own—with positive outcomes in terms of employment.

Coventry City Council established the Clothing Centre as far back as 1989 in order to furnish services and assistance to small local clothing companies and to encourage them to innovate and strengthen their position in the local economy. Traditionally, in fact, this is a sector with a reputation for inefficiency and poor working conditions, and characterized by destructive competition. Over time, the Centre has offered a wide range of training projects to develop the skills of personnel and management. It has encouraged the use of functional flexibility or working hours flexibility, the regulation of home work, and employment creation. Through its commitment to the delivery of services required by companies, it has fostered networks within the sector, earning the esteem and respect of a set of firms accustomed to operating covertly and in isolation. 'The Centre has been able to build upon this to create influences and initiatives that had a considerable, if uneven, impact on the clothing sector in Coventry. This included the creation of an environment in which regulation of work organisation and employment became an important matter in the environment agenda' (Marginson, McIlroy, and Gilman 2001). In 1998, during a difficult economic period, on the initiative of the City Council, the Centre's governing committee was restructured to reflect a greater diversity of partners, including trade unions. It undertook a series of joint projects designed to raise the sector's production standards and to foster competition based on quality rather than costs through the definition of shared rules. With the support of the Clothing Manufacturers Association, a charter was drawn up which established a set of voluntary standards covering production methods, work organization and working conditions to which all local clothing companies should aspire. Because these are initiatives joined by companies on a voluntary basis, their impact has been uneven. But there is no doubt that they have helped to improve the employability of workers threatened by redundancy, to safeguard employment levels, and sometime to increase them.

6.4.2. *Coalitions Among Employers*

Employment protection may also be provided by forms of coalitions among employers. Perhaps the most interesting example is the establishment of local-level associations among employers for the collective engagement of specific human resources which they might not be able to afford individually, thus offering them better conditions and forms of job security—a case in point being the '*groupements d'employeurs*' (employers' groupings) in France (Mériaux and Duclos 2001). These initiatives are of particular interest because they combine employment stability for workers with the flexible use of labor for employers. In fact, by unifying jobs undertaken temporarily for various employers under a single permanent contract, the *groupement d'employeurs* (GE) provides an alternative to the internalization of work within the firm, while still guaranteeing its security.

This particular solution to the dilemma between job security and employment flexibility was first used in the agricultural sector, and was then extended to industry, especially among small and medium-sized firms. But as analysis of three different cases by Mériaux and Duclos (2001: 18) has shown, two conditions must be in place for a GE to develop: (i) a system of local firms must be willing to share the use of specific human resources (which requires recognition of a shared interest and the construction of trust relationships among the participants); (ii) the firms concerned must be able to predict their joint labor demand. A GE differs from a temporary agency, in fact, because it responds to recurrent or cyclical demands for temporary labor; but it can cope with unexpected peaks only with difficulty. This means that the volume and types of skills required must be established *a priori*. In exchange for this prior commitment, companies benefit from a more loyal workforce, whose investments in training are not lost but capitalized upon, and whose commitment is long-term.

As regards the first of these two conditions, the ways in which it comes about vary significantly among the three cases examined. In one case it is the product of familiarity, being constructed over time among the members of a club of small local entrepreneurs, and of the initiatives that they have begun to develop together also using facilitated access to European structural funds, so that the creation of a GE (open to other firms that may be interested) appears an almost natural consequence of previous experiences. Another case concerns the initiative taken by a 'social entrepreneur', who had accumulated local experience as the manager of a company, head of a temporary labor agency, and promoter of an association of local entrepreneurs, to persuade small firms in this rugged and inaccessible area to organize themselves to create a pool of workers with hard-to-find skills, who could be shared once they had been suitably trained. In a third case—that of an agricultural GE—constructing the preconditions for it was more straightforward because the social relations of the small farm-owners concerned already displayed a certain propensity to cooperation, and the project was put forward by the local chamber of commerce and agriculture, which enjoyed a good reputation.

As to the second condition for a GE—the ability of its member firms to predict the amount of labor demand to be met by sharing human resources—this was never already in place. Instead, in all the cases considered it was constructed in a preliminary phase during which specialist agencies were commissioned to conduct an accurate survey of demand. This phase was followed by definitive design of the project (definition of strategies and the association's governing bodies, human resources management and development policies, selection of the appropriate collective agreement, and so on) with the direct and indirect contribution of the various actors involved.

Overall, the case studies have shown that this solution can only work successfully if solutions are found for the many structural difficulties associated with employers' collective action, which requires either a considerable endowment of local social capital or substantial investments in its construction, as well as major investments in institutional engineering.

6.4.3. *New Ways to Use Collective Bargaining*

The final examples to be cited belong more or less clearly to the more traditional category of collective bargaining, but from which they differ in certain respects.

A first example consists of local-level collective agreements. In various cases (as documented especially in Rhône-Alpes, Veneto, and Tuscany), a collective agreement among the local social partners may be intended to establish rules and procedures which restrict unfair competition in the use of human resources (e.g. by seeking to regularize illegal workers, as has occurred in relation to Chinese labor in the textile district of Prato), to increase (again in Prato) the supply of vocational training relevant to local needs (Bortolotti and Giaccone 2001), or to regulate and stabilize seasonal work, to coordinate and incentivize the allocation of local workers to different jobs and their mobility between different activities.

On the topic of the stabilization and 'de-precarization' of seasonal work, of particular interest is the district collective agreement reached in the tourist area of Vercors (Rhône-Alpes) in France for the first time on an experimental basis in 1994 and then renewed, in view of its positive results, in 1997. This agreement is also interesting because it highlights the possible limitations of innovative initiatives that originate at the local level but require national-level recognition (Mériaux and Duclos 2001: 24–9).

The overall aim of the agreement was to transform the seasonal employment contract into permanent jobs with annualized part-time contracts. The signatories—a number of local employers' associations and one of the largest unions, the CFDT, supported by an association for local development—expected numerous advantages from the agreement. The employers foresaw an improvement in tourist services because they could use more stable, better-known and more highly motivated personnel, in whose training they could invest, and they would also benefit from the reduced social security contributions provided by the law on part-time work. The workers concerned expected to enjoy more predictable and less precarious conditions. Benefits were also expected by the local administration, which envisaged a gradual reduction of the irregular work widespread in the sector. But in order to make full use of these advantages (relief on social contributions, universal application of the new rules to reduce irregular work), it was necessary to obtain an extension of the district collective agreement from the Ministry of Labor.[7] This extension, however, which was formally requested by one of the signatory employers' organizations was not granted, despite the strong pressures applied by local authorities and politicians. It was opposed twice, in fact, by both the main employers' organizations and some of the leading national trade unions, which raised doubts as to the representativeness of the signatory organizations and the ability of the agreement to take adequate account of collective bargaining in individual sectors. The parties concerned nevertheless continued to apply the agreement on a voluntary basis; but it was not renewed upon expiry, largely because its contents were superseded by the new rules of 2000 on part-time and intermittent work.

In the case of the footwear district of the Riviera del Brenta (in the Veneto), during a period of short labor supply due amongst other things to the traditional precariousness of work in a sector subject to sharp seasonal oscillations and in which much use is made of homeworking, at the end of the 1990s the social partners reached territorial agreements (which also gave rise to a territorial pact) intended to redefine local working conditions in the sector (Bortolotti and Giaccone 2001). And for the first time the measures introduced (on

---

[7] In this way the agreement became valid for the companies not represented by the signatories.

vocational training, skills certification, health and safety programs, protection against unemployment) concerned female homeworkers as well.

A distinctive case in point is the attempt to intervene by contractual means in the local labor market of Prato by redefining working time and the use of overtime (Bortolotti and Giaccone 2001: 14–15). In the textile district of Prato, a particularly high level of overtime has traditionally been the basis for implicit agreements between companies and workers based on a trade-off between high wages and temporal flexibility. Companies guaranteed to maintain a certain amount of overtime which ensured high pay in exchange for workers' willingness to work extra hours whenever necessary. The mechanism was able to work because it was possible to rely on the wage guarantee fund in periods of particularly low demand. In the mid-1990s, however, stricter controls by INPS (Istituto Nazionale Previdenza Sociale, the social security fund which provides income support) and the advent of the first company-level productivity agreements provided employers and unions with an opportunity to dispense with an arrangement which was by now perverse and no longer acceptable to either party. Excessive recourse to overtime, in fact, resulted in extremely high labor costs, and it hampered both employment expansion and organizational and technological innovation. After long negotiations, in 1997 the parties signed a local agreement (or better 'protocol') which established the terms for a new trade-off, to be defined operationally at the company level, between on the one hand reduced overtime use and employment expansion, and on the other, union-sanctioned recourse to further forms of flexibility: specifically, the greater use of non-standard forms of employment (part-time, temporary work) with the consequent growth of employment and greater working-time flexibility. Under the slogan 'from compensated flexibility to negotiated flexibility', the in-company implementation agreements then signed, albeit with some difficulty, provided that about one-third of the previous amount of overtime would be maintained, that another one-third would be converted into greater working-hours flexibility, and that the remaining third would be absorbed by new hires on non-standard contracts. But the results of the agreement were less encouraging than expected, both because some of the normative solutions envisaged were soon regulated by the 1998 labor-market law, which dealt with similar issues, and perhaps even more so because the agreement failed to take sufficiently realistic account of local customs (on the firm's side) and the scant interest of large sections of the local labor supply targeted by the agreement (young people, women) in part-time jobs or ones with highly variable working hours.

In various ways, therefore, initiatives of this kind help increase employment protection at the local level by acting on both the demand side (more stable and yet more flexible contracts, redistribution of job opportunities, increased training opportunities and greater security) and the supply side (willingness to accept more variable working hours, to participate in training programs, to accept a possible reduction of income). However, the available studies show that they achieve highly variable degrees of success, and they depend closely on whether the participants are able to gain short-term advantages from them, under constraints deriving from national systems of industrial relations.

Forms of self-organization by non-standard workers are infrequent but not impossible. In Italy, as shown by Ballarino *et al.* (2001), in the mid-1990s various kinds of self-help association were set up by groups of professionals and freelances in the business services and social-welfare sectors. On the basis of these experiences, in 1997 a union representing atypical workers, (Nuove Identità di Lavoro, NIdiL) affiliated to the CGIL was set up. Today, the national NIdiL organization operates in three areas: (a) institutional action for the general representation of atypical work; (b) industry and company-level representation of particular occupational categories in national and local collective bargaining; (c) the provision of individual assistance and services (on tax, legal-contractual matters, social security) both on its own and through the CGIL offices. Similar features are displayed by the organizations for atypical workers set up by CISL (Associazione Lavoratori Atipici e Interinali, ALAI) and UIL (Comitati per l'Occupazione, CPO). The explicit objective of the various initiatives undertaken to represent atypical workers is to increase the protection afforded to self-employed or temporary workers. In the long term, the aim of NIdiL is to contribute to the definition of a more universalistic guarantee system, under which three levels of rights are to be recognized: basic social rights (independent from employment); rights connected with employment (such as unemployment benefits, accident insurance, maternity leave, continuing training); and rights connected with specific activities and employment relationships. In the future, according to these organizations, this should eliminate the typical/atypical antithesis, replacing it with a varied set of forms of employment, among which workers may choose in the same way as employers.

For the moment, these new unions have relatively small memberships. But they received significant recognition during the elections in 2000 of the worker representatives on the committee that manages the recently established INPS social security fund for coordinated freelance workers. Noteworthy too are a number of examples of new forms of collective bargaining at local level. The most interesting case is probably the signing in 2000 of the first collective agreement for specialist interviewers working for market survey companies. Signed by NidIL and by the association of market survey companies in Milan, but with national coverage (and concerning around 7000 freelancers), the agreement deals with issues such as the form of individual contracts, minimum pay levels for various job categories, rules on the reimbursement of expenses, pay rates for night and weekend work, guarantees in the case of contract annulment, injury, illness, maternity, the criteria used for performance assessment, rules on vocational training and the recognition of trade-union rights, the creation of conciliation boards and ones for the periodic re-appraisal of the agreement (Ballarino *et al.* 2001: 17–18). Similar though less elaborate agreements have been reached in several other cases: for example in Treviso (Veneto) to regulate the employment relationships of the teaching assistants employed on coordinated freelance contracts by the provincial administration in order to integrate blind children into the school system, or in Florence to give greater employment stability to freelance archivists and data processors working for a large public childcare institution (Bortolotti and Giaccone 2001: 12–13, 19–20). Of particular interest in these cases, and especially in the last two, is that they concern situations in which workers with medium-to-high level skills are looking for a clearer, more predictable and more advantageous definition of their employment relationships, but without this entailing their being taken on as employees. For the first time, there is some progress toward achievement of these goals. But this development also highlights the marked heterogeneity among the interests of the non-standard workers which NidIL and similar organizations seek to represent, as well as their difficulty of finding general criteria valid for everyone. It also demonstrates the need to deal with the problems surrounding their relations with the industrial unions already present in the workplaces concerned.

Finally, further forms of employment protection may derive from company-level formal/informal collective agreements. Studies on decentralized bargaining in the European countries suggest that agreements on working time, in particular, make it possible to negotiate reductions in the use of temporary labor, or increased hirings, in exchange for the greater flexibilization of working time and annual schedules and/or greater internal flexibility.

But there are still other types of agreement. One is exemplified by company agreements on the use of agency workers, as in the case of the arrangement between Rover Cars, the Manpower employment agency and the Transport and General Workers Union at one of Rover's sites in the West Midlands (Marginson *et al.* 2001: 12–13), or an agreement at a Dutch-owned bank in Milan (Ballarino *et al.* 2001: 18–19). In both cases, under the collective agreement the unions consent to the use of a form of employment traditionally viewed with suspicion in exchange for guarantees for both the employees that they represent and for the external temporary workers.

Another example is provided by the company agreement on the use of fixed-term work at Malpensa airport (Lombardy), in which 'the key objective for the partners is to establish an open dialogue on the theme of fixed term work in order to make the most out of the advantages allowed by this form of employment while reducing unwanted effects on the workers and the organization' (Ballarino *et al.* 2001: 22). Of especial interest are some of the company agreements negotiated as part of the programs carried out under the already-mentioned Vallès Occidental Employment Pact in Catalonia. These are job security agreements which state criteria for the use of various forms of temporary work and their gradual conversion into less contingent positions.

Compared to more traditional company bargaining, the novel feature of these agreements is that they seek to provide protection which covers both insiders and outsiders. This is not only in the sense that protection is extended to occupational categories (temporary workers, even freelancers) traditionally outside the circle of trade-union representation, but also in the sense that, in all the cases considered even if to differing extents, this extension has repercussions on the conditions of insiders: it alters their working hours (which become more flexible and less predictable), restricts their access to overtime, and also exposes them to competition by workers who may work with greater diligence and commitment (as sometimes happens when agency workers are used).

Hence, although the unions seem more able than they used to be to represent and protect the interests of new occupational categories, they risk new tensions in their relationships with the rank and file. From this perspective, too, the intervention of external institutional actors may be useful if it facilitates definition of a new framework within which to foster innovation.

6.5. Different Logics of Intervention

I conclude my discussion by first summing up the objectives that these various forms of decentralized intervention are intended to achieve, paying particular attention to how attempts have been made to regulate the use of new and more flexible forms of employment. I then offer some general remarks on the future prospects of territorial regulation.

The main objectives can be grouped into five broad categories:

1. There is a first broad category whose main aim is to promote employment growth and to reduce unemployment, and in particular to foster entry or re-entry into the labor market by the unemployed categories that find it most difficult. This endeavor is typical of the majority of the concertation initiatives promoted by local institutions—both because of external inducements or incentives (by EU programs or national legislation) and independently— which seek to involve the social partners in the pursuit of goals of local

development and employment growth. Examples are provided by the various types of territorial employment pact and other forms of multi-lateral concerted initiatives. In this case, there is generally no explicit concern to improve the regulation of non-standard forms of employment, either because of an implicit belief that the problem will resolve itself through economic growth or because such forms are viewed as a temporary and transitional phenomenon (and therefore of little social importance), or because they are considered to be a better solution than unemployment (or irregular work). The risks to be reduced are those of unemployment on the workforce's side and, secondarily, of a possible lack of sufficient human resources on the firm's side. The resources available are provided mainly by the institutions, often making recourse to European funds. Beyond being used to cover the running costs of the initiatives, these resources are usually invested in training programs to increase employability, and to improve information systems on trends in labor demand and supply, to which access is free or at any rate at very low cost.

2. A second broad category of initiatives is explicitly designed to provide non-standard employment (mostly temporary in form)—flanked by incentives and specific forms of protection—for disadvantaged categories of workers and the unemployed residents of depressed areas; but also vice-versa for underemployed or inactive workers in labor-market situations where there is a shortage of supply (examples of this are the Pact for Milan or the activity envisaged by the Not-for-Profit Temporary Agency in Birmingham, or the various projects envisaged by the territorial Pact of Eastern Veneto). In this case, too, the intention is to foster the access or re-integration to work of the unemployed. But the underlying logic is that of positive and promotional action on the supply side, subordinate to a specific interest in using the workers involved in the program on the demand side. In other words, the aim is to combine the advantage of having a job (albeit temporary), on the one hand, with the availability of flexible labor on the other. This explains why in this case the promoters of concerted action may also be firms. Beyond the creation of mechanisms to match demand and supply (examples being the concertation committee that evaluates projects submitted by firms and technical support bodies in the case of the Pact for Milan, or the special not-for-profit agency set up jointly with firms in the case of the Birmingham initiative), specific action is taken to support programs such as vocational training targeted on firms' needs, transport services, housing, social services (crèches, care for the elderly) to promote female labor supply, and so on. Specific mechanisms to increase job security may be also introduced, like fixed-term contracts of relatively long duration and/or a guarantee of re-employment within the local labor market. While the advantages to firms are evident (availability of a flexible labor supply trained according to their needs), those to workers are more variable. Beyond the reduced risk of being excluded from the labor market and greater opportunities to increase their human capital, workers

may benefit from greater job security and from the new services provided for them. The difference lies mainly in the combination of labor-market characteristics, the aims of the promoters, and the capacity to apply pressure of the workers and (where they are active) of the organizations that represent them (the unions). In short, the intention is to promote non-standard work while trying to link it with compensatory benefits and advantages, as a transitional solution for which the benchmark is the standard employment relationship.

3. For a third category, the aim is to reduce the insecurity of non-standard forms of employment by means of initiatives designed to facilitate transition from more to less precarious forms of employment: from irregular or 'black' work to temporary agency work; from temporary agency work to fixed-term contracts (of greater or lesser duration); from fixed-term contracts (e.g. seasonal) to permanent part-time jobs. Most of the company and territorial collective agreements pursue goals of this kind as part of negotiations which concern permanent workers as well: examples are territorial agreements on seasonal work, or company-level agreements on temporary work, which provide for the gradual transformation of agency contracts into fixed-term ones, and of fixed-term contracts into permanent ones. In these cases, the initiative is taken mainly by the trade unions, although these single out problems and risks that concern the firm as well. And they also concern the local authorities, especially as regards the regularization of 'black' labor. This type of initiative implicitly presupposes the idea that the various forms of non-standard work can be organized along a continuum ranging from the maximum to the minimum divergence from the standard model of employment. This spectrum can be viewed as a sort of locally-based atypical internal labor market where the main threshold is the passage from a temporary contract to a permanent part-time one. Note that the pursuit of a concerted strategy of this kind by the trade unions requires not only reaching agreement with management and/or employers' associations but also, to some extent, mobilizing the solidarity of permanent workers, whose terms and conditions of employment may be damaged by it.

4. A fourth category concerns initiatives intended to 're-internalize' non-standard temporary work within a new organized space, one wider than the individual firm but still with a limited compass, and defined on a local basis. The clearest example is provided by the French GE. Other examples are schemes for seasonal alternation among different spells of work, or those for the shared use of (usually scarce) human resources sometimes found in industrial districts. The project of a not-for-profit agency in the area of Birmingham airport may evolve in this direction (and so too may a similar project suggested for the area surrounding Malpensa airport in Lombardy), as well as some of the activities of the non-profit temporary labor agency, Obiettivo Lavoro, in Italy. We must use 'may' here, given that the majority of these initiatives exist more on paper than in

practice. The overall pattern, however, is an effort to create job security for workers whose exclusive use cannot be afforded by any individual firm, but whom many firms want to have available, so that a new perimeter of corporate citizenship may be defined in a co-operative way. The numerous difficulties that arise in this case are similar to those encountered when arranging collective goods.

5. The final category consists of initiatives whose aim is to use a certain amount of creativity in defining rules for non-standard labor external to the firm, without seeking to 're-internalize' it—not even in the new sense indicated above. The clearest examples are a few Italian initiatives to lay down the employment conditions of employer-coordinated freelance workers, in which the recently-created trade unions for 'atypical' workers (NIdiL, ALAI, and CPO) have been involved.[8] Another example is provided by the project for the organization of a network of multi-activities considered in the Albertville (Rhône-Alpes) territorial pact (Mériaux and Duclos 2001).

To sum up, the foregoing survey has shown that the decentralization of employment protection is under way, although it is still largely in its initial stages, and its prospects of success are by no means clear. We have also seen that the process may assume various forms, and that it may be driven, if we concentrate on protection of the more precarious or at any rate less protected forms of employment, by various logics: the minimal and traditional (but prevalent) logic of regulation implicit in schemes for employment creation in general; that of compensated regulation, in which promotion of the use of non-standard forms of employment (which firms need) is flanked by incentives and benefits for the workers concerned; the logic based on progression (in general negotiated by the unions) along a continuum which gradually converges on the standard model of employment (the logic of the non-standard internal labor market); that of the re-internalization and stabilization of non-standard work within an organized perimeter which extends beyond the individual firm; and the logic of providing protection and rights for workers who do not belong to any particular organization in a stable way.

Note that the first three logics implicitly confirm the substantial central feature of the standard model, on which they seek to converge, or for which they seek to provide compensatory measures. The last two instead distance themselves from the standard model and seek to modify it, either by redefining the boundaries within which workers are entitled to stability and protection, extending them beyond the individual firm, or by releasing workers

---

[8] It should be emphasized that in some of these cases workers did not want to be hired as employees, showing that a preference for a non-standard form of employment, under certain circumstances, may be expressed by labor as well.

from the need to establish permanent relations with a firm in order to enjoy rights and security.

This is as much as it is possible to say by generalizing from cases which have not always been successful, or whose results it may be too early to assess. Under what conditions, can we imagine the solutions observed succeeding?

To return to the above classification, we may say that the first three logics are also those which require less revision of the entrenched practices envisaged by the social partners and the local authorities. But given that the regulatory solutions largely concern forms of employment different from those around which relations between the social partners have revolved in the past, to be successful in these cases, the proposed solutions need above all to be based on agreements among all the actors concerned which commit them to the goals to be pursued, avoiding both exclusions and an excessive reliance on voluntarism. For this to occur, there must be a surplus of resources to bring into play, thereby encouraging participation, and the creation of a promoting body able to mobilize interests. It is for this reason that programs of this kind usually develop through the use of additional external resources and are based on cooperation among the interested parties, with the local government often playing a major role. In this case the availability of European structural funds proves to be particularly important because it may furnish the incentive that enables possibilities to be translated into concrete initiatives.

In the other two cases, the traditional practices and consolidated behavior of the local actors are subjected to powerful pressure. In the first case, it is a matter of devising and implementing rules for the acquisition and coordinated use of human resources within a specific territorial area, and by coalitions of firms rather than by single organizations. But this raises all the difficulties connected with the production of collective goods. In other words, success requires the mobilization of local actors according to dynamics not dissimilar to those necessary for the emergence of collective social movements, but with the extra complication associated with the need for inter-firm cooperation—whose promotion is particularly complex, as the literature on employer collective action has long emphasized (Schmitter and Streeck 1981). It is therefore necessary that there be (i) great interest—however latent—at the local level in the creation of this collective good, namely the pooling of human resources to be used in turn by employers; (ii) material or symbolic resources to be brought into play; (iii) local leaders able to put cooperative action into practice through the launching of information and consensus-building programs, the acquisition of support resources, the creation of alliances, the definition of procedures for operational decision-making (e.g. reaching a territorial-level collective agreement, the creation of a new association of firms, the creation of a specialized coordination agency); and (iv) that rules for access to and utilization of the collective good be established.

In the second case it is a question of defining and implementing conditions and rules which protect non-standard workers (especially the more mobile and temporary, or the self-employed) whether or not they belong to a structured employment setting, and without proposing their 're-internalization'. This not only requires imagination and inventiveness, given that it amounts to defining the bases for a different logic of employment (that of work which remains external to the firm, or external to settings that we may call 'quasi-firms'); it also raises problems of redefining the relationships between external labor and the firm in a manner which necessarily affects the employment relationships of internal workers.

The aim in this case is to provide more inclusive 'light' protection for everyone rather than more exclusive 'heavy' protection for only a few. The conditions for change are therefore much more demanding. This is because they require the existence of an interest in reinventing the rules (and thus changing the *status quo* for both firms and labor); that this interest finds a voice able to assert it and place it on the political/trade-union agenda; and that a sufficiently broad coalition willing to intervene is created. It is no coincidence that some first examples, however timid, have emerged in cases where bodies representing the interests of the new forms of employment have been set up. It is, moreover, in this area that one discerns forms of work regulation and employment protection particularly suited to the ways in which the world of production and work is changing.

6.6. Conclusion

To return finally to our point of departure, the evidence has confirmed the importance of labor market policies rooted at the local/regional level. Measures at this level are in fact functional to the delivery of quality employment services, targeted on specific and difficult problems, which would be impossible to deal with from the center and which spring from the new characteristics of highly differentiated and segmented labor markets. From this point of view, the local dimension increases the efficacy of such measures.

The local dimension may also prove to be more efficient to the extent that it gives rise to beneficial linkages among different programs. This, however, requires the activation of horizontal linkages among programs that are not only distinct but promoted by different actors with at least partly different logics of action. It is this capacity to network programs or projects of differing complexity together, without placing them under excessive strain, that constitutes one of the most promising opportunities in which to invest imagination, planning and resources.

Within a distinct territorial unit it is also possible to make reliable forecasts (as regards employment and training needs, for example) on which to base policies and define the means to implement them, overcoming the limitation of overly circumscribed and short-term perspectives or ones that are too broad and general (Zeitlin 1992; Mériaux and Duclos 2001).

On the other hand, the cases examined indicate that the more actors search for *ad hoc* solutions to overcome obstacles and/or grasp new opportunities experimentally, the more necessary the consensus-based coordination of initiatives becomes. Joint definition of pacts or agreements, or at any rate of shared reference norms, serves to establish common parameters or to set limits and constraints on actors' discretion. This is necessary in an area or at a level where parameters and constraints deriving from norms fixed by national laws or agreements do not exist or are inadequate, or where the intention is to modify them experimentally.

The advantage of jointly agreed solutions is that they can be innovative (see the agreements on the 'stabilization' of seasonal work, on the organization of alternation among different activities, etc.). Their disadvantage, however, is that they are fragile (see also Sabel 1992), because they depend on adherence by all the main actors involved and are therefore subject to the disruptive effects of exit or opportunistic behavior, or of collusive coalitions.

All this has two important implications. One is that it cannot be taken for granted that innovative potential—even when on paper it promises advantages or reduced risks for all the actors involved—will actually be realized. Although this is a rather obvious observation, it is often ignored. Yet, it is important for explaining why, in the face of the difficulties of cooperation, companies or unions may prefer the sub-optimal solution of adapting to already-existing rules, even if imposed from above, which may be less convenient but do not involve the costs of designing and participating in innovation processes.

The second implication is that the role of the resources available and of incentives for cooperation becomes particularly important. The cases observed have frequently highlighted the importance of the availability of European structural funds, or of other sources of funding outside the local system, as a factor which facilitates concerted actions. But the availability of these resources is neither a sufficient nor a necessary condition, since on the one hand it may give rise to local coalitions of a purely opportunistic nature, incapable of producing innovation, and on the other the concerted definition of new rules may occur even if financial resources are not made available (e.g. when collective agreements are reached).

What instead always matters is either the presence of a tradition of cooperative relations among the main actors, or the active role of local authorities and institutions in promoting innovation.

Although my analysis has focused on the importance of the local dimension, its results also prompt reflection on the role of higher levels, national and/or European, in labor-market policy. As we have seen, this role is indubitably important from two fundamental points of view: that of definition of the general normative framework, and that of promotion (sometimes indirect and unintentional) of change and innovation by making resources and incentives available.

Bearing in mind the necessarily very heterogeneous nature of the concerted initiatives examined—from the point of view of both their goals and the means to achieve them, as well as their results—it seems that, in addition to these functions, higher levels of governance must assume responsibility for the 'light' coordination of measures and *ex-post* monitoring of output. This higher-level coordination and monitoring seems especially necessary to prevent harmful forms of competition and/or a socially unacceptable diversification of standards.

References

BALLARINO, G., BOLOCAN, M., FONTANA, C., LIZZERI, B., MASCELLI, E., and PASQUI, G. (2001). 'The Regulation of New Forms of Employment and Work in Lombardy between Institutionalised Concertation and Experimentation'. *LocLevConc Working Paper* WP/01/16/EN, Milan: Ires Lombardia (also available on www.ireslombardia.it).

BARBERA, F. (2001). 'Le politiche della fiducia. Limiti e possibilità dei Patti territoriali', unpublished paper.

BOBBIO, L. (2000). 'Produzione di politiche a mezzo di contratti nella pubblica amministrazione italiana'. *Stato e Mercato*, 1: 111–41.

BOLOCAN GOLDSTEIN, M. (2000). 'La via milanese alla concertazione. Il patto per il lavoro'. *Quaderni Rassegna Sindacale-Lavori*, I/3: 91–106.

——, PASQUI, G., and PERULLI, P. (2000). 'La programmazione negoziata e la concertazione territoriale dello sviluppo in Lombardia: l'indagine empirica'. *Ires Working Paper*, Milano: Ires Lombardia.

BORTOLOTTI, F., and GIACCONE, M. (2001). 'The Regulation of Non-Standard Employment in the Italian Small Firms Systems. A Comparison between Tuscany and Veneto'. *LocLevConc Working Paper* WP/01/18/EN, Milan: Ires Lombardia (also available on www.ireslombardia.it)

CERSOSIMO, D. (2000). 'I Patti territoriali', in D. Cersosimo and C. Donzelli (eds), *Mezzo Giorno*. Roma: Donzelli, 209–50.

Consiglio Nazionale dell' Economia e del Lavoro (CNEL) (1994). 'La società di mezzo. Le rappresentanze sociali fra territorio e competizione'. *Documenti*, No. 38, Rome.

COOKE, P., and MORGAN, K. (1998). *The Associational Economy*. Oxford: Oxford University Press.

CROUCH, C., LE GALÈS, P., TRIGILIA, C., and VOELZKOW, H. (2001). *Local Production Systems in Europe: Rise or Demise?* Oxford: Oxford University Press.

ESPING-ANDERSEN, G., and REGINI, M. (2000). *Why Deregulate Labour Markets?* Oxford: Oxford University Press.

FERNER, A., and HYMAN, R. (eds) (1998). *Changing Industrial Relations in Europe*. Oxford: Blackwell.

GREWER, H. G. (2001). 'Institutional Continuity in Change. Main Results of the German Report on NFEW and Local Level Concertation'. *LocLevConc Working Paper* WP/00/3/EN. Milan: Ires Lombardia (also available on www.ireslombardia.it).

LEONARDI, S. (2001). 'Contrattare i parasubordinati'. *Quaderni Rassegna Sindacale-Lavori*, II/3: 105–23.

LOPE, A., GIBERT, F., and ORTIZ DE VILLACIAN, D. (2001). 'The Local Regulation of the New forms of Employment and Work. The Case of Catalonia'. *LocLevConc Working Paper* WP/01/17/EN. Milan: Ires Lombardia (also available on www.ireslombardia.it).

MARGINSON, P., McILROY, R., and GILMAN, M. (2001). 'The Regulation of New Forms of Work and Employment in the West Midlands: Local Territorial and Local Company Case Studies'. *LocLevConc Working Paper* WP/01/14/EN. Milan: Ires Lombardia (also available on www.ireslombardia.it).

MÉRIAUX, O., and DUCLOS, L. (2001). 'Agencements locaux et internalisation de la responsabilité de l'emploi. Etudes des cas menées en Rhône-Alpes'. *LocLevConc Working Paper* WP/01/2/FR. Milan: Ires Lombardia (also available on www.ireslombardia.it).

MIRABELLI, C. (2000). 'Concertazione e sviluppo locale: l'esperienza dei Patti territoriali in Calabria'. *Rassegna Italiana di Sociologia*, 3: 363–88.

OECD (1999). 'Employment Outlook 1999'. Paris: OECD.

PYKE, F. and SENGENBERGER, W. (eds) (1992). *Industrial Districts and Local Economic Regeneration*. Geneva: International Institute for Labour Studies.

QUI NORD-OVEST (2000). 'I Patti Territoriali in Piemonte'. *Quaderni di indagine sul Nord-Ovest per l'Artigianato e le P.M.I.*, June 1.

REGALIA, I. (1998). 'Industrial Relations at Regional Level in Europe: Strengths and Weaknesses of an Intermediate Level of Social Regulation'. *European Journal of Industrial Relations*, 4/2: 157–76.

——(2000). 'Dealing with New Forms of Employment and Work', A Survey of the Use and Regulation within Workplaces of New Forms of Employment and Work in Selected Regions of Five European Countrie's. *LocLevConc Working Paper*, WP/01/13/EN (also available on www.ireslombardia.it).

——(2001). 'The Possible Role of Local Level Concertation in the Regulation of New Forms of Employment and Work. The Results of Six Regional Studies in Europe'. *LocLevConc Working Paper* WP/01/20/EN, Milan: Ires Lombardia (also available on www.ireslombardia.it).

REGINI, M. (1995). *Uncertain Boundaries. The Social and Political Construction of European Economies*. Cambridge: Cambridge University Press.

REYNERI, E. (1999). 'Unemployment Patterns in the European Countries: a Comparative View', *DML-online*, n. 1 (www.lex.unict.it/DML-online).

SABEL, C. F. (1992). 'Studied Trust: Building New Forms of Co-operation in a Volatile Economy', in F. Pyke and W. Sengenberger (eds), *Industrial Districts and Local Economic Regeneration*, Geneva: International Institute for Labor Studies, 215–49.

SCHMITTER, P. and STREECK, W. (1981). 'The Organization of Business Interests'. Discussion Paper, IIM/LMP, 81-13. Berlin: Wissenschsftzentrum.

STREECK, W. (1991). 'Industrial Relations in a Changing Western Europe'. Paper Presented at the Third European Regional Congress of the International Industrial Relations Association, Bari, Italy, September 23–26.

SUPIOT, A. (ed.) (1999). *Au delà de l'emploi: transformations du travail et devenir du droit du travail en Europe*. Paris: Flammarion.

TRAXLER, F. (1996). 'Collective Bargaining and Industrial Change: A Case of Disorganization? A Comparative Analysis of Eighteen OECD Countries'. *European Sociological Review*, 12: 271–87.

TRIGILIA, C. (1992). *Sviluppo senza autonomia*. Bologna: Il Mulino.

URBANI, P. (2000). 'Agire per accordi. Studi di caso'. *Quaderni Rassegna Sindacale-Lavori*, I/3: 47–60.

ZEITLIN, J. (1992). 'Industrial Districts and Local Economic Regeneration: Overview and Comment' in F. Pyke and W. Sengenberger (eds), *Industrial Districts and Local Economic Regeneration*, Geneva: International Institute for Labor Studies, 279–94.

7

Local Labor Market Policies and Social Integration in Europe: Potential and Pitfalls of Integrated Partnership Approaches

ADALBERT EVERS

7.1. Introduction

Unemployment and social exclusion seem to have established themselves as key problems at the turn of the millennium. The unemployment rate in the European Union stands at nearly 10 percent representing some 16 million people. Approximately 50 million EU citizens are considered to be poor. The growth of productivity as a consequence of technological innovation and the effects of economic globalization may aggravate the situation in the future. Evidently, the model of social integration and inclusion developed over the past 50 years by Western European welfare states can no longer be expected successfully to curb unemployment, exclusion, and poverty when these are no longer temporary individual risks, but widespread and lasting social phenomena. The need for recasting European welfare states (Ferrera and Rhodes 2000) is strongly felt across political borders.

Against this background, the 1990s saw the growing importance of public policies addressing poverty, social exclusion, and unemployment. The latter problem—exclusion from paid work—has been at the heart of labor market and employment policies and programs that have steadily evolved at levels above and below the nation-state: both at the EU level, in terms of concepts and strategies initiated by the European Commission, and at the local level, where regional and municipal authorities have assumed special responsibilities in this area. Moreover, such trends have led these levels to draw closer to one another, with state and national authorities serving as intermediate agents in decision-making over the distribution of EU funds to local development and social and occupational integration programs. One of the prerequisites for the successful 'localization' of EU programs and financial transfers is, obviously, the existence of shared perspectives and understandings concerning the challenges and possible solutions between the Commission in Brussels and regional or municipal authorities in such diverse settings as southern Italy or eastern Germany.

This chapter presents a brief account of the findings of an international research project (Evers and Koob 2001) that examined two central elements of EU policies for social and occupational integration: the idea of an 'integrative approach' that puts employment issues on the agenda of all policy sectors, and the idea of 'pacts', 'partnerships', and 'cooperative' strategies, both vertical and horizontal. The latter idea involves public–private partnerships that include not only public authorities and business but also the 'third sector', comprising civic associations, especially those that run services and act as employers on a non-profit basis.

The chapter opens with a brief sketch of policy developments in the European Union (Section 7.2), goes on to clarify the objectives and assumptions of the international research project on which it builds (Section 7.3), and then presents an overview of developments in three countries: France, Germany, and Italy (Section 7.4). Section 7.5 draws out the common trends and cross-national characteristics visible in the localities and regions studied, while Section 7.6 concludes with some critical reflections on the potentials and pitfalls of the EU concept of an integrated partnership approach to local social integration.

7.2. Above and Below the Nation-state: Local, Regional, and EU Action for Social and Occupational Integration

In the past decade EU local policies, concepts, and programs have acquired greater visibility. But this should not obscure the fact that national policies still play a key role in determining and designing policies for social and occupational integration. All EU countries have an inherited legal and institutional framework. And despite differences between them, social and occupational integration usually builds on two pillars:

1. The weaker pillar—developed to a varying extent in different countries—comprises measures for social assistance, which even in a national regulatory framework have usually a strong regional and local flavor due to specific financial and administrative responsibilities of municipalities, districts, and so on. This traditional pillar was not designed to solve unemployment problems and therefore few or no instruments were available to help those who had fallen

into dependence on social assistance to re-enter the labor market. Gradually, the barriers between social assistance and labor market policies were removed, and forms of financial social assistance have been combined with social work, training, and placement programs.

2. The stronger pillar in all countries is formed by the set of rules and institutions responsible for the bulk of labor market policies, that is, the labor market administration, which is sometimes semi-independent from the state (even though traditionally it was strongly centralized) and represented locally by public employment offices. This pillar has been stronger because there are many more people who are able to work and yet dependent on unemployment benefits, compared to the number of those who are solely dependent on social assistance. But it has also been stronger due to the tradition of 'activation' measures which require special finance and organization, such as training, subsidies, consultation, placement services, and so on. The demarcation from social assistance (historically related to sanctions) has become blurred, as job offers, services, and rights in this policy sector are becoming increasingly dependent on special characteristics of the recipients and tailored to particular problem groups.

But the new concepts and practices of social and occupational integration at the local level, operating somewhere between the local employment and social assistance offices, cannot be understood without taking into account at least two other related policy fields. First, municipalities and districts usually have their own economic policy departments working to improve local conditions in order to retain and attract business. Obviously, unemployment can be both a challenge and an additional stimulus for them. Second, there are urban development policies designed both to boost prosperous urban districts and to keep other parts of a city or region from disintegration and decay. Such policies are increasingly required to frame developmental concepts in which investments in social and economic projects reflect the challenges of occupational and social integration.

Recent developments throughout Europe should therefore be located in the 'tension field' comprising the following four areas: (1) labor market policies and programs; (2) social assistance; (3) economic development concepts; and (4) programs of rural and urban (re)development. The primary challenge is to adapt them to new realities of unemployment and exclusion for which they were not originally designed, such as: regional unemployment that may affect a much broader segment of the population than was originally expected; youth unemployment that not only requires measures different from social assistance but also different from placing trained jobless adults; or situations, where exclusion from gainful employment turns into social exclusion and emergence of an 'underclass' experiencing a gradual loss of basic social competencies required in standard work situations. Furthermore, insofar as problems and challenges differ for various sub-groups and regaining a job means regaining a perspective on and competencies for life and work more generally, the interrelationship between administrations, services, and their clients becomes more complex and ought to be tailored to individual needs. Finally, policies formulated in these cases will rely on a form of governance that is different from the traditional highly regulated and hierarchically administered practices.

In the European Union the debate is structured by two different discourses which need not be mutually exclusive.

Workfare and individually tailored measures.   The first approach deals with problems of social and occupational integration as a challenge to the individual and public authorities in finding the right activation measures. It is assumed that most people's problems can be solved by occupational integration and that sooner or later they will find a job, assuming that the right kind of activation strategies preparing them for a niche in the regional labor market can be developed. What is needed then is a sensible way of classifying the unemployed in groups that range from those who can be easily placed to those for whom placement in an ordinary job is only possible after a series of mid- or long-term measures to enhance their social competencies, work skills, and qualifications. Against this background, new types of workfare strategies have developed across previous ideological divisions, for example, in Scandinavia (Kildal and Keysers 2000; Arnkil and Spangar 2001). These strategies operate everywhere with individual contracts and case management techniques that require the recipient of assistance to accept some clearly stated duties in a jointly negotiated plan for reintegration. The sanctions, in case the client cannot fulfill the contract, vary. So do the levels at which public authorities are willing and able to invest—in terms of the quality of job offers and the budgets for re-socializing clients and for training provision. It should be noted that these approaches are used in settings where there seems to be a realistic chance of the labor market absorbing the problem groups.

Development and job creation.   A second, less prevalent, discourse is more centered on the problem of how to create additional jobs and at the same time stimulate a more integrative socioeconomic and urban/rural development. In France and the new federal states of Germany where there exist wide economic and employment imbalances, large-scale programs have been introduced to finance short-term work for particular target groups (in Germany *Arbeitsbeschaffungsmaßnahmen*/ABM; in France, above all, *Revenue Minimum d'Insertion*/RMI and *Emploi Jeune*). It is not always clear, however, whether such 'second labor markets' offering a springboard for creating new jobs represent a transitional phase to the 'primary labor market', or merely a social reservoir to be placed mostly in the public and the 'third sector' (private business hesitates to hire even very 'cheap' labor if the people to be hired do not appear 'fit for the job'). This discourse has generated much debate as well as produced government programs addressing the capabilities of the third sector which runs all kinds of 'employment-intensive' services, contributing significantly to job creation. Furthermore there have been debates and programs which address the challenge of social integration from a broader perspective, that is, by designing concepts of urban and community revitalization which embrace all kinds of participation: from community and volunteer work, training, and self-help to participation in job creation programs. Obviously, the creation of a 'second labor market' through additional short-term jobs almost exclusively financed from public funds, as well as revitalization projects for decaying city districts, find greater support where there is a wide gap between employment opportunities and demand and/or when exclusion from work is accompanied by marginalization and pauperization.

As will be demonstrated below, various types of policies, programs, and practices can be found at the local and regional level, some closer to the former and others to the latter discourse, or representing a hybrid of the two.

As far as the European Union is concerned, the Treaty of Amsterdam (1997) established the basis for a coordinated European Employment Strategy (EES). As earlier chapters of this book explain in more detail, each year the European Union adopts employment guidelines following which Member States submit a National Action Plan and annual report on their employment-promotion activities. Interestingly enough, from an early stage, EU concepts and programs have demonstrated sensitivity for the role of the local level. The Delors Commission initiated the first programs for local development and employment, designed by a special unit reporting to the president (Commission of the European Communities 1996). EU policy has remained strongly committed to the importance of the local and regional levels, as can be seen from the Commission's paper on *Acting Locally for Employment: A Local Dimension for the European Employment Strategy* (Commission of the European Communities 2000).

Particularly interesting is the fact that the European Union places much greater emphasis on a developmental rather than individualized workfare approach. In this respect it clearly differs from the perspective of a number of OECD studies and recommendations on local employment policies (see, e.g. OECD 1999). *Acting Locally for Employment* speaks of 'developing employment' and not 'putting people back to work'. Proceeding from this principle, however, it draws a harmonious picture, where every sector does its best to stimulate locally a type of growth that results in 'developing employment'. Based on this understanding, EU documents underline the special role of small and medium-sized enterprises and the contribution of the non-profit 'Third System/Social Economy' (which creates new services in local communities for individual and collective needs), as well as the importance of improving the services of local public employment offices and strengthening the social partners' commitment. Together such measures should result in an 'integrated approach' whereby, as the Commission states, 'all policies operated at the local level must, for maximum efficiency, be integrated into a single strategy' that should lead to 'mutually supportive economic, structural and social policies'. Obviously, in order to reach this goal the Commission recommends 'partnership' where 'employment policy is no longer seen as the exclusive concern of political decision-makers and economic operators, but as a concern of society as a whole'. In this view 'local partnerships that bring together all forces in an area must be regarded as a fundamental condition for successful local employment development strategies' (Commission of the European Communities 2000: 20–1). It should be mentioned that a considerable part of EU funding for local and regional socioeconomic development goes to programs that make subsidies dependent on such local coalition-building. One of the most prominent examples is the EU program which helps to fund 'Territorial Pacts'—cooperative approaches to local and regional action that envisage not only the participation of the traditional 'social partners' but also the 'third sector', or the 'Third System', in EU jargon (see also Chapter 6 above). This sector, comprising advocacy and community groups and non-profit service providers, who are simultaneously economic actors and employers, has been targeted by special EU pilot programs (Campbell 1999) and has been the object of extensive research on its potential effects on employment growth (Ciriec 2001). Linked to this is a debate on the contribution of a 'social economy' consisting of non-profit organizations as 'social enterprises' (Borzaga and Defourny 2001) which act in an entrepreneurial way and at the same time integrate social effects, such as social inclusion or community support, into their agenda.

But how far does this ambitious concept of (a) developing employment through integrative policies and (b) developing governance mechanisms and partnerships beyond hierarchical administration or the traditional triangular corporatism of public authorities and social partners reflect the realities that have taken shape locally? What are the potential benefits, and also the specific challenges and pitfalls, of policies designed from this perspective?

7.3. Background Assumptions and Concepts

The following observations and reflections draw on evidence from the aforementioned research project (Evers and Koob 2001), which investigated the types of partnerships and cooperative policies established to promote social and occupational integration. This project focused primarily on the practical development of new programs and forms of network-building that contribute to an integrated and partnership-based approach. Policy-makers modify their routines and programs because the 'old' paradigm supporting their previous strategies is no longer congruent with the new challenges of the economic and social environment. The general hypothesis proceeds from the recent EU assumption that the effectiveness of innovative policies for social integration depends on how far local and regional levels of governance involve actors outside the political administration. Such involvement should facilitate adjustment of national programs to specific local and regional conditions and favor the capacities of policy diffusion as regards, for instance, new social policy norms and paradigms in occupational and social integration. But the connection between new 'open' forms of cooperation and policy innovations has not been taken as given, even though such a link is implicit in EU concepts and funding structures. Based on a comparison of different national systems of collective action and detailed local and regional case studies in Western Europe (France, Germany, Italy, and Switzerland) and Eastern Europe, the project sought to identify characteristic forms of networks and partnerships among and between actors and institutions which are conducive to policy innovation.

Since both EU concepts and local experiments are centered on active support for integration, the following discussion leaves aside pure income support schemes, such as unemployment insurance and social assistance. These programs are only discussed in relation to 'active labor market policies', which in addition to providing some financial compensation, involve support for activation through social work, training (short-term) jobs, and other combinations of work, participation, and income generation.

Furthermore, it should be noted that depending on the form of particular policies and programs, the groups considered are broader than the 'work-ready' unemployed, but narrower than all those threatened by social exclusion. Obviously, the concern with social integration, or as it is often referred to in EU discussions 'social cohesion' and 'social exclusion', is focused on more than just those forms of disintegration that result from unemployment. Nevertheless, unemployment is at the core of most integration problems. Thus the focus of the analysis is on a variety of policies and programs insofar as they create some explicit link with occupational integration in labor market policies (as, e.g., is often the case with social assistance programs, local development concepts, or policies to combat urban decay).

All these considerations lead to the basic framework which can be presented visually (Fig. 7.1). This arranges policies and programs on a *vertical axis* with

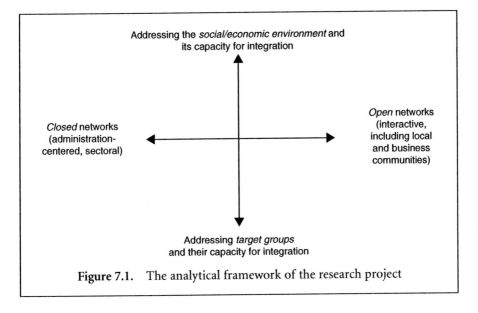

Figure 7.1.   The analytical framework of the research project

policies *addressing target groups* at one pole, and policies *addressing the social and economic environment* at the other. The idea is to capture the differences between narrow labor market policy and social work approaches of a workfare character (aimed at adapting people through training and placement to available jobs) and wider concepts of 'developing employment', which include a link to policies influencing the structures of industrial and labor market development (e.g., by developing new service activities offering employment to low-skilled people, as well as through urban renewal or economic modernization).

The *horizontal axis* between '*closed*' and '*open*' *networks of cooperation* needs some clarification. Between a strong corporatist tradition with exclusive partners on the one hand and the mushrooming of new public–private partnerships in various local policy fields on the other, three main dimensions can be said to characterize the distinction between the two poles: the number of actors, the degree of cross-sectoral participation, and the style of cooperation. For instance, closed networks are scarcely open—at least formally—to actors other than the social partners (corporatist model). At the same time 'open' systems have been identified with what are often called 'policy networks' (Scharpf 1997) wherein public and private partners from different sectors (e.g. municipal representatives, the labor market administration, social partners, and other civil society associations, such as chambers of commerce, voluntary organizations, social enterprises, and so on) cooperate in a multi-polar network on a semi-formal basis. It is assumed here, that current developments in occupational and social integration policies include a difficult shift from traditional hierarchical decision-making and sectoral corporatist partnerships to new forms of 'local partnership' (Geddes 1998).

In the following discussion, just as in the original research project (Evers and Koob 2001) we use this framework to organize a comparative discourse around the findings from local and regional case studies in three fairly representative countries—France, Germany, and Italy.

7.4. Difficulties of Integration and Local Partnerships: Findings from Three Countries

7.4.1. *France*[1]

Even though the French economy is currently strong, it suffers from widespread unemployment marked by a relatively high share of long-term and youth unemployment (the latter currently stands at about 15 percent, but has been significantly reduced over the past few years as a result of programs targeting this group). Public–private relations and local capacity-building for social integration have been shaped by the historical path of French state-formation and recent attempts at decentralization, as well as by efforts to use these rearranged structures for the implementation of various central state programs. In addition, however, one can observe attempts at building local capacities, matching central funds and programs according to local needs and priorities (such as the PLIE: '*Plans Locaux d'Insertion et d'Emploi*' or Local Plans for Integration and Employment). Given this background, our four French cases—Aubervilliers, Saint Denis, Grenoble, and Valenciennes—are interesting in terms of the degree to which local actors succeed in integrating different central programs into stable coordination structures and Local Plans for Integration and Employment. All of these localities, except for Grenoble, are marked by high unemployment ranging between 15 and 20 percent.

As far as the implementation of central policies and programs is concerned, two programs are of special importance in France.

The RMI (*Revenu Minimum d'Insertion*, or minimum insertion income) aims at combining the preservation of some kind of social assistance payment (to be financed by the state) with an additional task, the 'I' of RMI: offering places for short-term training and work provided by various organizations, especially in the public and third sectors; this program dates back to 1988.

---

[1] This section is based on Bafoil *et al.* (2001).

In 1997, given the fact that the persistence of high unemployment among young people had led to a debate on the larger problem of social exclusion, a new program 'New Jobs—New Services' was introduced, also called the 'Jobs for Youngsters' program (*Emplois Jeunes*). Through this program the government seeks to provide, for a limited time, access to work to about 350,000 young people. Partners in implementation are usually local public employment services.

These two most important programs are surrounded by a multitude of smaller and more limited initiatives (also noteworthy are the CES, solidarity employment contracts in the public service sector, targeted at young people from 16 to 25). As a result it is often difficult for those in need to obtain effective assistance: the expression 'bush' or 'jungle' was frequently used in the many interviews conducted in France. To achieve both greater transparency for the potential users and better coordination between different programs, many municipalities have developed Local Plans for Integration and Employment, which are created from the 'bottom up' and used as a coordinating framework for the implementation of central government programs, such as those discussed above.

Unlike other countries, the old paradigm in the French programs to be overcome is not so much shaped by tripartite corporatism but to a much greater extent by state centralization. Even now that decentralization has occurred, the forms of cooperation in local councils and other bodies are prescribed by central legislation and administration and are a product thereof— except for the Local Plans for Integration and Employment. With each measure having its own steering group there is a lot of overlap and uncertainty with regard to areas of competence and means of coordination. The multiplication of central initiatives has both increased the need for coordination and posed obstacles to it.

One way to deal with this dilemma is through the creation of a 'social enterprise'—a non-profit organization (association) which is closely related to municipalities and yet semi-independent. The objectives of the social enterprise known as 'Target Employment' (*Objectif Emploi*) are to identify organizations which can offer (short-term) employment that matches the training and subsidy programs it works with. These can be third sector organizations or local public administrations that try to develop new services for their constituency in areas such as day care for children, services for the elderly, and so on, as well as private firms. Similar forms of local coordination have been found in all the cases studied. With the shift from passive to active programs oriented toward occupational integration, the local bodies share the task of overcoming a one-sided linkage with local social (assistance) policies and of getting closer to the sectors dealing with employment and economic policy. This obviously creates conflicts between different professional legacies and understandings, such as those of social workers on the one hand and business people on the other. But in addition to seeking a cooperative approach to improved economic and employment performance, a key objective of such coordination centers and social enterprises is to create a single entry point for young unemployed people and to establish a consultancy tailored to specific needs of different subgroups and individuals.

There is, however, some room for maneuver in locating relevant policies and programs between the poles represented by the programs which target problem groups and those that seek to change local conditions. Some local projects rely on centrally developed programs integrating job placements and income support mainly as 'shock absorbers'. For example, in the context of the RMI measures, departments often fail to provide the job placements and training programs, which should be complementary to central state transfer payments. Program beneficiaries receive the money without necessarily taking part in an activating program (and often without a chance to do so). In contrast to such situations, in some cases departments and cities are eager to set up programs to create jobs for such people, which may be secured even after the initial program financing is over through establishment of new public, third sector, or even commercial services and products. Establishment of local coordinating structures has contributed to the diversity of local situations. It underscores the salient role of different types of local cooperation in the interpretation and implementation of central programs. Given the strong dominance of these programs over initiatives that combine jobs and income, like the *Emplois Jeunes* program, it is not surprising that the private sector is frequently underrepresented relative to the public and third sectors in the existing policy networks.

7.4.2. Germany[2]

Since the 1970s, the unemployment rate in Germany has increased from 2.2 percent (1974) to about 9 percent (2001), reaching a peak of more than 11 percent in 1998. Specific to Germany is the sharp difference between growth regions unaffected by unemployment (like the Munich area) and regions where unemployment exceeds 20 percent (as in many parts of the new Länder of the former GDR, whose industrial base has been decimated by reunification). Obviously this greatly influences the composition of unemployment. Where unemployment is low, it tends to be concentrated among a rather small group of long-term jobless people, who lack skills and suffer from erosion of social competences, as well as sometimes from deterioration of their overall health status. In those regions of the former GDR which have experienced a sudden

---

[2] This section is based on Evers *et al.* (2001).

collapse in employment (especially among women whose employment rate used to be very high), joblessness is concentrated instead among people over 45 and youth seeking first-time employment and apprenticeships. There exclusion is much more a problem of low demand for labor than of insufficient skills or competences, and many of those who are able to do so migrate to the West.

Since the benefit period for unemployment insurance is limited, most of the long-term unemployed have to rely on social assistance which is financed locally by municipalities and districts. Hence unemployment has created a lot of stress not only on the national social security system, but also on the social assistance budgets of cities and districts.

The federal system of labor market administration, represented locally by public employment offices, operates through a number of programs, the most important being those that offer training opportunities and the aforementioned ABM program, which subsidizes more than 80 percent of the wages of those employed under it. Public employers and third-sector organizations have been the primary supporters of this initiative. Private employers, on the other hand, looking mostly for skills and quality, are reluctant to hire and train people on the job, even when ABM funding (which is limited to a maximum of two consecutive years) covers most of the initial labor costs. There are thus considerable barriers to the employment of the long-term unemployed.

In the past few years, under the pressure of increasing unemployment, social assistance offices have been using their mandate to provide support in the form of workfare: those who are found, upon inspection, able to work are required to take a job from a pool set up by the city or district of residence (mostly in the public sector or in the third sector and social enterprises). If they refuse, their social assistance can be reduced, even if this requires a difficult legal process. These measures are financially attractive for districts and municipalities because after having worked for some time on social assistance-based jobs, people are entitled to renewal of unemployment insurance if they fail to find a non-subsidized position. Thus they are at least taken off the social assistance records and excluded from locally funded programs.

Special organizations are often created by municipalities, churches, or through local grass-root initiatives to set up training facilities, offer short-term jobs (e.g. for such labor intensive work as repair services or environmental clean-up and so on), and sometimes even to provide placement services. In Germany these 'social enterprises' are often referred to as BQGs (*Beschäftigungs-und Qualifizierungsgesellschaften*, or 'employment and qualification agencies'). ABM or social assistance-based jobs created by these initiatives or by districts and municipalities (in public services, such as gardening and repair of social housing) make up what is called in Germany the 'second labor market'. Public agencies in charge of economic development are also involved in such job creation schemes.

The Länder and, more recently, the federal government have launched schemes such as the national 'social city' program seeking to link occupational and social integration with programs for social and economic development, which create additional jobs. Apparently, such investment in local programs of urban revitalization provides additional opportunities to strengthen links with social enterprises and civic and community groups, as well as to facilitate integrative approaches to economic and social recovery. But only a few states have enough experience with such programs and their quantitative impact, especially on employment, is very limited.

Our Germany research analyzed six cases of collective action, covering typical approaches wherever cities and districts have built a local policy capacity beyond the execution of routine tasks. The cases were chosen to represent eastern and western Länder, urban and rural settings, and different degrees of 'problem load'. The existing forms of cooperation were found to be very diverse, ranging from cooperation between social assistance offices and local employment agencies to an institutionalized round table bringing together social groups and representatives of an urban neighborhood which has initiated collective action to combat urban and economic decay. Three different approaches illustrate the range of available options.

1. *A social enterprise dealing with specific problem groups without much need for cooperation among local actors.*   In cities, such as Leipzig in the East and Dortmund in the West, a municipally owned social enterprise is a frequent solution. It offers short-term jobs and training facilities in the enterprise itself, in the public sector and in various municipal services. Cooperation here is mostly a matter of ensuring that departments and services in the municipal public sector offer such places. Beyond that, only 'negative cooperation' characterizes this approach, such as efforts to avoid conflicts with artisans (*Handwerker*) or trade unions who feel threatened in different ways by the expansion of ABM-subsidized public-service employment. As opportunities to get outside jobs are very limited in these settings, such strategies can only be justified by the enormous initial pressure to somehow absorb the shock of mass unemployment (as in Leipzig) or as attempts (Dortmund and other cities) to curb local social assistance costs.

2. *Public authorities and employers of different types cooperating in a social enterprise.*   There are however many examples of a more promising way to use a social enterprise. In Ortenau, a rural but industrialized district in West Germany with low unemployment, all those involved in occupational integration (private, public, and third sector employers) were brought together through a cooperative model as stakeholders in a social enterprise and its constituency. Once such a network of employers representing various segments of

the regional and local labor market has been set up and the partners are truly committed to combating unemployment, much better chances exist for the social enterprise to serve as a real bridging institution, whose stakeholders are prepared to employ those who have worked or been trained in it.

3. *Cooperation between public and private partners for social and occupational integration with a common concern for urban and regional development.* In Dortmund (western Germany) employment has become part of programs for urban improvement and renewal in potentially vulnerable city districts. These programs operate through a broad multi-polar network which includes, besides the usual organizations, various community groups and representatives of the local economy. Leipzig (eastern Germany) has a formalized and continuous model of cooperation, with a slight corporatist flavor, in technological innovation and economic modernization. In Güstrow, a rural district (eastern Germany) with very high unemployment and enormous difficulties in formulating a concept of local and regional economic development, there is special concern to create a 'labor intensive' developmental model which would combine public services and tourism, ecological sustainability, and use of cultural heritage, building on wide participation from all social sectors. The idea is to use grants from social assistance, ABM, and EU territorial pact funding to create jobs and services which may later become self-sustaining.

It should be stressed that while these three models represent a broad range of local approaches to cooperation, the first two types are much more prevalent than the third. Cooperation is therefore usually limited to social assistance and employment agencies, a social enterprise for job creation and training and a few partners that are willing to hire people on the basis of short-term ABM grants. This is all the more true, since there is currently an increasing tendency to contract with commercial agencies to place the long-term unemployed directly in regular jobs in the private sector as quickly as possible, using a mix of measures for opening places in contact with local business and an individual approach to select, motivate, or even force people to accept low-paid jobs not infrequently provided under such arrangements.

7.4.3. *Italy*[3]

The Italian research highlights the persistent dualism between northern and southern Italy. In the prosperous North, unemployment is below 5 percent, that is, well below the EU average. The South, though accounting for only one-third of the total resident population, comprises nearly two-thirds of all those in search of employment and more than 70 percent of all those below

---

[3] This section is based on Ferrera *et al.* (2001).

the official poverty line. These observations are discussed within the context of regional development, since after the enactment of decentralization legislation in 1997, this has become the most interesting level to study.

The policy packages operating in the two selected northern regions—Lombardy and Emilia Romagna—are oriented toward occupational integration. The main instruments are (a) vocational training initiatives designed for the long-term unemployed on the one hand and highly educated young people on the other and (b) flexible labor contracts, such as fixed-term contracts. Both measures aim at integrating groups at risk as soon as possible into the primary labor market. Economic and urban development as well as passive policies figure only as marginal issues for cooperation in an 'industrial' model of integration, which works when the level of unemployment is quite low and when it is mainly a result of a qualitative mismatch between labor demand and supply.

As to the institutional background, these two northern regions have long relied for on a closed network of trilateral corporatism, represented by regional employment commissions whose suggestions were often linked with recommendations to municipalities concerning traditional passive policies of social shock absorption. But both regions have shifted to varying degrees toward a more open pattern of cooperation, including, on the local level, a more important role for municipalities and associations in offering training and integration services.

This model of cooperation between regional and local administrations with expanded capabilities and a limited number of directly involved actors mainly representing the social partners is the product of continuous evolution and a homogeneous and fairly stable political culture, in which relationships among the actors are generally characterized by consent and cooperation.

The situation appears to be remarkably different in Calabria, Apulia, and Campania, the three southern regions analyzed in our research. There, the degree of 'problem load' is much higher than in the North. The total unemployment rate exceeds 20 percent, while youth unemployment in some areas is over 40 percent. Local bureaucracies there still lack the culture, skills, and capacities for autonomous problem-solving and innovation. Until the early 1990s, the southern regions had depended on the national policies, finance, and regulation, i.e. mainly passive policies based on state-funded 'short-term work compensation' benefits and massive financial transfers to support existing employment at numerous state-owned enterprises. Since there is limited scope for industrial integration, the situation is marked by the coexistence of:

(1) various passive policies still in place and linked with clientelism and reliance upon family ties and networks; and
(2) the increasing influence of regional and economic development concepts as formulated, in particular, by EU territorial pacts and area contracts, which

require cooperation between all sectors, including third-sector associations. In the three regions, 24 territorial pacts had been established by the end of the 1990s. The task is to encourage measures that would bring together industrial modernization, service creation, and urban development.

As far as models of cooperation are concerned, the regional and provincial administrations still lack to varying degrees the culture and capacity to innovate and change. Widespread suspicion and mistrust are the main features of local bureaucracies where party connections and clientelism still dominate. Civic culture and social capital have developed at a slow pace. But since the early 1990s an *externally induced* change has been taking place: the need to apply for EU Structural Funds and new rules for local prerequisites and program administration, have somehow 'awakened' the various labor market institutions. In particular, the initiative of the municipalities and their mayors (whose influence has been strengthened by direct election since 1993) has contributed to the emergence of a less clientelist model of vertical cooperation, combined with an increased number of partners in more challenging programs on the horizontal local and regional levels.

The Italian research underscores the need (and certain signs of a growing potential) in the southern regions for a far-reaching cultural shift from passive clientelist policies to a local development paradigm, arguably easier to achieve in the better-equipped regions of the North. To meet this challenge, institutional capacity-building in the South is recommended in order to go beyond mere modernization of local administration and to strengthen cooperative interaction by encouraging dialogue between local actors and providing targeted incentives to discourage those forms of 'exit' which deprive the local context of such capacities. Although these recommendations for 'rescuing the South' focus on institutional capacities, such as the creation of a more professional politico-administrative elite and organizational and technical prerequisites (many of the southern interviewees complained about the lack of personal computers), the prospects for success largely depend on the development of civil society and social capital.

7.5. Common Trends and Cross-national Patterns

To sum up, one basic assumption behind the EU concept of 'Acting Locally for Employment'—the first part of our working hypothesis—has been validated: the role of cooperation and partnerships in occupational and social integration is increasing. New partnerships have developed in many localities where they never previously existed. Sometimes these partnerships have taken shape alongside the trend to open up narrow labor market policies and programs to other policy sectors. The latter may include workfare schemes where social assistance departments deal with people threatened by exclusion, or local policies for economic and technological promotion, as well as community-building and urban revival. Such policies, in turn, may directly address employment issues.

The increasing role of various forms of partnership and networking coincides with a clear trend toward decentralization of competencies and activities in labor market policies, enhancing the role of regional and local levels, which used to be either inadequately developed or even totally absent. In most cases there is a shift in emphasis from passive to active measures. This is partly a top-down process, although in many cases a bottom-up approach is used when the local level demonstrates readiness for action. At the same time municipalities themselves do not always serve as the driving force behind new cooperative developments, which can also be spurred by civic initiatives or 'nodal points' in the political administration. What became evident in France, for example, is the key role of local political authorities, given the relatively recent emergence of the municipality as a partner in governance. The flip side of the coin is the inertia of regional government and administration, as reported in southern Italy. This also demonstrates how unemployment, by leading to social exclusion and general local decay, may be a key factor in accounting for local (in)action, although there is no automatic link between 'problem load' and response.

Three mediating factors shape readiness for action:

(1) general concern with modernization of governance and public management reform;
(2) associational traditions and vitality, along with the social capital gained over time, whose impact is manifested in how civic associations, trade unions, or church-based groups deal with those threatened by unemployment and social exclusion;
(3) policies and programs designed at higher levels of governance, including incentives for new forms of co-operation.

These observations can be linked with three key factors operating across each of these countries:

1. There is a wider recognition of the complex links between economic and urban/territorial development on the one hand and social cohesion and integration on the other, even though this does not always translate into policy change.
2. The distance between policy concepts and action at different levels of governance, from the national and the EU to the municipal and the regional levels has been significantly reduced.
3. There is a growing awareness of new and more cooperative forms of governance and public–private partnership as critical success factor in all public policy spheres.

Five points of convergence and common trends may be adduced in elaboration of the preceding analysis.

Programs designed at upper levels of governance have an important role both as incentives for local action, and as frameworks and rules that simultaneously support and restrict it. The findings from all three countries demonstrate that central programs have largely initiated—or at least facilitated—local action for social and occupational integration. Moreover, the German and Italian cases underline the important role of EU level programs. But our research did not assess whether the EU programs' impact is just a question of making additional funds available for local and regional purposes or whether these programs are also a catalyst for changing practices and attitudes on the ground. While it would be clearly misleading to portray the developments as based on bottom-up initiative restricted by hierarchical rules and practices, it should be recognized that wherever initiatives and programs multiply, they create double structures and thus additional difficulties for concerted action at the local level. This aspect of central incentives is most clearly illustrated by the French cases, while the Italian cases underline the modernizing impetus provided by central programs. At the same time the German findings point to the relatively high degree of freedom of action enjoyed by local actors despite the administrative costs resulting from the higher levels' playing on many different program-strings.

The findings from all three countries testify to the enrichment of policy instruments for occupational and social integration. In the core area of local labor market policy, consultancy and an individualized approach are becoming more popular; the design of vocational training services has improved; and new case management techniques—similar to those increasingly used in social assistance and job placement agencies—are being employed. Other examples of new institutions and services include different kinds of specialized consultancy and networking agencies serving as intermediaries as well as social enterprises with multiple objectives which range from securing training and placement services to creating jobs and promoting new socially useful services.

Innovation in the forms of collective action manifests itself:

(1) in concepts and programs adopted. A number of the cases investigated reveal the presence of comprehensive programs, plans, outlines, and other similar policy documents indicative of a clear shift from traditional sectoral administrative routines to new forms of action which—beyond the higher level of interaction—are pursued with greater awareness of their interdependence with other actors and policy fields;

(2) by means of linking labor market policy with related policy sectors. The most frequent examples here demonstrate a closer cooperation between municipal

social assistance agencies and local employment offices; between sectors responsible for economic development and the aforementioned departments; and finally, between labor market and social assistance policies on the one hand, and urban and community development policies, as well as policies addressing various specific issues (such as youth unemployment measures and so on), on the other;

(3) by unconventional forms of networking and interaction. These can, for example, involve a decision to support a social integration enterprise, created by a local association, or developing a new style of personal contacts with local employers, or more individualized services for clients belonging to relevant target groups.

Nevertheless, insofar as such networks need to bridge the gap between different sectors (e.g. the private commercial sector which relies on economic approaches and the third sector with its genuinely social approach), the challenge of finding common perspectives becomes stronger as compared to more traditional corporatist settings or types of cooperation dominated by a single actor or sector. It is quite a task to develop shared perspectives between such different actors as employment officers, social workers, economic developers, representatives of the business community, urban planners, community leaders, and managers of non-profit organizations.

Finally, a common feature in all these countries is that in most forms of cooperation, whether 'closed' or 'open', a rather technical and managerial approach prevails over civic commitments. Yet all the country studies underline the importance of a civic culture, trust, experience in problem-solving, and diversity of associational forms. At the same time, while the practices of cooperation everywhere build on that social capital, it remains unclear to what extent the mechanistic forms of management and networking are suited to its further cultivation.

7.5.1. *Toward a Cross-national Typology*

The second part of our hypothesis dealing with the importance of new forms of 'open' cooperation and their nexus with policy innovations, had to be modified in the light of the empirical findings of the project. We have found *different* recurrent forms of cooperation that are *loosely* connected with various approaches to occupational and social integration. The most obvious (traditional) approach consists in sustaining simple shock-absorbing programs. These forms of action, however, are rarely developed into interactive and cooperative initiatives. Therefore we distinguish two other approaches to be found *across* the national landscapes, even though their impact in different national contexts may vary considerably.

Type 1. Collective action as active labor market policy for training and placement with a focus on private labor market. The underlying rationale derives from the fundamental problem of a mismatch between labor market needs and the availability of skills and qualifications within particular population segments. Hence local action has to address the issue of training provision for these groups and effectively channeling them (back) into the labor market. Even if traditional corporatist approaches involve only administrations and private employers, there is a difference in that the new concepts call for innovative forms of cooperation between employment and social assistance agencies or for personalized interaction between these centers/offices and local enterprises. Moreover, the networks can expand, for example, by involving third sector organizations as additional employers or providers of special services. Such types of sectoral policies can build on the traditional identities of the parties concerned—the identities of firms as employers and the identities of trade unions as defenders of workers' interests. There is, however, a challenge for social assistance or similar departments in turning the logic of preservation into that of activation.

Type 2. Local development action. All the country studies demonstrate, to different degrees, types of cooperation oriented toward economic and social development, involving the redevelopment of a neighborhood, an urban district, or a whole region. Labor market and employment concerns figure in these initiatives as just one dimension alongside broader concerns with cultural, social, economic, and technological modernization. This can mean turning existing economic concepts into a framework for employment and integration, but it can also mean a revision and change of goals of urban and economic development resulting from unemployment and exclusion problems that were not initially anticipated. Obviously, such concepts will move closer to the 'open' policy pole as the goals of development strongly imply the need to address not only the business community and trade unions but also civic associations and a variety of third sector groups. Some of these diverse partners resist categorization merely as employers (e.g. the third-sector organizations) while others (representatives of the business community or trade unions) may find the role of 'corporate citizens' problematic.

Type 3. Collective action as cooperation for additional jobs, focusing on the third and the public sectors. This is a local type of cooperation in programs for job creation, like the German ABM or the French *Emplois Jeunes*, aimed at reviving social skills, training, and short-term employment, as well as developing new products and services for creation of new employment facilities. Therefore, organizations of the third sector are often privileged partners to be addressed not only as potential providers of short-term training and work facilities but also as social entrepreneurs who are expected to create new

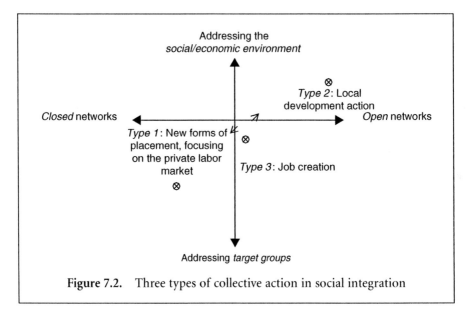

Figure 7.2.   Three types of collective action in social integration

sustainable jobs and services. This makes cooperation more challenging. In addition, however, our research has identified deep ambiguities concerning the objectives which are supposed to hold the cooperating actors together.

The best case may be that the initiatives are seen as promoting local development where the specially created 'second labor markets' serve as incubators for new jobs to be gradually implanted and stabilized and as 'transitional' toward the existing primary labor market.

A second possibility is that these initiatives may aim to create a protected pool of short-term jobs, a bridge to help people in their transition to jobs in regular labor markets.

In the worst cases, these initiatives represent or may turn into mere pools of 'sheltered employment' with no opportunity of progression to new stable jobs and with a constant fluctuation and 'recycling' of temporary job-holders who never acquire appropriate skills or gain opportunities to secure a job in the 'real' labor market.

As indicated in Fig. 7.2, in many cases it is difficult to determine which of the three outcomes will finally prevail.

7.6. Potential and Pitfalls of Integrated Partnership Approaches

If the analysis behind the typology developed here is accurate, it highlights some inconsistencies in the European Commission's present effort to map out ways of 'acting locally for employment'. Our initial overview has already indicated that the European Union has tried to develop 'a local dimension for the European Employment Strategy' (European Commission 2000) aimed at closing gaps and bridging sectoral divisions between social integration and labor market measures on the one hand, and general concepts of economic and urban development on the other, thus making employment an import-ant issue in all municipal policy fields and ultimately in the wider local approach to development. To achieve this, the European Union advocates all-encompassing 'pacts' and 'partnerships' to pull together the energy and resources of the public sector, social partners, private firms, and enterprises of the 'Third System'/social economy.

In many instances this perception corresponds to the developments found in the French, German, and Italian cases. Thus certain conclusions can be limited to organizational and technical recommendations, such as support for key innovations (individually tailored case management and social enter-prises), improvement of evolving multilevel governance, or more consistent monitoring and evaluation not just of outcomes, but also of processes which increase local action capacity.

But our findings also point to some visible strategic problems in the EU concepts, which should be acknowledged and addressed. The EU concept of an 'integrative approach' is based on the assumption that in each case policy integration can and should be achieved by integrating employment into eco-nomic and territorial development issues, gathering thereby a wide range of local partners around both. In reality, however, existing development approaches often remain unchallenged, so long as they are believed to form the best available framework for achieving full integration and employment in the future. In this case (a), cooperation for social and occupational integration of problem groups is all that appears necessary, with a few partners (e.g. enter-prises or other organizations willing to hire people on special terms) helping local authorities responsible for social and occupational programs. It should be noted, however, that this limited form of cooperation between few partners can very well take innovative forms. Only in case (b), where the existing develop-ment concepts are no longer considered appropriate for overcoming mass unemployment and social disintegration, cooperative action for new ways of integrating developmental and occupational challenges can ensue.

So far, the EU concepts have not taken into account the considerable differ-ences in 'problem load' or differences in perceptions and political and cultural prerequisites for action, which can lead to quite diverse understandings of an integrated approach and local partnerships. In case (a), the goals of coopera-tion around active labor market policy may require a limited number of parti-cipants and, even when innovative instruments are used, they remain within the traditional framework of a sectoral labor market policy. Beyond employers and labor market and social assistance officials, the presence of 'Third-System' actors may only be occasionally required, for example, when a need arises for specialized training and employment measures (Type 1 in Fig. 7.2). Promotion of employment and integration will possibly remain a separate issue ranking far behind other issues and the networks that promote them.

Only in case (b) is it likely a broad multi-polar cooperation network may emerge to create the collective action capacity needed, for instance, to revitalize an old industrial area or city district, including the creation of new services and jobs (Type 2 in Fig. 7.2). In such cases, where occupational and social disintegration is perceived as a vital challenge to the future development of a city or a region, there may be a real chance to make these issues a focus of concern for all relevant actors.

Taken together, this means first of all, that contrary to the EU concepts, broad cooperation and partnership that encompasses actors from all sectors on a more or less equal footing will very often not be perceived as necessary. Moreover, when such an approach is adopted, it may be much more difficult than portrayed in the EU proposals. The shared concept of (re)development may challenge established approaches to economic and urban growth that have been successful in many respects. Furthermore, the social partners, business community, and trade unions may have particular difficulties in switching over from 'industrial' and sectoral to 'local' and public partnerships.

Finally, particular ambiguity is produced by the fact that the EU concept of local action and employment is unclear about the future status of the widespread and massive programs that have helped in many countries and regions to create a 'second labor market' that is a special zone of short-term jobs (Type 3 in Fig. 7.2). To what degree should these programs be part of a strategy aimed at creating additional services and work places; or a 'transitional zone', where work is a special social component of an active labor market policy, that continues to focus exclusively on the private sector; or a mere dumping ground for those groups that are economically 'superfluous'? The answer to this question will also determine the future status of third sector organizations as partners in cooperation.

Three recommendations can be derived from this argument as a contribution to the debate on how EU concepts treat the issue of 'integrated approaches' and building 'local partnerships':

1. First, the concepts should acknowledge the plurality of existing forms of collective action and partnerships, many of which demonstrate capacity for innovative action. New forms of 'workfare' as used, for example, in Scandinavia, also need partnerships and integration, even though they may involve fewer partners and cover fewer aspects of the overall problem.

2. Second, the concepts should be more sensitive to the challenges of switching over from active labor market policy to a revision of local development approaches, and from exclusive social partnerships in the corporatist tradition to pluralist and cross-sectoral forms of local action. While some partners, such as community action groups, have evolved as part of local public initiatives, others, such as chambers of commerce or trade unions have generally little experience beyond their role as pressure groups in industrial relations to be able to assume the role of corporate citizens with responsibility for integrated approaches to local development and employment.

3. Finally, the concepts should state more clearly the final objectives of the programs that offer a combination of employment and income, in particular, with regard to the decisive question of the role of partners, especially from the 'Third System'. Should they be regarded solely as 'soft' administrators of a marginalized part of the workforce or are they welcome as partners with clear comparative advantages in creating new services for individual and community needs, which imply additional jobs of different quality? Earlier EU documents and rhetoric about the central importance of the 'Third System' point in the former direction, while reality frequently indicates the latter.

References

ARNKIL, R. and SPANGAR, T. (2001). 'Comparing Recent Danish, Finnish and Swedish Labour Market Policy Reforms: Key Themes for the Reform Agenda of Employment Services'. Unpublished paper.

BAFOIL, F., DEMONQUE, B., GUYET, R., and LOZACH, V. (2001). 'Policies of Social Integration in France'. Grenoble: Centre de Recherche sur le Politique, l'Administration, la Ville et le Territoire (CERAT), Université de Grenoble.

BORZAGA, C. and DEFOURNY, D. (eds) (2001). *Social Enterprises in Europe*. London: Routledge.

CAMPBELL, M. (1999). 'The Third System, Employment and Local Development', 1, Synthesis Report. Policy Research Institute: Leeds Metropolitan University.

Ciriec (International Center of Research and Information on the Public and Cooperative Economy) (ed.) (2001). *The Enterprises and Organizations of the Third System in the European Union*. Liège: Ciriec.

Commission of the European Communities (1996): 'First Report on Local Development and Employment Initiatives'. SEK (96) 2061. Brussels: Commission of the European Communities.

—— (2000). *Acting Locally for Employment: A Local Dimension for the European Employment Strategy*, COM (2000) 196 final. Brussels: Commission of the European Communities.

EVERS, A. and KOOB, D. (2001). 'The Policies of Social Integration in Europe. Systems of Collective Action'. Final report of an international research project within the TSER Programme of the EU. Frankfurt am Main: Institut für Sozialforschung, Johann Wolfgang Goethe Universität.

EVERS, A., KOOB, D., and LIEB, A. (2001). *Policies of Social Integration in Germany*. Frankfurt am Main: Institut für Sozialforschung, Johann Wolfgang Goethe Universität.

FERRERA, M. and RHODES, M. (2000). 'Recasting European Welfare States: An Introduction', in M. Ferrera and Rhodes (eds), *Recasting European Welfare States*, London: Frank Cass, 1–10.

FERRERA, M., GUALMINI, E., GRAZIANO, P., and ALTI, T. (2001). 'Policies of Social Integration in Italy'. Milan: POLEIS Centre for Comparative Political Research, Bocconi University.

GEDDES, M. (1998). *Local Partnership: A Successful Strategy for Social Cohesion?* Luxembourg: Office for Official Publications of the European Communities.

KILDAL, N. and KEYSERS, F. (2000). 'Workfare Tendencies in Scandinavian Welfare Policies'. Paper presented at the European Research Seminar 'The Activation of Welfare States. New Ways of Fighting Poverty and Social Exclusion in Europe'. Lund University, Sweden, October.

MERRIEN, F. X., BERTI, ST., BERTOZZI, F., BONVIN, J. M., and BUDDE, S. (2001). *Policies of Social Integration in Switzerland*. Lausanne: Institut des Sciences Sociales et Pédagogiques, University of Lausanne.

OECD (ed.) (1999). *The Local Dimension of Welfare-To-Work. An International Survey*. Paris: OECD.

SCHARPF, F. W. (1997). *Games Real Actors Play. Actor-centered Institutionalism in Policy Research*. Boulder, CO: Westview.

Part 2

Experimenting with the Work–Welfare Nexus: The United States

8

US Welfare Reform: The Big Experiment*

JOEL F. HANDLER

America has 'ended welfare as we know it'. Welfare has been 'abolished' by The Personal Responsibility and Work Opportunity Reconciliation Act of 1996 (PRWORA). The most notorious welfare program, the welfare 'crisis' in American Aid to Families with Dependent Children—the program for single mothers—has been replaced by Temporary Assistance to Needy Families (TANF). The welfare rolls have fallen by half since 1996. They are at their lowest levels. And of 1.6 million parents still on assistance, nearly a third are working, a threefold increase from four years ago (Ellwood 2000). What was this great reform?

Welfare (which we will now call the cash program for single-mother families) is no longer a guaranteed federal entitlement. State authority—already considerable—has been greatly extended by converting the federal open-ended matching payments to the states into block grants which are no longer an entitlement.[1] Congress must enact new legislation by October 1, 2002, otherwise the federal funding stops for many of the provisions of the new law. Under the prior law, if a family left the welfare rolls, the state would lose the federal cost-sharing (about 50 percent). Since the block grant funding level is fixed, the states retain all the funds for that family. Thus, there is an incentive for the states to reduce the rolls.[2] There are restrictions on the states under the

---

* This draft is a revised and expanded version of 'Reforming/Deforming Welfare' (2000) *New Left Review* 4, Second Series, July–August 2000: 114–36. I would like to thank Danielle Sarah Seiden for her excellent research and editing.

[1] State block grants were calculated as the highest amount of federal money a state received under the AFDC program in either 1994, 1995, or the average of 1992, 1993, and 1994 (Haskins and Blank 2001).

[2] States are required to maintain their spending at a level equal to 75% of the amount they spent from state funds on AFDC and JOBS programs in 1994. These are called Maintenance of Effort (MOE) funds.

block grants, but whether and how these restrictions apply depends on previously granted state waivers and recent regulations expanding state authority (The Children's Defense Fund 1996). As will be discussed below, over forty states have waivers (see Handler 1995 for a description of state waivers).

The major thrust of the reform is work—'get a job quickly, any job, or cash assistance will stop' (Gaid *et al.* 2001). States are required to move an increasing percentage of welfare recipients into the work force (at least 30 hours per week) over the next six years, starting with 25 percent of the adults in the single parent family in 1997 and increasing to 50 percent by 2002. States are required to reduce grant amounts for recipients who refuse to participate in 'work or work activities'. These welfare-to-work requirements are to be enforced by funding cuts in the block grants (The Children's Defense Fund 1996). That is, the funding structure of the block grant places a premium on rapid caseload reduction because the state's federal funding remains constant whether the caseload goes up or down (Stawn, Greenberg, and Savner 2001).

Work requirements, as will be discussed, are not new; they are as old as welfare itself. What is new, and what is the most significant change are the time limits. Previously, welfare would last as long as the youngest child was under eighteen. Now, there are two sets of time limits for assistance. There is a two-year time limit on continuous cash assistance (several states have shorter periods) and there is a cumulative five-year limit (with exceptions for no more than 20 percent of the caseload). It is the combination of work requirements *and* time limits that are the most important basic change in TANF.

In addition to work requirements, States may provide any mix of cash or in-kind benefits or altogether eliminate cash assistance to selected groups based on grounds, such as school enrollment status or drug-related felonies. Moreover, in the initial legislation, PRWORA denied most means-tested assistance to non-citizens who arrived after August 22, 1996, when the legislation was signed ('post-enactment immigrants'), and limited the eligibility of many non-citizens already living in the United States—'pre-enactment immigrants' were to lose their SSI and food stamps within a year (Borjas 2001). In 1997, several of the more draconian restrictions on immigrants were dropped.

PRWORA also modified other programs which impact the well-being of welfare recipients. Welfare families are no longer automatically eligible for Medicaid; instead, they must apply separately. Some percentage will undoubtedly not enroll.[3] In addition to narrowing immigrants' eligibility for Supplementary Security Income (SSI), the Act and the related Contract with

---

[3] The number of persons receiving Food Stamps declined by 27% from 1996 to the first half of 1999. Medicaid enrollment began to fall in 1996—for the first time in nearly a decade—and has fallen steadily since then (Pavetti 2000: 44–50).

America Advancement Act of 1996 also tightened the definition of disability for children and eliminated the drug addiction and alcoholism diagnosis from SSI and Disability Insurance (DI) (Karoly, Klerman, and Ragowski 2001). Moreover, funding was reduced or eliminated for child nutrition and meals programs, including programs in family day care, the Summer Food Program, the School Breakfast Program, and other meal services. Yet, while several childcare programs were ended, the total childcare funding was increased by around $4.5 billion over 6 years. States were given more flexibility, and by 1999, states were using almost $3 billion in TANF funds to purchase childcare.

This chapter will concentrate on the work requirements, which, along with the time limits, are the heart of the welfare reform. I will briefly review the history of the work requirements during the post Second World War period, and then turn to the current reforms. Then, after reviewing some of the key provisions of the new law, I will concentrate on the work programs and the assumptions behind these provisions. I then discuss whether the reforms will succeed, drawing on the recent experience of several states' welfare-to-work demonstration programs. I will review what has happened since the reforms have been enacted. As stated, there has been a very dramatic decline in the welfare rolls. Why? Are the welfare-to-work programs succeeding in getting recipients to work? Are families leaving welfare because of sanctions or denied entry? How are the families who have left welfare coping? This part involves an analysis of the low-wage labor market. I then briefly discuss the other PRWORA changes. I raise questions as to the future of welfare reform and conclude with a discussion of proposals for reform.

8.1. In the Shadow of the Sturdy Beggar

Not surprisingly, the current welfare reform is being hailed as 'new'—a fundamental change. Welfare is no longer an entitlement. Instead of a lifetime on welfare, recipients will have to work, and welfare will only be for relatively short periods of time. In some respects, this is a sharp departure. There never have been legislatively determined time limits. But in a fundamental sense—the emphasis on work rather than welfare—the current reform is as old as welfare history. The very first welfare statute—the Statute of Laborers of 1342—prohibited the giving of alms to 'sturdy beggars'. There was a labor shortage (the Great Plague) and the concern was that welfare would act as a disincentive to work on the part of the able-bodied. Only the disabled were 'worthy' of support. Over the years, the English welfare laws tried repeatedly to separate the 'deserving' from the 'undeserving' poor, culminating in the Poor Law Reforms of 1832, which tried to abolish outdoor relief and confine all recipients in the poor houses. The test of necessity would separate the 'deserving' from the 'undeserving'.

This is what welfare policy *purports* to do—support the 'deserving' but not the 'undeserving'. Yet, in many circumstances, especially with single-mother families, it is often less costly and less difficult administratively to provide welfare benefits (however meager) than to impose sanctions and risk homelessness and breaking up the family. Thus, welfare policy, at least for this category of recipients is often symbolic politics, the affirmation of values that serve to make majoritarian society feel better (Handler and Hasenfeld 1991).

Starting in the late 1950s and 1960s, for a variety of reasons—migration to the cities, civil rights, Democratic Party politics—welfare grew rapidly and the demographics changed from largely white widows to divorced, deserted, and disproportionately never-married women as well as families of color. Welfare now became a 'crisis'. Even though the Federal Government responded to this new situation by introducing mandatory work requirements, AFDC rolls went from 2 million to about 13 million over the next three decades while costs skyrocketed from about $500 million to about $23 billion. The welfare controversy continued to boil until the 1996 reforms.

What explains our continuing fixation on welfare reform? It is surely not the costs. AFDC at its height cost $23 billion (both federal and state), whereas the budget for Social Security pensions is more than $300 billion, and Medicare is $280 billion. As always, it is the fixation on the 'undeserving' poor that drives the never-ending debate on welfare. While US welfare policy is centrally concerned with the work ethic, the stigmatization of the 'undeserving' poor is much broader than failing to become gainfully employed. It encompasses race, gender, and other forms of deviant behavior. While contemporary welfare policies are often described in so-called objective terms—labor markets, wage rates, incentives, demographics—they are heavily laden with moral judgments. Who the poor are, whether they should be helped, and under what circumstances, are social processes that affirm moral norms of work, family, gender roles, morally 'proper' behavior, and attitudes toward race and ethnicity. The term 'welfare' is the code word for the inner-city, African–American young woman, most likely a substance abuser, having children to stay on welfare, and breeding a criminal class. This is the 'underclass' (Gilens 1999).

8.2. The 'Work First' Strategy

The heart of the contemporary welfare-to-work reform is the 'work first' strategy. The consensus behind this work strategy is that welfare encourages dependency. Recipients, instead of seeking to improve themselves and become self-sufficient, have children to get on welfare and stay on welfare, which then becomes a way of life from generation to generation. Thus, welfare recipients, according to this stereotype, threaten both the two-parent family and the work ethic. Tough work requirements, enforced by time limits, will not only reduce welfare costs, but more importantly, replace the entitlement status and permissiveness of the current system with the values of responsibility and self-sufficiency. This will not only benefit the parents, but also provide positive socialization for the children.

The idea is to move both current recipients and applicants into the labor market as quickly as possible rather than place them in longer-term training or education programs. The assumption is that there are plenty of jobs for those who want to work. Moreover, by taking any job, even an entry-level job, and sticking with that job, a person will move up the employment ladder. Presumably, it is therefore not the job market that accounts for the malaise but the welfare recipients who do not have the motivation or the incentives to leave welfare and enter the paid labor markets (Mead 1986).

8.3. The State Workfare Programs

Prior to TANF, over thirty states had approved waivers which imposed work requirements enforced by some form of time limits (Handler 1995). The reported experience of these welfare-to-work projects was used to justify the 'work first' strategy despite the fact that the evaluations of these programs were seriously flawed. It is unclear as to which policies—for example, time limits, work requirements, the reduction in welfare benefits, or macroeconomic conditions—account for the 'successes' (Seiden and Prehoda 2001). Despite the fact that it was unclear as to which policies actually helped recipients become self-sufficient (Corbett 2001), the 'success' of pre-PRWORA state experiments had a decisive influence on the 1996 welfare reform.

The California GAIN program and, in particular, the program in Riverside County is considered the standard-bearer for the 'work first' strategy.[4] Overall, this program was hailed as a success: welfare recipients who worked earned more than the controls, welfare payments were reduced, and the programs showed a positive cost–benefit ratio. Yet, the results were modest in terms of increases in employment rates and income. The earnings of the participants in the experiment averaged less than 10 percent more than the controls. Moreover, about two-thirds of the experimentals were *not* working at the end

---

[4] For a discussion of the Riverside program, see Handler and Hasenfeld (1997).

of the three-year demonstration and almost half *never* worked during the entire three-year period. And this was true of other programs as well.[5] Thus, despite the political claims for success, the gains for welfare-to-work recipients were very modest, and often failed to account for the costs of working— transportation, reciprocity in child care, missed days, and so forth. Most recipients remained in poverty (Pavetti 2000: 48–9). Nevertheless, the Riverside 'work first' strategy has become the standard.

These modest results can be explained by the misconceived assumptions about the participants of welfare-to-work programs and the low-wage labor market. We will first evaluate the characteristics of the low-wage labor market and then consider the match between the welfare recipients and the jobs. We will discuss what has been happening to the welfare leavers.

8.4. The Low-wage Labor Market

The 'success story' of the US economy is well known. Since 1990, over 20 million new jobs have been created. Until recently, unemployment was approximately 4 percent, and there seemed to be no sign of inflation. On the other hand, there has been stagnation in the real wages of the less skilled, less educated workers (Freeman 2000). Poverty fell in the 1990s, given economic growth, and poverty among female-headed households with children is at an all-time low—although still 35 percent. However, many more people have left the welfare rolls than have escaped poverty (Blank 2001). Despite the economic expansion and the rise in productivity between 1973 and 1993, the household income of the poorest fifth declined (US Census Bureau 1998; Heclo 1994). Similarly, while child poverty has fallen from 21.8 percent in 1994 to 18.9 percent in 1998 (Greenberg and Laracy 2000: 9), it is still higher than it was 20 years ago. In particular, nationwide, more than 13 million children are poor, 3 million more than in 1979 (Lee 1999).

Even though wages began to rise among the less-skilled workers after the mid-1990s (Blank and Schmidt 2000), jobs are increasingly contingent or short-term, and without benefits (Lee 1999). Moreover, the US employment market has become increasingly characterized by low paying jobs that do not lead to improved career opportunities over time. As a result, the holders of these jobs remain close to the poverty line throughout their lives. Very few of the poor work full time—in 1998, only 13 percent of the poor were fully employed. Considering that not even full-time employment can help

---

[5] Similar findings also hold for MDRC's 20 welfare-to-work programs and the evaluation of 11 state TANF programs.

unskilled workers find their way out of poverty, it is not surprising that part-time work is even more unrewarding: only 17 percent of part-time workers receive health insurance and only 21 percent are included in pension plans. Furthermore, 17.5 percent of part-time workers have combined family incomes of less than $ 15,000 a year (Wenger 2001). Thus, despite the booming economy, despite the very low unemployment, and despite the fact that most Americans are better off, the bottom fifth of the population is *worse* off. The average after-tax household income of the poorest one-fifth of households, adjusted for inflation, has *fallen* 12 percent since 1977. The average annual income of this group is $ 8800, down from $10,000 in 1997.[6]

Similarly, despite the decline in unemployment, there is considerable evidence that, at least in the less-skilled segment of the labor market, there are more job applicants than available positions (Lerman, Loprest, and Ratcliffe 1999). Moreover, many jobs remain inaccessible to the low-wage worker. Low-skilled jobs are in the suburbs; many of the less-skilled lack the necessary networks; and many of the urban jobs require higher levels of skills.[7] Job tenure has also declined, and re-employed workers usually suffer a decline in wages. Unsteady employment with frequent and long spells of unemployment (*ibid.*: 8) continues to be a major problem for the less-skilled and disadvantaged workers (Burtless 1999: 31–5). Lastly, employment mobility is also a myth. Whether or not true in the past, there is increasing evidence today that low-wage workers are not moving up the economic ladder (Mishel *et al.* 2000; Wright and Dwyer 2000/2001). Thus, although more Americans are working harder, inequality and poverty remain severe among the working poor.

8.5. The Work Experience of Welfare Recipients

Contrary to the stereotype, most welfare recipients are adults with small families (1.9 children, on average) and are on welfare for relatively short periods—between two and four years. Long-term dependency (five years or more) is rare—perhaps as low as 15 percent. Furthermore, it turns out—again contrary to myth—that the largest proportion of welfare recipients are connected to the paid labor market. Many package work with welfare, and the most common route off of welfare is via a job. In other words, most welfare recipients have little or no problem with work ethic. However, those who

---

[6] Johnston (1999: 14) discusses the recently published analysis by the Center on Budget and Policy Priorities.

[7] '[T]he Educational Testing Service estimates that individuals with 'minimal skills' will qualify for only 10% of all jobs generated between now and 2006' (Katz and Allen 1999: 33).

leave welfare often have to return. The low-skilled labor market produces cycling back and forth between work and welfare.

Welfare recipients, especially African Americans, do not fare particularly well in the competition for these low-skilled jobs. On the basis of a survey of 900 employers in Michigan, for instance, Harry Holzer found that while employers, in general, indicated a willingness to hire welfare recipients, only about 6 percent of the jobs would likely be 'available to women with few skills, little experience, and poor reading and math skills' (Holzer 1996: 28–9).[8]

It is not surprising that most recipients are in and out of the labor market. But why welfare? Because in most states, they do not qualify for Unemployment Insurance. Many do not satisfy the minimum earnings and hours requirements; others fail to satisfy the 'non-monetary' requirements (i.e. the separation from work has to be 'involuntary') (Gustafson and Levine 1998; Williams 1999). Less-skilled workers with far more unstable work patterns experience significantly far more cyclical unemployment than higher-skilled workers. Hence, for these women, AFDC is the equivalent of unemployment compensation.

8.6. The Supply Side: How Job-ready Are Welfare Recipients?

The rapid decline of the welfare rolls with record employment levels probably means that those still remaining on the rolls have the most serious barriers to employment and the likelihood of working steadily declines as the number of barriers increase. In addition to education, the more significant barriers are few work skills, transportation, poor health, drug dependency, depression, and perceived workplace discrimination (Danziger *et al.* forthcoming). There is a relatively high incidence of physical and mental health problems (especially depression) among adult recipients, disabilities among their children, alcohol and drug abuse, domestic violence, low education levels and cognitive abilities, and limited work experience. Not all of these problems prevent work or render recipients eligible for SSI. Nevertheless, many may find it difficult to hold a job (Zedlewski and Loprest 2001).

To date, we know very little about what works for TANF families who face a diverse set of challenges that limit their ability to leave welfare successfully (*ibid.*). Service delivery for the disadvantaged may be the states' most difficult challenge. Post-employment services are often necessary, but this

---

[8] According to Holzer's study (Holzer 1996), most of the jobs already filled by welfare recipients required basic cognitive skills, computers, or contacts with customers. Most (more than 75%) had a high school diploma or GED; only 14% had neither education, skills, nor experience.

poses a significant challenge to the states in building institutional capacity to address these needs and develop linkages with other organizations and agencies. Some programs connect clients to specialists, for example, domestic violence counselors, health care, substance abuse; others use services that deal with multiple barriers to work. Nevertheless, these activities are limited in scope and coverage. The majority of programs serve only a couple of hundred disadvantaged recipients. There is little information on outcomes. Most states have not moved beyond their 'work first' strategies.[9]

8.7. Leavers: How Well Are They Doing?

Shortly after termination of their welfare benefits, between half and two-thirds of leavers (former welfare recipients) find jobs. Most of the jobs are in sales, food preparation, clerical support, and other service jobs. Despite the relatively high number of weekly hours of work, there are substantial periods of unemployment. While the pay is between $5.67 and $8.42 per hour, the average reported annual earnings range from $8,000 to $15,144. Consequently, this leaves many families in poverty. Most do not receive employer-provided health insurance, paid sick or vacation leave (Pavetti 2000: 48).

Overall, the findings on leavers are consistent across studies (Haskins 2001; Primus 2001; Cancian *et al.* 2000; Bavier 2000). The majority of recipients leaving welfare are working but most remain in poverty. There is a subset that is not working. In particular, 19 percent of leavers are not working, have not recently worked, and do not have a working spouse or partner. Some in this group receive disability assistance. The remaining 'at risk' group (about 17 percent) show no evidence that they will become self-sufficient. They have far higher levels of personal barriers than employed former recipients. Significantly more have a disabled child (19 percent), very poor health (50 percent), or less than a high school education (38 percent). They have about the same number of barriers as long-term TANF recipients (Zedlewski and Loprest 2001).

8.8. Impacts on Children

The number of children in deep poverty has been increasing steadily. The declining effectiveness in reducing poverty is due in part to the emphasis on

---

[9] Zedlewski and Loprest (2001). In 1997, Congress passed the Family Violence Amendment, which allows states to screen for domestic violence and exempt those recipients from program requirements. State adoption of the Family Violence Option will allow them exceed the 20% limit.

reducing caseloads, the declining participation rates in both food stamps and TANF, and the immigrant restrictions. If the anti-poverty effectiveness of means-tested cash assistance and food stamps had not declined between 1995 and 1999, about 400,000 fewer children would be poor today, and the poverty gap would be about $6.7 billion lower (instead of $17.1 billion) (Primus 2001).

Two recent studies by the MDRC indicate that mandatory welfare-to-work programs have very mixed impacts on children: some programs seemed to improve academic achievement, social behavior, and overall health, others produced the opposite effect (Morris, Huston, and Duncan 2001).[10] However, large positive impacts were the exception rather than the rule; in particular, health and developmental problems, such as alcohol or behavior problems were quite widespread (Duncan and Chase-Lansdale 2001).

8.9. Childcare

The crisis in child care—especially for low-wage workers—cannot be over-emphasized. Millions of infants, children, and adolescents are at high risk of being compromised both developmentally and in health because of mediocre childcare. Yet, the current welfare reform requires mothers of young children—in some cases, three-month-old infants—to enter the paid labor force. Childcare centers are at capacity, and even if there are vacancies, the cost is usually too high for welfare recipients.[11] Consequently, most welfare recipients use unregulated relative or family day care. Even here, costs are high, and expenses—as well as availability—vary as children are younger and the mother has to engage in shift work (White 1999). Moreover, there seems to be a lack of care for parents who work part-time, during non-standard hours, and/or parents with infants or children with special needs.[12] Needless to say, childcare challenges limit the ability of many women to remain employed (Corcoran *et al.* 2000).

8.10. Health Care

Because of poorer health, low-income people tend to use more health care than higher-income people, but they have greater difficulty getting health insurance and health care. AFDC/TANF recipients qualify for Medicaid, and

---

[10] Even though the study did not produce any large or consistent effects, there seems to be some evidence that increased employment has unfavorable impacts on school-aged-children.

[11] Market-level childcare costs between $150 and $175 per week.

[12] Current data is very uneven. Most results are based on four experiments in periods before the current welfare reform. Here, too, it is hard to separate out the various factors since the welfare reform packages differed (Besharov 2001).

under the new law—as well as several of the state reforms—Medicaid continues for a period, but no more than a year. Moreover, since under the new law, welfare recipients no longer automatically qualify for Medicaid and food stamps, there has been a serious drop in enrollments. Yet, not surprisingly, women on welfare as compared to working and non-working leavers had better overall access to health care, including health insurance and a regular health care provider.

Considering the coverage discrepancy between welfare recipients and low-income workers, some states developed health care programs in conjunction with welfare reform in order to improve the insurance rates of the working poor. Ultimately, these programs were a means to demonstrate that welfare reform could help people work in decent jobs that provide health insurance. Consequently, in 1999 Wisconsin adopted 'BadgerCare', an insurance program for low wage families ($26,000 for a family of three) that did not have access to employer-based health insurance. The program soon became very popular and enrolled a surprisingly high number of people (66,545 people in 2000). What accounts for this success? According to Louise Trubek (this volume) and other researchers the program's popularity was based on a clever strategy that marketed the program as an insurance—rather than a welfare—program; thus, people were much more willing to apply for the plan.

8.11. The Decline in Food Stamps and Medicaid

As stated, many who have left welfare are not getting food stamps or Medicaid, even though they are eligible. Families who are no longer eligible or deterred from cash assistance may also think that they are no longer eligible for other programs or are not informed of these programs. Evidence is growing that changes in how the food stamp program is administered have increased the difficulties facing eligible families in enrolling and retaining benefits: for example, families are required to return frequently to food stamp offices to reapply and for verifications. This can cause working parents to miss work, forgo wages, and possibly jeopardize working relations (Greenstein and Guyer 2001). Consequently, as only 40 percent of eligible working poor families receive food stamps and only one-third receive Medicaid (Greenberg and Laracy 2000), the reduction in means-tested programs is one of the reasons that poverty has not declined as fast as welfare caseloads. Moreover, fewer former recipients are working full-time, full-year (Danziger *et al.* forthcoming). Most employed recipients do not receive benefits (vacations, sick leave, health), and many are not covered by the federal Family and Medical Leave Act (Greenberg and Laracy 2000).

8.12. The Decline in the Welfare Rolls

If employment is so uncertain, then what accounts for the dramatic decline in the welfare rolls? Politicians—state as well as national—are, of course, claiming that welfare reform is 'working', despite the fact that rolls were declining significantly before many of the work requirements were enacted (DeParle 1997; Brito 1999; Pear 1996). Most economists argue that the macro economy is responsible for the decline. Yet, they differ as to the relative importance of the economy versus welfare reform. Estimates as to the effect of welfare reforms, as compared to the economy, range from 'trivial' to 30–50 percent (Figlio and Ziliak 1999: 4; Meyer and Rosenbaum 1999; Ellwood 1999; CEA 1999: 5).

A major difficulty in explaining the drop in caseloads involves the previously discussed deficiencies of welfare program evaluations. Another complication arises from the use of discretion in administering these reforms: not only the states but the *individual* offices vary greatly in how they interpret and apply these rules.[13] Then, there has been a significant increase in benefits, such as the Earned Income Tax Credit (EITC) that provides strong incentives to work but is not considered part of 'welfare reform'. Some experts actually consider the EITC to be the single most important influence on the decline in welfare rolls. For instance, in the late 1980s working families were eligible for about $5 billion (1997 dollars) in federal aid; by 1997, the total was above $50 billion. About half of this growth is attributable to the EITC (Meyer and Rosenbaum 1999; Ellwood 1999).

8.13. Sanctions

The welfare reform dramatically expanded the range of circumstances in which a family could have its benefits reduced or canceled. In fact, sanctions—financial penalties for noncompliance with program requirements—and time limits have become central features of most state TANF programs (Pavetti and Bloom 2001). While sanctions have always been a part of welfare policy, the TANF sanctions have much more significance, in part owing to the 'full-family' sanctions whereby a family loses its entire grant. The usual practice in the past was that only the adult violator would lose her grant and the children would keep theirs.[14]

---

[13] This has convinced some economists that they cannot look at data since 1996 (Figlio and Ziliak 1999).

[14] Thirty-five states use full-family sanctions, and 19 states eliminate food stamps for failure to meet work requirements (Haskins and Blank 2001).

Federal law restricts the use of TANF money as a means of assistance for most families no more than 60 months, starting from the date of the state's TANF program. 'Assistance' generally means payments designed to meet a family's ongoing basic needs. States are free to set time limits of less than 60 months, but they may also exempt up to 20 percent of the average monthly state caseload, which is calculated after the families begin reaching the 60-month limit—2001 at the earliest. At the same time, they may also use state maintenance of effort (MOE) funds to assist families beyond the 60-month limit. For the most part, federal law does not specify what categories of families are exempt from the 60-month limit, other than child-only cases that do not include any adult recipient. As with sanctions, there is great variation among the states.[15] Most states have chosen to exempt some families from the work requirements and/or time limits.[16]

8.14. Implementing Sanctions

Implementing sanctions and time limit policies is a complex process. Primarily, states have to decide who should be subject to the work requirements, the sanctions and time limits. At the same time, they must opt how to communicate the policies to the recipients and how to encourage and support compliance with the program requirements. Yet, some offices have difficulty in communicating the most basic information about sanctions and time limits and how they work, especially when these messages are combined with other information regarding benefits, reporting requirements, and so on. Moreover, when families begin to reach the time limits, states are going to have to decide who gets an exemption and who gets terminated. Lastly, state authorities must determine whether and how to support families who are sanctioned.

It is now clear that states make widespread use of sanctions. While the sanctioned families are heterogeneous, the hard-to-employ are over-represented. In Tennessee, 60 percent of the sanctioned families did not have a high school diploma or a GED compared to 40 percent who left welfare for work. In South

---

[15] Twenty-six states have imposed a 60-month time limit. Seventeen have imposed time limits of less than 60 months. Six of these have imposed a lifetime limit of less than 60 months; others have imposed fixed period time limits, for example, a limit of 24 months of benefit receipt in any 60-month period. And eight states have not imposed termination time limits. Six of the eight states have 'reduction' time limits that eliminate benefits for adults but not the children. Two states have no time limits at all (Pavetti and Bloom 2001: 3–5).

[16] Forty-four states exempt adult recipients who are caring for a young child (although these exemptions are typically more narrow than under previous law); thirty-four exempt disabled or incapacitated recipients.

Carolina, 36 percent of high school dropouts were sanctioned as compared to 22 percent of high school graduates. Long-term recipients are over-represented: in South Carolina, 38 percent of long-term recipients as compared to 21 percent of short-term recipients. In addition to childcare and transportation problems, many sanctioned families experienced personal or family challenges at a higher rate than other recipients, such as chemical dependency, physical and mental health problems, and domestic violence (Pavetti and Bloom, 2001).

8.15. Diversion

Diversion seeks to dissuade potentially eligible people from applying for benefits. A widespread practice is to require applicants to conduct job search while the application is pending. Requirements range from 2 to 6 weeks and from 2 to 40 employer contacts before benefits can start. Many states offer a one-time, lump-sum level of cash assistance in exchange for a period of ineligibility for TANF. Twenty states have such cash diversion programs, of which 13 demand 3 months ineligibility. In 15 states, agencies can impose job search requirements before applications will be accepted (Blank and Schmidt 2001). Again, there is considerable caseworker discretion as to who is required, who is excused, what constitutes an excuse, and so on (Diller 2000).

8.16. Do Sanctions Make A Difference?

Sanctions often fall on the weakest recipients in the system.[17] Moreover, even though a great percentage of recipients in fact comply with welfare regulations, many are sanctioned because of bureaucratic errors (Diller 2000). Some states are just beginning to track what happens to these families. Most are coping, but the question is at what level (Fein and Lee Wang 1999). While the evidence is contradictory as to whether sanctions are effective in encouraging compliance, studies have shown that sanctioned leavers are substantially less likely to work than individuals who left welfare for other reasons. Similar findings also apply to the receipt of food stamps (Pavetti and Bloom 2001).

Is this, then, the meaning of the 'new' 'welfare reform'? 'Success' is now defined as not being on welfare which, in turn, is considered the same as working and supporting one's family. Denying aid to the needy is hardly reform.

---

[17] Sanctioned recipients often include women who reported being highly depressed, having been physically abused, or having a child with a serious health problem (Polit, London, and Martinez 2000).

8.17. Positive State Experiments

There are some programs which have been able to improve recipients' overall life quality while decreasing poverty. In contrast to the 'work first' strategy, the most successful programs were those that employed a mixed rather than a single strategy approach. Instead of merely forcing recipients to work, they offered a multitude of opportunities, ranging from childcare to education classes. New Hope, a program administered in Milwaukee, Wisconsin in the 1990s, offered four different program components: an earnings supplement to raise participants' income to the poverty level for their household, affordable health insurance, childcare subsidies, and a full-time job opportunity for those unable to find one. Overall the program was a success: employment and earnings increased not only during the study period but also during the follow-up, and recipients' stress level reduced significantly while their children displayed both greater academic and social achievements (Bos *et al.* 1999). The welfare-to-work program in Portland, Oregon, had similarly promising results: in comparison to 10 other programs, its mixed strategy, which stressed employment-focused activities in addition to offering education and training, yielded the most significant increases in employment and earnings (Freedman *et al.* 2000). Another successful program was the Canadian Self-Sufficiency Project (SSP), which was in operation between 1992 and 1998. The core of the project was to make work pay. Consequently, in order to become eligible for income supplements, recipients were required to leave Income Assistance (Canada's welfare system). Yet, work was voluntary, as SPP's monthly earnings supplement payments were tied to work effort and were paid on top of earnings from employment, for up to three years, as long as individuals worked full-time and remained off Income Assistance. Ultimately, the program not only increased earnings but also employment (Berlin 2000).

8.18. The Future

Predictions as to the longer-term effects of major programs is always uncertain. So much depends on the state of the economy, which now appears to be weakening. In California, by 2002, welfare will be terminated for 575,000 children. If the economy does continue to weaken, and welfare growth resumes, welfare will be terminated for 994,000 children in 2005. There are additional rules that can result in welfare terminations—paternity establishment requirements, additional children born to current welfare recipients. Moreover, children born to unmarried mothers will be denied benefits until the mother turns eighteen. The combined effects of the welfare cut-offs will affect 1,158,000 children.

What will happen to these children? Whether working or not, poverty will increase for this group, and poverty is the single most important predictor of poor outcomes for children. In particular, risks are increased for abuse and neglect, poor health, school failure, teen pregnancy, crime, and delinquency. One of the most serious problems is the potential impact of the cut-offs on the foster care system. So far, there has not been a significant increase in foster care as a result of the welfare reform, as the more stringent cut-offs have not really started (Sengupta 2000). However, in California, if only a fraction of the children subject to the welfare cuts enter the foster care system, the costs will skyrocket.[18] And the consequences for children in foster care are not good. Foster care children have higher rates of both acute and chronic medical and mental health problems, higher rates of growth problems, and three times the national average for asthma.

If the past is any guide, one would not predict dramatic changes in welfare. Throughout history, welfare policy has always been largely symbolic. Myths and stereotypes gain prominence; drastic reforms are enacted; but policy at the field level is usually de-coupled from administration. Under the present reforms, states as well as counties and municipalities have plenty of room to fudge. Welfare rolls have declined significantly, which reduces the number of recipients that states have to place in work programs. In addition, the states can decide what constitutes work or 'best effort', and can excuse up to 20 percent of the caseload. So far the states have met their quotas, but even if they do not, serious federal penalties are not likely. States always excuse their failures and their congressional delegations lobby against federal penalties.

The present situation, however, looks very different from past welfare reforms. Four kinds of changes have been occurring. One is a continuation of the recent past—the gradual erosion of benefits (House Committee on Ways and Means 1998: 402). The second change is the dramatic decline in the case-loads. The third change has been the vast increase in *privatization*. There is money to be made by private companies who take over parts or even all of the public welfare. Thus far, most of the privatization has occurred within specific parts of welfare. Examples are the work programs, day care, child support collections, and Medicare (Handler and Hasenfeld 1997; Hartung and Washburn 1998). Private contractors promise to reduce the rolls.

---

[18] Assuming no change in TANF rolls, if half of the children who lose TANF benefits need foster care, the cost to the state would be $80 million in additional funds per month. If only 10% need foster care, the cost would be $16 million per month. If 5% of these children are older and have to go to group homes, the cost would be $81 million in additional funds per month.

They control the data; besides, states do not have a burning desire to find out, as long as the rolls and the costs go down. Actual developments will become even more difficult to track. Fourth, as a result of the decline in the economy, in many of the states, the surplus welfare money has already been spent, often for other state programs. And all states are hurting financially (De Parle 2001). Congress is scheduled to re-consider TANF by October 1, 2002. In the meantime, the national surplus has disappeared and the TANF reauthorization will have to compete with many other programs that are struggling to survive (Blank 2001).

8.19. What Can Be Done?

There have been some significant developments in the past couple of years. With the declaration of 'victory' in 'ending welfare as we know it', the stereotypical negative media image of the welfare family has been replaced by positive but sobering accounts of the struggles of single working mothers (e.g. see Boo 2001; Frank 2001). At the same time, there has been a significant increase in the support for low-income working families—by 1996, total expenditures approached $50 billion, about half of which was the EITC. At least 10 states have an additional EITC. Another significant change was the extension of Medicaid coverage to all children 18 years of age or younger living in poor families as well as increases in child care subsidies (Ellwood 1999: 189–90).

On the other hand, there appears to be a lack of concern as to how welfare leavers are doing. Approximately half of the leavers are unaccounted for, and most of the leavers who are working are in poverty. Child poverty, while it has declined somewhat, is still very significant. Yet, the debate over welfare reform equates the *absence* of welfare with *self-sufficiency*. We cannot assume that meeting children's needs depends only on whether their mothers make successful transitions from welfare to paid employment. Many ex-welfare recipients are not working; others are working part-time, and job tenure is uncertain. The large increase in funds to help the working poor will not help these poor families. The public discourse needs to be broadened beyond caseloads and maternal employment to address the larger issues of family poverty (Duncan and Chase-Lansdale 2001: 22–3).

Serious proposals to help the poor cost money. But, as stated, there are now budget deficits at both the state and federal level. The prospects for low-wage, low-skilled workers, for welfare leavers, and for those currently still on the welfare rolls are not good. As stated, these groups of workers, even under relatively good conditions, suffer repeated spells of unemployment. But under the present law, the welfare time clock is running out. Today, the image is of the ex-welfare heroine. In tough times, the image is the negative stereotype.

8.20. Recommendations to Make Welfare Reform Really Work

Making Work Pay.   Since the great majority of welfare recipients are presently working, have recently worked, are trying to work, and will eventually leave welfare via work, the most obvious reforms involve improving the low-wage labor market so that more jobs are available, and earnings and benefits are increased. Nationally, this means job creation where unemployment is still high or when unemployment begins to rise and jobs become less available, continuing to support the EITC, modest raises in the minimum wage, and providing health and child care benefits.

There are also other ways to help the working poor. These options include the reduction of payroll taxes and refundable child tax credits. At the same time, it is crucial to reduce transportation and housing costs. Perverse incentives on the working poor such as the marginal tax rates on federal and state taxes and Medicaid and EITC have to be reduced (*The Economist* 2000: 29).[19] As discussed, the Unemployment Insurance system has to be reformed to take account of the changes in the labor market. This would include re-calibrating the base period and a re-definition of the 'involuntary' quit requirement to take account of family responsibilities and childcare and transportation needs.

The time limits clock should stop for working recipients. Policies that combine disregard of time limits and earnings send a mixed message: time limits encourage recipients to leave the rolls and bank their lifetime-limited number of months; incentives encourage them to stay on the rolls and combine welfare and work. Implementing the two policies virtually guarantees that a substantial number of people will unwittingly exhaust their months of welfare eligibility. At the same time, incentives should be kept separate from the welfare system by amending TANF so that states have greater flexibility in administering time limits.

8.21. Food Stamps and Medicaid

The food stamp program needs to overhaul its outdated quality control system to eliminate disincentives for states. Moreover, food stamp programs need simplification to make access easier (Greenstein and Guyer 2001).

---

[19] For a discussion of the high marginal tax rates on low-income households, see Shaviro (1999).

Federal changes have recently granted states options and established proce-dures to make food stamps more accessible to working families. For example, states can now fix benefits for working families for 6 months at a time unless the family's income climbs over the eligibility limit. But more needs to be done (*ibid.*).

Similar issues concern Medicaid. Children of leavers continue to be elig-ible, but enrollments have declined. Mothers may be unaware that eligibility continues for up to a year after leaving welfare. There is some evidence that state Medicaid programs have responded to this issue, and enrollments have gone up in many states (Haskins and Blank 2001). Changes are needed to make it easier for these families to apply for and maintain benefits. Medicaid has to extend coverage to more low-income parents and to reduce the wide-spread disparities across states. Families should not be made worse off by los-ing health insurance and food stamps when they leave welfare for work. Neither should they have to return to welfare to obtain such assistance. The federal government should consider greater financial incentives to extend eligibility to more low-income working families and added flexibility to simplify enrollment procedures. There should be a family-based coverage initiative that draws on lessons from SCHIP and other child health outreach campaigns. Moreover, Temporary Medical Assistance (TMA) needs improve-ments, as only a small minority of families working their way off of welfare receive TMA even though they qualify (Greenstein and Guyer 2001).

8.22. Immigrants

As noted, post-enactment immigrants are generally ineligible for Medicaid and SCHIP for the first five years in this country. Thus, legal immigrants with a substantial need for preventive or remedial health care, including pregnant women, and children are not covered. If states wish to extend coverage, they must do so at 100 percent cost. Individuals who entered the country legally and otherwise meet eligibility criteria should have health insurance, espe-cially children, pregnant women, working parents, and those who have become disabled after coming to the US (Greenstein and Guyer 2001).

8.23. Child Support

Under current law, states may retain child support payments while the mother is on welfare. In addition, once the mother leaves welfare, half of the overdue payments are retained by the states. The federal government should provide incentives to the states so that more money can go to mothers who leave welfare (Haskins and Blank 2001). To prevent the accrual of unreasonable and unjust arrearages, states should be required to establish child support obligations which are not disproportionate to the father's ability to pay. Disincentives to marry and co-habit should be reduced both for child support and TANF. Irwin Garfinkel has proposed that Congress should create a publicly financed minimum child support benefit that is conditioned on the mother being legally entitled to receive child support. This will increase incentives to establishing paternity and securing a child support award (Garfinkel 2001).

8.24. The More Difficult Cases

Many welfare recipients have multiple barriers to employment. Some of these families need sustained and expensive assistance. Some are probably unlikely to ever become fully self-sufficient. Others may be able to do part-time, low-wage work. The 20 percent exemption should be changed to give the states more options in providing help for the disadvantaged families (Haskins and Blank 2001). There should be a division of responsibility between the two programs: TANF as a time-limited program for those who are reasonably expected to work, and SSI as a non-time-limited program for those who cannot reasonably be expected to work (Karoly, Klerman, and Rogowski 2001).

There is a need to provide work experience for the hard-to-employ (Haskins and Blank 2001). After-school and community programs should be available for older children. Fathers should be encouraged to become more involved with their children (Duncan and Chase-Lansdale 2001). Education and training must be provided and participation in these programs should count as fulfilling work requirements.[20]

The more successful welfare-to-work programs are those that combine strategies—the 'mixed strategy programs' which have a flexible, balanced approach that offers a mix of job search, education, job training, and work activities. They have more individualized services, a central focus on employment, ties to local employers, and high expectations for participants. Some of these mixed strategies have not only increased employment but also succeeded in helping welfare recipients find better jobs (Stawn, Greenberg, and Savner 2001).

---

[20] Haskins and Blank (2001) (this is Blank's proposal, not Haskins').

To respond to these needs, the government must create employment-related organizations that make available information, post-employment support, monitoring, and advocacy services for the working poor. This is especially true since most employment is obtained through informal networks, and many welfare recipients lack these connections. In addition, poor single mothers often require post-employment support when there are breakdowns in childcare or transportation or when their children are sick. There is also a great need for information concerning the EITC, health benefits, the availability and quality of day care, and related programs, such as disability and unemployment insurance.

Community-based agencies could provide this information, monitor health and child care services, and provide counseling and advocacy services for low-income working mothers (Handler and Hasenfeld 1999). It will be necessary to keep monitoring the changes in the welfare programs. Many decisions are of low-visibility. Organizations serving the poor should engage in systematic data gathering—tracking families who leave welfare, monitoring families needing shelter, food, and so on—and publicize the impact of the welfare changes.

There should be an expanded and more focused role for philanthropy. Philanthropy can continue and expand its efforts to disseminate findings of evaluation and assessments, organize grassroots, create public will, search for new ways to assist the 'hard-to-serve', support living wage campaigns and other strategies to help the working poor, forging coalitions, and so forth (Greenberg and Laracy 2002).

These are some of the things that can be done for most of the welfare recipients. They are universal programs that will, at the same time, help the working poor. In addition, they will help the men who have to be brought back into the discussion if progress is to be made with families. But then, there will be those who need more help. This population is varied. Some recipients will need relatively small amounts of training, help in networking, building self-esteem, and so forth. Others will need moderate amounts, and some will need considerable support. The success of service programs varies, of course, with the relative difficulty of their cases—the more ambitious the program, the more problematic the results.

Despite the success of some programs, we still know very little about what 'works' and even less about how to replicate good programs. People with serious problems need patience, understanding, and resources. Above all, sanctions must be avoided. They rarely change behavior; they produce considerable harm; and they largely serve the function of making the rest of the society feel superior and in control.

References

BAVIER, R. (2000). 'A Look at Welfare Reform in the Survey of Income and Program Participation'. Unpublished paper, May.

BERLIN, G. L. (2000). 'Encouraging Work, Reducing Poverty: The Impact of Work Incentive Programs'. *MDRC*, March.

BESHAROV, D. (2001). 'Child Care After Welfare Reform'. In R. M. Blank and R. Haskins (eds), *The New World of Welfare*. Washington, D.C.: Brookings Institution Press.

BLANK, R. (2001). 'Welfare. and the Economy'. *Brookings Institution Policy Brief* No. 7, September.

—— and SCHMIDT, L. (2001). 'Work, Wages, and Welfare'. In R. M. Blank and R. Haskins (eds), *The New World of Welfare*. Washington, D.C.: Brookings Institution Press.

BOO, K. (2001). 'After Welfare: Working Two Jobs, Elizabeth Jones Does Her Best for Her Family. But Is It Enough?' *The New Yorker*, April 9, 93–107.

BORJAS, G. (2001). 'Welfare Reform and Immigration'. In R. M. Blank and R. Haskins (eds), *The New World of Welfare*. Washington, D.C.: Brookings Institution Press.

BOS, H., HUSTON, A., GRANGER, R., DUNCAN, G., BROCK, T., and McLOYD, V. (1999). 'New Hope for People with Low Incomes: Two-Year Results of a Program to Reduce Poverty and Reform Welfare'. *MDRC*, April.

BRITO, T. (1999). *The Welfarization of Family Law*. Unpublished paper.

BURTLESS, G. (1999). 'Growing American Inequality: Sources and Remedies'. *Brookings Review*, Winter, 17/1: 31–5.

CANCIAN, M., HAVEMAN, R., MEYER, D., and WOLFE, B. (2000). 'Before and After TANF: The Economic Well-Being of Women Leaving Welfare'. Special Report No. 77, May. Madison, WI: Institute for Research on Poverty. Available at http://www.ssc.wisc.edu/irp/sr/srlist.htm

CORBETT, T. (2001). 'Evaluating Welfare Reform in an Era of Transition: Are We Looking in the Wrong Direction?' *Focus*, Spring, 21/3. Madison WI: University of Wisconsin, Madison.

CORCORAN, M., DANZIGER, S. K., KALIL, A., and SEEFELDT, K. S. (2000). 'How Welfare Is Affecting Women's Work'. *Annual Review of Sociology* 26: 241–69.

Council of Economic Advisors (1999). 'The Effects of Welfare Policy and the Economic Expansion on Welfare Caseloads: An Update'. Technical Report. August 3: 5.

DANZIGER, S., CORCORAN, M., DANZIGER, SH., HEFLIN, C., KALIL, A., LEVINE, J., ROSEN, D., SEEFELDT, K., SIEFERT, K., and TOLMAN, R. 'Barriers to the Employment of Welfare Recipients'. Forthcoming in R. Cherry and W. M. Rodgers (eds), *Prosperity for All? The Economic Boom and African Americans*. New York: Russell Sage Foundation, forthcoming.

DEPARLE, J. (1997). 'Lessons Learned: Welfare Reform's First Months—A Special Report: Success, Frustration, as Welfare Rules Change'. *The New York Times*, Dec. 30, A1.

—— (2001). 'A Mass of Newly Laid-Off Workers Will Put Social Safety Net to the Test'. *The New York Times*, Oct. 8, A12.

DILLER, M. (2000). 'The Revolution in Welfare Administration: Rules, Discretion, and Entrepreneurial Government', *N.Y.U. Law Review*, 75: 1121–1220.

DUNCAN, G. and CHASE-LANSDALE, P. L. (2001). 'Welfare Reform and Child Well-Being'. In R. M. Blank and R. Haskins (eds), *The New World of Welfare*. Washington, D.C.: Brookings Institution Press.

The Economist. September 30, 2000, p. 29.

ELLWOOD, D. (1999). 'The Impact of the Earned Income Tax Credit and Social Policy Reforms on Work, Marriage, and Living Arrangements'. Unpublished paper. Cambridge MA: Harvard University, Kennedy School of Government.

—— (2000). 'Anti-Poverty Policy for Families in the Next Century: From Welfare to Work—and Worries'. *Journal of Economic Perspectives*, 14/1: 187–99.

FEIN, J. and LEE WANG, S. (1999). 'Carrying and Using the Stick: Financial Sanctions in Delaware's A Better Chance Program'. Abt Associates, Inc., January 1999. 301-913-0500.

FIGLIO, D. and ZILIAK, J. (1999). 'Welfare Reform, the Business Cycle, and the Decline in AFDC Caseloads'. Unpublished paper.

FRANK, E. (2001). 'The End of Welfare As We Know It: Media Depictions of Welfare in an Era of Reform, 1997–2001'. Unpublished Masters Thesis, UCLA, Afro-American Studies.

FREEDMAN, S., FRIEDLANDER, D., HAMILTON, G., ROCK, J.-A., MITSCHELL, M., NUDELMAN, J., SCHWEDER, A., and STORTO, L. (2000). 'National Evaluation of Welfare-to-Work Strategies: Evaluating Alternative Welfare-to-Work Approaches: Two-Year Impacts for Eleven Programs'. *MDRC*, June.

FREEMAN, R. (2000). 'The Rising Tide Lifts...?' *Focus*, 21/2: 27–37.

GAID, T., NATHAN, R., LURIE, I., and KAPLAN, T. (2001). 'Implementation of the Personal Responsibility Act of 1996'. In R. M. Blank and R. Haskins (eds), *The New World of Welfare*. Washington, D.C.: Brookings Institution Press.

GARFINKEL, I. (2001). 'Child Support in the New World of Welfare'. In R.M. Blank and R. Haskins (eds), *The New World of Welfare*. Washington, D.C.: Brookings Institution Press.

GILENS, M. (1999). *Why Americans Hate Welfare: Race, Media, and the Politics of Antipoverty Policy*. Chicago: University of Chicago Press.

GREENBERG, M. and LARACY, M. C. (2000). 'Welfare Reform: Next Steps Offer New Opportunities'. June. Washington, DC: Neighborhood Funders Group.

—— —— (2002). 'Welfare Reform: Next Steps Offer New Opportunities: A Role for Philanthropy in Preparing for the Reauthorization of TANF in 2002'. Neighborhood Funders Group, http//:www.nfg.org/publications/welfare.htm

GREENSTEIN, R. and GUYER, J. (2001). 'Supporting Work Through Medicaid and Food Stamps'. In R. M. Blank and R. Haskins (eds), *The New World of Welfare*. Washington, D.C.: Brookings Institution Press.

GUSTAFSON, C. and LEVINE, P. (1998). 'Less-Skilled Workers, Welfare Reform, and the Unemployment Insurance System'. Working paper 6489. Washington DC: National Bureau of Economic Research.

HANDLER, J. (1995). *The Poverty of Welfare Reform*. New Haven: Yale University Press.

—— and HASENFELD, Y. (1991). *The Moral Construction of Poverty: Welfare Reform in America*. London: Sage.

—— (1997). *We the Poor People: Work, Poverty, and Welfare*. New Haven: Yale University Press.

—— (1999). 'Community-Based, Employment-Related Services for Low-Wage Workers', in J. Handler and L. White (eds), *Hard Labor: Women and Work in the Post-Welfare Era*. Armonk, NY: M. E. Sharpe.

—— and WHITE, L. (eds) (1999). *Hard Labor: Women and Work in the Post-Welfare Era*. Armonk, NY: M. E. Sharpe.

HARTUNG, W. and WASHBURN, J. (1998). 'Lockheed Martin: From Warfare to Welfare'. *The Nation*, 2 March.

Haskins, R. (2001). 'Effects of Welfare Reform on Family Income and Poverty'. In R. M. Blank and R. Haskins (eds), *The New World of Welfare*. Washington, D.C.: Brookings Institution Press.

—— and Blank, R. (2001). 'Welfare Reform: An Agenda for Reauthorization', in R. M. Blank and R. Haskins (eds), *The New World of Welfare*. Washington, D.C.: Brookings Institution Press.

Heclo, H. (1994). 'Poverty Politics' in S. Danziger, G. Sandefur, and D. Weinberg (eds), *Confronting Poverty: Prescriptions for Change*, Cambridge MA: Harvard University Press.

Holzer, H. (1996). *What Employers Want: Job Prospects for Less Educated Workers*. New York: Russell Sage Foundation.

House Committee on Ways and Means, 103rd Cong. (1998). 'Green Book: Background Material and Data on Programs Within the Jurisdiction of the Committee on Ways and Means'. Washington, DC.: US Government Printing Office.

Johnston, D. (1999). 'Gap Between Rich and Poor Found Substantially Wider'. *The New York Times*, September 5, 14.

Karoly, L., Klerman, J., and Rogowski, J. (2001). 'Effects of the 1996 Welfare Reform on the SSI Program'. In R. M. Blank and R. Haskins (eds), *The New World of Welfare*. Washington, D.C.: Brookings Institution Press.

Katz, B. and Allen, K. (1999). 'Help Wanted: Connecting Inner-City Job Seekers with Suburban Jobs'. *Brookings Review*, Fall, 31–3.

Lee, D. (1999). 'Nature of Work Has Changed'. *The Los Angeles Times*, September 6.

Lerman, R., Loprest, P., and Ratcliffe, C. (1999). 'How Well Can Urban Labor Markets Absorb Welfare Recipients?' Washington, DC: Urban Institute.

Mead, L. (1986). *Beyond Entitlement: The Social Obligations of Citizenship*. New York: Free Press.

Meyer, B. and Rosenbaum, D. (1999). 'Welfare, the Earned Income Tax Credit, and the Labor Supply of Single Mothers'. Working Paper Series, W7363. Washington DC: National Bureau of Economic Research.

Mishel, L., Bernstein, J., and Schmitt, J. (2000). *The State of Working America*. Ithaca, NY: Cornell University Press.

Morris, P., Huston, A., and Duncan, G. J. (2001). 'How Welfare and Work Policies Affect Children: A Synthesis of Σ Research'. *MDRC*, January.

Pavetti, L. (2000). 'Welfare Policy in Transition: Redefining the Social Contract for Poor Citizen Families with Children'. *Focus*, 21/2, Fall, 44–50.

—— and Bloom, D. (2001). 'State Sanctions and Time Limits'. In R. M. Blank and R. Haskins (eds), *The New World of Welfare*. Washington, D.C.: Brookings Institution Press.

Pear, R. (1996). 'Most States Find Goals on Welfare Within Easy Reach'. *The New York Times*, September 23, A1.

Polit, D., London, A., and Martinez, J. (2000). 'The Health of Poor Urban Women: Findings from the Urban Change Project'. *MDRC*, December.

Primus, W. (2001). 'Comments on R. Haskins,' Effects of Welfare Reform on Family Income and Poverty. In R. M. Blank and R. Haskins (eds), *The New World of Welfare*. Washington, D.C.: Brookings Institution Press.

Seiden, D. M. and Prehoda, S. (2001). 'The Influence of Welfare Reform Policies on Caseloads, Food Stamp Participation, Employment Earnings, and Income. Applied Policy Project', Los Angeles: UCLA School of Public Policy and Social Research. Unpublished paper.

Sengupta, S. (2000). 'No Rise in Child Abuse Seen in Welfare Shift' *New York Times*, August 2000, A1.

Shaviro, D. (1999). 'Effective Marginal Tax Rates on Low-Income Households'. New York: NYU School of Law, Employment Policies Institute.

Stawn, J., Greenberg, M., and Savner, S. (2001). 'Improving Employment Outcomes Under TANF'. In R. M. Blank and R. Haskins (eds), *The New World of Welfare*. Washington, D.C.: Brookings Institution Press.

The Children's Defense Fund (1996). *Summary of Legislation Affecting Children in 1996.* Washington, DC: The Children's Defense Fund.

US Census Bureau (1999). *Poverty in the United States*, 1998. Washington, DC: US Census Bureau.

Wenger, J. (2001). 'The Continuing Problems with Part-Time Jobs'. *Economic Policy Institute Issue Brief*, # 155, April 24. Washington, DC: EPI.

White, L. (1999). 'Quality Child Care for Low-Income Families: Despair, Impasse, Improvisation', in F. Handler and L. White (eds), *Hard Labor: Women and Work in the Post-Welfare Era*. Armonk, NY: M. E. Sharpe, 116–42.

Williams, L. (1999). 'Unemployment Insurance and Low-Wage Work', in F. Handler and L. White (eds), *Hard Labor: Women and Work in the Post-Welfare Era*. Armonk, NY: M. E. Sharpe, 158–74.

Wright, E. O. and Dwyer, R. (2000/2001). 'The American Jobs Machine: Is The New Economy Creating Good Jobs?' *The Boston Review*, 25/6: 21–6.

Zedlewski, S. and Loprest, P. (2001). 'Will TANF Work for the Most Disadvantaged Families'. In R. M. Blank and R. Haskins (eds), *The New World of Welfare*. Washington, D.C.: Brookings.

9

Organizing the US Labor Market: National Problems, Community Strategies

PAUL OSTERMAN

The American welfare state which emerged out of the New Deal and the Second World War is notable for its many weaknesses: incomplete coverage and stringent means testing come immediately to mind. However, in the realm of labor market policy there was a logic to the American system. The policies which were put into place were based upon a common understanding of how the American labor market itself was structured. There was at least a rough match between policy and reality. However, in the last two decades as the American labor market has radically changed, public policy has been very slow to catch up. Overcoming this mismatch between American labor market policy and the new labor market realities is one of the central challenges we face.

I will begin this chapter by describing how the American labor market has changed. I will then briefly lay out how these changes create problems for labor market policy as currently structured. I will then describe in more detail important local responses to these challenges and I will emphasize the activities of the Industrial Areas Foundation, a network of community organizations which have developed innovative responses to changes in the labor market.

9.1. How the American Labor Market Has Changed

When commentators think about what is new in the American labor market they tend to emphasize the remarkably long run of low unemployment experienced in the 1990s. However, this cyclical pattern is not my focus. Instead I want to emphasize the changing long run structure of the job market. To do this I will first describe what I see as the central characteristics of the labor market before the transformation. The postwar, or New Deal, system had several distinctive characteristics.

9.1.1. *The Firm as Family*

One way of thinking about the evolution of employment relations during most of the postwar period is to conceive of two competing models. One of these, the industrial union model, was best typified by the employment practices which emerged in the automobile industry, an employment system which was strongly shaped by bargains between the United Automobile Workers and the Big Three auto firms. This was a system in which seniority, not individual merit, played a key role in wages, in which job duties were tightly specified by contract, and in which the firm was free to adjust employment levels by layoffs although most layoffs were followed by recall.[1] These patterns were extended not only throughout the union sector but were also widely imitated by many large non-union employers.

The competing employment model was the aggressively non-union approach perhaps best typified by IBM. Under this system the firm sought to establish direct relations with employees via numerous communications programs and employee surveys. Wages had a larger individual component and job descriptions were flexible. At IBM there was a strong implicit job security commitment. IBM was one of the most powerful and most successful firms in the nation and not many firms could imitate it in all respects. However, IBM was consistently cited as among the most admired employers in the country, and among those firms which sought to avoid unions or union-like employment systems the IBM model was the target to be chased.

While it is true that at some level these were two competing systems my point is quite different. In a deep sense the IBM and the Big Auto systems shared a great deal in common. They were both premised on the assumption that the firm and the employee had long-term attachments to each other and that a web of mutual obligations existed between the two parties. Both models accepted the idea of a firm as a coherent organizational form with relatively fixed boundaries and relationships. They were not the same kind of family in all the details, just as real families may differ in how the members get along, but they shared a deep underlying assumption about stable relationships and long-term attachments. Since these were the two dominant employment models in the postwar period it seems fair to say that their commonalties fundamentally define what was the core of the postwar employment model.

---

[1] For an excellent description of the evolution of this employment system see Katz (1985).

In important measure what IBM and the union model shared in common was grounded in the academic literature termed the Human Relations School (Bendix 1956; Barley and Kunda 1992; Guillen 1994). This line of thought, which began with Elton Mayo and was elaborated by numerous management theorists, reached the peak of its influence in the postwar period. The central idea, as Mauro Guillen points out, was that 'neglecting the morale, sentiments, and emotions of both the worker and manager would set limits to the firm's productivity and profitability' (Guillen 1994: 58). This perspective, very different in spirit than the engineering-oriented scientific management approach to boosting performance, led to the diffusion of human resource practices such as morale surveys, suggestion systems, and various communication techniques. More to the point, Human Relations reinforced the view that ideally the firm should make a long-term commitment to its labor force.

9.1.2. *Internalized Careers*

A corollary of the foregoing argument is that the postwar period was characterized by a particular system for shaping careers. For most people, the typical career pattern was to enter a firm at the bottom of a job ladder and to move up that ladder over time. This system implied a fairly high degree of job security because both individuals and firms made mutual investments in each other (particularly in training) and were loath to lose those investments. Indeed, early in the 1980s researchers comparing American and Japanese workers were surprised to discover that the Americans seemed to enjoy nearly as much job stability as the Japanese despite the much ballyhooed Japanese system of lifetime employment (Hall 1982).

It was never the case that this relatively secure closed system was universal. Some people held good jobs but under different arrangements. An example is craft workers who moved from employer to employer, or work site to work site, but who were protected by their high level of skills. Other people were trapped in a low-wage casual segment of the labor market, unable to break into the security of the more protected sector. However, despite these exceptions the dominant image and paradigm of postwar employment was very much the 'organization man' who lived his (and sometimes her) life within one organization.

Even during the golden years of American economic dominance the economy ebbed and flowed and firms needed to adjust their labor force. How they did so, however, was played out in the context of the internal career structure outlined above. Managers and other senior white-collar employees faced very little employment risk. They were treated as a fixed factor of production and their layoff rates were very low. Blue-collar workers were laid-off but most typically these were temporary layoffs which were followed by recall.

9.1.3. *Wage Setting*

Nothing is more central to our understanding of how the labor market works than wage determination. How wages are set is one of the key elements of any theoretical picture of labor markets and to show that there was indeed an identifiable postwar institutional structure it is important to be able to convincingly characterize the process of wage determination.

One element of the old system was high valuation of internal equity in the firm's wage structure. Sociologists studying the shop floor discovered that employees, particularly those in stable work groups, developed norms about the relative wage structure (Roy 1952; Ross 1948). These norms, which were couched in the language of fairness, dealt with the relative pay of different jobs as well as the weight which should be given in wage setting to personal characteristics such as skill and seniority. Even in the absence of collective bargaining these norms could be enforced by collective withholding of effort by employees. Firms in turn recognized the importance of these norms in their own approach to pay administration. A great deal of care was devoted to developing job evaluation procedures (typically the awarding of points to jobs based upon their skill, responsibility, and so on) which were used to rationalize and stabilize the internal pay structure. Merit pay, which on its face appears to emphasize individual differences, was typically administered in a way which led to everyone receiving relatively equal raises.

A second characteristic of the old system was a stable set of pay relationships among firms and industries. This was captured in phrases such as 'pattern bargaining' and 'wage contours' used by scholars to describe the phenomena. In pattern bargaining the wages of workers in one industry, for example agricultural implements, were tightly connected to those in another industry, for example automobiles. Although the word 'bargaining' strongly points to the role of unions it was also accepted that via spillovers and imitation the patterns were often extended into the non-union sector. Researchers set about showing that the dollar value of wage agreements in one industry were imitated (plus or minus a stable mark up or mark down) elsewhere even though 'objective' economic conditions such as unemployment or product market developments might have implied a different outcome.[2] In a similar spirit, wage contours or orbits or coercive comparison referred to the interrelationship

---

[2] The most influential early formulations of these ideas are found in the chapters by Dunlop and Ross in Taylor and Peirson (eds) (1957). Typical early empirical work is Maher (1961) and Eckstein and Wilson (1962).

of wages within a community and the linkage between the wages in one job and another.

An additional element in pay-setting in the old regime was the important role played by the firm's financial capacity. Virtually all observers noted that a key consideration in pay-setting was the company's balance sheet: when times were good employers shared the profits with their employees.[3] There was an asymmetry to the system given that in bad times wages may have been held down but they did not fall in nominal terms. Nonetheless, whatever the level of conflicts which might emerge in the workplace, the role of 'ability to pay' created some degree of shared community interest.

Taken as a whole what did this picture of wage setting add up to? To begin, these considerations did not necessarily suggest a coherent theoretical structure and in particular 'ability to pay' poses problems. The pattern bargaining and wage contours of institutional theory have difficulty accommodating 'ability to pay' since different firms within the pattern or contour may be at different points in their profit cycle. The thrust of patterns and contours is to push for uniformity while 'ability to pay' can create centrifugal forces in the wage structure.

What this account of wage setting does clearly suggest is that the wage structure of the economy was very sticky, that is, slow to adjust to conventional economic forces. The source of this stickiness was a set of considerations—particularly the role of equity, custom, and comparisons—which have no place in simple market-oriented models nor in their more sophisticated extensions. These factors meshed very well with the broader picture of stable employment relationships described earlier and created an overall system for wages and careers which placed a heavy emphasis on continuity and fairness.

9.1.4. *The Broader Context*

This postwar system of careers and wages did not emerge in isolation nor was it sustainable without a broader set of supports which were consistent with it. One of these elements was a secure and influential industrial relations system. Unions, while never representing a majority of the labor force, played an important role in structuring the labor market. Many of the practices and norms regarding how employers behaved and what employees could expect were derived from union–management agreements.

At their high-water mark unions represented 35.5 percent of the private sector labor force (in 1945). The influence of unions, however, extended

---

[3] The role of 'ability to pay' is discussed in Reynolds, Ross, Dunlop, Lester (Taylor and Peirson (eds) (1957)), and numerous other expositions of postwar wage setting.

beyond the firms and industries in which they were strong. Unions played a central role in structuring the postwar labor market. They did so in several ways. Non-union firms typically organized work and paid wages in line with the union standards and they did so for two reasons. The first was fear: due to what industrial relations scholars termed the union 'threat effect' the non-union sector sought to match union patterns in order to avoid being organized. In an important sense the unions established a 'minimum wage' for significant regions of the labor market.

Perhaps as significant was the impact union models had upon other firms' images of what was the 'right' or 'accepted' way of structuring themselves. The unionized system of seniority, job classifications, and temporary layoffs followed by recall was widely influential even in the non-union manufacturing sector. A good example of this is my experience in Digital Equipment Corporation (DEC), a militantly anti-union company. When DEC began its first round of layoffs in the 1980s I happened to be conducting interviews in the firm and it turned out, much to my surprise, that the basis for the blue-collar layoffs was employment date, that is, seniority.

If the industrial relations system helped support the postwar system from perspective of the shop floor and office another important contextual feature was the nature of corporate governance. American corporate law gives the owner of stock primacy in the governance of the firm and the maximizing welfare of the stockholder is supposed to be the guiding objective of managers. However, as Berle and Means (1968) observed as far back as 1933, the reality was that executives enjoyed a great deal of autonomy. The ownership of stock was widely dispersed and boards of directors provided very little effective oversight.

The important question, therefore, is what were managers trying to achieve. There is a great deal of evidence that they placed substantial value on maintaining, indeed growing, employment and on sharing profits not only with stockholders but with the broad employee base. This was not necessarily because managers had humanitarian values. The strongest correlate of executive pay during this period was the size of the firm and hence there was a clear incentive to grow. Furthermore, it is simply more pleasant to manage in a situation in which people are treated well and conflict is low than in other circumstances. Managers also enjoyed being considered good corporate and community citizens and were willing to expend stockholder resources in order to achieve this. It was also true, as noted earlier, that managers had been schooled in the human relations perspective and their relative freedom from oversight gave them the slack necessary to implement these policies even when the immediate payback was hard to demonstrate.

9.2. The Collapse of the Postwar Structure

The institutional structure which shaped the postwar labor market is disappearing. Each of the symptoms of labor market distress—stagnating earnings, heightened insecurity, uncertainty about what it means to hold a job—reflect this collapse. For the purposes of this paper the most important change has been the erosion of long-term careers but it is worth noting in passing the other major developments.

With respect to wages, the central fact in the new era is their rapid dispersion, that is, the sharp growth in wage inequality as well as the sluggish growth of real wages for most people. These developments have been widely noted and generated a burgeoning literature. However, relatively little attention has been paid to the implications for our understanding of wage setting. Recall that at the heart of the postwar model was a wage system which placed very heavy emphasis on stability and equity. Implicit in the growth of inequality is that these considerations have lost force and that when employers set wages other concerns are now paramount. The postwar wage system was also characterized by de facto profit sharing yet in recent years the average level of wages has stagnated even in the face of rising profits. Clearly, then, our previous understanding of how wages are set is obsolete and this signals a radical shift from the old system.

Internal equity considerations play much less of a role in wage setting than in the past. The evidence for this lies in the explosive spread of new systems of pay centered around identifying and rewarding individual performance. These innovations have two main effects. The first is to put employees more at risk by tying their pay to firm performance. Various forms of profit sharing and bonuses are part of this. In many cases these innovations were tied to concession bargaining in the unionized sector (Mitchell 1985) but they had a broader reach. The second set of innovations move employers away from standard across-the-board increases and instead make pay increasingly dependent upon the performance and characteristics of individuals. The most dramatic of these are so called 'forced distributions' which are the real world equivalent of grading on a curve. Taken together these innovations naturally lead to the erosion of stable wage differentials, in part because of the variation across firms in how they perform and in part due to variation across individuals which are no longer dampened by attention to equity. As these new compensation systems spread the old wage structure was undermined and inequality surged.

Another significant development has been the erosion of union power. It would be a mistake to equate the collapse of the postwar institutional structure with the decline of union power. Even at the height of their power American unions only organized 35 percent of the private sector labor force and the norms, ideology, and behaviors which characterized the postwar system extended deeply into the non-union sector. Indeed, in some respects—for example commitments to employment security—the non-union sector represented by firms such as IBM, DEC, and Proctor and Gamble, was more advanced than unionized employers. Nonetheless, the erosion of union power is an important element in the destruction of the postwar regime.

As the perimeter of union power has shrunk the ability of unions to shape employer behavior in both union and non-union settings has diminished. The weakened capacity of unions to influence the behavior of unionized employers, who are now able to be more aggressive in setting wages and working conditions, is obvious. More important, perhaps, is the impact of debilitated unions upon the much larger non-union sector. The earlier generation of institutional economists recognized this broader effect of union power and coined terms such as the 'threat effect' or 'spillovers' to capture the idea that non-union employers modified their actions either to avoid unionization or simply out of imitation. Using data drawn largely from the 1970s, Freeman and Medoff (1984) estimated that the wages of employees in large non-union firms were raised by between 10 and 20 percent as a consequence of these spillovers. Today most employers are free to determine their employment conditions without fear of being organized.

The decline of unions is due to the convergence of many factors, ranging from fierce employer resistance to the failure of many unions to adapt their appeal to an increasingly well educated white and pink collar labor force. The weakened power of unions then becomes part of the explanation for the broader collapse in the postwar labor market structure. However, it is important to recognize that the decline of unions is also a symptom of this shift, not the cause. An important component in the decline of unions is the same transformation in attitudes and norms which underlies some of the other changes I have described. This is illustrated by the substantial increase in unfair labor practice filings coming out of efforts to organize new local unions. An index of unfair labor practices per union member jumped from 95.5 between 1960 and 1968 to 162.9 in 1969–77 to 285.2 between 1983 and 1988. A similar index of employer-sponsored union decertification petitions grew from 158.2 in 1969–77 to 358.0 in 1983–88 (Mitchell 1989). More generally, firms are simply more willing to oppose unions. As Kochan, Katz, and McKersie (1986) have shown, a cottage industry of consultants has emerged whose expertise lies in teaching employers how to resist unions.

9.2.1. *The Erosion of Internalized Careers*

The development with the most significant implications for labor market policy has been the loss of stable secure careers. One way to see what has happened

Table 9.1.   Median years of job tenure

Age	Men		Women	
	1983	1998	1983	1998
35–44	7.3	5.5	4.1	4.5
45–54	12.8	9.4	6.3	7.2
55–64	15.3	11.2	9.8	9.6

Source: Bureau of Labor Statistics.

is to examine data on job tenure. Job tenure represents the number of years an employee has been with his or her current employer and as such is an important clue about what is happening to careers. Table 9.1 shows the distribution of tenure for men and women in three age groups (Osterman 1999: 41–3). These data show a sharp drop in tenure for men and a mild gain in tenure for women which is most likely linked to the growing commitment of women to the labor market. Overall in the workforce tenure has fallen.

Perhaps an even more fundamental shift is that in the past several decades a rapidly growing fraction of the workforce find themselves working in what has come to be termed 'contingent employment'. In the past temporary work arose either because of seasonality (consider, for example, Christmas hiring of store clerks) or to fill in for absent employees on a short-term basis. Today the use of contingent workers has become a much more central and intrinsic part of a firm's operations. Indeed, in 1996 office and clerical jobs accounted for only 30 percent of the revenue of the staffing industry (which is the industry's term for contingent work) (Staffing Industry Analysts). In some instances companies use employees of temporary help firms to permanently staff significant portions of their operations. A very common example is call center, or customer service, operations (Batt 1995). In other instances firms replace the traditional probationary period, in which the new workers were on their payroll, by contracting for temporary workers and then selecting some of these as permanent hires. In these cases temporary help agencies perform a labor market recruitment and intermediary function. In yet other instances temporary workers and permanent employees work side by side with the employer retaining the flexibility to easily reduce staffing by cutting back on the temporary portion. In this case, of course, there is also the possibility of gradually shifting a larger fraction of the work to the contingent group.

The broader significance of this shift in nature of temporary work is threefold. First, it represents a re-thinking on the part of firms of their relationship and obligations to their workforce. Second, the employees who find themselves in these jobs are almost certain to be more mobile than 'standard'

Table 9.2. Fraction of the labor force accounted for by different types of contingent workers (in %)

	1995	1997	1999
Independent Contractor/Freelance	6.7	6.7	7.1
On-call	1.6	1.6	2.1
Agency temporaries	1.0	0.9	0.8
Contract workers	0.6	0.5	0.6

Source: CPS, 1995, 1997, 1999; http://stats.bls.gov/news.release/conemp.toc.htm

employees and hence will face the challenges described earlier of a more unattached and insecure labor force. Third, although a considerable fraction of contingent workers are content with their circumstances, for many others these jobs provide less pay and fewer benefits than received by employees with comparable human capital in more regular positions.

The general impression of contingent work is that it has grown substantially (e.g. between 1991 and 1996 the fastest growing industry was Personnel Supply Services) however it is important to move beyond impressions and examine broadly representative national data. One such source is the Current Population Survey (CPS) which in 1995, 1997, and 1999 asked employed people about the nature of their work and data from that survey are shown in Table 9.2.

While the fraction of employees who are contingent has doubtlessly grown since the early 1980s, nonetheless as a proportion of the labor force the numbers are not very great. This should not be a big surprise given that even small percentage changes can lead to large absolute numbers in an economy as large as ours and hence can catch people's attention.

In addition to the CPS there is, however, another source of data that suggests larger numbers. This is the Current Employment Statistics (CES) series, which is generated by surveys of establishments (as opposed to the CPS which is a survey of individuals). The CES collects data on employment by industry and one industry is Personnel Supply Services, which is basically equivalent to temporary help firms. For reasons which are not well understood, the CES shows employment levels well above those of the CPS. The CES data are shown in Table 9.3. It is still worth noting, however, that even the CES shows that under 3 percent of the labor force is employed in temporary help firms. However, these data do show impressively rapid growth rates.

In assessing these numbers it is also important to remember that they represent the stock of employees who, at any point in time, are contingent. Because contingent assignments are often short-term it is very likely that a larger

Table 9.3. Employment in Personnel Supply Services

	Number employed	As percent of total employment
1979	507,800	0.5
1989	1,454,500	1.3
1999	3,600,000	2.7

Source: http://www.bls.gov/cestabs.htm

fraction of employees are contingent at some point over a year. The National Establishment Survey found that the median duration of a contingent or temporary job was five months.[4] Hence, depending on whether the same or different people move through a series of short-term assignments, it is possible that the fraction of employees who are contingent at some point of the year could be up to twice as large as the fraction contingent at any particular time.

9.3. Rebuilding the Labor Market

The collapse of the old labor market structure and the halting emergence of a new one have not been matched by similar transformations of public policy. As a consequence there is a mismatch between current labor market policy, premised on old assumptions, and new realities. The central challenge facing us is to devise new approaches to deal with two issues: increased mobility and the loss of employee power. With respect to mobility we lack strong institutions for linking together a series of short-term work opportunities into a continuous stream of employment and income now that this function is no longer performed within large enterprises to which workers are permanently attached. We lack institutional guidance for workers negotiating their careers through a sequence of skills developed by moving across the borders of different firms. Unemployment insurance coverage, originally conceived as an income replacement for workers on temporary layoffs, is declining at the very moment when the risk of permanent job loss has increased. With respect to power, the decline of unions is obviously an issue and the question is both whether unions can be revived and whether new employee institutions can emerge.

---

[4] The median duration of a temporary job (i.e. an assignment from a temporary help firm) was three months and the median duration of an on-payroll contingent job was nine months. There are twice as many temporary as contingent jobs hence the five-month figure.

In the remainder of this chapter I will focus on an organization and set of strategies which, in my view, have been successful in addressing the issues of both mobility and power and in linking the two together. I will describe the activities of the Industrial Areas Foundations (IAF), a network of community organizations. While the IAF is national in scope I have researched their activities in the American Southwest and it is these organizations which I will highlight here.

The IAF network in the Southwest comprises 20 cities and 21 organizations. Most of these have embarked upon labor market initiatives. In order to provide depth to the discussion I will emphasize two areas—San Antonio and the Lower Rio Grande Valley—which represent somewhat different approaches to labor market issues and which also represent different economic environments.

9.3.1. *An Introduction to IAF Organizing*

The IAF is an 'organization of organizations'. When the IAF comes into a city (or region), whether Baltimore, Los Angeles, San Antonio, or the Rio Grande Valley it puts together a membership of other organizations, most frequently churches. These constituent organizations commit to participating in the IAF and to paying annual dues.

Today's IAF organizations are successors of the pioneering work of Saul Alinsky, the man who virtually invented community organizing in America.[5] Alinsky, a graduate of the University of Chicago sociology department, began organizing during the 1930s. Closely associated with the union organizing drives which were exploding during this era and with the Catholic hierarchy in Chicago, Alinksy invented a style of organizing which proved remarkably durable. In Chicago he founded the Back of the Yards organization in a white working class area and later initiated the Woodlawn organization in an African–American community. He sparked organizations in Rochester, New York, New York City, and California and trained several generations of organizers including Cesar Chavez. Alinksy was famous for his combination of media-wise hardball tactics (e.g. threatening to fill the seats of Rochester's opera with his members after having eaten a large baked bean dinner) and also for his tough minded pragmatism and willingness to accept half a loaf or 'the world as it is, not as it should be'. Indeed, more doctrinaire leftists attacked Alinksy for his lack of ideology (Horwitt 1992: 535). With his death in 1972 his protégé Ed Chambers took over the organization, deepened its strategy of organizing through institutions such as churches and professionalized its training of new organizers.

---

[5] For a biography of Alinsky, and the source of the material in these paragraphs, see Horwitt (1992).

While the building blocks of the IAF are these member organizations, the power of the model depends on the kind of connections it builds among individuals. Participants have an affiliation to one of the member organizations, but are connected to other participants and to the IAF by way of relational meetings (so-called 'one-on-ones'). At these meetings, two people, who might be members or organizers, tell each other their stories so that they can develop a shared understanding of what is important to each of them. Relational meetings are primarily organized to accomplish the key IAF goal: to build strong connections among people based on a shared understanding of each person's experiences, their self-interest, and the aspects of their life and their community that frustrate and anger them. House meetings, larger get-togethers where members define the local and regional issues that are important and determine which of them are actionable, are also important to the IAF model.

These relationship-building activities are central to the IAF's goals and are not merely means to get to programmatic or action ends. These relationships and shared stories that develop out of the one-on-ones and house meetings form the undergirding of the organization and are what make the IAF different from protest campaigns or social service agencies. The IAF builds strong organizations by establishing long-lasting relationships among people.

Within an IAF organization, the professional staff (the organizers) obviously play a key role. The biographies of the Southwest organizers are diverse, ranging from former garment workers born in the Valley, to college graduates drawn to the work, to nuns who believe that engagement in community organizing is the best way to express their religious commitment. The dominant figure among the organizers is Ernesto Cortes who, twenty-five years ago, founded Communities Organized for Public Service (COPS) in San Antonio. A winner of a McArthur genius award, Cortes is part tough street organizer and part college professor who virtually always has read more than anyone in the room.

The focus is not, however, on the organizers. A tremendous amount of effort is aimed at identifying and developing 'leaders', the IAF term for active members. These leaders, as well as other less active members, are given numerous opportunities to attend workshops and training sessions on public speaking and political organizing. In public forums it is the leaders, not the organizers, who represent the IAF and these leaders are trained to function effectively in these settings.

Unlike national interest groups, even progressive ones, which only ask that their members write a check, the hallmark of the IAF is that its members become active and confident political actors. As a result of the relationship building and training, people who had previously never spoken in public nor felt that they had any say in politics find themselves researching policy, developing strategies, and taking on public officials. The testimonies of personal transformation are extensive and impressive. These organizations create citizens in the true sense of the word.

The IAF is a power organization: its mission is to build and grow a base of power by identifying issues, training citizens who have a stake in those issues, and then spinning off the efforts to the control of local, independent organizations. By doing so, it shifts the nature of discussion and discourse in communities across a broad range of issues and creates a group of citizens who feel entitled to have a voice and have the personal tools to achieve their goals.

The IAF has had success in issues ranging from school reform to job training programs to living wage campaigns and in efforts to shape patterns of local economic development. In each of these arenas their successes stand as national models of effective programs. The IAF organizations are, however, about more than enacting successful programs or policies. They seek to transform the nature of local and regional politics, and they have been successful in their efforts. Their success ranges from the very local, re-drawing city council districts, to the far broader: forcing local and state politicians to take into account, and indeed court, a previously unrecognized and powerless constituency.

9.4. Labor Market Strategies

In thinking about how to address via labor market policy the problems generated by the changing institutional structure of the labor market two broad choices come to mind. The first is to find better ways to enable workers to navigate through a more uncertain labor market. This approach, which takes as its main problem the increased mobility of the labor market, implies an emphasis on skill and on matching or intermediary services. The second broad strategy is to find new ways to build up employee power given the weakening impact of unions. This implies new worker organizing strategies. The IAF has followed both paths.

9.4.1. *Training and Intermediaries*

There are two IAF organizations located in San Antonio, COPS and Metro Alliance. For most purposes these organizations work in tandem and they share a lead organizer.

In January 1990, Levi Strauss closed a plant in San Antonio that had employed more than 1000 people, many of them connected to COPS and

Metro Alliance. Following this closure COPS and Metro Alliance started to investigate the economic situation of members of their organizations. The IAF organizations initially sought to develop a grassroots understanding of the on-going economic dislocation and characteristically started with house meetings. In the meetings people told stories of past unsatisfactory experiences with training programs, particularly those in which no recognized certificate or diploma resulted, or in which there were no available jobs after the training period. Through discussion of such stories, three principles were developed that would guide Project QUEST: first, training must be long-term; second, training must be job-driven because, as one IAF leader stated, 'our people had enough disappointments in their lives'; and third, there must be financial support through the training that is tied to the individual.

In the spring of 1991 a job training core committee was formed of 40 COPS and Metro Alliance leaders. This committee met bi-monthly for almost two years and worked on three fronts. The first was the design of the program itself. Second, the committee and the IAF organizations worked hard to obtain job commitments from the business community. In the end, they were able to generate 650 commitments to hire QUEST graduates. As a result, the people entering the program knew that there were jobs on the other end and the training itself could be tailored to actual job requirements. Third, the organizations struggled to raise funds. To accomplish this the organizations put considerable pressure on the city via accountability sessions and lobbying. In addition, because the IAF networks had played an important role in the election of Ann Richards as governor (not via endorsements—which the IAF does not do—but rather because of her strong performance in accountability sessions and the IAF get out the vote effort) the organizations were able to tap into state funds.[6]

The IAF does not want to be in the service-providing business and QUEST was organized as a distinct entity with its own staff. The board of QUEST comes from the IAF organizations, as well as members of the local business community, and the IAF organizations play a central role in obtaining continued funding for QUEST and in promoting it and protecting it. COPS and Metro were very careful not to treat QUEST as a patronage operation or source of jobs for their members as has happened with some other efforts organized by community based groups. The first two directors of QUEST were Anglo ex-military men with no connection to the IAF and since the beginning of the program the IAF has insisted on entirely merit-based staffing.

In order to see what makes QUEST special it is necessary to understand the nature of the typical job training program. Most programs are short term

---

[6] A good account of the fund raising efforts is in Warren (2001: 170–5).

and they provide no financial support to enrollees. These two features are obviously interrelated: a long-term program is difficult to sustain without some kind of assistance. Another reason for quick and dirty efforts is that these enable public officials to serve the largest number of people possible, a politically desirable goal even if the results are poor. In addition, most training programs operate 'on spec'. That is, they train people and hope that jobs will be available. What all this adds up to is very modest results. The evaluation literature suggests that the gains from typical training programs are not very large and are sometimes zero.

QUEST broke with this model and was very self-conscious about doing so. The program began with a commitment from firms of 650 jobs for the program's graduates. This meant that the training could be designed—in cooperation with the employers—for what would be needed upon graduation and it also meant that the trainees had a goal which maintained morale throughout the effort. The power of COPS and Metro Alliance was obviously crucial in obtaining these commitments. At the end of the day some of the commitments did not materialize but most did and all the firms felt a moral commitment to find jobs for the graduates.

QUEST training was long term, averaging around 18 months, and took place in community colleges. The long-term character of the effort meant that real skills were taught. The use of the community colleges relieved the program of the need to invest in costly infrastructure and meant that all training would be done by professional staff. Throughout the program QUEST was able to provide modest financial support to trainees to help them deal with life's emergencies: a rent crisis, medical issues, childcare, and the like. Although the trainees provided most of their own financial support, via part-time jobs or family support or welfare, the availability of some emergency funds was crucial and further distinguished QUEST from standard programs.

A key component of the program is the intensive attention counselors give to the trainees. Part of the counselor's time is spent speaking to instructors, tutoring, and keeping in touch with what is happening in school. They also ran motivational group sessions called VIP meetings (for Vision, Initiative, and Persistence). These meetings are held once per week and attendance is mandatory for QUEST participants. In these sessions, counselors keep students updated on program information, such as when new ID cards must be made and when forms must be completed. The VIP meetings also provide a forum for students to air their concerns and for counselors to track student progress in class. Counselors also advise participants how to budget their resources, provide references to other private and public aid that is available, and administer QUEST support which consists of tuition, books, childcare, and transportation funds as well as limited emergency aid for other living expenses.

In 1996 I evaluated Project QUEST quite carefully. Over the course of a year I collected pre-enrollment data on all people who had attended QUEST, whether or not they had completed the program, and did a follow-up survey to learn their post-program status. The quantitative evaluation showed that QUEST led to substantial gains for its participants, gains which far exceed those of typical training efforts. My estimated annual earnings gain was between $4900 and $7500 with the expected payoff of costs being a very short three years. At that time costs were about $10,000 per client but this has since been reduced to $6000 due to the success of the program in tapping into newly available child care funds from the state. As of December 2000 the program had served 2345 people. About 60 percent of QUEST placements are in health care and this has remained stable.

The QUEST model has been replicated in the IAF network although different cities have modified it in various ways. In the Valley Project VIDA offers shorter-term customized training in cooperation with firms as well as the standard QUEST model. This works well provided that the hiring commitments from the firms are very strong and are at acceptable wages. Capital IDEA, the program in Austin, also offers the customized option and has a component of the program aimed at high school drop-outs, which brings them up to the level that permits them to enter the 'classic QUEST' track. In Tuscon Job Path requires that its graduates pay the program back either financially or via community service. QUEST-like programs have also been established in El Paso and Dallas. The IAF network is aggressive in promoting learning across the projects and holds frequent training workshops.

Most training programs, no matter how good, are limited in their achievements to the gains (if any) experienced by their clients. This is a problem because these programs are ultimately small relative to the size of the labor market and their overall impacts are consequently modest. QUEST has been more ambitious, and has had more extensive impacts, in three respects: it altered the hiring practices of employers, it improved the community colleges for all of that system's students, and it was linked to the broader organizing goals of COPS and Metro Alliance. It altered employer hiring patterns by demonstrating that skilled employees can be drawn from pools of workers which the San Antonio employer community had previously ignored. Employers reported that their recruitment patterns had changed as a result of their experience with QUEST. QUEST also led to important changes in how the local community colleges operate, changes which redounded to the benefit of many more students than just the QUEST enrollees. These changes include the creation of a Remediation Institute (which prepared people to pass the entry exam and hence take credit courses) open not only to QUEST trainees but to all people who attend the schools, and various forms of curricular reform which make the programs more accessible. As a consequence of these efforts the impact of QUEST is greater than simply the gains achieved by clients.

Given the success of QUEST, and the substantial positive publicity it generated, it is surprising but nonetheless true that the program has had difficulty securing a stable funding base. The original funding was a combination of city and state support, with a modest amount of foundation financing, but over time the public resources have fluctuated. This has meant that enrollment levels have not been stable and it also required that the organizations engage in an annual or bi-annual struggle for resources. In response to this problem, and also as a way of linking the training program to organizing efforts in San Antonio, the state network launched a drive to permit the use of economic development funds for human development programs. The economic development funds were generated as a small fraction of the city sales tax but state law required that these funds be used only for physical projects. The IAF's proposed state legislation permitted their use for training programs, after-school programs, and the like.

Achieving passage of this legislation, dubbed the Human Development Fund, proved to be a major battle, a battle which was waged on two fronts. The Mayor of San Antonio supported the idea but wanted the funds to be controlled by an independent public/private corporation. The IAF viewed this as a tactic to remove control of the monies from politics, that is, from the purview of COPS and Metro Alliance. At the state level economic development officials from various cities, all of whom had plans to use their local sales tax funds for physical projects, opposed the effort. The IAF network mobilized to pass their version of the bill, with COPS and Metro Alliance taking the lead. Elizabeth Valdez, the lead organizer in San Antonio, virtually lived in Austin in the Spring of 2001 and everyday carloads, and on some occasions busloads, of leaders from around the state traveled to Austin to lobby their legislators. As is typically the case, the IAF used this campaign not simply to obtain the legislation but also as a fulcrum for organizing, in this case for re-energizing COPS and Metro-Alliance leaders. In the end, a compromise was reached with the Mayor of San Antonio on how the funds would be managed and due to vigorous work in Austin the bill passed through the Republican legislature and was signed by the Republican governor.

Another way in which the training effort is linked to organizing is via efforts to keep in touch with the programs' graduates. QUEST created an alumni association which is building up slowly and Capital Idea has established a members association which trainees join while they are enrolled. Over the long run these alumni associations have the potential to become institutional members of the IAF organization in the same way as do congregations, schools, and unions.

9.4.2. *Making Bad Jobs Good*

The IAF organization in the Valley, Valley Interfaith, has followed a two-pronged labor market strategy. In 1996 it established a job-training program (called VIDA) which is based, with some modification, on Project QUEST. To date the program has graduated nearly 1000 people. The second element is a living wage campaign which is currently aimed at public employees and which is poised to be expanded into other sectors.

The living wage campaign began with Valley Interfaith's involvement in passage of a half cent sales tax measure in McAllen. In return for their support of this measure (which had repeatedly failed and which finally passed with Valley Interfaith's support) the organization insisted on a voice in how the funds were to be spent. Out of a series of house-meetings emerged an agenda which included support for VIDA, a branch library, recreation centers, and after-school programs. The new tax revenue was also earmarked for school construction projects.

With this success in hand the organization began to think about how the construction funds would be spent and focused on the question of living wages. The leaders began a study ('research action' in IAF parlance) and came to the conclusion that living wages were indeed an important issue. At a convention in March, 1998 (attended by 7000 people) elected officials agreed in principle to support living wage policies.

The initial IAF strategy was to target construction jobs associated with new school building. Indeed, the organization engaged in considerable research regarding the economics of the local construction industry and its wage setting practices. However in the face of opposition they asked for an opinion by the Texas Attorney General regarding the legality of their efforts. After some delay he ruled that while living wage ordinances were acceptable under the Texas constitution, they required state legislative action to make them permissible. The IAF is currently organizing to pass such legislation but in the interim Valley Interfaith decided to target the employees of school districts in the Valley.

In August 1998 Valley Interfaith succeeded in McAllen and the school district raised the wages of 400 full time workers from the minimum wage to $7.50 an hour. Similar campaigns met with success in Pharr, San Juan, and Alamo. These were all administrative decisions by school committees. In June 1999 Valley Interfaith was able to get an ordinance passed in Hidalgo County raising the wages of 1000 county employees. A struggle is currently underway to pass a similar ordinance in Cameron County. A total of 8500 persons have had their wages increased as a direct result of these campaigns. The success of these efforts is impressive and even startling given the long history of low-wage employment and relative powerlessness of poor people in the region.

9.5. Cross-cutting Themes

With this material in hand, I will now discuss some broader themes regarding the IAF labor market strategy.

9.5.1. *Program vs Organization*

One way to think about what the IAF is doing is that they are experimenting with and devising innovative programmatic approaches to addressing the difficulties of low-income labor markets. As such, the IAF could be considered a 'program-generating organization' and when we want to assess how well it is doing we would ask about the performance of each of its component programs.

There is certainly good reason to take this perspective. The bottom line for many people in the policy community is the tangible, and measurable, impacts of specific programs. A typical question is how many people were served and what were their income gains. By this standard the IAF has performed well: Project QUEST appears to be one of the most successful job training programs in 'the nation and the living wage campaign in the Valley has improved the wages of thousands of people and it also looks likely to expand. Other IAF organizations in the Southwest are undertaking job-training programs modeled on QUEST (although some have made various modifications) and living wage campaigns are also increasingly popular.

As intuitive as this perspective might seem, however, it is limited in its perception of what the IAF is trying to accomplish. Obviously the organizations are interested in the programs in their own right and do a great deal to assure that the programs are successful. However the overall goal of the IAF organizations is considerably broader than simply creating and administering programs, no matter how good. It is better to think of the IAF as having two fundamental objectives. The first is to enhance the ability of its members to participate in civic life. The second is to build an organization which has the power necessary to be a respected and influential actor in the community and which can, by deploying this power, improve the circumstances of its members in an on-going way.

The centrality of these goals helps explain several aspects of how the IAF operates. The prominence of the education and training sessions which are frequently held for members of the organizations can be understood by reference to the value placed on building the capacity of people to fully participate in their communities and in economic and social decisions.

The importance of these objectives also explains the conscious efforts of the IAF to maintain an administrative distance between the organizations and the training programs (recall that both QUEST and VIDA are separate organizations with their own staff). One of the challenges confronting the IAF organizations is to avoid slipping into the mind-set of a program operator. This is a danger because conceiving, funding, creating, and maintaining the programs is so difficult that it is easy to be satisfied with these achievements.

The distinction between traditional program objectives and civic culture/ power goals does not represent an inherent conflict and the two sets of goals are compatible. However, tradeoffs may have to be made, for example, in terms of the time and energy of leaders and organizers, and these will typically be shaded toward the civic culture/power objectives. The complex set of objectives also will prove important when it comes to thinking about assessing the overall impact of the IAF efforts.

9.5.2. *Scale and Objectives*

The foregoing implies that to see the IAF efforts as 'program generating' or 'program administering', while not literally inaccurate, represents a limited perspective on the organization's objectives. A related issue concerns the scale of impact to which the IAF aspires.

Issues of scale always haunt employment and training programs. It often seems that the best received programs are small efforts which, while helping a limited number of people, are not easily expanded or exported. As such the impact is constrained and the programs do not offer a way of addressing the difficulties which confront entire communities or large groups.

From the perspective of a program operator this concern may seem understandable but not really central. The program operator wants to do the best job for its clients and to keep the organization viable. The broader concerns are more distant. However, the IAF's ambitions are considerably more expansive. Because the IAF is a broad-based organization representing a large geographic area and because the IAF has a fundamentally structural view of the origin of the difficulties of the people it represents it cannot be satisfied with running a good program and keeping that program going. Instead, the IAF has to take as the ultimate programmatic objective of the work strategies, structural change in the labor market. This structural change will ultimately rebound to the benefit of far more people than those who are served in the program itself.

To some extent these concerns regarding scale are obviated in the IAF strategy of replication: the QUEST model and variants on it are being implemented in a large number of other cities by IAF organizations. Specifically, training programs based on QUEST (though with modifications) have been implemented in the Rio Grande Valley (Project VIDA), Austin (Capital

IDEA), El Paso (ARRIBA), Tucson (Job Paths), and Dallas (Workpaths 2000). Furthermore, these replications demonstrate real learning as will be discussed below.

A second response to the scale concern is the current success of the interventions in having broader impacts than the direct effects for their clients. For example, we saw that Project QUEST led to considerable changes in the curriculum of the community colleges, changes which will rebound to the benefit of substantial numbers of people.

The broader response to the issue of scale and impact is to examine the logic of how the programs evolve, or might evolve. The experience of QUEST and of the living wage campaign in the Valley illustrate two different aspects of this dynamic.

The COPS and Metro Alliance in San Antonio have fundamentally pursued a human capital strategy, as exemplified by QUEST and the Alliance Schools. The potential scale of this approach is constantly under threat due to budgetary issues. For example, QUEST, despite its widely acknowledged success, was allowed to shrink to about a third of its original size. Although this has temporarily been resolved by the city revenue described above, annual city appropriations are uncertain. The logical solution is to obtain a dedicated stream of revenue and this is what the organizations achieved in their recent campaign for a Human Development Fund. The statewide IAF network obtained state legislation enabling cities to expend funds on training and education which had previously been reserved for physical capital projects.

The Valley's living wage campaign follows a different path of expansion. In order to understand this it is worth thinking a little more carefully about the dynamics of living wage campaigns. Living wage campaigns have two logics, one economic and one political. The economic logic is that the campaigns seek to establish a new baseline 'going' wage for adults in the community which is above the Federal or state minimum wage. It may be acknowledged that the minimum wage is acceptable for youth and other people with casual labor market attachment but for adults whose earnings are important for family support the minimum is unacceptable. The power which can establish the new living wage as the baseline 'going' wage lies partly in legislation, for example, requirements that city contractors pay the living wage, and partly in shifts of expectations. A long line of research on wage settings shows that such expectations can play an important role in local labor markets.

Living wages are also an important organizing tool. First, the beginning of a campaign provides a venue for people to research their local economy and learn about the wage structure. Second, establishing the initial ordinance provides a goal around which considerable energy can be mobilized.

Third, once living wages have gained a foothold, for example, via the ordinance, then it is possible to approach a new group of workers and ask them whether they realize they are not being paid the living wage. This provides an on-going basis for organization.

The living wage campaigns in the Valley have thus far directly affected 7500 people and, while this is substantial, much the same set of concerns about overall impact that were raised in the training case can be raised here. However, as in San Antonio, an expansion is underway. First, as already noted, Valley Interfaith, along with Texas IAF, is pushing for legislation which will permit passage of ordinances extending living wage requirements to contractors who do business with a municipality.

Beyond this, Valley Interfaith is engaged in active consideration of strategies for pushing into the private sector. In part this has been stimulated by the fact that groups—school cafeteria workers, bus drivers, and former Levi's employees—have approached them about living wage issues (thus illustrating the points about standard setting and the political dynamic of these campaigns) and in part by the idea of building an employees' association which can mobilize power with respect to private sector targets. To the extent that these efforts can change norms in the local labor market and push into the private sector, the impact will be quite substantial.

In summary, scale is a major concern for all labor market interventions and the IAF is no exception. It addresses the scale issue in several ways: through replication of successful models, by consciously seeking to achieve structural change in labor markets, and by following the logic of expansion built into its initiatives.

9.5.3. *Learning*

The foregoing discussion describes the ways in which programs have evolved. There are two ways to deepen this discussion even further. The first is to examine how the IAF has learned over time. The second is to discuss the interaction of programs and organizing.

Understanding how organizations learn is very much a concern in management practice and literature. As already noted, the IAF devotes considerable effort to working on this topic and frequently brings in outsiders to talk with organizers and leaders. At the core of the learning process within the IAF is the Interfaith Education Fund. This central organization has, among its other responsibilities, organizing seminars, developing models of best practice, and diffusing the lessons of experience throughout the network.

An illustration of how this can play out is the evolution of the QUEST model. The original QUEST model required that trainees have at least a high school education. The rationale for this was that the training was for high-level work for which a high school degree provided both necessary skills and a level of credibility with employers, an especially important consideration given that QUEST was a new and untested initiative. A corollary of this set-up was that the training was very long-term.

This model worked very well. However it did have limitations: a substantial number of people were excluded, either because they lacked the high school degree or because they were unable or unwilling to commit to such a lengthy training period. The IAF organizations have responded to this by modifying elements of the QUEST model. The best elaborated of these modifications is the Austin program (called Capital IDEA) which has three tiers. The first is a pure remediation component with no job training. The second is short-term (six months or so) job training aimed at relatively rapid placement into jobs which, while they may not have high initial wages, provide internal training and career ladders. The third tier is the full QUEST model. Individuals can enter into any of the tiers (depending, of course, on their circumstances and qualifications) and, should they wish, move from one tier to another over time. QUEST in San Antonio is now planning to adopt this model with the new round of funding mentioned above. This process illustrates quite well the learning dynamics within the IAF network.

Another example of organizational learning is the feedback between programmatic interventions and the actual organizing strategy of the IAF. Traditionally the IAF adds new members by increasing the number of congregations who are affiliated with the organization. The labor market strategies of the IAF open new possibilities. One of these is to add unions as affiliates and this is being done in various IAF cities around the country. The training programs and the living wage campaigns open another possibility, namely organizing the individuals who are beneficiaries of these efforts. These people may not be members of an IAF-affiliated congregation, but they owe a good deal to the IAF and are potential members. A promising step would be to organize them into an employees' association. The IAF is actively considering steps along these lines and this dynamic illustrates the interaction between program and organizing. Furthermore, the creation of an employees' association would open new paths for programmatic activity, for example initiatives around health insurance and a broader living wage thrust into the private sector.

9.6. Conclusion: A Framework for Thinking About Labor Market Policy

This chapter began by arguing that shifts in the nature of American labor markets require a new formulation of labor market policy. Clearly some of those new policies, for example, benefit portability, will require national initiatives. However, a great deal can be accomplished at the local level and, indeed, the American experience in social policy is that national policies often emerge from local experimentation. In many respects, despite the gloomy national political climate, there is reason for optimism because throughout the country there is a great deal of local energy around this experimentation. I have highlighted the IAF model for two reasons. First, it has engaged in some of the most substantively interesting initiatives. Second, it links political organizing with labor market policy and in doing so uses the political efforts to improve the policy initiatives and uses the policy initiatives to build up its political capital. This linkage makes the IAF distinctive.

In thinking about the nature of the labor market efforts launched by the IAF it is useful to distinguish between different underlying strategies. Human capital interventions are supply-side efforts aimed at improving the skills of individuals. The skills can range from basic education to technical skills such as nursing or mechanics to soft skills such as teamwork. The overwhelming majority of training programs fall into this group and certainly QUEST and VIDA have important elements of this approach.

Demand-side programs seek to alter the behavior of individual firms by increasing their willingness to employ a program's clients or an organization's constituency. This might be accomplished by helping the firm expand its markets or improve its performance (as is attempted by various so-called sectoral programs or manufacturing extension services) or simply by using persuasion and power to pry open the hiring gate. QUEST with its success in securing employment pledges and VIDA with its linkage of tax abatements to hiring and training also contain elements of this strategy.

The third approach is much more unusual in labor market policy and is what makes the IAF efforts distinctive. This is to change the structure of local labor markets. The focus here is broader than individuals or specific firms but rather on the norms, rules, and institutions which influence outcomes. One example is the effort of QUEST to reform the community college system. Another is the attempt via living wage campaigns to alter wage norms in a community. A third example is the use of QUEST as an intermediary to facilitate mobility in the labor market. If the IAF moves in the direction of building an employees' association this would be a fourth example.

The IAF is distinctive in that it seeks to draw upon elements of all three approaches to labor market interventions. Clearly the human capital strategy is the most trod path and the easiest to undertake while changing the structure of labor markets lies at the other extreme. However, in terms of scale, it is the latter strategy which holds the most promise.

References

BARLEY, S. and KUNDA, G. (1992). 'Design and Devotion; Surges of Rational and Normative Ideologies of Control in Management Discourse'. *Administrative Science Quarterly*, 37/3: 363–99.

BATT, R. (1995). 'Performance and Welfare Effects of Work Restructuring: Evidence From Telecommunications Services'. Ph.D. Dissertation, M.I.T. Sloan School of Management.

BENDIX, R. (1956). *Work and Authority in Industry, Ideologies of Management in the Course of Industrialization*. Berkeley: University of California Press.

BERLE, A. and MEANS, G. (1968). *The Modern Corporation and Private Property*, rev. edn. New York: Harcourt, Brace, and World.

DUNLOP, J. (1957). 'The Task of Contemporary Wage Theory' in Taylor and Peirson (eds) (1957), 117–39.

ECKSTEIN, O. and WILSON, T. (1962). 'The Determination of Manufacturing Wages In American Industry'. *Quarterly Journal of Economics*, LXXVI/3: 379–414.

FREEMAN, R. and MEDOFF, J. (1984). *What Do Unions Do?* New York: Basic Books.

GUILLEN, M. (1994). *Models of Management*. Chicago: University of Chicago Press.

HALL, R. (1982). 'The Importance of Lifetime Jobs in the U.S. Economy'. *American Economic Review*, 72/4: 716–24.

HORWITT, S. (1992). *Let Them Call Me Rebel; Saul Alinsky, His Life and Legacy*. New York: Vintage Books.

KATZ, H. (1985). *Shifting Gears*. Cambridge: MIT Press.

KERR, C. (1957). 'Labor's Income Share and the Labor Movement', in Taylor and Peirson (eds) (1957), 260–98.

KOCHAN, T., KATZ, H., and MCKERSIE, R. (1986). *The Transformation of Industrial Relations*. New York: Basic Books.

LESTER, R. (1957). 'Economic adjustments to Change in Wage Differentials', in G. Taylor and F. Peirson (eds), *New Concepts in Wage Determination*. New York: McGraw Hill, 206–38.

MAHER, J. (1961). 'The Wage Pattern In the United States'. *Industrial and Labor Relations Review*, 15/1: 3–20.

MITCHELL, D. (1985). 'Shifting Norms In Wage Determination'. *Brookings Papers on Economic Activity*, 2: 575–608.

—— (1989). 'Wage Pressures and Labor Shortages: The 1960s and the 1980s'. *Brookings Papers on Economic Activity*, 2: 191–232.

OSTERMAN, P. (1999). *Securing Prosperity : the American Labor Market: How It Has Changed and What to Do about It*. Princeton: Princeton University Press.

REYNOLDS, L. (1957). 'The General Level of Wages', in G. Taylor and F. Peirson (eds), *New Concepts in Wage Determination*. New York: McGraw Hill, 239–59.

ROSS, A. (1948). *Trade Union Wage Policy*. Berkeley: University of California Press.

—— (1957). 'The External Wage Structure', in G. Taylor and F. Peirson (eds), *New Concepts in Wage Determination*. New York: McGraw Hill, 173–205.

ROY, D. (1952). 'Quota Restriction and Goldbricking in a Machine Shop'. *American Journal of Sociology*, 57/5: 427–42.

Staffing Industry Analysts. *Staffing Industry Reports*. Los Altos, California, vii/14.

TAYLOR, G. and PEIRSON, F. (eds.) (1957). *New Concepts in Wage Determination*. New York: McGraw Hill.

WARREN, M. (2001). *Dry Bones Rattling: Community Building to Revitalize American Democracy*. Princeton: Princeton University Press.

10

Part of the Solution: Emerging Workforce Intermediaries in the United States

LAURA DRESSER AND JOEL ROGERS

Faced with the unsettling changes in competitive practice, work organization, and workforce demographics explored throughout this volume, many in Europe look to the United States as a model for labor-market 'flexibility' in responding to them. As used conventionally in policy circles, 'flexibility' carries the positive connotation of agile firm and broader labor-market adjustment to changing market demands and opportunities, an adjustment that may be painful to some but is good for the broader society. The most thoughtful US observers are less impressed with flexibility, however, at least as exercised here, since here it has largely been one-sided, negative, and evidenced less social invention than *lacunae*—in particular the distinctive absence in the United States of effective constraints on employer discretion to lower employment, restructure work, withdraw employment security, or otherwise alter wage or benefit norms in ways generally unfavorable to labor. As we review in a moment, this 'negative flexibility' appears to bring little general benefit, and its social costs are exceedingly high—an experience that recommends caution to any who would seek to adopt the 'American model' elsewhere.

Of greater and more positive interest may be some of the institutional experimentation that has followed from such negative labor-market restructuring. Of particular note are a variety of new 'workforce intermediaries' (WIs)—serving both workers and employers, and sometimes performing functions previously assigned the state—that have become more evident in recent years. These new institutions help solve vexing workforce and employment policy problems, for example in aligning shifting employer demand for skills and public workforce training systems. They mitigate some of restructuring's worst effects among the least advantaged by widening their opportunities at work—both in gaining job access, and gaining resources for advancement once there. They smooth adjustment to new employer demands among incumbent workers, developing new career paths where the old job ladder system of advancement has broken down. They integrate parts of generally fragmented economic development and workforce systems. In the limiting case, indeed, they appear to offer, under the radically changed labor-market conditions of the present, some promise of reinserting a worker voice throughout the micro-institutional choices involved in restructuring—perhaps even to the point of making it again better serve the general welfare.

At once we emphasize that this promise should not be overstated. The existing WIs are relatively small in scale, uneven in effect, and in no case authoritative for broad labor-market outcomes. Still, we believe they are worth looking at, something we do here in three steps. First, we set the institutional and policy stage for the emergence of these new intermediaries. Second, we explore a series of examples of them. Third, we speculate on how their positive effects might be amplified and made more secure by supportive policy, or linkage to the broader strategy of key market actors.

10.1. Institutional and Policy Background: Before and After 'Welfare Reform'

More than any other advanced capitalist economy, the United States relies on competitive labor markets to determine pay, employment, and other aspects of worker welfare.[1] Outside the public sector, only nine percent of workers belong to unions, a level that has declined steadily over the past quarter century and now in fact is lower than a century ago. Union collective bargaining agreements, moreover, generally cover individual firms or establishments, rather than entire industries or regions, and are not extended to non-union employers as they widely are elsewhere, so collective bargaining coverage in the United States is not much greater than union membership. Public regulation of labor markets is also minimal. The minimum wage applies to a relatively small number of workers, has no obvious spill-over on the overall level of wages, and is now more than a third below its late 1960s peak, despite massive increases in productivity since that time. Unemployment insurance is more time-limited than in other countries. Outside a cluster of 'means tested' programs directed to the very poor, the welfare state is largely limited to old-age pensions and insurance. Exclusive of occupational health and safety regulation and equal employment opportunity laws protecting groups from discrimination, the state has few national policies safeguarding workers. Job

---

[1] This discussion of the broad institutional and policy features of US labor regulation in part draws directly from Freeman and Rogers (1996).

security, training, and even the provision of medical insurance are all determined at the workplace—through collective negotiations for a small number and through employer policy and individual negotiations for the vast majority. The bottom line is that for most Americans, how one fares in the economy depends overwhelmingly on how one fares in the labor market and thus upon the employer.

For more than two decades now, this market-driven system has led the advanced world in job creation. Since 1983, the US unemployment rate has consistently been 3–4 percentage points lower than Europe's (Mishel, Bernstein, and Schmidt 2001: 404). From 1974 to the mid 1990s the US employment/population ratio grew from 65 to 71 percent, while Europe's fell from 65 to 60 percent (Freeman and Rogers 1996). Compared to Europeans, US workers also put in more than 200 more hours at their jobs annually (a difference that itself widened during the period), further underscoring relative US success in generating work (Mishel, Bernstein, and Schmidt 2001: 400). But while the United States is brilliantly successful in generating jobs, it has been less successful in generating wages, or spreading the fruits of prosperity.

Wages have stagnated or declined for much of the US working population. For example, the real hourly wages of men with less than 12 years of schooling dropped 27 percent over 1979–99; wages of high school graduates fell 15 percent; only male college graduates experienced absolute wage increases, and at those were modest: a 10 percent increase over 20 years (Mishel, Bernstein, and Schmidt 2001: 153). Income erosion was especially severe among the young, with the wages of male high school graduates 19 to 25 years of age, for example, falling 24 percent over the period (*ibid.*: 158). And fewer workers experienced life-cycle wage improvement—earning more as they aged and advanced in their careers, gained skills, and attained seniority. In the 1970s the ratio of such life-cycle winners to losers was 4–1. In the 1980s it was halved to 2–1, meaning that one-third of workers actually lost ground as their job experience increased (Freeman and Rogers 1996).

Given a rapid secular shift in labor demand toward more-skilled workers compared to the supply of those workers, flexibility in wage determination assures rising inequality. In the US, men's college/high-school wage differential more than doubled over the last two decades, rising from a 20 percent advantage for college graduates in 1979 to a 42 percent one in 1999 (Mishel, Bernstein and Schmidt 2001: 153); over the same period, the pay of CEOs skyrocketed relative to that of other employees (*ibid.*: 211). But inequality has also increased within educational and occupational strata suggesting the increased importance of sheer luck in labor-market outcomes. Over the same 1979–99 period, for example, the ratio of earnings of female high school graduates in the 90th/10th percentiles increased 25 percent; at the same time, similar changes are found within detailed occupations (*ibid.*). Here flexibility benefited the lucky few and harmed the unlucky many.

With real wage drops concentrated on young workers—those most likely to be starting families—poverty has increased, especially among children. For historical reasons, 'poverty' in the United States is defined as an income below three times the cost of a minimal diet 'fit only for temporary or emergency use'. The share of the population living below this level rose in the 1980s and early-1990s, returning to the 1979 poverty rate of 12 percent only after the sustained growth of the late 1990s (Mishel *et al.* 2001: 289). Over the same period, child poverty actually grew from 16 to 17 percent (*ibid.*: 291). At present, nearly one-in-five American children are growing up in such poverty.

A comparison of the earnings of the bottom decile of US workers to their European counterparts may help put these trends in crossnational perspective. Within their respective systems, the bottom decile of US workers earn 36 percent of the US median wage, while the bottom decile of European workers earn 67 percent of the European. On a cross-system basis, using a purchasing power parity measure—contrasting the cost of a comparable basket of commodities across countries—US bottom-decile workers earn just 69 percent of what bottom-decile European workers earn; compared to their colleagues in a rich country like Germany, they earn just 45 percent (Freeman 2000: 44, table 8b; Freeman and Rogers 1996).

Wretched earnings at the bottom of the wage distribution, and the difficulty of making even normal gains in income over the life cycle, contribute to the growth of an 'underclass' in the United States—concentrated in our cities, often violently criminal. Lacking any social or economic policies to prevent or remedy this problem, US policy increasingly deals with the underclass through physical incarceration. In absolute terms, all this yields a very large number of people behind bars or under criminal justice supervision. The inmate population of state and federal prisons has increased by more than 600 percent since 1970, growing from 200,000 then to 1.3 million in 2000. And a much larger population of some 6.3 million Americans—that up 240 percent from 1980—is either institutionalized, or on probation or parole (Dickey, Rogers, and Smith 2001).

Such social costs might be thought worth bearing if they somehow contributed to gainful employment among the less-skilled. But this turns out not to be the case. Massive drops in the real wages of less-skilled American men (not to mention massive increases in their incarceration) did *not* improve their employment prospects absolutely, or relative to high-skill workers. In fact, the gap in unemployment between workers with less and more education is substantially higher in the United States than in other OECD nations: high school graduates are more than twice as like to be unemployed as college grads—compared to a 1.5 ratio for other OECD nation—and those with less than a high school education are 4.5 times more likely to be unemployed—compared to a ratio of 2.3 for the rest of the OECD (Mishel, Bernstein, and Schmitt 2001: 405). Thus, US experience provides no support for the proposition that downward wage flexibility helps cure unemployment.

Nor, finally, is there much evidence that the work restructuring accomplished by employers in the past 20 years has reconfigured labor market skill demand in ways that, in the future, might promise alleviation of these trends—for example, by generalizing higher skill requirements. On the demand side of the training equation, while US labor markets have shown, since the late 1970s, a strong secular increase in relative demand for skilled as against unskilled labor, overall employer demand for skilled labor remains relatively weak. Indeed, as measured by occupational trends, business demand for more educated workers is actually projected to *slow* over the next decade, not increase. Such occupational measures of course do not capture intra-occupational shifts, but more nuanced investigations of such changes—themselves driven by changes in work organization and technology—are not particularly comforting. Particularly among 'foundation' firms employing fewer than 250 workers, rates of investment in new technology are flat. And only a minority of firms—on no estimate accounting for more than 20 percent of overall employment—are making the broad changes in work organization that can be expected to drive long-term increases in the demand for new and deeper skills (Osterman 1999).

Much of the present US labor market, instead, appears to approximate a 'low-wage, low-skill' equilibrium. Given a low-skill environment, and little rigidity in wages, even firms operating under increased competitive pressure have continued with low-skill forms of work organization that require little more than obedience and a good work attitude from direct production or service workers. Having chosen such a strategy, however, the skill demands of these firms are low. While they may wish to remedy deficiencies in very basic worker skills, or provide training to a few in the application of expensive new technology, they generally do not demand or promote broad and continuous skill upgrading among their frontline workforce. Such low-skill, low-wage strategies of course lower overall living standards, but that makes them no less profitable or attractive to firms, and their adoption weakens the political thrust for a stronger training effort.

In US employment policy discussions, it has become common to distinguish two broad employer strategies of response to new competitive pressures—a 'low road' strategy that typically focuses only on reducing the costs of production or service delivery, and a 'high road' strategy that additionally focuses on improving service or product quality or distinctiveness, with some

of the customer premium paid for such innovation passed along to the typically better-trained workers who help produce it. Generalized, low-road
strategies lead to sweated workers, economic insecurity, rising inequality,
poisonous labor relations, and degraded natural environments.
Generalization of high-road strategies, conversely, is associated with higher
productivity, higher pay and better labor relations, reduced environmental
damage, and greater firm commitment to the health and stability of surrounding human communities needed to attract and keep skilled workers
and managers. In terms of social benefit, it is obvious which set of strategies
are to be preferred. But there are few market pressures encouraging the 'right'
choice, which would have to be deliberately aimed at by public policy, and
this the US has generally failed to do. Somewhat more specifically, moving to
the high road is associated with various transition costs, which are difficult to
sustain given the continued presence of low-road competition. It also
requires a series of supports, quasi-public goods, that are typically beyond the
capacity of individual firms to supply. These include effective educational
and training institutions; better functioning labor markets, with fuller information about requirements for job access and advancement; advanced infrastructure of all kinds; modernization services and other means of diffusing
best practice; and, throughout, barriers to low-road defection. Making
a high-road transition then in employment policy would require a mix of
policies and new institutions variously designed to close off the lower-
road options that make high-road transition more difficult, to 'pave' the high
road so that more firms can take it, and to support high-roading directly.
But this policy and institutional mix has generally been lacking in US labor
markets.

It was in this context that the US, in the mid-1990s, ended a 60-year commitment to cash assistance for unemployed female heads of households with
dependent children. In the rhetoric of the day 'welfare as we know it' was
superseded by a commitment to 'work first'. The Personal Responsibility and
Work Opportunity Reconciliation Act of 1996 established a new program:
Temporary Assistance for Needy Families (TANF). Under TANF, assistance
was time-limited to no more than two years, though states were permitted
very substantial variation in the precise level and kinds of benefits required,
with wide resulting variation in the availability of day care, training, transportation, or other assists to former welfare recipients heading off to the
world of work (Pavetti 2000). The stated rationale behind this welfare reform,
encapsulated in what became an administrative mantra of 'work first', was
that 'rapid attachment' of the formerly dependent unemployed to jobs, however poor, was the best guarantor of their long-run income growth and
self-sufficiency (Mead 1997).

In the years since, welfare caseloads have been reduced by more than half—dropping from 12 to 5 million in the first five years of reform. (US Department of Health and Human Services 2002). By this simple measure, indeed, the program is widely counted a success. The evidence on where former recipients have gone, however, is more troubling. Early jobs taken by them pay, on average, well below that needed to support the average family at the poverty level, while studies of former recipients show very little subsequent advancement (Gottschalk 1999). Three, four, and five years out, most still remain well below the poverty line. As a way to purge the rolls, then, welfare reform is a success. As a way to ensure self-sufficiency, it is a clear bust.

There is little surprise from this result, as some of the preceding review of general labor markets conditions might have suggested. Former welfare recipients in the US have effectively been dumped into a much larger population of Americans—some 40 million workers—who are 'stuck' in 'dead end' jobs showing little to no earnings growth even after long periods of job tenure. Even amid the giant job expansion in the United States over the past two decades, the share of the workforce finding itself in this predicament has increased. Of young workers who entered the labor market in the early 1980s, well over a quarter had become trapped in low-wage dead-end jobs by the mid-1990s—or double the rate of entrants in previous decades (Bernhardt *et al.* 2001*a*). Nor is this 'dead-end' effect limited to the less-skilled. Of college-educated women who held a low-wage job in 1990, half were still holding such a job five years later (Rose 1999). What appears to have happened—with the worst consequence for the less-educated, but extending well beyond their ranks—is that a large and growing portion of the American workforce is simply stuck in poverty or near-poverty jobs, with no serious prospects of income growth.

This period of increasing instability and job quality decline has corresponded with the emergence of alternative work arrangements—defined by the US Bureau of Labor Statistics as temporary work, independent contractors, on-call workers, and contract company workers. While these sorts of jobs still account for less than 10 percent of the total laborforce (US Bureau of Labor Statistics 1999), employment growth has been strong. By the 1990s, growth of the temporary employment sector alone accounted for 20 percent of all job growth (Segal and Sullivan 1997). There is a growing body of evidence documenting that workers who use temporary agencies are generally paid less and have poorer benefits than similar workers employed in 'permanent' positions (Barker and Christensen 1998; Hudson 1999; Carré *et al.* 2000). There is also evidence, however, that the temporary help industry is not homogenous, and that some workers voluntarily use temporary agencies, presumably for the valuable placement services they provide (Polivka 1996; Polivka, Cohany, and Hipple 2000).

At the bottom of the labor market, the prevalence of such contingent arrangements is twice as high (Lane *et al.* 2001). Many public agencies have looked to temp agencies to help place their workers, often resulting in low-wage, low-benefit, and unstable work (Lane *et al.* 2001). Bernhardt *et al.* (2001*b*) also found that in some instances temp agencies themselves allowed or encouraged negative work restructuring, downgrading job quality in general. The growing importance of these private-sector intermediaries in the labor market has brought policy and academic focus to both public and private workforce intermediaries.

10.2. The Resistible Rise of Workforce Intermediaries

At the same time that for-profit temp agencies have grown conspicuous, a number of non-profit and public efforts, led by labor and community leaders have emerged. We focus here on these efforts, which aim to improve job quality and job prospects for low-wage workers. Throughout the country, these emerging workforce intermediaries are building institutions with standing power to perform sorting and placement functions in the labor market. More important, these local efforts are doing so with explicit goals of improving the long-term career trajectory of workers.

The emerging workforce intermediaries have brought actors into new roles in labor markets. For example, while many of these institutions operate with the support or leadership of unions, they are not in the business of collective bargaining or organizing new members. Likewise, the intermediaries led by community groups tend to focus on regional labor markets and broad industry strategies, rather than neighborhood boundaries and traditional community development schemes. Even the public-sector intermediaries have broken with common public program rigidities, finding new ways to engage businesses and deliver services.

The WIs' targets of intermediation are diverse. Some WIs were formed by the 'rapid attachment' focus of welfare reform, but have branched into training and organizing as a means of securing self-sufficiency for their clients and members. Other WIs started by developing programs for incumbent workers and tight labor markets pushed them into programming for recruitment and training of new workers. Still others began with expressly political goals, working to build stronger floors under wages, and have resorted to training as one means to help secure that floor. Most WIs have become more comprehensive over time, evolving as industry and workforce needs change.

In this section of the chapter, we have chosen to highlight a handful of interesting and promising intermediaries that have emerged over the last decade. This is surely not expressive of the entire range of activity in the nation. It would be impossible to simply identify all labor-market programs in the nation, let alone to catalog their strengths and weaknesses. Rather, here, we offer a limited list to indicate some of the exciting programs at the local level, to consider their strengths, discuss their replication, and to begin to illuminate the weaknesses of these responses to labor-market problems. In some instances, our information is extremely good because we designed the projects ourselves. In other instances, the projects appear promising but our information is less complete.

10.2.1. *Beyond 'Rapid Attachment' at the Bottom of the Labor Market*

In the past decade, training programs in the United States, especially those targeted at disadvantaged populations like the TANF caseload, have fallen from favor. Formal evaluations of many public and non-profit training programs have struggled to find any significant impact on workers' earnings (Jacobson 1995; Grubb 1996) and helped increase the popularity of rapid attachment strategies.

But it may be that it is traditional approaches to training, rather than training itself, that should have been discarded by policy-makers. New intermediaries across the nation are developing programs which involve training, and the results suggest the new approaches are working. Many of these intermediaries have found success in pursuing 'sector'-based strategies where the intermediary focuses on specific industries and occupations, and works with industry leaders to improve systems of connecting disadvantaged workers with their jobs. Evaluation of a handful of these initiatives suggests training by these sectoral WIs has substantial and positive effects on participants' earnings (Aspen Institute 2002).

The programs we highlight in this section are focused at the bottom of the labor market where 'dead end' jobs are prevalent. Programs in this area attempt to restructure work in order to make it more financially and personally rewarding. Programs also attempt build new pathways out of the dead-end jobs and into better jobs in the sector.

10.2.2. *Paraprofessional Healthcare Institute/Cooperative Home Care Associates*

Home health aide is a classic and predominant 'dead-end' job. The jobs offer low-wages, unstable hours, poor benefits, and isolation from co-workers. Aides work with clients in their homes generally bathing, feeding, and otherwise supporting independent living. Founded in 1985 in the South Bronx as an employee-owned, for-profit company, Cooperative Home Care Associates (CHCA) has developed a range of programs in order to improve the quality of these jobs. CHCA employs roughly 300 women of color as home health care aides on a contract basis to large service providers and major hospitals.

In a sector characterized by part-time work, low wages, little training or upgrading, high turnover, and uneven service quality, CHCA has approached the problem of simultaneously improving the quality of home care and upgrading poor-quality jobs in three related ways. First, its worker–ownership structure gives employees a voice, encourages firm loyalty, and informally confers quasi-professional status on its member-employees. Second, it provides entry-level training, counseling and support to all, and follow-on training to some, members. Third, and perhaps most importantly, CHCA offers senior aides a guaranteed-hours program, which effectively transforms their work from temporary to full-time.

Results have been significant: wages and benefits are 20 percent above industry average and the typical member is able to work 34–35 hours a week. A nurse education program has enabled several CHCA aides to become licensed practical nurses. Meanwhile, both training and reduced turnover (half the industry average) have improved care: contractors acknowledge that CHCA aides are more reliable and responsive.

The Cooperative's training program is run by a non-profit agency, the Home Care Associates Training Institute, which receives one-third of its funding from public sources and the remaining two-thirds from foundations. Trainees must be low-income; all are minorities, and the vast majority are women. Most test between the 5th and 8th grade reading and math levels; less than half have completed high school or a Graduate Equivalent Degree. Entry-level training includes four weeks of on-site classroom instruction and 90 days of on-the-job training. The pedagogy emphasizes non-traditional forms of instruction, including role-playing, games, simulations, and hands-on demonstrations.

While skill upgrading is touted as CHCAs 'primary innovation', the cooperative's most important contribution may well have been to demonstrate that upgrading 'temporary' workers requires a prior transition to 'permanent' status, and that any such transition requires organization and focus on increasing and regularizing hours.

Moreover, CHCA has used its experience in the industry and strong connection to workers to become a significant voice on state and national policy issues. The Paraprofessional Healthcare Institute (PHI), a CHCA affiliate, has been a prominent force behind the development of the Direct Care Alliance which brings together patient and workforce advocates to improve jobs through improvements in Medicaid and Medicare reimbursement policy.

Additionally, PHI has released a number of influential reports, documenting the staffing crisis in the health care industry and the workforce development, reimbursement, and other policies which can improve the quality of jobs and care. PHI also works to develop worker-owned home health cooperatives to further extend its philosophy of quality care and quality jobs.[2]

10.2.3. *San Francisco Hotels Partnership*

Work in hotels, especially housekeeping and food and beverage work is often also seen as a dead-end job. Wages can be poor, hours variable and unreliable, and job stability low, given the tourism sector's vulnerability to the economic cycle. Unions in the industry have done much to improve the quality of jobs in traditional ways, but in San Francisco, a labor/management partnership has been founded to develop new solutions to industry challenges.

The Partnership was created in 1994 as part of a multi-employer contract between 11 first-class hotels and the largest union in the industry. The logic of the partnership is to continue to provide job security and solid compensation to workers, while also allowing for increased competitiveness at the member hotels. These goals are achieved through the 'living contract', which establishes an unprecedented structure for labor–management collaboration on productivity issues.

At the core of the partnership lies a series of problem-solving teams in the hotels that address long-standing workplace issues. These teams are staffed by workers, managers, and neutral facilitators and translators, always with the objective of developing joint solutions with sustained input from all sides. Often there is coordination or information sharing with teams at the other member hotels so that a partnership-wide standard emerges. An early initiative was to implement team-building and communication training at all levels of the hotels—this was critical to any future progress, given the history of hostile labor–management relations. Other initiatives include classes in Vocational English as a Second Language (ESL) and basic skills, alternative grievance resolution, and a welfare-to-work training center for housekeepers. Another project trained more than 200 entry-level workers to be higher-paid banquet servers, allowing the banquet hiring hall to have the best-ever performance in filling job orders for the holiday season. Funded with more than $1 million in state funds and an additional $500,000 from employers, these programs have offered more than 223,800 hours of training to more than 1500 labor and management participants.

---

[2] For more information on PHI/CHCA, see their website: www.paraprofessional.org and also aspeninstitute.org/eop/eop_sedlp.html. See also the website of the Direct Care Alliance, www.directcarealliance.org.

Finally, and perhaps most important, problem-solving teams at several hotels have focused on issues of work content and cross-training in the context of organizational restructuring. In one pilot project, the entire kitchen area was restructured: 27 kitchen job categories were collapsed into three, and two job titles were eliminated altogether. This reorganization spoke directly to one of the main concerns of the employers, that rigid job titles hindered flexibility in how workers were deployed and that therefore put unionized hotels at a competitive disadvantage with non-unionized ones. The union and its workers were involved in every part of the reorganization, and wages were raised and seniority rules were renegotiated in the process. While such joint projects are not yet the norm, the direct and sustained participation of workers in decision making is the hallmark of the partnership model in fully realized form.

As in the CHCA case, local success has ensured expanding influence. The San Francisco Partnership has recently started to work with employers, unions, and community colleges in San Diego, San Jose, and Los Angeles on a long-term program to solve the problem of upward mobility in the industry. While still in the planning stage, the ultimate goal of this project is to create formal career ladders for entry-level workers, both within and across job categories, at the same time meeting the growing need for skilled workers in California's hotel industry (which is predicted to grow twice as fast as the overall economy in the next decade).

On the 'demand side', labor–management teams in each hotel will work on redesigning jobs and promotion policies in order to eliminate existing structural barriers to mobility for entry-level hotel workers. On the 'supply side', workers in participating hotels will receive paid training in a job category different than their own—complemented by education and career counseling and vocational ESL. The Project staff itself serves as a critical intermediary here, by providing hotels with the technical assistance to implement the workplace reorganization, by facilitating the sharing of information among the 29 participating hotels, and by facilitating the complex process of working with local community colleges on training programs. The project is supported by a combination of employer contributions and state training funds.[3]

10.2.4. *The Culinary & Hospitality Academy of Las Vegas (CHA)*

Also working in the hospitality industry, the Culinary & Hospitality Academy of Las Vegas (CHA) was established in 1993 by a consortium of local hotel casinos and unions to provide job training for all union members, as well as

---

[3] For more information, see Bernhardt, Dresser, and Hatton (2002) and Working for America Institute (2000).

classes in ESL, high school GEDs, and soft skills. Additionally, the academy works closely with the union's hiring hall, so that graduates are first in line for new job openings at the hotels. Since the CHA's inception, more than 16,000 workers have graduated from the academy and over 70 percent have been placed in jobs. Union hotels report that turnover is 50 percent lower among academy graduates as compared to off-the-street hires. Both the placement and retention statistics, as well as the sheer scale of the program, easily surpass other programs in the region.

The CHA is funded almost entirely by contributions from employers, and they are getting a good deal. The training is highly tailored to the industry (there is an employer board that gives advice on curriculum) and the cost is significantly cheaper than at the local community college ($780 vs $6,000 per graduate). The system works so well that at this point, employers effectively treat the training center as their main source of entry-level workers—even non-union hotels want to hire the academy trainees. The CHA has been able to secure this central role because it solves two critical problems facing the hotel and gaming industry, which is the primary employer in Las Vegas. First, the academy has solved severe recruitment and retention problems by providing a steady stream of workers to union hotels. Second, by successfully training recent immigrants and welfare leavers, the academy has addressed the growing problems of lack of skills and work experience in the new workforce.

On the worker side, the CHA has become known as the premier source of training and good jobs in the region. The training is free, everyone qualifies for it, and at the end there is a decent paying job—it is this last point, the direct feeding of graduates into the industry's hiring hall, that most distinguishes the academy from the workers' standpoint.

Having gone to scale, the CHA is now focusing on broadening and diversifying its services. While the bulk of the academy's training is currently focused on entry-level skills, ultimately the goal is to provide advanced training in order to open up career ladders that have historically been closed to front-line workers. There is already scattered evidence of increased mobility for CHA graduates (e.g. housekeepers who have become assistant managers, cooks who have become executive chefs). The challenge will be to systematize such career ladders and structure them as part of a formal training program.[4]

10.2.5. *Creating a Way Out*

Each of these three programs has taken on the structure of dead-end jobs, and built training, restructuring, and advancement strategies to improve the jobs. These programs have responded to industry demands, but have also

---

[4] For more information, see Bernhardt, Dresser, and Hatton (2002) and also Working for America Institute (2000).

attempted to restructure those demands in ways that are friendly to workers. In so doing they offer some of the best examples of the ways that low-wage unstable work can be improved. Moreover, each of these programs has established credibility and used that to spread into more and more difficult issues of work restructuring. In the case of CHCA/PHI, the strategy has been not only to extend their work-owned model throughout the country, but also to help build a coalition of organizations all advocating for improved job and care quality in health care. The San Francisco Partnership has become a model for multiple cities in California (and beyond) and their work is now extending to workers throughout the state. In Las Vegas, the CHA is expanding the influence of the union, and programming is beginning to encourage more mobility in the industry. In each case, the competence, ambitions, and influence of these projects have grown over time.

10.2.6. *Ensuring Access and Advancement in Better Jobs*

Even if they are not caught in the poverty-wage, transient employment that characterizes dead-end jobs, many workers find themselves stuck in jobs with no real opportunities inside their firm and no clear signals on opportunities outside it. These workers may have made it off the first rung of the ladder, but they do not have jobs with a secure future and clear career trajectory. For example, non-professional tracks in insurance, financial services and business services have extremely short ladders—in many instances the only step up is to shift supervisor. Advancement in clerical work usually requires a college degree, not the kind of training that is easy to get on the job or after work. The health care sector often looks the same way; most hospitals discourage movement from food service to patient care to technical work. In manufacturing, competitive pressures have pushed many firms to cut back on training, just when training investments are most needed. In these firms, workers are expected to produce more with the same skills, or firms shift inexorably toward lower-end product market strategies. Projects that connect workers only with the first job in an industry often falter as the workers find themselves stuck with no way up. A handful of projects have taken on expansive roles as multi-purpose intermediaries in their respective labor markets. Osterman's chapter in this volume on Project QUEST offers one example of a training program that helps build access and advancement for disadvantaged workers. Here we discuss a few other important examples.

10.2.7. *Hospital and Health Care Workers Union Training and Upgrading Fund, Philadelphia*

In Philadelphia, the Hospital and Health Care Workers Union has been placing, training, and upgrading skills for its members and prospective members since 1974. The fund has been managed by labor and management partners to ensure that workers and firms interests are well represented. An employment center functions as a hiring hall, connecting members and other interested workers with openings called in by employers. Programs allow workers to build new skills and move into better jobs in the industry. Some training programs are focused on union members. But many programs reach not only members, but other workers as well. For example, workers displaced by economic restructuring receive career counseling, placement, and occupational training at the training center. Additionally, since the mid-1990s, the union has used the infrastructure provided by its training and upgrading fund, its connection in the industry, and its reach into the community to provide training for prospective workers for the industry. Presently, about 60 percent of training and program participants are union members, while the remainder come from outside the union.

The union employs a range of strategies in its training programs and explicitly focuses on building career paths in the industry as a strategy in the interest of members. Training programs offer everything from basic education (literacy, ESL, etc.) to specific health-care certifications. In any given year, the program serves literally thousands of union members and prospective members. Perhaps most important, the Fund has leveraged its resources, industry connections, and community legitimacy to attract public funding for work with Philadelphia's underemployed workers.

The union's programs are impressive, not only because they have been so effective for workers, but also because they contribute to a comprehensive union strategy. Efforts in the training programs build community legitimacy by offering good jobs, serve members by improving job quality and career progression, and secure an important role for the union in the local health care labor market by serving employer needs. Moreover, the union has used its credibility and experience in health care in devising strategies to help organize the region's childcare industry as well. The union's child care efforts include not only traditional organizing of the sector's workforce, but also pulling together providers, workers, parents, and advocates in a coalition to lobby for improved child care funding. Thus, their success in health care is providing a foundation for success in child care as well.[5]

10.2.8. *Wisconsin Regional Training Partnerships (WRTP)*

The WRTP now has a membership of more than 100 firms collectively employing approximately 60,000 workers in southeastern Wisconsin.

---

[5] For more information, see www.1199etjsp.org and also Working for America Institute (2000).

While the most established programming supports workers and firms in the region's manufacturing industry, a number of new partnerships have been founded bringing joint labor/management attention to building quality jobs and a quality workforce in hospitality, health care, information technology, and construction. The original manufacturing partnership was founded in 1992 and the WRTP is the largest sectoral training consortium in the country with the most-advanced program goals.

The WRTP develops programming in three major areas of activity: incumbent worker training, modernization, and future workforce development. As regards the first, new technologies and new work organization require workers with new skills. For many workers, the transition to a 'continuous innovation' environment is impossible without considerable training. WRTP members have prioritized activities that can aid firms as they seek to develop and/or improve their workplace education centers. The WRTP provides assistance as firms develop new centers. WRTP staff direct firms to external resources available for workplace skills centers, such as funding sources and curriculum developers; they also work inside firms to help develop the labor/management collaboration on which any successful skills center relies. Without labor collaboration on the project, the skills taught at the center can easily be irrelevant to worker needs and shop-floor skill gaps. Without the context of workforce buy-in and contribution to the development of the skills center, the significant investment in a workplace skills center can be wasted. The WRTP facilitates cross-site and cross-union learning about workplace skills centers and has also helped a series of small shops develop jointly operated centers. Finally, the WRTP helps firms and unions develop workplace awareness of the centers through peer advisor networks.

Competitive pressures require that firms have access to and adopt rapidly advancing technology. In response to this industry need, the WRTP focuses considerable attention on modernization of member firms. Often, new technology and new work organization go hand-in-hand. Many firms, especially the WRTPs smaller member firms, do not have sufficient resources to commit to modernizing their own firms. The State of Wisconsin has developed a Manufacturing Extension Program (MEP) to assist firms as they identify, adopt and adjust to needed technological modernization. The WRTP is collaborating closely with the state MEP to ensure that member firms have access to its resources and that those resources will help to serve member firms. Again, collaboration between member firms can improve learning and knowledge of technologies and the challenges that come with modernization. Both management and labor union members can investigate options and discuss the effects of modernization with firms that have already adopted new technologies. This shared experience can ease the process of modernization and improve the efficiency with which new technologies are adopted by allowing firms to avoid common mistakes.

Finally, as regards future workforce needs, WRTP programming is directed to both school-to-work initiatives and programming for dislocated and disadvantaged workers. In the last few years and in partnership with the Milwaukee Jobs Initiative (itself a labor, business, and community partnership to help extend good jobs to economically isolated residents of Milwaukee's central city), more than 500 workers, mostly African Americans and Hispanics, have been placed at WRTP member firms at an average wage of over $10.00 per hour. This is most usefully compared to welfare to work results in Milwaukee where wages average in the $7.00 or $8.00 per hour range (Bernhart, Dresser, and Rogers 2001).

As the WRTP has expanded its work into new sectors, the WRTP's role as a new kind of intermediary has become more apparent. The WRTP does not seek to replace the services provided by community-based organizations (recruiting and supporting new workers), the local technical college (which trains workers in preparation for jobs or at the work site), or employers and unions (which hire and establish work rules). Rather, the WRTP seeks to integrate the system by facilitating communication across sectors and establishing standards and norms for performance. The WRTP provides infrastructure (in the form of information and connections) required to improve the performance of other players in the labor market so that each can focus on what it does best. And, as in the case of many other examples in this chapter, the success of programming in one sector—in this case manufacturing—has provided a foundation for extending programs in new sectors.[6]

10.2.9. 'Jobs With a Future' in Dane County

In 1995, the Dane County (home of Madison, Wisconsin) Board of Supervisors constituted the Economic Summit Council—a blue-ribbon commission comprised of leaders from Dane County business, labor, public and non-profit sectors. The Summit Council was charged with developing a strategic vision for economic and workforce development in Dane County. One element of this plan is a community career ladder project to make 'jobs with a future' (JWF) available to all Dane County residents. The Center on Wisconsin Strategy (COWS) has provided lead technical and design assistance for the project.

Following a review of our experience with the WRTP, of best practices from around the country, and detailed quantitative and qualitative analysis of

---

[6] For more information, see www.wrtp.org and Bernhardt, Dresser, and Rogers (2001).

local labor-market conditions and needs, COWS identified three key sectors for development of sectoral intermediaries that could support high performance work organization on an industry wide basis. In these sectors—manufacturing, health care, and insurance and finance—COWS then conducted extensive interviews with human resource and training personnel at leading firms to identify the skill and workforce needs shared by the firms in each industry: this work recently led to decisions in each sector to establish sectoral consortia to address these needs.

The JWF Manufacturing Partnership has pursued a number of skill development programs for incumbent staff. Perhaps most impressive has been the development of basic skills programs at five member firms in conjunction with the technical college. None of these firms would have been able to develop the basic skills programs, or fill classes, on their own, but their workers now have a range of basic skills classes and supports available to them. Manufacturing partners have also worked on recruitment and developed a pre-employment training program in order to recruit new workers to the industry.

The JWF Health Care Partnership has focused on improving the quality of entry-level jobs in the industry. One identified means of improving the jobs is to improve pathways into other health care careers. To that end, local employers and the local technical college have developed short-term training for workers to move up. They have also begun discussions on industry turnover and the best means of increasing retention of frontline care-giving staff. One identified means of increasing retention was providing more opportunities for skill development. To that end, local employers have increased the training on skills for incumbent workers. Recently, the Health Care Partnership has begun to explore the state's nursing shortage and look for a role in facilitating conversations and developing programming to solve it.

Originally, the JWF Finance and Insurance Partnership focused on the development of training for technical programming positions. However, more recently the focus has been on business strategies for retaining customer service staff. Member firms now benchmark performance against each other, and participate in strategy roundtables to discuss means of improving retention of workers. The Partnership has also worked with the Dane County Job Center to improve recruitment in the city's economically disadvantaged communities.

The JWF experience suggests that there is a real role for intermediaries which pull together employers for discussions of workforce development issues. Firms participate because they gain better knowledge and services through the discussion. Workers at member firms get access to improved training opportunities and upward mobility. The public sector gains by having an easier way to identify and respond to industry needs—the technical college has created literally dozens of courses on the basis of information gathered in partnership meetings and projects. Finally, disadvantaged workers gain better information about the labor market and career opportunities in specific industries. Like the WRTP, and many other emergent WIs, JWF does not seek to replace elements of the system. Rather, JWF provides the infrastructure for communication and problem-solving and private-sector leadership that the local workforce development system lacked.[7]

10.2.10. *Strategic Focus, Increasing Scope, and Growing Ambitions*

Whether focused on improving entry-level, dead-end jobs, or aiming to improve training and advancement for workers throughout a sector, these WIs and others like them are helping to forge local solutions to labor-market problems. By targeting multiple employers, and building workforce development solutions for them, these programs have begun to show real promise as a means of improving outcomes for workers and the unemployed. Perhaps most important, as the scale of these projects grows, they become increasingly able to confront the restructuring of work, both through aiding in positive restructuring and by blocking negative forms. For example, the WRTP has begun to work with member firms to begin limiting those firms' use of temp agencies to fill open positions. The WRTP is using its own knowledge of the firms and offering its successful model of training and recruitment as a concrete alternative to recruitment by temp agencies. In so doing, they are turning 'temp jobs' back into permanent work at participating firms. Similarly, training and recruitment services of CHA in Las Vegas have reduced casinos' resistance to unions and helped leverage organizing victories in new properties. The projects are as unique as the localities and sectors that have spawned them, but they do tend to move towards increasing scale and influence on the structure of work as they grow.

The infrastructure supporting, informing, and extending these local efforts is fairly weak, but it too has grown. In some instances, the organizations themselves have helped build it. This is most clear with CHCA/PHI, where the connections in the health care industry allowed them to play the key role in developing a national coalition to advocate for quality jobs and care. It is also clear in the case of the San Francisco Hotel Partnership which is now extending its model to cities across California. Given the central role of labor unions in many of these projects, the national AFL-CIO and its Working for America Institute have played a central role in documenting and

---

[7] For more information, see Dresser (2000).

disseminating the success of union-led projects. Additionally, the national AFL-CIO has helped facilitate peer-to-peer learning and technical assistance across regions and sectors. As is also shown by Louise Trubek's chapter in this volume, such horizontal networks are important and likely become more so as this field of practice grows.

10.3. An American Model for Training?

While still in their infancy, we believe these sorts of 'high road' workforce intermediaries show considerable promise as the foundation for a new sort of 'American model' in training. In effect, they provide at the regional level what is not provided nationally—a genuine infrastructure of industry and union collaboration that both drives industries toward more demanding skill demands and provides the flow of information, and assurances against free-riding, needed to meet them. Given pressures for devolution, moreover, there is no reason why such efforts could not be more effectively integrated into public labor-market administration.

A large share of such WIs self-consciously set themselves the task of organizing particular industry sectors. And here, despite their variation, they commonly seek three sorts of efficiencies not delivered by existing labor market institutions. First, there are economies of scale obtained by expanding the breadth of employer participation within a regional labor market. Unlike modernization, workforce development, or job connection activities that adopt a narrowly customized firm-by-firm approach, a sectoral approach makes it possible to benchmark public and private sector efforts to advanced industry practices. And information sharing and standard-setting processes across organizations that account for a significant share of the market enable the participants to share the cost of replenishing the skilled labor pool. With enough market share, they gain the capacity to leverage accountability from modernization and training institutions to high-road production or service delivery. Instead of reinventing the wheel in one workplace after another, scaling up new programs spreads out the cost of their development and delivery.

Second, sector-based WIs leverage economies of scope by extending the range of policy areas responsive to the shared needs of organized firms. The development of a diversified program aligns modernization, training, and related labor-market services to the most advanced practices in the sector. Just as the scale of the initiative can capture the accumulated wisdom of learning across firms to augment common elements of curriculum and training routines, the scope of the project achieves efficiencies in program development across policy areas defined by the segment of the workforce they are intended to serve. The same set of core competencies apply whether the individual is employed, unemployed, under-employed, disadvantaged, still in school, or returning to the paid laborforce. The alignment of institutional and public policy supports for skill upgrading with a progression of proficiency standards enables workers to build on what they already know to get to where they want to go throughout their careers.

Third, a successful sectoral initiative develops positive network externalities as a growing number of employers, unions, public sector, and community-based partners come together and find ways to solve recurrent problems and meet convergent needs. By sharing information, identifying the best practice models, conducting experiments, defining curricula, and routinely benchmarking among themselves, the participants are able to sustain and diffuse high-road production or service delivery. Legitimating and disseminating advanced practices throughout a growing share of the sector facilitates joint investments made by all the stakeholders in the formation of a skilled and committed workforce. As the sector becomes more competitive relative to the low-road, the high-road firms within it may become more tied into the regional economy. With the institutional and public policy supports knitted together by a successful intermediary in the regional labor market, the sector contributes to job opportunity and career security within the region. As these initiatives help tie together their economies, they also help tie individuals into more promising careers. Like the best community-based training programs, sectoral initiatives help provide provide 'bridges' across social boundaries to better jobs (Harrison and Weiss 1998; Melendez and Harrison 1998).

Summarizing across these efficiency effects, successful sectoral initiatives create a 'win–win' situation for firms, workers, and new labor-market entrants from the community. Such initiatives may increase demand for a skilled and committed workforce; enhance learning across business, labor, and community organizations; facilitate benchmarking and standard-setting across them; enable related firms to pool their investments in human capital; leverage the accountability of public institutions to the high road; realize efficiencies in the delivery of supports and services; build the capacity of a wider range of players in the labor market; clarify entry-level skill requirements and advancement opportunities; and improve the employment relations climate in the area.

10.4. Getting to Scale, Building a System

It is not much of a step from the sectoral base to the more functional integration of regional labor-market services, with representatives of regional sectoral consortia providing the natural ballast and direction for program administration. Whatever the many confusions of US training reform at present, the clear and broad direction is toward greater state discretion in the administration of workforce development systems. The recent Workforce Investment Act (WIA) explicitly invites state experimentation, and provides resources either directly or through 'individual training accounts' to capture resources to sustain it. Many states have accepted this invitation, albeit in the context as well of the massive dislocations associated with welfare reform. And many of the most advanced changes have inclined toward some version of the 'partnership' model, assigning intermediaries a greater role in setting standards, monitoring training, determining the regional content of training, and so on. Gradually what seems to be happening is that sectoral intermediaries are taking on a more and more formal role in the public system, in effect filling out the membership as well as program of many of the 'Workforce Investment Boards' (WIBs) that are mandated by WIA on a regional basis. Thus, one could easily imagine that were the independent impulse to sectoral consortia more fully realized, these changes in the public system themselves could accelerate.

Consolidation of labor-market services, moreover, might be naturally extended to include elements of the fledgling MEP program that has grown up in the United States. While presently under attack in the budget pro-posals of the Bush administration, this program enjoys broad business support. Federally supported but essentially state-based, it provides technical assist-ance to small- and medium-sized manufacturers to upgrade their operations through better use of new technology, information systems, and work organization. It is now capable of reaching tens of thousands of firms annually with such assistance on upgrading. Operating at some $300 million annually, it is the most significant US program acting directly on the demand side of the training equation.

The result would be, in effect, a series of regional labor-market boards, with financial resources to apply to both the supply and demand sides of that equation, and considerable leverage within a more organized private sector.

How movement to such a system might be encouraged is also straightfor-ward enough. Without mandating such industry organization, participation in it could reasonably be offered as a condition for discounts on public train-ing assistance—the rationale being that public dollars are best spent where private leverage and representativeness is demonstrated—with reciprocal premia applied to supports for non-participating firms. Such boards could be charged as well with local implementation of the national skills standards, providing some baseline coordination of their activities. And the process of organizing regional industry and labor—based on our experience, perhaps surprisingly, not a desperately hard thing to do—could be supported through demonstration grants and a minimal national technical assistance infrastructure. The Department of Labor has recently signaled its interest in doing just this, with 'Regional Skills Alliance' grants provided for replicating high-road partnership work on the order of $20 million annually.

Of course, whether any of this happens fast enough to capture the energies now unleashed by reform-mindedness and devolution is not something we can confidently predict. But it is certainly a development worth watching, and for Europeans the fact that it is already happening unselfconsciously, without almost any explicit public support, may carry some interesting lessons. Based on the experience in the most liberal of polities, with the greatest hostility to government, with the weakest associational structures in business and the most decimated labor movement, it appears that there is at least a plausible way to functional, flexible, and politically supported labor-market administration—at the regional level. That level of administration appears to capture the operative efficiencies of associational action, while being sufficiently tutored by local experience, and allowing a speed and flexibility in government response, to satisfy firm demands for such attention to their new competitive realities.

10.5. The Role of Organized Labor

Finally, however, a note on the future role of one of the most important 'players' in the new intermediary discussion, namely organized labor. Unions have perhaps the most to gain through higher valuation of intermediary functions, since they themselves, at least in part, are such an intermediary. They enjoy a loyal if shrinking base of members that generally trust their leadership, and certainly the importance of the role they play in navigating present labor-market conditions. Their competitive advantage in the intermediary world derives in part from this obvious resource, but in part too from their close historical understanding of the micro-politics of standard setting, training, evaluation, job placement, and job advancement. But the real prize of involvement, of course, would be greater union ability to influence the terms of employment beyond its organized base, greater ability to respond to changes within it, and through the harmonization of those two conditions greater ability to reduce or simply overcome the employer resistance that is currently killing unions as an important institution in American life.

But organized labor has been relatively reluctant to get into the intermediary game, at least relative to the obvious opportunities it would seem to offer. This is chiefly because it has seen such involvement as a distraction from its most immediate problem, namely declining membership. Under the 'new voices' leadership team headed by John Sweeney, which took charge of the national AFL-CIO in 1995 after the first contested leadership election in the federation's history, labor has sought to make 'changing to organize'—that is, to make the internal organizational changes to expand its dwindling membership base—the centerpiece of all its efforts. But at least as organizing has traditionally been understood, WI activities of the sort described here have been accorded a distinctly secondary importance in achieving it.

Now, however, it is commonly recognized that the 'changing to organize' program has been a failure. Seven years into the 'new voices' team's leadership, union density is even lower than when they took office. And so there are signs that labor will alter this view, as it looks more broadly to different strategies for advancing its power. Suggestions on these abound, but the most promising all involve a break with the single-minded concentration, characteristic of the postwar American labor movement, on achieving majority membership in individual employment settings, in order to be the exclusive bargaining agent on behalf of workers there, and eventually to achieve and then administer a collective bargaining agreement with their employer.

Instead, the new thinking is some old thinking—to return to earlier aspirations in American labor to be 'the voice of many that speaks for all', to care less about immediate achievement of majorities and more simply about building worker presence in the economy, to be less concerned with jumping the many hoops of the existing legal system, to be more directly political in its local operations, to be more intent on changing broader opportunities for employment at work under acceptable terms: economic democracy linked to social democracy. The natural direction of taking these suggestions seriously would be a labor movement that was much more dependent on its ties to friends outside its immediate ranks, more accommodating and inclusive of diverse membership, and more concerned in general with establishing itself as the conscience and steward of the broader economy. It is too soon to tell if American labor will move in this alternative direction. If it does, however, the emerging WI considered here will, we are quite certain, be seen as vital to its future course.[8]

References

Aspen Institute (2002). *Working with Value: Industry-specific Approaches to Workforce Development*. Washington DC: The Aspen Institute.

BARKER, K. and CHRISTIANSEN, K. (1998). *Contingent Work: American Employment Relations in Transition*. Ithaca: ILR Press.

---

[8] For discussion of some of the debate around this choice, and its particular implications for labor's structure, see Rathke and Rogers (1996) and Freeman and Rogers (2002).

BERNHARDT, A., DRESSER, L., and HATTON, E. (2002). 'The Coffee Pot Wars: Unions and Firm Restructuring in the Hotel Industry'. Unpublished paper.

———— and ROGERS, J. (2001). 'Taking the High Road in Milwaukee: The Wisconsin Regional Training Partnership'. *Working USA: The Journal of Labor and Society*, Winter 2001/2002. 5/3: 109–30.

——Morris, M., HANDCOCK, M., and SCOTT, M. (2001a). *Divergent Paths: Economic Mobility in the New American Labor Market*. New York: Russell Sage Foundation.

——PASTOR, M., HATTON, E., and ZIMMERMAN, S. (2001b). 'Moving the Demand Side: Intermediaries in a Changing Labor Market'. Paper presented at the Industrial Relations Research Association Annual Meeting. New Orleans, LA.

CARRÉ, F., FERBER, M. A., GOLDEN, L., and HERZENBERG, S. (eds) (2000). *Nonstandard Work: The Nature and Challenges of Changing Employment Arrangements*. Champaign, IL: Industrial Relations Research Association.

DICKEY, W., ROGERS, J., and SMITH, M. (2001). 'Punishing Inequalities: Race and Criminal Justice in Wisconsin', *Wisconsin Academy Review*, 47: 16–23.

DRESSER, L. (2000). 'Building Jobs With a Future in Wisconsin: Lessons from Dane County', in F. Carré, M. A. Ferber, L. Golden, and S. Herzenberg (eds). *Nonstandard Work: The Nature and Challenges of Changing Employment Arrangements*. Champaign, IL: Industrial Relations Research Association.

FREEMAN, R. (2000). 'Single-Peaked vs. Diversified Capitalism: The Relation Between Economic Institutions and Outcomes'. *NBER Working Paper* 7556. Cambridge MA: National Bureau of Economic Research.

——and ROGERS, J. (1996). 'Die Quintessenz: Der Inneramerikanischen Debatte'. *Mitbestimmung*, July–August: 12–17. Available at http://www.boeckler.de/mitbestimmung/index.cgi?ihv=56#inhalt

——(2002). 'Open Source Unionism'. *Working USA*, 5: 8–40.

GOTTSCHALK, P. (1999). 'Work as a Stepping Stone for Low-Skilled Workers: What is the Evidence?' in K. Kaye and D. Smith Nightingale (eds), *The Low-Wage Labor Market: Challenges and Opportunities for Economic Self-Sufficiency*. Washington DC: The Urban Institute, 171–85.

GRUBB, N. (1996). *Learning to Work: The Case for Reintegrating Job Training and Education*. New York: Russell Sage Foundation.

JACOBSON, L. (1995). *The Effectiveness of the Employment Service*. Washington, DC: Advisory Commission on Unemployment Compensation, US Government Printing Office.

HARRISON, B. and WEISS, M. (1998). *Workforce Development Networks: Community-Based Organizations and Regional Alliances*. Thousand Oaks: Sage Publications.

HUDSON, K. (1999). 'No Shortage of "Nonstandard" Jobs'. Economic Policy Institute Briefing Paper. Washington DC: Economic Policy Institute.

LANE, J., MIKELSON, K. S. SHARKEY, P. T., and WISSOKER, D. (2001). *Low-income and Low-skilled Workers' Involvement in Nonstandard Employment*. Washington DC: The Urban Institute.

MEAD, L. (1997). *From Welfare to Work: Lessons from America*. London: Institute of Economic Affairs.

MELENDEZ, E. and HARRISON, B. (1998). 'Matching the Disadvantaged to Job Opportunities: Structural Explanations for the Past Successes of the Center for Employment Training.' *Economic Development Quarterly*, 12/1: 3–11.

MISHEL, L., BERNSTEIN, J., and SCHMITT, J. (2001). *The State of Working America 2000–2001*. Washington DC: Economic Policy Institute.

—— and TEIXEIRA, R. (1990). *The Myth of the Coming Labor Shortage: Jobs, Skills and Incomes of America's Workforce 2000*. Washington DC: Economic Policy Institute.

OSTERMAN, P. (1999). *Securing Prosperity: The American Labor Market: How It Has Changed and What to Do about It*. Princeton NJ: Princeton University Press.

PAVETTI, L. (2000). 'Welfare Policy in Transition: Redefining the Social Contract for Poor Citizen Families with Children.' *Focus*, 21/2,44–50.

POLIVKA, A. (1996). 'Into Contingent and Alternative Employment: By Choice?'. *Monthly Labor Review*, 119: 55–74.

—— COHANY, S., and HIPPLE, S. (2000). 'Definition, Composition, and Economic Consequences of the Nonstandard Workforce', in F. Carré *et al.* (eds), *Nonstandard Work: The Nature and Challenges of Changing Employment Arrangements*. Champaign, IL: Industrial Relations Research Association, 41–94.

RATHKE, W. and ROGERS, J. (1996). 'A Strategy for Labor'. *Dissent*, 43 (Fall): 78–84.

ROSE, S. (1999). 'Is Mobility in the United States Still Alive? Tracking Career Opportunities and Income Growth'. *International Review of Applied Economics*, 13/3: 417.

SEGAL, L. M. and SULLIVAN, D. (1997). 'The Growth of Temporary Services Work.' *Journal of Economic Perspectives*, Spring, 11/2: 2–19.

US Bureau of Labor Statistics (1999). 'Contingent and Alternative Employment Arrangements, February 1999'. Available at ftp://ftp.bls.gov/pub/news.release/History/onemp.12211999.news.

US Department of Health and Human Services (2002). 'Percent of Total US Population on Welfare, 1960–1999.' Available at http://www.acf.dhhs.gov/news/stats/6097rf.htm.

Working for America Institute (2000). 'The High Road Partnerships Report'. Available at www.workingforamerica.org/documents/HighRoadReport/highroadreport.htm.

11

Health Care and Low-wage Work in the United States: Linking Local Action for Expanded Coverage

LOUISE G. TRUBEK

11.1. Introduction

In Winter 2001, two unlikely allies—a health advocacy group (Families USA) and the trade association for health insurance companies (Health Insurance Association of America)—announced an agreement to develop a meaningful proposal to extend health coverage to the uninsured, stating 'it is not an intractable public policy problem but could be addressed if the various health care stakeholders could only find common ground' (Kahn and Pollack 2001: 20). The announcement provided few details of the proposal. However, the optimism underlying the announcement of a consumer-health plan alliance is a reflection of events over the last eight years.

The Clinton health plan was an effort to achieve a seamless universal system through an elaborate, federally controlled, and all embracing system. The United States provides health coverage to people in three different systems: employment-based health insurance, public programs, and *ad hoc* treatment for the uninsured. Each system has its own complex regulatory and eligibility mechanisms that are governed at the state, federal, and local levels, as well as by the private market. The Clinton health plan was defeated in part because it was viewed as an attempt to replace these complex health coverage institutions with a mammoth bureaucracy. When the Clinton health plan failed, a gap was created in possible approaches to achieving the regulatory confluence. It left a public policy vacuum.

In the intervening eight years, viable new approaches to expand health care coverage, termed 'incremental' have been emerging to fill the vacuum. The

I would like to thank Barbara J. Zabawa for her knowledgeable research and her imaginative insights into health care policy and law. Some material contained in this chapter was published in *Health Matrix*, 12/1: 157–79.

consumer-health plan alliance proposal reflects the belief that an incremental approach could be politically viable and effective. This belief reflects two major shifts: the movement down and the movement out. The movement down is the devolution of public programs and planning from the federal level in Washington, DC to the states. The movement out reflects privatization, which is an increased reliance on private institutions to satisfy public needs. The interaction of these two phenomena is creating a set of institutions that enable a vision of state-based public–private approaches to expanded health care coverage. The viability of these new institutions will be tested by the first downturn in the economy experienced since the boom economy that followed the demise of the Clinton plan. People are losing their jobs and employers with falling profits are cutting back on benefits. The ability of this new system positively to react and provide coverage will be tested.

This chapter proceeds in three sections. Section 11.2 identifies the policy goals, authority and funding that created the climate for transferring health coverage initiatives to the states. Section 11.3 documents the emerging public/private mechanisms that are developing to link the state-based health initiatives, allowing a seamless and horizontal structure. Section 11.4 describes the challenges to the emerging new system and proposes solutions to expand coverage in a weakening economy. These challenges include: (a) linking public and private plans; (b) effectively meeting workplace and workforce needs; and (c) integrating the safety net into the mainstream health care financing system.

11.2. The Move to the States—The Movement Down

The public policy vacuum created by the failure of the Clinton plan is being filled by state-based initiatives that provide coverage and access for low-income people. The moving down to the states for the expansion of health coverage to low-wage people can be viewed as another example of devolution of public services and functions to lower government levels. A report summarized the trends in state-based initiatives in the past 25 years pointing out that the states 'in their roles as regulators, purchasers, and providers have created state-funded programs, expanded and restructured Medicaid, experimented with individual and small business subsidies, established purchasing alliances, and indigent care programs and crafted children's health coverage' (NASHP 2000a: 1). The Floodtide report analyzed the state-based programs by studying how state officials used their bureaucratic roles to create more coverage. The report divided state initiatives into two sections: comprehensive approaches and incremental reforms. These examples included a quarter of the states, demonstrating the strength of the state-based approach. The report states, 'In serving as laboratories, states have tested reforms that have later been enacted federally'. Two examples of states that in the early 1990s envisioned a comprehensive approach are Minnesota and Washington. Minnesota's program was a result of an express commitment on the part of the government to a universal health coverage program. They used provider and tobacco taxes and premiums to pay for the program which provided coverage to people up to moderate income (DHS/Health Care: MinnesotaCare web site). Low-income adults without children are eligible. Washington relied on an employer-based approach requiring employers to offer coverage and premium subsidies for low-income workers. This was an early effort to achieve expanded access at the state level and was not very successful.

These preliminary efforts to develop state-based programs were the precursors to the accelerated creation of ambitious state programs that developed after the passage of welfare reform in 1996. There are two major factors for this rapid acceleration: welfare reform intersecting with the lack of health coverage in the workplace, and the enactment of a children's health program combined with flexible federal standards. One of the striking aspects of this acceleration is that states used different mechanisms and strategies to exploit this opportunity to increase coverage. The approaches taken by the states to some extent reflected their earlier experiments of the late 1980s and early 1990s. One overview states that the general findings of the early state experimentation was that the success of various strategies differ, Medicaid has been an important platform for state-based reform and provides critical resources to finance access initiatives, and state solutions respond to local needs and capacities (NASHP 2000*a*: 42).

This chapter relies on a Wisconsin case study of the evolving state-based public–private approach to providing health care coverage, which reflects the possibilities created by welfare reform and the passage of the Children's Health Insurance Program. This is not because Wisconsin is a unique, ahead-of-its-time exemplary project. The state-based efforts at creating widespread access following welfare reform are evident in other states as well, such as New York. The State of New York enacted the Health Care Reform Act 2000, which expands access to health care coverage for up to one million New Yorkers. The motivation for this expansion is similar to that displayed in Wisconsin. However, New York's program also incorporated an indigent care pool and restructuring of health facilities (NASHP 2000*b*).

11.2.1. *Brief History of BadgerCare*

Wisconsin has addressed the needs of the working uninsured with a new program titled 'BadgerCare' (the state mascot animal). It is an outgrowth of the

Medicaid program, which is the United States' public health insurance program for low-income people (KFF 1999). BadgerCare went into effect in 1999 to cover low-income families using a combination of Medicaid and a new federal program, the State Children's Health Insurance Program (SCHIP). BadgerCare was developed as part of Wisconsin's welfare reform initiative.

To be eligible for BadgerCare, a family must meet three general criteria. First, the family must be currently uninsured, have an income under $26,000 for a family of three, and have no access to employer-based health insurance (Wisconsin Administrative Code § 103.03(1)(f)(2) 2000 making the provision that the family currently does not have health insurance and that the family did not have health insurance coverage in the three months prior to becoming eligible for BadgerCare). Many families in BadgerCare at the higher income levels must contribute towards the health insurance premium. To a limited extent, these premiums help defray the cost of BadgerCare to the state (Peacock 2000). However, federal funds pay the bulk of the program. Those that qualify for BadgerCare receive care under one of the most expansive public health insurance programs in the nation.[1]

Since the program's inception on July 1, 1999, BadgerCare has attracted more eligible people than expected (Peacock 2000: 2). After one year, 66,545 people have enrolled in BadgerCare, including 18,535 children and 48,010 adults (DHFS 2000*b*). BadgerCare's popularity extends into the political arena. For example, at the federal level, the focus during the Senate confirmation hearings approving former Governor Tommy Thompson to head the federal Department of Health and Human Services was on the success of BadgerCare (Sen. Peggy Rosenzweig at the 'Covering Kids' Wisconsin Meeting, Madison, WI, March 21, 2001). In Wisconsin, at the state level, politicians from both major parties are heavily invested in BadgerCare and want to see the program continue. The program is also popular among both rural and urban groups. Some legislators have attributed BadgerCare's bipartisan support to the efforts of local community collaborations and activists (*ibid.*).

In Fall 2001 the success of BadgerCare in enrolling participants began to assume a more negative view to some. The emerging weakening of the economy was immediately reflected in BadgerCare enrollment. In October 2001 the BadgerCare enrollment jumped to 90,592 people. One newspaper reported that formerly upper income people were now enrolling in BadgerCare and other public programs (*Wisconsin State Journal* 2001). As of October 2001 the number of people in Medicaid programs including

---

[1] 'Wisconsin is one of only 10 states that pay for medical social workers' services; Wisconsin is one of 28 states that pay for chiropractors' services; Wisconsin is one of 38 states that pay for dentures; and Wisconsin is one of 14 states that pay for respiratory care services' (*Wisconsin State Journal* 2000). For a comprehensive list of BadgerCare services, see Wis. Stat. § 49.46(2) (1999).

BadgerCare stood at an all-time high of 539,450 people covering one in ten Wisconsin residents (Memo from Mary Bradley, December 6, 2001). In addition to the increases in costs of enrollees, the State also faces a declining budget prospect with the weakening economy. It faces hard choices with the popularity of BadgerCare, which it created, and the tight fiscal situation. Wisconsin shares this dilemma with other states. One National Governors' Association official stated 'States cannot provide services for new people coming on to the Medicaid rolls in their current financial situation' (NGA 2001*a*).

11.2.2. *Welfare Reform Interacting with Workplace Health Coverage Gaps*

The welfare reform efforts of the mid-1990s converged with the lack of workplace coverage to create a driving force for state-based health coverage expansion. The combination of the commitment to making work pay of the welfare reformers, the lack of health insurance coverage at the low-wage workplace, and the movement of authority and funding to the state level created an atmosphere for state-based initiatives in providing health coverage for low-wage workers. Change in the welfare system occurred at the federal level under the 1996 Personal Responsibility and Work Opportunity Reconciliation Act (PRWORA). This Act eliminated the Aid to Families with Dependent Children (AFDC) program and replaced it with a block grant program (called 'Temporary Assistance to Needy Families'—TANF) to help needy parents end their dependence on government benefits by promoting job training, work, and marriage (PRWORA 1996). The block grant system gave states wide latitude on how to design their own system within broad federal standards. This is part of the trend toward devolution in public programs. Before welfare reform, people who received government income assistance under AFDC were automatically eligible for health insurance under Medicaid (NCSL 1999). Under the new TANF program, however, Medicaid is separated from government income assistance. Consequently, many former welfare recipients were dropped from Medicaid, even though they were still eligible. Furthermore, the separation of Medicaid from income assistance complicated state attempts to 'reposition the Medicaid program to help boost the transition to work' (*ibid.*).

Parallel to PRWORA, Wisconsin enacted its own legislation to replace the AFDC program with 'Wisconsin Works' (or W-2. Wisconsin Laws 1995: 289). W-2 has been characterized as 'an employment and training program, rather than a means of providing income support' (Coughlin *et al.* 1998). To help make 'work pay', Wisconsin had to create a health insurance program for low-wage workers who were forced off the traditional welfare system and whose income would make them ineligible for the traditional Medicaid program: 'welfare reformers realized that changes in health insurance for low-income families were essential in order to have a work-based strategy succeed' (Trubek 1999: 148–9). Federal and state welfare reformers realized that people leaving welfare are less likely to work in jobs that offer health insurance, due to low-wage labor market characteristics. In the first years after welfare reform, one study found that 'fewer than 25% of families leaving welfare for work reported having employment-based health coverage' (NCSL 1999). Welfare reformers also recognized the importance of health coverage in promoting and sustaining work. For example, 'health care promotes job retention; illness contributes to job loss'. Additionally, postponing health care needs results in more costly care later on (*ibid.*).

However, the issue of the relationship between low-wage workers and health care coverage propelled the welfare reformers to develop a program broader than covering those just leaving the AFDC system. They understood the resentment of the low-wage worker struggling without health care coverage who never was a welfare recipient. Thus, the advocates for BadgerCare intended the program to cover any family who had no coverage and was low-income. They were therefore forced to confront the complexity of the relationship between low-wage work and health care coverage. To understand the complexity of the relationship between work and health care in the United States, one must look at the sources of health coverage. Fifty-one percent of low-income people are covered by employer-based health insurance, 35 percent are covered by public programs such as Medicaid, and 15 percent are uninsured. Although they are not required to provide health benefits to their employees (Matthew 1996), US employers carry the primary burden of providing health insurance coverage to workers.[2] This burden, however, has translated into a popular desire (and perhaps expectation) by US workers to obtain health insurance coverage through employers, and not the government (Schoen, Strumpf, and Davis 2000). Unfortunately, employer-based insurance is not uniform across all types of jobs and workplaces. Low-wage workers over the past 50 years have moved from large-employer, manufacturing jobs to small employer, service jobs (Dresser and Rogers 1997). As a result, rather than acquiring a permanent job with upward mobility possibilities, today's low-wage worker finds herself in 'dead-end jobs' (*ibid.*). These jobs are found, for example, in the service, clerical, hospitality, and health care sectors (*ibid.*: 2–10; Middleton 1996). Dead-end jobs are characterized as low-wage, having no upward mobility and offering few (if any) fringe benefits (Schwab 1995; Dresser and Rogers 1997). Furthermore, these jobs are often

---

[2] Eighty-four percent of people who were covered by health insurance in 1999, 62.8% of those had coverage through their employer as opposed to 24.1% of insured people who were covered by a government program (*ibid.*).

contingent (i.e. temporary, leased, or part-time), and are prone to a high rate of turnover.[3] Low-wage jobs offer inadequate health insurance. Although Wisconsin's unemployment rate has been steadily decreasing since 1990 and is below that of the United States as a whole (BLS 2000*a,b,c*)[4] many low-wage employers may still find it difficult or unappealing to offer health insurance to attract low-wage workers.[5] 'Many employers of part-time and temporary workers either cannot afford to pay insurance for their employees or simply do not want to invest in these workers who will not be around for the long term' (Schroeder 1995). For example, in a recent interview with a large Wisconsin call center, which employs many low-wage, part-time workers, the employer revealed that it only offered health insurance to full-time workers because those workers were the most committed to the company.[6]

Thus, the welfare reformers undertook the mammoth job of creating a state-based health insurance program for low-wage families in order to demonstrate that welfare reform could produce people who were working in decent jobs with health care coverage. BadgerCare was their creation. Since the reformers wanted to market the program to make it successful, they designed it to look like an insurance program rather than a welfare program. BadgerCare marketing reduced the stigma that often attaches to public benefit programs and thus has contributed to the program's popularity. Wisconsin has strategically marketed BadgerCare as an insurance program rather than public assistance. Researchers suspect that the stigma related to enrolling in public assistance programs such as Medicaid deters people from applying for coverage (Garrett and Holahan 2000). Particularly in the wake of welfare reform, studies attributed some of the decline in Medicaid enrollees to the stigma attached to the program (*ibid.*). According to one state official, 'no one in the general public thinks of BadgerCare as welfare Medicaid. They think of it as an insurance program without the welfare stigma'.[7] A Wisconsin Legislator partially attributed BadgerCare's large enrollment to the program's

---

[3] Dresser and Rogers (1997) provide an example of one employer, in the hotel business, as having a turnover rate of 100%. The employees view this employer's jobs as 'something to do for a couple of months and they're gone'. See also Dietrich, Emsellem, and Ruckelshaus (1998).

[4] From this series of data, one discovers that Wisconsin's unemployment rate in September 2000 was 3.6%, compared to the national rate of 3.9%. According to the statistics, Wisconsin's unemployment rate fell from 4.6% in January 1990 to 2.8% in January 2000. Nationally, for the same time period, the unemployment rate fell from 5.4% to 4.0%.

[5] According to one small business group in Wisconsin, 81% of the group's members indicate that health insurance is needed to attract employees. But, because of cost pressure, small businesses are struggling to continue with health insurance benefits. Interview with Bill Smith, State Director, National Federation of Independent Businesses, in Madison, WI (14 November 2000).

[6] Interview by Barbara J. Zabawa with Wisconsin shoe retailer, 10 October 2001.

[7] Interview with Angela Dombrowicki, Director, Bureau of Managed Health Care Programs, DHFS, in Madison, WI (3 November 2000).

'cute name' and disassociation from welfare.[8] The brochures that advertise BadgerCare describe the program as 'Health Insurance for Working Families' and convey no connection to Medicaid (DHFS 1999). Consequently, more low-wage employees may be willing to participate in BadgerCare, especially since the program is a much better deal than most employer-sponsored insurance and is not viewed as a welfare program.

A remaining issue is how to interweave the private health care coverage, which is offered by many employers to low-wage workers, while offering BadgerCare to uninsured workers. The welfare reformers had to design a program that would not discourage employers from offering health coverage to workers, since the employer-based system was still necessary in order to reduce the overall number of uninsured families. It is an especially difficult task since even if a low-wage employer offers health insurance, the cost of that insurance may be prohibitively high or the benefits comparatively low to those offered in public programs such as BadgerCare. According to one study, 'low-wage firms tend to pay a smaller percentage of premium costs and to offer policies with fewer benefits' (Jecker 1994: 262). For example, one temporary worker who earned $11.50 per hour paid $300 per month for health insurance to cover both herself and her children, absorbing a significant amount from each paycheck (Henly 1999). However, to receive the comprehensive benefits offered under BadgerCare, the most a family of three earning about $26,000 annually would have to pay per month would be $60 (DHFS 2000*a*).[9] Therefore, the benefits low-wage workers receive in employer-sponsored plans pale in comparison to the benefits offered in BadgerCare, especially when one compares the cost to the employee.[10]

Wisconsin attempted to weave BadgerCare into the employer-based system through at least two techniques. One technique prohibited the potential enrollee from enrolling in BadgerCare if they had been covered by an employer-based plan in the prior three months. The second technique is the Health Insurance Premium Payment (HIPP) program. If the employer of a BadgerCare applicant pays for at least 80 percent of the cost of a group health insurance plan, the applicant is not eligible for BadgerCare (Wisconsin Administrative Code § 103.03(f)(3) (2000)). If the applicant's employer pays between 60 percent and 80 percent of the cost of a group health insurance plan, the applicant is eligible for BadgerCare, but may be required to participate in the HIPP or 'buy-in' program (Wisconsin Administrative Code § 108.02(13) (2000)). The buy-in program allows the State to purchase the coverage offered by the applicant's

---

[8] Interview with Judy Robson, Wisconsin State Senator, in Madison, WI (15 November 2000).
[9] BadgerCare monthly income limits for a family of three earning between 185% to 200% FPL range from $2,139.83 to $2,313.33 (*ibid.*).
[10] Interview with Angela Dombrowicki; Interview with Bill Smith.

employer if the purchase is more cost effective than providing coverage under BadgerCare (*ibid.*).

New York also implemented a program, 'Healthy New York' that attempted to expand coverage through the employer-based system. This program subsidizes health insurance for small businesses and individuals who buy their own health insurance. It offers a basic health insurance product to those entities at a lower cost than what those entities can purchase outside the program. The state participates by purchasing coverage for high cost claims experienced by individuals or small businesses. This program demonstrates New York's commitment to sustain the private insurance system and to use state resources as a safety net (NASHP 2000*b*).

11.2.3. *Children's Health Coverage Funding Intersection with Flexible Federal Standards*

The ambition of the Wisconsin welfare reformers to create expanded health care coverage for low-income workers might have foundered on fiscal constraints if the infusion of additional federal dollars had not occurred. The enactment of the State Children's Health Insurance Program (SCHIP) in 1997[11] created a new federally funded program, tied to Medicaid, for states to expand health care coverage. The quick passage of SCHIP was due in part to the national emphasis on children as a priority and was a direct outcome of the public desire to improve children's lives. The strong public support for coverage of children allowed the SCHIP program to have substantial outreach and consumer-orientation as states developed their programs. The significant outreach and streamlining that are part of the SCHIP program have now affected the view of how to design public programs. Wisconsin has used SCHIP funds to help support BadgerCare. Wisconsin applied for a waiver, which was eventually approved, allowing BadgerCare to cover both children and parents (Sirica 2001). Wisconsin argued that covering parents would increase enrollment of children. This waiver pushed BadgerCare into the national limelight, helping the program serve as a model to other states that wanted to expand health coverage to more workers.

The development of relatively easy waivers to obtain significant amounts of federal funding from both Medicaid and SCHIP have allowed the states to develop their own unique health-care coverage programs. The use of federal waivers has become popular since 1993 with respect to Medicaid, and state application for federal waivers is steadily increasing (*ibid.*). Although the federal government sets the terms and conditions by which states must abide in

---

[11] Balanced Budget, Pub. L. No. 105–33, § 4901, 111 Stat. 251, 275 (1997).

order to receive federal funding for programs such as Medicaid and SCHIP, the federal government does allow states to apply for 'waivers' to experiment outside the federal rules. According to one health policy expert, 'after 1993, you can begin to see that the flexibility has become increasingly visible. The use of waivers to accommodate state diversity is pretty phenomenal under the Clinton administration' (*ibid.*: 8). The Floodtide paper, referred to earlier, points out that the SCHIP demonstrates that the greater the flexibility the states have in tailoring their programs to meet local needs, the greater their response to expand coverage. Since the enactment of the Children's Health Plan, Washington, for example, is developing a program that uses Medicaid and Children's Health Program funds to expand coverage to underserved groups through greater use of co-pays and less generous benefit packages (DSHS 2001).

Thus, devolution in health-care coverage has been rapid and diverse. The concern that welfare reform would leave many uninsured, the strong economy producing low-wage jobs, the availability of new federal funding and the loosening of federal control on the states have all allowed the explosion of diverse state-based programs. The embedded nature of devolution is demonstrated by the current debate on the reauthorization of PRWORA. Despite widespread participation of many groups attempting to change specific policies and laws within the legislation, there is little effort to return the power to the federal government. State and local agencies that are now running the programs have coalesced in alliances to support the devolution (Haskins and Blank 2001).

11.3. The Move to Public/Private Coordination—The Movement Out

The first section of this chapter discussed the devolution of authority and funding to the state level. This 'movement down' is allowing a variety of state-based initiatives expanding health-care coverage. The second section describes another phenomenon in health care: the movement out. The movement out is a series of systems that link public and private organizations and is related to what is often called 'privatization', an increased reliance on the private institutions of society to satisfy public needs. The institutions involved in this shift are quite diverse, ranging from the marketplace to corporations, to charitable organizations and the family (Handler 1996). A contradictory situation was created when the welfare reformers pushed for state initiatives in health-care coverage. The federal legislation known as the Employment Retirement Income Security Act (ERISA) of 1974, which regulates employer-based coverage, limited the regulatory power of the states over employer-based plans. Therefore, the states were given a space in which to provide programs, but have been limited in their abilities to coordinate with employer-based programs. The mechanisms for linking across states are emerging to fill this regulatory gap.

These mechanisms that link public and private organizations occur both within states and across states. They create the potential for seamless coverage through encouraging transfer of knowledge, funding, and influence. These linkages overcome the fragmentation of local level experimentation and the isolation of singular state innovation. They accomplish this through the intermeshing of a knowledge base and of actors. These knowledgeable actors are in a position to implement health programs and policies.

An example of this new movement out is the Kellogg Foundation's Community Voices Initiative, an ambitious effort to achieve expanded access through using community providers as a learning community. The Kellogg Foundation is funding 13 communities to 'form the building blocks of a national effort to heal the health care system'. The goal of the project is to build from the community level and give the underserved a voice to help make health care access and quality part of the national debate. The Kellogg project funds learning communities to sort out what works from what does not in meeting the needs of those who receive inadequate or no health care. The projects are located throughout the nation. The Foundation provides consultants to assist each project, including evaluators. Each local project includes a public and private partnership. The goals of these learning communities is to share the results so that a policy outcome can be reached that can be part of what is viewed as a forthcoming debate on universal health care coverage (Meyer and Silow-Carroll 2000).

The ability to develop local collaborations across the traditional public and private divide is the first step. Even more important is the ability of these local collaborations to share information and findings, allowing them to participate in the development of how society can expand health care access. This collaborative learning process can provide a scale that overcomes the limits of fragmentary programs and local parochialism by connecting the plethora of small locally-based initiatives appearing in diverse settings. A scale requires reciprocal interaction: sometimes the local action helps create the state action, and vice versa. It is an interactive process.

11.3.1. *Collaborations and Delivery Systems Across the Community*

11.3.1.1. *Local Collaborations*
For comprehensive and accessible coverage, it is essential to bring together local actors who share the necessary information. The complexity of local conditions that affect coverage requires detailed knowledge to insure that the

system responds both to the local labor force and the types of health-care coverage that are available. The collaborative model allows the variety of actors to share their information and 'problem-solve' by collectively allocating responsibilities for program development and implementation. These collaborations encompass representatives from traditionally antagonistic or separate spheres.

Wisconsin's BadgerCare program in Milwaukee had unique needs that required an approach different from the implementation in the rest of the State. Milwaukee has a distinctive experience with W-2. The W-2 population remaining in the State is concentrated almost exclusively in Milwaukee County. The entire county was divided into five regions and contracts were given to private for-profit and non-profit agencies to provide welfare services. The State, with the cooperation of local leadership, rapidly dismantled the former public system. One result of the confusion and inadequate community input was a substantial reduction in Medicaid enrollment.

The BadgerCare Coordination Network was formed to 'promote healthy individuals and families by providing easy access to publicly funded resources through collaboration and coordination by community organizations and local and state government agencies' (BadgerCare Coordination Network 2001). The Committee consists of the contracting W-2 agencies, state agencies, schools, health maintenance organizations (HMOs), community clinics, and major health-care providers that meet regularly. The Commissioner of Health for the City of Milwaukee indicated, 'he has never participated in such a successful collaboration. We all look each other in the eye and will not leave until we have decided on an approach to a problem' (Foldy 2001). The Committee is largely responsible for the development of a simplified form for applying for BadgerCare. The Committee has also led the initiative to coordinate closely with Milwaukee Public Schools in identifying and enrolling low-income families into BadgerCare.

Providing health-care coverage to small businesses is the goal of the Wisconsin Coalition of Health Insurance Reform. Members include small business groups, government agencies, insurers, providers, and health advocates. Agencies that administer public health insurance programs such as BadgerCare are unaware of the workplace conditions that the program enrollees and their employers experience. This information, however, is essential if the public and private systems are to merge successfully. The Coalition meets regularly to share information and to agree on advocacy for their proposed programs. Two major initiatives of the Coalition are to ensure that small and rural business voices are heard in the administration of BadgerCare and to secure passage of funding to initiate a small business health insurance pool, which would assist small businesses in obtaining quality and affordable private coverage. The collaboration sees the availability of health insurance as crucial to small and rural business viability.

11.3.1.2. *Community-based Delivery Systems*

Community collaboration at the local level reveals the gaps in not only coverage but also service delivery. Local knowledge on the problems of access within a community is essential in order to provide accessible services to all people; 'because they are so local in nature, clinics have the ability to see trends in their communities and to adapt to them' (Solomon and Asaro 1997). Two particular groups are often identified as having especially distinctive problems in delivery: women and illegal workers. There may be reluctance by women, especially teenage minority women, to use traditional facilities for birth control, abortions, and other health care services (NARAL 2000). Community health programs allow secure spaces for clinical and educational services related to reproductive care (Planned Parenthood web site). The group with the highest number of uninsured are Hispanic (Weil 2001); undocumented aliens comprise a large percentage of the Hispanic uninsured. This shows not only in lack of insurance coverage, but also in the low access and use of health-care services among low-income adults (*ibid.*). Community clinics and specialized migrant clinics have developed trust among these communities through their provision of culturally sensitive services and bilingual providers.

These community programs, sometimes called safety net providers (hospitals, community health centers, and public health clinics), are often supported through private and public subsidies that enable these providers to deliver accessible and culturally appropriate services to these difficult to reach populations (Brown and Sparer 2001). These clinics are increasingly emerging as necessary participants in the overall health-care delivery and financing system. Many serve as initial entry points into the health-care system, and can serve as enrollment and outreach mechanisms as health-care coverage expands. The health-care delivery mechanism under BadgerCare are the HMOs that are serving Wisconsin residents, including Medicaid patients. That system encourages the HMOs to collaborate and contract with community clinics to provide services and ensure quality health care (Trubek 1999: 144–5). For example, Wisconsin requires HMOs to use 'community groups, public health units, and schools to provide prenatal care, immunizations, and transportation to health care services' (*ibid.*: 145). The contracting process between Wisconsin HMOs and community clinics is a subsidy that allows the maintenance and development of these clinics. Without the specific encouragement by the state to use these community clinics, the clinics may have disappeared because they would have been unable to compete with the traditional providers.

These community clinics are beginning to realize their importance in the overall system and are organizing for increased funding and advocacy. One example of linking community-based delivery systems is the Free Clinics of the Great Lakes Region (FCGLR). The FCGLR was established in 1996 to 'formalize a grassroots network of free clinics in the Great Lakes states and draw attention to the hundreds of thousands of uninsured working poor in the United States'. The FCGLR is producing local and regional data on the uninsured population and distributing this information throughout the network and community. They are also encouraging 'partnering' with mainstream hospitals and clinics, linking with educational institutions who prepare health-care professionals, and engaging of the community at large through churches, service organizations, and media. The FCGLR has also developed electronic networking using web pages and listservs. The development of the group has been greatly assisted by small grants from national foundation funders (FCGLR brochure).

11.3.2. *Networks*

The tremendous expansion of networks is notable. These networks provide sharing of experiences and actors across states. The critique that incremental approaches cannot lead to a universal system is overcome by these networks; they allow scaling up of the local programs. These networks permit knowledge and learning to spread rapidly (see Sturm 2001 for an interesting discussion of a similar phenomenon called 'intermediaries'). They also allow rapid revisions when problems arise. There are three networks, which are having a significant effect: government networks, advocate networks, and policy/foundation networks. It is notable that the three networks are in fact intertwined through shared funding and projects. It is also evident that these networks are significantly involved in local community collaborations and community service delivery.

The government networks include the National Conference of State Legislature (NCSL) and the National Governors' Association (NGA). In 1995 NCSL created the Forum for Health Policy Leadership ('the Forum') to 'improve the capacity for informed decision-making and leadership among state legislators with respect to current and emerging critical health policy issues'(NCSL brochure). The Forum is funded by private foundations such as Robert Wood Johnson, Kellogg, Kaiser Family, David and Lucille Packard, and Commonwealth. The Forum publishes joint papers with the NGA, the Center on Budget Policy Priorities, and the Alzheimer's Association. The Forum also hosts audio conferences with state leaders to learn about various approaches to expanding health coverage, such as school-based application processes for SCHIP programs. Their participant list consists of providers, advocates, and insurers, which ensures communication between various stakeholders about major health policy reform. The confidence among state government leaders in their ability to deal with complex health issues is substantially amplified by the staff support they receive from the Forum. The Forum's publications allow 'state legislators and others to compare notes and further stimulate innovative and responsive public policy' (NCSL 2001*a*).

Advocate networks are emerging to share local and state information. The Center for Budget and Policy Priorities has developed the 'state fiscal analysis initiative' to build capacity in state-level nongovernmental organizations in state fiscal policies. By 1999, the initiative has grown to 22 state-based organizations. For example, the Center for Budget and Policy Priorities funds staff at the Wisconsin Council of Children and Families to track BadgerCare legislation and enrollment progress, and electronically transmit this information to a wide array of community groups. The importance of the Center for Budget and Policy Priorities' project is the use of non-profit organizations to advocate at the state level using shared information on best practices across states. Thus, states generally viewed as having fiscal policies unresponsive to social needs, such as Alabama, have easy access to data from other states that provide more services. The linkages allow more uniformity in health coverage programs, since the budget process is crucial to health-care decisions. The Center for Budget and Policy Priorities is establishing a parallel project on health care reform. Another important program is the Covering Kids project funded by the Robert Wood Johnson Foundation. This is a major financial investment in the creation of collaborative networks in many states to monitor and improve outreach and quality of the coverage of children under the SCHIP program. Specifically, Covering Kids seeks to increase the enrollment of low-income children in available health coverage programs by simplifying enrollment, conducting outreach and coordinating program coverage (Trubek and Farnham 2001). Non-profits play an important role in the organizing and administering of these collaborative outreach efforts.

Supporting the governmental and advocate networks are a group of committed foundations that are providing millions of dollars in support. These foundations also fund policy groups to produce data analyses and proposals on health. One example is the Assessing Federalism Program of the Urban Institute, which is a multi-year project to monitor and assess the devolution of social programs from the federal to the state and local levels. Of particular interest is the Urban Institute's own national survey of American families which allows a much more reliable and targeted statistical indicator on health for low-income families. The Assessing Federalism program provides information for free and informs thousands of people of their reports' availability through email networks and websites. The Kaiser Family Foundation has developed 'State Facts Online'. 'This new resource contains the latest state-level data on demographics, health, and health policy, including health coverage, access, financing, and state legislation' (KFF 2001).

The success of these networks is directly related to the developments in technology, which allow rapid dissemination of information through use of audio conferencing, email listservs, and websites. In addition, states themselves provide access to their statutes, regulations, and legislative and administrative processes through their respective websites, information which was previously very difficult to obtain and share across states.

11.3.3. *Creating a System for Outcomes and Processes*

The emergence of data-driven systems for health-care access and quality is a manifestation of the movement out. Starting with the Clinton Administration, the Federal grip on what states could do loosened, allowing an easier route to state experimentation. This loosened grip allowed states to differentiate their programs and try different ways of providing service. The regulatory gap could have allowed a variety of coverage options to develop without standards for access and quality across states since Congress was unwilling to provide a federal set of standards. This effort to fill the gap has been led by large employers, and government agencies in conjunction with other nongovernmental organizations. These actors have created and participated in systems for data collection and analysis that permit health-care providers, insurers, state and local agencies, and community organizations to participate in, obtain information on, and monitor health-care access and quality. There is now an increased use of data collection analysis and benchmarking systems.

State, federal, and private agencies are creating a series of organizations that create standards that provide comparative information that operates across state lines. These allow centralized monitoring of the access and quality of health care delivered at local levels. Private, non-profit organizations such as the National Commission for Quality Assurance (NCQA) have fostered a system of voluntary certification on quality utilized as a benchmark by the industry and increasingly referenced by government agencies. The information is based on standards developed by NCQA in a consensus process. NCQA develops systems based on this process to measure and compare HMOs on quality indicators, dubbed the Health Plan Employer Data and Information Set (HEDIS). Wisconsin now statutorily requires quality assurance standards, and is relying on private accreditation systems. These certification systems not only allow actors to review quality across state lines, but may also affect health-care coverage. For example, NCQA requires the HMOs they certify to serve Medicaid enrollees (Foldy 2001).

State agencies, are also using data collection and benchmarking systems as methods to monitor privatized contracting systems. When welfare reform began in Wisconsin, health advocates realized that the new system, which included contracting out of services, could have a potentially negative effect on the number of recipients of health-care coverage provided through Medicaid. Since there was confusion about the Medicaid entitlement and the potential for people to have income exceeding the traditional limits, BadgerCare was created specifically to provide a bridge program. However, there was the hope that many recipients would obtain jobs that provided private health-care coverage. To encourage the contracting agencies to seek jobs with health-care coverage, the advocates sought and obtained evaluative standards in the contracts between the state and the agencies administering the program. It placed responsibility on the private agencies that were administering the benefits program to reach a benchmark figure. To ensure continued efforts to reach and exceed the benchmark, local agencies regularly report on their compliance with the standard. Moreover, there are regular meetings among state officials, contracting agencies, and other community advocates to monitor compliance and progress in meeting the benchmark. The standards and data that come out of these meetings are available to the public, and much of the work, including the minutes of the monitoring committee meetings, is made available on the state website (W-2 Contract and Implementation Committee 2001).

11.4. The Next Steps

The enthusiasm for a new expansion of access to health care in the United States is based on a combination of state initiatives, the creation of public and private partnerships and understanding of the relationship of work and health. The recent consumer-health plan alliance, which places expanded health care on the table, is based on their assessment of the importance of emerging state initiatives and development of horizontal linkages. The alliance states that the time is ripe for 'solving a proposal for common action'. They argue that a meaningful proposal should achieve 'a balance between public and private sector approaches, focus attention on those who are most in need of assistance (low-income workers), and build on systems that work today' (Kahn and Pollack 2001).

This new system, which emerged in the balmy days of the late 1990s, is now subject to its first real test—the economic downturn at the dawn of the twenty-first century. There is now the double problem of falling state revenues and the increasing number of people potentially eligible for public health programs. There is awareness in the health-care world as well as with state and federal officials that access to health-care coverage is under pressure and competing with other priorities. There is substantial debate and disagreement among local and state organizations, health-care analysts, employers, and academics about how to react to the test of this emerging system.

State officials are concerned that their Medicaid expansion programs cannot be sustained without federal assistance either through tax credits, increased federal contribution towards the cost of the programs, funding the mandatory continuation coverage for unemployed workers, and expansion of unrestricted funding for health care coverage programs. According to the NGA, the ideal proposal would both stimulate the economy and provide health care for low-income individuals (NGA 2001). A state-based approach will also maintain and expand the devolution that has been described. Other approaches such as block grants to the states will encourage the continued development of public–private collaborations. Funding unemployed workers through continuing their private insurance will allow a continuation of the employer-based health coverage system. Approaches that cut back on medical benefits and provider reimbursements will undercut the support of health care providers and the health-care system for maintaining coverage. Therefore, the type of approaches implemented to address the economic downturn will be crucial in allowing these larger reforms that are discussed in this chapter to move forward or be quashed (Lambrew 2001).

Thus, the challenges to achieving a workable system that utilizes the state-based public–private system are sobering. There are three challenges to conceptualizing a workable proposal: linking public and private plans, effectively meeting workplace and workforce needs, and integrating the safety net into the mainstream health-care financing system. For the seamless knitting of public and private insurance, collection of data about health plans from employers is essential. For instance, there are legal and managerial challenges to coordinating BadgerCare with private health insurance. The potential for mixed coverage, where the private employer is subsidized through a buy-in from the public programs, can only be achieved through intensive knowledge of the employer-based health plan. Wisconsin statutes allow a buy-in program, where the State may buy into the employer-sponsored health plan if such buy-in proves to be more cost-effective than covering the low-income family solely in the BadgerCare program (*ibid.*).[12] However, the lack of information

---

[12] See also Interview with Don Schneider, Chief of Coordination of Benefits Section, DHFS, in Madison, WI (23 February 2001) noting that cost-effectiveness is based upon the cost of a BadgerCare enrollee in a managed care plan compared to the cost of the wraparound coverage and extra administrative costs provided in the HIPP program. The HIPP program pays the wraparound costs of the employer plan so that the HIPP enrollee receives the same benefits as they would under straight BadgerCare. As of the end of February, 2001, approximately 34 families were enrolled in the HIPP program, mostly with smaller employers (*ibid.*).

about workplace coverage is a barrier to the utilization of this statutorily allowed program. For example, according to a recent study of former welfare recipients in Milwaukee County, women who work full time for firms that offer health insurance are more likely to take up BadgerCare than women who do not work full time or in firms that offer health insurance. To improve the efficiency of the BadgerCare program, the state must better understand why these women elect BadgerCare over their employer's health coverage program (Wolfe 2001). The rapid turnover of low-wage workers also requires a health-care coverage system that can be moved with the worker from job to job without losing coverage. This requires close coordination between the patterns of employment and characteristics of the workplace with access and cost of health-care coverage. Another reason why linking public and private programs is essential and challenging, is the disparate reimbursement rate for health care professionals among public and private health plans. Public programs reimburse providers at a much lower rate than private health plans. This has been justified, historically, as a type of 'charitable' contribution. This is no longer viable with increasing number of for-profit provider groups and the expanded coverage by public programs. Unifying the public and private programs requires the support of these health-care professionals. A reimbursement system that is adequate and not based on whether the coverage is public or private is essential (Watson 2001).

A second challenge is expanding the eligibility of people without dependent children and part-time and self-employed workers. Currently, 18 percent of the uninsured are people without dependent children (Weil 2001). There is a proposal to expand BadgerCare, for example, to cover people who have an obligation to support children, though the children are not living in their household. These people are currently not covered by BadgerCare. The argument is that these 'non-custodial parents' are often unemployed and have poor health conditions because they are uninsured. Expanding BadgerCare to cover this group would encourage them to find and keep steady employment that would help support their families (Foldy 2001). Another uninsured group of workers are part-time and self-employed. Traditionally, no health coverage is available for these workers and there is an increase in these types of jobs.

Third, incorporation of community delivery systems into the health-care coverage financing streams is essential to sustain health-care coverage and access of disenfranchised groups. Groups such as teens and undocumented workers are reluctant to access coverage even if they are eligible for programs. The community agencies providing care for these groups are underfunded and often unable to provide in-hospital care.

These challenges can be overcome through clarifying how the health-care system is to be governed. ERISA can be amended to encourage state-based approaches. ERISA makes it difficult for states to access pertinent health information and coordinate public benefits with employer-sponsored plans (NGA 2000).[13] Any new proposals require federal laws that address health coverage to work in conjunction with one another. Second, the horizontal mechanisms now developing should be amplified and studied. The intersection of local collaborations with national programs and funding is a move in the right direction.

The foundation for a strong alliance to confront these challenges seems to be emerging. The consumer-health plan initiatives demonstrate an assessment that the time may be near to take on these challenges. There are two interest groups who may be interested in joining the consumer-health plan alliance to achieve expanded coverage: businesses and physicians. Large business has been a major beneficiary of the regulatory gap since it has allowed them to control health-care costs with little government intervention. Out of this control has evolved innovative quality and benchmarking systems, which are affecting the way health care is delivered through using public and private agencies across the nation. Large businesses may be willing to support some standard-setting by the federal government as long as they maintain control over the financing of their health coverage programs. Small businesses realize that in order to compete for skilled workers, they must provide health-care coverage. Many small businesses are now willing to endorse proposals that include public programs which enable them to maintain their businesses. Physicians have been ambivalent in their support for public programs since their reimbursement rates are significantly lower in those programs than in employer-based insurance. They may be willing to support expanded public programs that create a more uniform relationship between public and private coverage in order to achieve a more uniform and reasonable reimbursement rate (Brown and Sparer 2001).

11.5. Conclusion

The failure of the United States to provide universal health care for all residents is a continuing policy disaster. It affects the health status of many people and contributes to the spread of illness and disease. The attention within the United States to the continuing puzzle of our inability to cover all our residents is now connected to the character of our workforce and our attitude toward welfare policy. Covering all workers has captured bipartisan political attention and is a focus of business concern.

---

[13] ERISA presents one of the 'greatest barriers to some state reform initiatives' (NGA 2000).

Proponents of expanded health coverage are now seizing on systemic changes in the relationship between local and national governance, and public and private agencies. The proponents envision using these paradigmatic shifts to create a new, broad consensus for health system reform. Many obstacles remain, including economic trends and fiscal constraints. However, the combination of broad collaborations at the local level and new, unlikely alliances among policy leadership demonstrates the potential for solving the health care puzzle.

References

BadgerCare Coordination Network (2001). 'Mission Statement'. On file with the author.

Balanced Budget Act of 1997, Pub. L. No. 105–33, § 4901, 111 Stat. 251, 275 (1997) (codified as amended at 42 U.S.C. §§ 1397aa–1397jj (1994 & Supp. V 1999)).

Brown, L. D. and Sparer, M. S. (2001). 'Window Shopping: State Health Reform Politics in the 1990s'. *Health Affairs*, 20: 50.

Bureau of Labor Statistics (BLS) (2000*a*). 'State at a Glance—Wisconsin', April–September. http://stats.bls.gov/eag/eag.wi.htm

Bureau of Labor Statistics (BLS) (2000*b*). 'Local Area Unemployment Statistics—Wisconsin, 1990–2000'. http://stats.bls.gov/eag/eag.wi.htm

Bureau of Labor Statistics (BLS) (2000*c*). 'Labor Force Statistics from the Current Population Survey, Series Catalog, Civilian Labor Force, 1990–2000'. http://stats.bls.gov/eag/eag.us.htm

Coughlin, T., Wiener, J., Marsteller, J., Stevenson, D., and Wallin, S. (1998). 'Health Policy for Low-income People in Wisconsin', State Report. Washington DC: The Urban Institute.

Department of Health and Family Services (DHFS) (1999). *BadgerCare Brochure*, June. Madison, WI: DHFS.

Department of Health and Family Services (DHFS) (2000*a*). 'Fact Sheet, BadgerCare Eligibility and BadgerCare Premiums', July 11. Madison, WI: DHFS. Available at http://www.dhfs.state.wi.us/badgercare/factsheets/bcpremium.htm

Department of Health and Family Services (DHFS) (2000*b*). 'BadgerCare Enrollment by Category', August 14. Madison, WI, Unpublished paper.

DHS (Minnesota Department of Health Services). 'MinnesotaCare Report'. Available at www.dhs.state.mn.us/hlthcare/asstprog/mncare/

Dietrich, S., Emsellem, M., and Ruckelshaus, C. (1998). 'The Other Side of Welfare Reform'. *Stanford Law and Policy Review*, 9: 53–7.

Dresser, L. and Rogers J. (1997). 'Rebuilding Job Access and Career Advancement Systems in the New Economy', Working Paper. Madison, WI: Center on Wisconsin Strategy (COWS).

DSHS (Washington State Department of Social and Health Services) (2001). 'State of Washington', Memorandum, August 22. Olympia, WA: DSHS.

Foldy, S., City of Milwaukee Health Commissioner (2001). Presentation to the Collaboration for Healthcare Consumer Protection, Madison, WI, April 19, 2001.

Garrett, B. and Holahan, J. (2000). 'Health Insurance Coverage After Welfare', *Health Affairs*, January/February, 175–81.

Handler, J. F. (1996). *Down from Bureaucracy: The Ambiguity of Privatization and Empowerment*. Princeton, NJ: Princeton University Press.

HASKINS, R. and BLANK, R. M. (2001). 'Welfare Reform: An Agenda for Reauthorization'. In R.M. Blank and R. Haskins (eds), *The New World of Welfare*. Washington DC: Brookings Institution Press.

HENLY, J. R. (1999). 'Barriers to Finding and Maintaining Jobs—The Perspectives of Workers and Employers in the Low-wage Labor Market', in J. F. Handler and L. White (eds), *Hard Labor: Women and Work in the Post-welfare Era*. Armonk, NY: M. E. Sharp, 48–66.

JECKER, N. S. (1994). 'Can an Employer-based Health Insurance System Be Just?', in J. A. Morone and G. S. Belkin (eds), *The Politics of Health Care Reform: Lessons from the Past, Prospects for the Future*. Durham, NC: Duke University Press, 259–62.

KAHN III, CH. N. and POLLACK, R. F. (2001). 'Building a Consensus for Expanding Health Coverage'. *Health Affairs*, 20/1: 40–8.

KFF (Kaiser Commission on Medicaid and the Uninsured) (1999). 'The Medicaid Program at a Glance'. Washington, DC: KFF.

KFF (Kaiser Family Foundation) (2001). 'State Health Facts Online'. Kaiser Family Foundation Brochure. Washington, DC: KFF.

LAMBREW J. M. (2001). 'How the Slowing U.S. Economy Threatens Employer-based Health Insurance', Pub. No. 511, November. New York: The Commonwealth Fund.

MATTHEW, D. B. (1996). 'Controlling the Reverse Agency Costs of Employment-based Health Insurance: Of Markets, Courts, and a Regulatory Quagmire'. *Wake Forest Law Review*, 31: 1037–42.

MEYER, J. A. and SILOW-CARROLL, S. (2000). 'Increasing Access: Building Working Solution'. June. Washington DC: Economic and Social Research Institute.

MIDDLETON, J. (1996). 'Contingent Workers in a Changing Economy: Endure, Adapt, or Organize?' *New York University Review of Law and Social Change*, 22: 557–65.

NARAL (National Abortion and Reproductive Rights Action League) Foundation (2000). 'The Reproductive Rights & Health of Women of Color'. Washington, DC: NARAL.

NASHP (National Academy for State Health Policy) (2000a). 'The Floodtide Report: Access for the Uninsured: Lessons from 25 Years of State Initiatives', January. Portland, ME: NASHP.

NASHP (National Academy for State Health Policy) (2000b). 'Access for the Uninsured: New York Health Care Reform Act 2000', September. Portland, ME: NASHP.

NCSL (National Conference of State Legislatures) (1999). 'Health Chairs Project: Issue Brief: Welfare Reform, Medicaid and Health Coverage', Washington DC, July. http://www.ncsl.org/programs/health/forum/tanf2ma.htm.

NCSL (National Conference of State Legislatures) (2001a). '2001 State Children's Health Insurance Program Chartbook'. March. Washington DC: NCSL.

NCSL (National Conference of State Legislatures) (2001b). *Forum for State Health Policy Leadership. 2001 State Children's Health Insurance Program Chartbook*. March. Washington, DC: NCSL.

NCSL (National Conference of State Legislatures). 'Forum for State Health Policy Leadership Brochure' (unpublished).

NGA (National Governors' Association) (2000). 'NGA Policy Position Detail. HR-37: Private Sector Health Care Reform Policy', § 37.2.1, 3.

NGA (National Governors' Association) (2001). Press Release, 'Governors Seek Increase in Federal Share for Medicaid'. Available at http://www.nga.org/nga/newsRoom/1,1169,C_PRESS_RELEASE^D_2798,00.html. December 4.

PEACOCK, J. (2000). 'Badger Care Coming of Age: Promise and Reality'. Madison: Council on Children and Families, Wisconsin Budget Project 1. http://www.wccf.org/BC.pdf

Personal Responsibility and Work Opportunity Reconciliation Act (PRWORA) (1996). Pub. L. No. 104-193, § 401, 110 Stat. 2105, 2113.

Planned Parenthood Website, www.plannedparenthood.org

SCHOEN, C., STRUMPF, E., and DAVIS, K. (2000). 'A Vote of Confidence: Attitudes toward Employer-sponsored Health Insurance'. *The Commonwealth Fund Issue Brief*, 5, Pub. No. 363, January. New York: The Commonwealth Fund.

SCHROEDER, P. (1995). 'Does the Growth in the Contingent Work Force Demand a Change in Federal Policy?' *Washington and Lee Law Review*, 52: 731–35.

SCHWAB, S. J. (1995). 'The Diversity of Contingent Workers and the Need for Nuanced Policy'. *Washington and Lee Law Review*, 52: 915–19.

SIRICA, C. (2001). 'The Origins and Implementation of BadgerCare', January. New York: The Milbank Memorial Fund. http://www.milbank.org/010123badgercare.html

SOLOMON L. D. and ASARO T. (1997). 'Community-based Health Care: A Legal and Policy Analysis'. *Fordham Urban Law Journal*, 24: 235–62.

STURM, S. (2001). 'Second Generation Employment Discrimination: A Structural Approach'. *Columbia Law Review*, 101: 458–568.

TRUBEK, L. G. (1999). 'The Health Care Puzzle', in J. F. Handler and L. White (eds) *Hard Labor: Women and Work in the Post-welfare Era*. Armonk, NY: M. E. Sharp, 143–57.

—— and FARNHAM, J. J. (2001). *How to Create and Sustain a Successful Social Justice Collaborative*. Madison, WI: Center for Public Representation.

W-2 Contract & Implementation Committee, http://www.dwd.state.wi.us/desw2/w2min/2001_minutes.htm

WATSON, S. D. (2001). 'Commercialization of Medicaid'. *St. Louis University Law Journal*, 45: 53–78.

WEIL, A. (2001). Presentation for the Free Clinics of the Great Lakes Region, 5th Annual Conference, in Madison, WI, April 27, 2001.

Wisconsin Administrative Code (2000).

Wisconsin State Journal (2000). 'BadgerCare Coverage Is Among Nation's Broadest', August 27.

Wisconsin State Journal (2001). 'BadgerCare Enrollment Hits Records', October 28.

Wisconsin Works Program Act, 1995 Wisconsin Laws: 289, 1933.

WOLFE, B. (2001). 'Take Up of Medicaid and Food Stamps among Former Welfare Recipients in Wisconsin', Presentation at UW, October 29, 2001.

Part 3

Governing Work and Welfare in a New Economy: Emergent Patterns and Future Possibilities

12

Work and Welfare: Toward a Capability Approach

ROBERT SALAIS

In a capability approach to work and welfare, what matters for public policies is what a person *can do and be* with the resources over which she has command. In other words, what matters is her achievement as a person (and, as a consequence, the effective freedom she has to do so), compared with what is judged normal (i.e. conventionally agreed) in a given society. Usually, welfare theories are centred only on incomes or on the basket of commodities (and services) a person enjoys, whatever the effective functionings she manages to achieve with them. For Amartya Sen from whom we take inspiration in this contribution, empirical evidence shows that, when faced with the same hazard, people are unequal in their capabilities of doing and being with the same basket of commodities or amount of money. The true problem for social policies is thus to struggle against inequality of capabilities.

Let us give a couple of examples. Taking into account the conventions in force in a number of countries, in most cases a married woman with young children will not be able to reach equal capabilities in taking a good job unless there is collective investment in childcare (not to mention other subsidiary conditions). Similarly, for the disabled to attain equality in access to transportation in relation to others, it is essential to ensure that means of public transport be fitted with specially designed entrance doors. A long-term unemployed person will have no capability of sustaining a job placement; he also needs treatment and training appropriate to his individual circumstances. This capability approach has a long-standing history in economics. Sen recalls the example given by Adam Smith that 'to be able to avoid shame, an eighteenth century Englishman has to have leather shoes'. This capability was necessary, 'not so much to be less ashamed than others, ... but simply not to be ashamed, which as an achievement is an absolute one' (Sen 1983: 159). To have or not to have the required capabilities is the question to address when judging situations in which help is needed. The capabilities in question are not minimalist ones (having shoes), but the ones everybody in the society under review considers as normal in that given situation (having *leather* shoes).

This shift toward capability has two key consequences for social policies.

1. As far as doings and beings (and not only beings) are concerned, work activities may be part of the sets of 'functionings' that an individual as well as the society can have reason to value. This perspective is proposed as a contribution to Sen's line of thought. The idea we defend is that such a valuation goes beyond obtaining money income on the labor market and includes conditions of work and life. As emphasized in Supiot (2001), changes in work in a knowledge-based economy call for such a conception. Skills become part of the wider concept of capabilities. In such a perspective, work means participating in an agency (for instance, creating a product or a service, via coordination with other persons in a firm, or the achievement of some personal goals via life at work). In welfare approaches, this suggests a shift away from freedom from want toward freedom to act.

2. For systems of social protection, this shift gives priority not to political debate between policy makers and experts about normative social theories, but to the objective informational basis of judgment on social justice (IBJJ) that is needed to evaluate the 'state of persons' in terms of capabilities. Criteria and procedures of evaluation must be developed which transcribe at a local level and aggregate as faithfully as possible the diversity of individual situations regarding work and life security. A capability approach is less concerned with macro-political regimes as in Esping-Andersen's (1990) work than with the diversity of the IBJJ that can be constructed.

To what extent the changing nature of work calls for a capability approach to welfare is the subject of Section 12.1, which distinguishes this approach based on the works of Amartya Sen from other classical approaches (the poverty line; equal freedom). Section 12.2 recasts Esping-Andersen's worlds of welfare from political regimes sustaining systems of social protection toward pragmatic worlds of welfare provision; a fourth world is added, the capability world. Combining OECD and International Social Security Association (ISSA) databases, Section 12.3 provides empirical evidence concerning the links between work and welfare in OECD countries. In Section 12.4, we briefly discuss the application of a capability approach to unemployment in Europe. We emphasize the urgent need for the so-called Open Method of Coordination (OMC) to develop informational bases that could really compare European countries with regard to their support for the development of capabilities.

12.1. Work and Capabilities

Work is changing; the labor market is changing. Any reform of social protection, if it is to succeed, must discover the trends that, in effect, lie behind these changes. We argue that, due to its transformation in a knowledge-based economy, work can less and less be considered as a disutility (whose only reward is a wage) and has more and more to be viewed as an agency (i.e. a goal, the achievement of which has its own value beyond a wage). Participation in the collective effort has to be valued. This raises problems for social policies in all their various domains (poverty, unemployment, health, and so on.). In order to take account of the changes in work, social policy principles need to shift away from 'freedom from want' toward 'freedom to act'.

12.1.1. *Changes in Work and Freedom to Act*

Access to freedom from want has been the main achievement of existing systems of social protection in developed countries. Providing people with the negative freedom to stay out of work and with the best income conditions as long as possible in case of major life-course hazards was a key innovation of most social systems of protection (except partly in the liberal welfare state in Esping-Andersen's typology). This strongly contributed to the regulation of the labor market by requiring employers to meet minimum requirements in terms of wages and working conditions in order to attract job candidates. This also created an incentive to enhance the standards of work and skills, which became the basis for raising both productivity and product quality in the long run. Such a great achievement still needs to be consolidated and, in some respects, improved. The question today is whether the transformation of work opens a path toward positive freedom, that is, an *effective freedom to act and to choose*.

Arguments in favor of positive freedom are twofold, pertaining to social justice and economic efficiency.

Social reform literature today repeatedly emphasizes the modernity of individual choice and of mastering one's own life and work career, specially for women and young people. A widespread consensus supports claims to a fair wage, a fair balance between work time and private time, participation in collective life within the firm, good career prospects, and the freedom to choose an appropriate job, and so on. The recent European Social Agenda puts these objectives at the top of its priorities. These issues are especially relevant in the case of achieving equality between women and men.

The economic aspect of positive freedom (notably its greater efficiency) is more controversial. Part of the management and labor economics literature (particularly on flexibility and uncertainty issues) focuses on the spread of new standards for employment, based on responsibility, initiative, autonomy, and relational skills. Efficient deployment of these qualities requires an adequate and reflexive situational use by workers of this freedom to act that no machinery can replace. Hence the importance of experience acquisition and job mobility, in order to cumulate various exercises of this freedom, in other words, the revival of professional skills in the new economy context (Supiot 2001, among others). This literature concludes that it is never the job itself which determines performance, but the person who holds it. Another more critical part of this literature insists on the precariousness and risks of exclusion that threaten the less skilled labor force. People who do not meet the requirements of the new norms of employment that emerge and who cannot sustain their employability in the job market tend to slip through the safety nets of existing systems of social protection (Salais and Raveaud 2002). In our view, the two statements are complementary rather than contradictory. It could be that effective freedom to act is not systematically required in all jobs, but it proves extremely difficult to say in advance in which jobs it is unnecessary, and in what circumstances. All these features emphasize that the need for adequate capabilities to participate in work and social life should be the major concern of any welfare reform.

Within a context of flexibility, hence of uncertainty, governance of work is more complex than managing opportunism or cheating. In response to efficiency concerns, it must allow some latitude of action to partners, in other words, a space of effective freedom and responsibility. Mutual expectations in this regard must be guaranteed by a security framework. The concept of capability thus refers to a set of qualities that are distinct from the traditional notions of employment skills and of individual employability. It is a broader concept, and is not narrowly defined in relation to a given job (which would impede mobility and adaptability). Capability refers to a person's potential, a capacity for work and for achievement. It addresses the scope of possibilities that, in a given situation and time, a person can effectively achieve. It is also grounded in a notion of work that is broader than the simple accomplishment of routinized tasks. For one thing, personal qualities are not derived from or exercised at work alone; they are also skills in everyday life. For another thing, individual control of the effective use of these qualities is a manifestation of personal liberty. The broader the 'capabilities', the wider and the more effective is the freedom to act. Developing capabilities is not purely an individual affair. It puts in question the effective operation of social institutions (notably the ways they judge individual situations and how they calibrate and deliver rights and resources), as well as the framing of the labor market.

This raises two heated points of debate between a neo-liberal and a capability approach, on individual responsibility and on the link to be made between work and welfare.

Neo-liberals consider that gaining positive freedoms is the individual's responsibility. Individuals can choose whether or not to invest in their human capital. In terms of public policy, employability has to be a strictly individual affair. This is the case, for instance, for the British 'New Deal' or for workfare policies. If necessary, the neo-liberals allow the state to create incentives and penalties to force the development of individual responsibility. Globally speaking, the main orientation they advocate for welfare policies resembles a refined poverty-line approach. Below the line, deserving people merit help on an incentive–penalty basis; above, they are left to their own devices. In a capability approach, for employability and responsibility to be effective, explicit rules and collective infrastructure are needed to guarantee equality of capabilities. Far from neglecting personal responsibility, a capability approach will aim to provide individuals with effective means to develop it. It acknowledges that these means should be collectively designed and provided.

For the neo-liberals, there is no possible positive and dynamic interaction between work and welfare. They view work essentially as a commodity sold and bought on a market, whose efficiency obeys the law of perfect competition. There are only two ways to escape from this 'iron law'. The first one is corporatism. Well-organized workers make political alliances with other social classes against the employers. They create protective rules for themselves with two consequences: they distort the law of competition on labor markets with the associated imperfections and inefficiencies; they reject non- or weakly-organized people (which gives rise to an insider/outsider problem). The other way out is to decommodify, that is, to provide everybody (not simply workers) with the negative freedom to escape from the labor market for as long as possible. As the only reward considered for work is income, this requires providing people with a replacement income in socially justified cases: old age, unemployment, childcare, illness, and so on. The labor market remains efficient and perfectly competitive, but people have no obligation to work at all costs. Welfare is a tax to be levied on everybody and on every income. As a result, welfare is basically inefficient for the society as a whole in both cases, a cost for the maintenance of political and social order.

12.1.2. *Equality of What?*

To avoid these dead-ends, welfare studies have to start from two contradictory facts. One is that everyone likes or would like to work because she values it intrinsically for a number of well-documented reasons. Thus work should be conceived, not only as a disutility, but also as part of an agency, in other terms, as a *valuable functioning* for people. The other fact is that, with rare exceptions, people feel dissatisfied with some or many aspects of their life at work and of their job, precisely because they are expecting some achievements in them. In particular, almost everybody, whatever her position, would like to have access to a better position in terms not only of income but also of effective freedom of choice.

In response to these facts, we propose to enlarge the focus of social policies: instead of dealing only with monetary resources or goods, they should deal with what people can achieve with the resources in their possession.[1] In theoretical terms, what is challenged are the metrics used by social policies to evaluate situations of people deserving help. To make this point, we shall first present the capability-based approach inspired by the works of Amartya Sen (Section 12.1.2.1) in contrast with other classical approaches. Roughly speaking, Sen has drawn on and defined his position in contradistinction to two major traditions in this field: the poverty-line and equal freedom approaches. Two points that differ from other well-known views are especially relevant in Sen's conceptions. First, to implement policies, the basic approaches of need (as measured by the poverty line) and equal freedom must be supplemented by a direct analysis of the actual freedoms of people. Beyond monetary benefits, the provision of help must also focus on services. A metrics of capabilities is then required. Second, doing so gives priority to the objective IBJJ that is needed to evaluate the 'state of persons' in terms of capabilities. Criteria and procedures of evaluation must be developed which transcribe at a local level and aggregate as faithfully as possible the diversity of individual situations about work and life security. In Section 12.2, we use this line of argument as a tool for analyzing existing and potential systems of social protection.

12.1.2.1. *Needs and the Poverty Line*

In the scientific debate about an adequate definition of poverty, one of the main disputed points has been the reference against which personal situations are to be measured. Is this reference to be absolute (a fixed amount of money, a fixed bundle of goods, etc.) or relative to the 'normal' living standard in a given country at a given date? With the obvious limits of a strictly absolute approach, by which almost everybody in our country is richer than most knights of the Middle Ages, the 'relative' definition of poverty has gradually taken precedence. But the standard to which one's situation is compared is to be built by the scientific researcher.

As advocated by Peter Townsend, the poverty line is relevant because 'below an approximate threshold of income, deprivation seems to intensify, accelerate or multiply disproportionately' (Townsend 1985: 662). That is, while poverty is a scalar phenomenon, it is nevertheless possible to draw a line underneath which a decent life is out of reach. Of course, Townsend is

---

[1] This subsection draws heavily on Salais and Raveaud (2002).

aware of the fact that money is not everything. But he argues that money is an overall good indication: 'the level of resources available (...) seems in the end to govern whether or not individuals within that community can satisfy social obligations, expectations and customs of such membership' (*ibid.*).

Identifying this line is therefore a crucial point. In Townsend's view, it is possible to draw such a line by the definition of 'scientific criteria by which we identify, or prioritize, human needs' (*ibid.*: 664). This position is questionable: being 'above' society, the scientific reseacher claims to have the ability to define what 'human needs' are, and in which order they are to be satisfied. This contradicts the widely shared view that it is a basic element of one's freedom to define one's own needs. Besides, there is a tension between this focus on 'needs' and the use of a poverty line: if the purpose is to guarantee the satisfaction of such needs, why not measure them directly? The poverty line here seems to be an unsatisfactory approximation: why not deal directly with the ways of meeting these needs, while taking into account the variety of lives people want to live?

12.1.2.2. *Fairness and Primary Goods*
For Rawls (1971), it is crucial to take directly into account the variety of 'conceptions of the good', as there is precisely no possible scientific definition of 'human needs'. This is because what people value in their lives greatly differs: some are greedy, others religious, others value music above all, and so on. But, according to Rawls, even if their needs and tastes differ, it is nevertheless possible to identify a bundle of goods that are useful, and even necessary as *a means*, to the satisfaction of *any* life plan. This is why he proposes to call them 'primary goods'.

'Primary' has two meanings here. First, these goods are *basic* in the sense that, without them, no one can lead the life he or she values. In Rawls's analysis, primary goods are ordered: they include first and foremost political and civil liberties. Without them, no valuable life can be led. Then, in a 'lexicographic order', they include all the necessary elements of life in society: income, health, the social bases of self-respect, etc. In this sense, the analysis is close to Townsend's. But for Rawls the focus on monetary resources is misguided. For instance, a wealthy person experiencing discrimination in the labor market because of his ethnic group will be above the poverty line, but may not obtain the social respect she is expecting. For Rawls there is no possible trade-off between civil and political rights and the distribution of primary goods: one cannot trade less liberty for more wealth. This draws attention to the fact that attempting to deregulate labor markets or to restrict access to social protection could threaten these basic liberties.

Second, primary goods are *elementary*, being the building blocks with which everybody will build their own life, whatever their tastes and preferences.

Rawls therefore escapes from Townsend's dead-end: it is not the scientific reseacher's role (nor anybody else's, whether a social worker, an expert, or a politician) to define 'social needs' that are to be satisfied for everybody. What is to be promoted is, on the contrary, a variety of trajectories and freedom of choice. Primary goods are a necessary means, independently of the social needs that could justify their provision.

Does Rawls's approach imply strict equality among the members of society? For Rawls, yes, but only when no gain for the least favored can be obtained from an unequal distribution. And it is very likely that some inequalities (like those implied by the division of labor) will promote the well-being of all, including the worse off. Therefore some inequalities can be said to be fair when they can be justified by a bettering of the conditions of the most deprived. Such a society will then have a proportion of relatively poor individuals, but their situation will be the best possible, after the distribution of primary goods. Poverty, in such an approach, is then compatible with fairness, as long as positions in the society are 'open to free competition' and accessible to all. Any change in the social status of people is far from being politically acceptable to Rawlsian citizens. First, it must be to the greatest advantage of the worst-off, as emphasized by Esping-Andersen *et al.* (2002). But another condition is that the choice has to be made 'under a veil of ignorance'. This means that everybody has to choose the best institutional arrangement, ignoring all the features of his personal current and future identity and position in society. If not, the only feasible change is the one which improves the situation of all.

12.1.2.3. *The Metrics of Capabilities*

Sen acknowledges the path opened by Rawls. But just as the definition of a poverty line was an indirect way for Townsend to assess the fulfilment of 'social needs', Sen considers that Rawls's focus on primary goods is an indirect—hence unsatisfactory—way to measure *effective* freedom. What really matters is not only the bundle of goods each person has, but what she can actually *do* or *be* with them (Sen 1983, 1990).

12.1.2.3.1. *Freedom and capabilities*   Consider the problem of finding a decent job. For Sen, this has to do with *focal personal features*, for instance, housing. Housing conditions can vary in quality, but living in some neighborhoods may also give a bad reputation to the families living there. That is, a *relatively* worse house can lead to an *absolute* distinction between those living in such a neighborhood and the others, the stigmatized and the normal. A relative deprivation of commodities (e.g. housing) can then lead to absolute deprivation of capabilities (inability to find a decent job). It can prevent these people from being integrated in any satisfactory way. This is because 'on the space of the "capabilities" (...) escape from poverty has an absolute requirement, avoidance of (...) shame. Not so much having equal shame as others, but just not being ashamed, absolutely' (*ibid.*: 161).

According to Sen (1985), assessing the situation of a person (her living standard) can then not be done from the goods in her possession alone, but from the evaluation of her actual possibilities, or 'capabilities', that is her actual freedoms: freedom to appear in public without shame; to participate in the life of the community; to move around freely, to choose an appropriate job, etc. Sen's preoccupations are exactly the same as Townsend's and Rawls's. But, instead of focusing on minimum income or on *means*, whatever their extension, one has to deal directly with the *effective freedoms* a person enjoys.

12.1.2.3.2. *Freedoms: collective and primary* Effective freedom requires a framework, both institutional and material. First, it is defined by legal texts and constitutions. Second, it depends on the environment in which the person lives. Sen takes the example of the possibility of living in a disease-free environment: such a possibility may depend on the individual's choices and health habits, but it depends above all on public policies. It is true that the examples chosen by Sen are frequently individualistic (metabolism rate, sex, race, age, etc.). But there is no reason to think of capabilities as an intrinsically individualistic notion. On the contrary, for an individual the effective possibilities are not only framed, but very often given by the institutions surrounding her. This is the case with health, but also the case with the labor market, education, housing, and so on.

Thus, evaluating the situation of the people requires us to *elaborate an IBJJ*, focused on the effective freedom people have to *achieve* the life they value. This requires a difficult exercise for the scientific reseacher: to take into account the range of possibilities (and the freedom of choice itself) offered to the person, and not only the elements of this set she has acquired at the time her well-being is evaluated. That is, what matters is also what she could have done and not only what she did. To illustrate this point, Sen compares the voluntary faster to the involuntary starver: both of them lack food, from a biological point of view. But the former could do otherwise whereas the latter has no other option.

This point is linked to the previous one: as the capabilities of a person depend on public policies, their evaluation does not imply defining *a priori* abstract categories. On the contrary, it relies on a situated methodology. If some characteristics appear *ex post* to be correlated with a given problem (metabolic rates with malnutrition, lack of education with unemployment), then targeted approaches may be required if these characteristics are not evenly distributed among the population. But this can only come as a result of the analysis, not as an *a priori* postulate, and categories should not be chosen for the sake of supposedly efficient and cheap public action. Categories must be built in line with their practical correlation with the issues at stake.

12.2. Four Worlds of Welfare and their Informational Bases in Relation to Work

To promote the use of capability in the shaping of social policies, the state–market relationship has to be reconsidered: one cannot simply choose one rather than the other, or subordinate the former to the latter. It is on the contrary the forms of intervention of the state in the market, which matter, especially with regard to the current changes in the labor market (Section 12.2.1). We hereafter characterize four types (or worlds as in Esping-Andersen 1990), not of social protection systems, but of public action according to the work and welfare relationship they rely on and promote (Section 12.2.2).

12.2.1. *Rethinking Work and Welfare through the State–Market Relationship*

One rationale for welfare-state intervention is to protect people from some selected risks by ensuring them protection when these risks occur. When dealing with work, the first point is to ensure 'negative' freedom, that is, to guarantee freedom from want. But the question of the relationship between work and welfare is less and less for people only to be free to opt out of work. This negative freedom is indeed a pre-condition for a decent living, and a minimal quality of life: a person does not have to work when he or she is sick, old, pregnant, or too young. But a more 'positive' freedom is to be promoted as well: the freedom to be and to do. In that conception, and using Sen's concepts, work should be considered as a valuable functioning. Such a freedom will prove fair and efficient simultaneously, in the context of the new environment and changing working conditions that characterize a knowledge-based economy. More broadly, the purpose of welfare intervention is to provide people with the necessary capability that allows them to act freely and efficiently at work.

Therefore the logic of decommodification of work, identified by Esping-Andersen as the only one, has to be opposed to another logic, the effective freedom to work. The state–market relationship is an interaction by which 'social policy has been systematically transformed so as to deliberately reshape the clearing mechanisms in the labor market' (Esping-Andersen 1990: 160). What we propose then is to recast Esping-Andersen's classical typology from this point of view. We identify four (and not three) typical state–market relationships: encouraging the market (liberal model); substituting for the market (social-democratic model); protecting against the market (conservative-corporatist model); and shaping the market (capability model). The typology no longer deals with macro-regimes, but rather with the plurality of public actions linking work and welfare. Hence Figure 12.1 suggests original names for the corresponding worlds.

Figure 12.1 presents the set of informational bases of judgment on just-ice linking work and welfare to which these state–market relationships lead. The rows show the grounds for assistance in terms of social justice. They oppose the two conceptions of work discussed above, in Section 12.1: work as an agency vs. an individual disutility. The columns show the grounds for assistance in terms of economic efficiency. They oppose two conceptions of the resources to be provided to the recipient: compensating for a loss (in monetary terms); providing people with adequate means (most often with services, but also, if necessary, with monetary allowances). In the first case, the hypothesis underlying public action is that everyone, whatever her singularity, possesses the full power to convert the income she receives into the actions required to succeed in her life and work plans. Monetary benefits are sufficient (the amount and the method of payment are second-order issues). In the second case, the hypothesis is that there is a high degree of inequality

Figure 12.1. Public action and its IBJJ

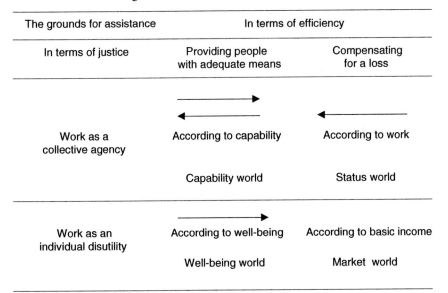

The grounds for assistance	In terms of efficiency	
In terms of justice	Providing people with adequate means	Compensating for a loss
Work as a collective agency	According to capability Capability world	According to work Status world
Work as an individual disutility	According to well-being Well-being world	According to basic income Market world

Note: In each cell, the arrows indicate the temporal orientation of assistance provision. For instance, the welfare delivered in a capability world looks both forward (to people's future) and backward (to their past). It is an in-process welfare adjusted to the evolution of their situation.

among people, in terms of their ability to convert money into concrete beings and doings that are adequate to their future life and the work they intend to do. The implications of this approach are more complex than for the other conception of the grounds for assistance, and lead to informational bases that are generally richer and more complex (Sen 1985).

12.2.2. *Four Types of Public Action Linking Work and Welfare*

The combination of the two preceding oppositions leads to four worlds linking work to welfare. These worlds do not claim to be normative models to be translated into equivalent global institutions. They are 'pragmatic worlds'. Their ambition is to guide the construction of the diverse informational bases that help to benchmark public action with regard to fairness and efficiency. Thus they are connected with the diverse practical and elementary rules that are used or suggested for welfare provision.[2]

In relation to any hazard, what should be assessed and which informational frame of reference should be used to reestablish the functionings relevant to the individual: the person's subsistence income (the market world); the person's work (the status world); the person's well-being (the well-being world); or the person's capabilities (the capability world)?

1. In the market world, it is sufficient for public action to evaluate the income of the individual, whatever its origin, and to compensate for any shortfall up to some minimum line. Hence its informational basis and subsequent rules focus on incomes, basic standard of life, and incentives. These are believed to work just as well for unemployment compensation as for pension or sickness benefits, etc.
2. In the status world, information and rules focus on past work commitments of the recipient and on wages earned. Welfare is justified by the contribution the person made to the creation of wealth. The objective is to determine the extent and duration of compensation for lost wages according to the rights previously acquired (a key statutory element). These principles are believed to work equally whatever the type of hazard.

   Both market and status worlds remain centred on freedom from want, though in different ways.
3. In the well-being world, emphasis is placed on reestablishing and developing the functionings of the person in terms of *beings*: health, nutrition, childcare, leisure, etc. (the list being an outcome of deliberation). Hence the greater importance of services in kind over labor market requirements (even if job tenure through public subsidized schemes may be considered as part of well-being).

---

[2] Three of these worlds are analogous to the familiar three worlds of welfare defined by Esping-Andersen. But, their theoretical and practical statuses are different. The fourth world, the most promising for the future of welfare systems in knowledge-based economies, does not exist in Esping-Andersen's work.

4. In the capability world, emphasis is put on both beings and doings. As an eminent doing, work becomes part of life activities and achievements. Thus the concept of work, taken as a basis for welfare provision (especially for services in kind), comes closer to the one we discussed in Section 12.1.1. Capability is neither that which allows the individual to adapt by being subjected to the vicissitudes of the labor market, nor that which keeps the individual out of that market as long as possible while preserving his or her welfare. Nor is it limited to preserving the person's status. Capability means developing positive freedom in life and in work. This has its own dynamic throughout a person's life and work career. It includes both freedom on the labor market (the freedom to choose to work or not to work; the freedom to choose the work one does) and freedom at work (professional skills, participation in decision-making, lifelong learning, development of mobility, etc.). This world has a strong dimension of procedural and substantive rights which deserve to be investigated with regard to responsibility and accountability.

Both well-being and capability worlds imply a complex informational basis. Judgments on the state of persons are contextual, in-process and deliberative; they use not only general state-centric categories, but also intermediate categories of their own (such as professions, districts, towns). They favor longitudinal inquiries rather than simple administrative general classifications. Probably too, since public action in these worlds is more synthetic and crosscutting, welfare provision is less separated along the strong institutional barriers that traditional social policies have up to now encouraged.

This line of approach should allow us in the last section to identify the capability approach as a desirable path for reforming European welfare states. Before that, a key issue is to appreciate how far Figure 12.1 helps us understand the diversity of systems of social protection in Europe and in the United States.

12.3. The Relationship Between Work and Welfare in OECD Countries

We have used and combined two databases, one from the OECD and the other from the ISSA (close to the ILO). The OECD provides social expenditure data; the ISSA describes the rules for entitlement and provision of the corresponding systems of social protection (ISSA, 2000).

The OECD database (SOCX) shows that social expenditure comprises a variety of collective systems and programs across the member countries.[3] For instance, the OECD distinguishes more than 400 basic expenditure items for France, about 150 for Germany, and 130 for the United Kingdom. Social

---

[3] This database is known as SOCX. See OECD (1998). We left aside other sources on education and training expenditure, because elaborating a capability approach to welfare does not require any extension toward education.

expenditure is divided in thirteen areas, built by crossing two principles. First, expenditure corresponding to cash benefits and services in kind to people are evaluated separately, which, following Section 12.2 and Figure 12.1, is crucial for our purpose. Second, categories are broken down according to the traditional classification of the so-called 'social risks' (old age, illness, unemployment, etc.). No distinction is made in relation to work activities as a basis for entitlement and provision, but the ISSA database will provide this information, which following Figure 12.1, is equally crucial. Mixing OECD and ISSA statistics gives us, for each type (old age, health, unemployment, etc.) and each OECD country, an approximation of social expenditure in four categories: cash universal expenditure; cash work-related expenditure; cash means-tested expenditure;[4] and expenditure on services in kind. Though arduous and raising some technical difficulties for which there is no exact solution, the exercise is feasible to some extent. ISSADOC uses the same type of expenditure classification as the OECD, though a little more aggregated: old age pensions (including disability and survivors); occupational injuries; illness; unemployment; and family benefits.[5] We will not go into the detailed computations, but look directly at the main findings (Section 12.3.1) and then discuss the concepts of corporatism (Section 12.3.2) and universalism (Section 12.3.3).

12.3.1. *The Main Findings*

At the OECD level three main characteristics are noteworthy:

1. Work-related welfare provisions dominate. They represent 108 systems out of a total of 163 (Table 12.1). Far behind, there are 33 universal systems and only 22 means-tested systems, most of the latter concentrated in Anglo-Saxon countries (Australia, Canada, the United Kingdom, Ireland, and New-Zealand). It is striking that the tighter the connection between work performance and the hazard dealt with, the more welfare is linked to work. That is, for instance, the case for occupational injury and disease, for old age (26 systems out of 37), for unemployment (24 out of 36) and even for sickness benefits (24 out of 36).
2. Universalism in its standard conception (see below) is mostly encountered in family allowances (15 out of 30), and family and health-care services. For the latter two, this is true whatever the country, with only rare exceptions (in particular the United States). But universalism very often does not mean in practice equal replacement income, but equal access to services in kind.
3. No OECD country is using the same rule for all risks, whether it be universal, work-related, or means-tested. Even the countries that most focus on a particular

---

[4] In some rare cases, universal or work-related benefits are subject to income or means-testing conditions. We have classified them as means-tested.

[5] Expenditure for social aid or housing benefits is missing, whereas it is included in SOCX: therefore we have excluded those from our analysis.

Table 12.1. Regimes of social protection according to type of rule and social expenditure in 1995[a]

Type of expenditure	Rule of provision			Total (dual regimes)
	Universal	Work-related	Means-tested	
1. Old age, disability, survivors	8	26	3	37 (10)
3. Occupational injury and disease	1	27	0	28 (1)
4. Sickness	9	24	3	36 (9)
7. Family	15	7	8	30 (3)
10. Unemployment	0	24	8	32 (5)
Total	33	108	22	163

[a] Belgium, 1994; Greece, 1993; Italy, 1993; Luxembourg, 1990; United Kingdom, 1994. 27 OECD countries (Hungary and Poland excluded).

Source: ISSADOC (2000).

Note: Row numbers refer to the OECD classification of social protection.

rule do not apply it to every risk, and often combine two, sometimes three rules for a single risk at the same time or in succession.

This again calls into question the adequacy of welfare macro-regime typologies for grasping intra- and international differences in the relationships between work and welfare. We will now look first at the 'corporatist' aspects of welfare regimes and then at the 'universalist' ones, as emphasized by the welfare-state literature.

12.3.2. *Founding Welfare upon Work is not Corporatism: Toward a Work and Welfare Social Agreement?*

More than sticking to corporatism, work-related systems of welfare could be better described during the 1990s as incorporating a work and welfare '*social agreement*' conception. Arguments are both contextual and general.

First, each partner pays for the funding of these systems, and the employer as much if not more than the worker. Out of the 108 contributory systems listed, the employer almost always contributes, and in 3 out of 4 cases at a higher rate than the employee; the insured person also contributes in 3 out of 4 cases. The state supplements the financing or compensates for possible defaulted payments. Second, for the majority of countries and systems, the relation between employer and employee generates rights and obligations on both sides that go beyond the payment of wages. Bearing in mind that current contributions relate to unpredictable future events (as in the case of unemployment or illness), it can be said that the labor contract relies on an exchange of expectations about mutual guarantees regarding the future of the relationship. In other words, for both partners work is neither a commodity, nor simply a physical factor of production. The convention between them[6] is that contracting now establishes the future reciprocity between work performance and, beyond the wage, welfare.

This kind of social agreement is different from a Rawlsian one. On the one side, it is supported by a set of legal and social institutions and by collective agreements. On the other, the positive link its rules create between efficiency and justice is not purely institutional. It operates above all within the work situation itself. Performing good work gives the worker a legitimate claim to security in the future in the event of a hazard. Providing this security to the employee gives the employer the right to expect a certain quality of work in return. Far from operating under a veil of ignorance, both employer and employees can evaluate the situation and their actual and future position in it. Furthermore, a contribution is not a tax. It is the foundation for social dialogue in welfare provision and its link with work. On the basis of their contributions, employers and workers are provided with rights to deliberate about objectives, rules, and reforms of these systems. In OECD countries, employers' organizations and trade unions participate in the management of one out of two work-related systems, alone or with the government. Even if affiliation has often become compulsory, these systems are not strictly part of the state administration. The fact that the state very often contributes is not primarily a sign of funding difficulties. Fundamentally, it means that the community devolves to the state the responsibility for ensuring the long-term viability of the prevailing social agreement.

This work-and-welfare conception sometimes extends beyond salaried employees, the unemployed and retired workers and quite frequently to the self-employed. The right to welfare is maintained beyond a change of employers or occupations. The amount of time worked is calculated in years of professional activity; periods of unemployment and of illness are generally covered, as is sometimes (probably increasingly) child care. Voluntary affiliation is possible in one out of five cases. Conversely, out of 33 universal systems listed, 5 are financed in part by the beneficiaries themselves (a percentage of income or wages) and 8 by firms (through a contribution calculated on the basis of the payroll). In some cases the two systems are combined (14 cases). For instance, Sweden, typically taken as an example of a universal

---

[6] This conception of work as deploying mutual expectations comes from a field of research known in France as 'the economics of conventions'. See, among others, *Revue économique* (1989), Salais (1989, 1998), Wagner (1994), Storper and Salais (1997), Storper (2000).

welfare state, currently has, according to ISSADOC, three systems based on the universal rule and four based on the work-related rule. Pensions and sickness schemes rely on dual systems combining universality and social insurance. Though subsidized by the state at 93 percent of the cost, unemployment compensation relies on some forty trade union funds organized by business sectors. Contribution to unemployment funds is compulsory for trade union members and voluntary affiliation possible for non-members.

This suggests, especially in Europe, a possible movement toward universalizing work-related regimes beyond the strict obligation of working as a dependent employee subordinated to an employer. Another issue is personalization (i.e. the search for greater adequacy of assistance in relation to personal needs). Universal systems shed most light on this point.

12.3.3. *Universalism Is Not Egalitarianism: Toward Personalized Welfare?*

Most often, in matters of welfare provision, universalism is identified with income egalitarianism (what could be better called weak universalism). Data do not confirm this. Among OECD countries, family cash benefits are the only type of benefits in which this rule of weak universalism prevails: residence criterion; and equal benefits for all for a given number of children (and/or dependants). In other cases, true universalism (that is equal access to services in kind) dominates. Services in kind (Table 12.2) account for almost 40 percent of public social expenditure, and are close to the level of cash work-related benefits. Flat-rate cash benefits account only for 22 percent: 15 percent come from universal systems and 7 percent from means-tested systems. Services in kind are more important proportionally, even if not by so much, than cash benefits in the Nordic countries.

Equal monetary benefit is in practice closer to the means-tested rule. According to this rule, every situation should be judged in relation to the income it will produce compared to a certain minimum threshold. Workfare reactivates that logic. The innovation consists in refining the criteria of merit by adding individual search effort. Welfare benefits are conditioned on proof of the person's active determination to reform and get a job.

This rejoins the debate on 'equality of what', discussed in Section 12.1.2. As Sen pointed out with the concept of capabilities, egalitarianism neglects the fact that for most issues people are unequal in their capacity to convert money into an effective and adequate improvement of their situation. In order to combat his inequality, equal access to services and treatment for each person according to his or her needs is required. If it proves necessary, each person must receive a specific kind of help, differing in quality and quantity from that given to others. True universalism goes together with equal access for all,

Toward a Capability Approach

Table 12.2. Social expenditure by type and nature in 1995[a]
(% of GDP)—non-weighted mean of all countries

Type of expenditure	Cash expenditure			Cash total	Expenditure on services	Total
	Rule of provision					
	Universal	Means-tested	Work-related			
1. Old age, disability, survivors	2.09	0.83	5.94	8.86	0.76	9.62
3. Occupational injury and disease	0	0	0.26	0.26	0	0.26
4. Sickness and Health	0	0.05	0.48	0.53	5.86	6.39
7. Family	0.88	0.22	0.20	1.30	0.45	1.75
10. Unemployment	0.13	0.23	1.26	1.61	0.56	2.29
Together	3.10	1.33	8.13	12.56	7.63	20.31

[a] Belgium, 1994; Greece, 1993; Italy, 1993; Luxembourg, 1990; United Kingdom, 1994. 27 OECD countries (Hungary and Poland excluded).

Source: SOCX reworked by the author.
Note: Row numbers refer to the OECD classification of social expenditure.

singularity of the treatment provided, and uniqueness of each person. This tends to be the case for health care access even if, in practice, there is a certain hierarchy in the quality of care provided depending on social stratification. For unemployment, expenditure on services accounts on average for one quarter of all expenditure—which is far from negligible.

To conclude, our conjecture from these data is that, among OECD countries (and even more so in Europe) welfare systems are empirically close to an architecture combining a long-term work-and-welfare 'social agreement' between employers, workers, and the state with more personalization of assistance. Welfare provision seems to be less general and more contextual than originally. These features are *a priori* compatible with the ongoing transformation of work and with positive freedom. But nothing ensures that these potentialities will be effectively grasped and prolonged. First, while combining, like other countries, diverse worlds in their social provision, Anglo-Saxon countries are more focused on the market world than the other ones and possibly more distant from such an architecture. Second, with these data we cannot properly disentangle which activation policies are inspired by a capability approach and which by a neo-liberal one. Nevertheless, as both assume that work has no intrinsic positive value, neither workfare nor decommodification seem truly to capture these features.

12.4. A Capability Turn in European Social Policy?

Could a capability approach as developed in the preceding sections, fit this empirical conjecture and serve as an appropriate path for reforming European welfare states? Any positive answer requires identifying, from our data, the IBJJs on which OECD systems of social protection relied in the 1990s. This requires us to address both conceptual and methodological questions (Section 12.4.1) before European countries can be compared in this respect (Section 12.4.2). Section 12.4.3 discusses the advantages and difficulties for Social Europe in advancing a capability approach.

12.4.1. *Conceptual and Methodological Issues*

12.4.1.1. *Social Expenditure as a Collective Investment*
In a capability approach, social expenditure is viewed above all as a collective investment in people's capabilities. This investment excludes no means and no rules, whatever their foundation and justification in a given world, insofar as these means and rules prove to be fair and efficient with regard to the individual situations at stake. This is a core message of Sen's work, whose importance comes from the basic objective of improving effective freedom and the range of possibilities made accessible to all (in the market and on the job). The issue at stake is not only whether to spend more or less (though a country spending much less than another one, can—*ceteris paribus*—be suspected of some neglect of capabilities), but also how to spend and on what type of help. Monetary aid on a short-term basis may be enough, at a given moment and a given place, for able and well-adapted people. The question is more complex for many others and calls for free and guaranteed access to services in kind, both collectively supported and provided on a personalized and in-process basis.

Hence, any comparison between welfare expenditures by type and country requires comparable data on the rate of investment in social expenditure and on the distribution of expenditure among the four worlds defined in Section 12.2. What immediately emerges are the differences of productivity and capacity to pay between countries, as well as between people. To take these differences into account, for each type of expenditure (in the OECD classification), we propose, first to estimate the expenditure per potential recipient, then to divide the result by the mean workers' remuneration in the country. At equal capacity to pay, the resulting ratio expresses the rate of investment *per capita* each country has accepted to subtract from its current spending. In the same way, this ratio also measures the percentage of mean individual remuneration reserved for collective solidarity, in other words 'the value of solidarity' in force in each country. Thus deflated, this benchmark renders actual efforts more comparable. For instance a country A whose mean expenditure per unemployed person is only 0.2 of the mean wage can be seen as investing less in the capabilities of the unemployed and valuing solidarity for them less in case of job loss than a country B which spends 0.4 of the mean wage,[7] even if, in absolute terms, country A might spend more than country B.

12.4.1.2. *From Worlds of Welfare to Social Expenditure*
In Figure 12.1, identifying the IBJJ requires two key empirical distinctions concerning social expenditure: between cash expenditure (monetary benefits), and expenditure on services in kind; and whether assistance is justified or not in relation to work. In effect, the former is, to some extent, correlated with the relative importance of monetary compensation vs. the provision of adequate means; the latter has to do with the opposition between work as an agency (hence the link with work) and work as a disutility. Fortunately these two empirical distinctions are available in the data built up in Section 12.3. However, no distinction of worlds of welfare can be made within services in kind, whereas their contextual dimension is key. Personalization of welfare could be (and sometimes is) focused on immediate individual adaptability and employability or on lifelong capabilities. In the case of unemployment, for instance, we classified active labor market policies as services in kind. Setting aside administrative costs and monetary incentives for hiring (like tax reductions),[8] these policies may be workfare-oriented, capability-oriented, more probably an unintentional mix of both, depending on the programs, countries, organizers, and users. Some ambiguity remains at a macro level, which calls for further qualitative investigation.

Nevertheless, some rough generalizations are possible. For instance, for a given country and program, the more social expenditure is oriented toward the delivery of services in kind and the more it is related to work, the higher the probability of belonging to the capability world. By contrast, the more social expenditure consists of monetary benefits with no work foundation, the higher the probability of finding the market world; the same applies to the other worlds.

12.4.1.3. *From Gross Public to Net Social Expenditure*
In OECD data, expenditure is evaluated according to the concept of 'gross public social expenditure'. This raises the questions of the public/private and

---

[7] Empirical inequality issues should also be treated in a later stage of research. At a given level of solidarity, the allocation of benefits and services could remain unequal, if it is inadequately based (for instance based not upon capabilities, but upon simple income redistribution). This does not exclude distributive measures, under the condition that they be well considered.

[8] Administrative costs have been excluded and tax cuts for hiring unemployed people (for instance, the young) allocated to work-related cash expenditure.

gross/net oppositions.[9] There are two main difficulties: how to classify social programs or institutions that, though not funded by the state budget and taxes, are nevertheless collective non-market devices? What is the role of taxation and of tax incentives?

Strictly speaking, 'public' expenditure is that which involves financial flows coming within the budget of the state. This means that flows are controlled by public authorities (central, regional, and local government).[10] Problems arise when social security institutions are created by social actors (with or without the participation of the state). When these are mandatory, it could be legitimate to consider them within public social expenditure. But, as a result, we lose sight of the professional origin of a number of these institutions and wrongly tend to identify mandatory social contributions with taxes. Thus with equal legitimacy, one could consider them as 'private', and not to be included as part of public social expenditure. Yet these welfare systems in which assistance financed and delivered by non-state collective institutions (funds managed by employers, professional mutual organizations, non-profit organizations, etc.), are not strictly private, but 'intermediate' between private and public. In these collective organizations, the state continues to play a public regulatory but non-financial role (defining rights, management schemes, guarantees in case of default, etc.). It would be better to consider that so long as membership is not subject to an individualized risk profile, these institutions do not fall entirely within the sphere of the market (and thus to reserve the term 'private' for direct recourse to the market on the part of individuals). The other difficulty is taxation. A portion of the benefits may be subject to tax. A few national examples show that, although means-tested benefits are generally not subject to tax, benefits under universal regimes tend to be, and work-related benefits are often taxed as well. Furthermore, through incentives or exoneration, taxation affects income inequalities, especially in the case of the family.[11]

In its recent work, the OECD has come to consider the best all-encompassing concept to be that of 'net total social expenditure', including the taxation effect as well as mandatory and voluntary 'private' social expenditure. The effect of switching to this concept has sometimes been spectacular for the six countries in relation to which the calculation was made. After correction, the percentages of national GDP devoted to social expenditure tend to

---

[9] See Adema *et al.* (1996); Adema and Einerhand (1998).

[10] In addition, part of the expenditure made by local or regional authorities (especially in countries with a federal organization) is not recorded either by OECD or by the national statistics. We do not deal with them here (see OECD 1998, 1999).

[11] Many countries use differential taxation or tax credits to help families with low or median incomes. These are becoming an increasingly central instrument of welfare policy in the Anglo-Saxon countries.

Table 12.3. From gross public social expenditure to net current total social expenditure in 1993 in six countries (as a percentage of GDP at factor cost)

	Germany	Sweden	United States	United Kingdom	Standard deviation (6 countries)
Gross public social expenditure	32.48	42.38	16.31	26.91	8.85
Net current public social expenditure +	27.17	32.39	16.96	23.92	5.03
Net current mandatory private social expenditure +	0.90	0.39	0.53	0.20	
Net current voluntary private social expenditure	1.45	0.97	7.82	3.19	
Net current total social expenditure	29.52	33.76	24.24	27.31	3.17
Other countries studied					
Denmark	35.25			—	27.13
Netherlands	34.02			—	28.20

Source: Adema and Einerhand (1998: 36, table 9).

become less divergent (Table 12.3). The expenditure rates in 1993 were initially spread between 16.3 percent (United States) and 42.4 percent (Sweden), but their dispersion narrowed after correction to between 24.4 and 33.8 percent.

What implications do these problems have for the interpretation of our data? Roughly speaking, taking account of the taxation effect would somewhat lower the effective level of benefits available to the recipients, and distributed through universal and work-related welfare systems. This does not affect services in kind. The omission of voluntary 'private' social expenditure underestimates the overall rate of social expenditure in the United States and the United Kingdom: this overwhelmingly applies to health-care and old-age cash expenditures.

12.4.2. *Comparing European Countries*

Figure 12.2 presents the deflated rate of social expenditure, broken down into the four types of expenditure: three in cash (means-tested, universal, work-related), the last on services in kind.[12] For reasons of space, we present the

---

[12] For Figure 12.2, we have left aside disease and injuries expenditure, for the services in kind in this category have not been isolated in the OECD database.

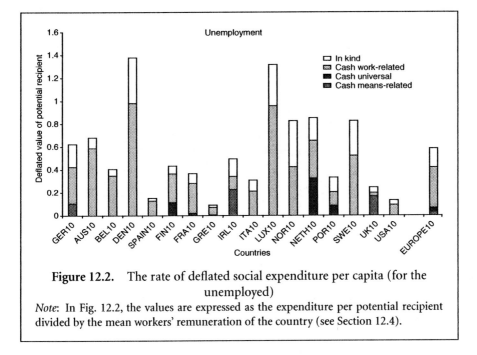

Figure 12.2. The rate of deflated social expenditure per capita (for the unemployed)

Note: In Fig. 12.2, the values are expressed as the expenditure per potential recipient divided by the mean workers' remuneration of the country (see Section 12.4).

unemployment case only. The number of potential recipients was the mean yearly number of the unemployed (in ILO definition).[13] The higher the ratio, the more the country at stake values social investment and solidarity, without hindering its competitiveness to a large extent.

Unemployment is a major specificity of the European social model, compared to the United States. Europe invests in supporting the unemployed and in recycling them into jobs. Some positive economic return on investment is expected from the future productive contribution of these people when at work. For Europe the mean deflated ratio for unemployment is 0.58, shared between cash benefits for three-quarters of it (mostly from work-related benefits) and services in kind (active policy measures) for one quarter. An unemployed person is valued a little bit more than half a worker. In some countries (Denmark and Luxembourg) the ratio rises to more than one and in some others (the Netherlands, Norway, and Sweden) it is almost equal to one. These countries combine important efforts in active policy measures with generous allocations from work-related systems (universal system added in the Netherlands). But there is a wide heterogeneity among European countries.

[13] As published in the OECD Active Population Statistics.

Some are close to the mean, slightly above, like Austria (0.68) and Germany (0.62), or just below, like Ireland (0.50). France (0.37) is below the line for benefits as well as for active policies. This is probably due to excessive selection of applicants. The Southern countries (Greece, Italy, Portugal, and Spain) and the United Kingdom (0.25) are well below. Whatever its political emphasis on the merits of workfare, the United Kingdom as a community simply does not invest in the recycling of unemployed people. Expenditure per unemployed person is very thin both in terms of benefits (0.20) and active policies (0.05). The ratio dropped to 0.18 in 1997, which has to be referred to the means-tested conception (what we called the market world) that dominates in the United Kingdom.

Further investigation is needed to tell whether these investments in supporting and recycling the unemployed pay or not. Figure 12.2 shows that the most investing countries combine work-related benefits with services in kind. Measures improving employability go together with fair income replacement measures, and cannot simply replace them. Are we observing in these countries some virtuous combination emerging between the status and capability worlds? Or is there some unconscious and bizarre mix between different types of public action? The Southern countries or the United Kingdom (but not only those) seem far from developing any capability approach. In order to do so, they should begin developing non-means-tested (or less conditional) allocations and policies. More generally, one can assume that preventive policies, which treat capabilities through within-job schemes, should be less costly and more efficient than repairing *ex post* damages. This could be achieved by training schemes in firms, sectors, or localities, as well as by procedures of consultation and information of workers in case of employment difficulties. This kind of experiment is likely to be easier to promote in countries far advanced in active policy measures (Nordic and some Continental countries).

12.4.3. *Is There a Capability Path for Europe?*

In a capability approach, choices in welfare provision are not made 'under a veil of ignorance' (as in Rawlsian approaches), but through the discovery and analysis of the relevant facts. Choices are, above all, a question of building adequate informational bases and of publicly debating them. The two keywords are pragmatism and effective improvement of situations at stake. For such choices, no strategic political agreement between governments of the Member States is necessary. The first step to be made at the European level concerns the statistical tools and methods for adequately benchmarking national social policies with reference to the capability world. Benchmarking national efforts is precisely a major aspect of the Open Method of Coordination that Europe has begun to develop. The second step could be to ask the

Member States to make explicit what they believe are their good practices in a capability-based approach (i.e. actions that, in social fields, aim to improve the capabilities of their applicants). Unemployment or social exclusion can once more become key domains for experimentation (or in which current developments can be reoriented toward capability improvement). Asking Member States to create their own indicators and to explain to others in detail their processes (categories, practical rules used by the public agencies, methodology, and so on) and how these fit with a capability approach would be politically fruitful. A public debate could then develop on the development of such a European approach and on how this approach could compromise with local conventions and policies.

One must say that the first developments of the OMC (in the European Employment Strategy and in the struggle against social exclusion) are disappointing in this regard. For instance, to deal with social exclusion, Atkinson *et al.* (2002) prioritized static indicators of poverty and the proportion of the least well-off people. Non-monetary and dynamic indicators should be developed concerning capability deprivation. The yearly reports on employment in Europe use the overall rate of employment (the number of jobs divided by the total population of 15–64 year-olds) to evaluate the performance of the Member States, in other words, the quantity of jobs, independently of their quality in terms of skills, wage, type of contract or welfare package, possible future careers, lifelong employability of their holders, freedom of choice in work, balance between work and private time, and so on— which are key characteristics of the capabilities that determine the scope of effective freedoms to achieve (precisely the focal features Sen speaks about, as seen in Section 12.1). These should serve to evaluate the inequality of capabilities between people and are essential to improve personal situations effectively. Empirical studies show that bad jobs (even if the fiscal poverty traps are corrected) cannot enable people durably to escape poverty.[14] As seen in the United Kingdom, and also in France (Observatoire national de la pauvreté et de l'exclusion 2002), the drift toward means-tested benefits accentuates this phenomenon. Both omissions, in European inclusion and employment policies, must be overcome for Social Europe to advance among a capability path. If not, there will be a strange ballet in which European employment and inclusion policies, hand in hand, will reproduce the mechanisms creating poverty more than effectively combating them.

Quality of work and of welfare must thus be implemented at the core of all the European policy coordination processes (including the Broad Economic

---

[14] According to ECHP, almost 18% of people of working age considered as 'partially excluded' are below the poverty line in Europe. 'Partially excluded' people are those whose time spent in employment is less than 50% over a 3-year period (Muffels and Fouarge 2002).

Policy Guidelines). The European Commission (especially the Employment and Social Affairs Directorate General) is aware of the crucial importance of these matters[15] and, at the end of 2001, the Belgian Presidency undertook very valuable work to launch the construction of appropriate indicators. Eight key indicators of quality in work ('to measure progress') and 23 context indicators ('to support the analysis') have been recommended in eight areas such as: intrinsic job quality; skills; lifelong learning and career development; gender equality; etc. But much remains to be done not only, as usually emphasized, on the availability of statistics and on their comparability, but on the principles guiding that work. The main danger is that the process of improving job quality will develop in isolation from macroeconomic concerns and actors. If so, it will satisfy, at least superficially for a while, social actors, but without effectively influencing European macroeconomic coordination or national policies. Evidence of this danger can be seen in the fact that the established list of indicators seems eclectic, too long, and lacks a theoretical or normative background. In such a perspective, statistical benchmarking risks favoring policies that manipulate indicators to achieve a better score. It puts countries in competition to discover, not true best practices, but rather strategies which improve their statistical profile (a well-known problem in economics). Conversely, by stressing informational bases of justice, a capability approach for Europe would seek to prevent such a drift.

Until now some oversights are striking. First, indicators of expenditure should be developed, not only indicators of outcomes however arrived at. When so doing, wide inequalities of expenditure would appear between countries that raise some doubts about true outcomes and should require the Member States to explain to others in detail their processes and indicators. Second, as for the European Employment Strategy as a whole, the debate on benchmarking is confined to a restricted circle of experts and policy makers. A public debate should develop on indicators and benchmarking that follows a capability path in employment and social policies. Social partners at all levels (local and sectoral as well as national and European) could have a core responsibility in organizing this public debate: for instance, in developing such a European capability approach and exploring how it could be reconciled with national conventions and policies. A key signal of true commitment to quality would be an effective interaction between the overall employment rate and indicators of quality of work. For instance, at what age limits to fix the

---

[15] See COM (2001) 313 final, 'Employment and Social Policies: A Framework for Investing in Quality', 20 July 2001; the minutes of the European Conference: 'For a Better Quality of Work' organized by the European Industrial Relations Observatory (EIRO) (Brussels, 20–21 September 2001); or 'Indicators of Quality in Work', EU Employment Committee, 23 November 2001.

overall rate of employment. Fifteen or 20 years old makes a big difference, in relation to whether casual jobs for young people are included in the computation. How to count part-time jobs for women and older people, to distinguish between involuntary and voluntary part-time work? Is it a serious proposition to define objectives impossible to achieve in the prescribed time? For many countries, reaching a 70 percent employment rate, as specified by the EU's Lisbon objectives, means yearly job creation rates beyond what has ever been achieved in the past.

Setting indicators aside, a capability approach would fit with some emerging themes of European social policy discourse. Viewed as a collective investment in people's capabilities, social protection would truly become a productive factor and link justice and efficiency positively. As solidarity is a basic value of the European Social Model, the defence of this value through renewed arguments, adapted to the more individualized nature of our societies, would be a fair strategy to promote the idea of Europe politically. Some of the decisive factors are beyond governments' control: economic trends and fluctuations; long-term expectations and behavior of workers, families, and future recipients, and so on. As seen in Section 12.4.1.3, the funding itself, far from belonging to the state budget and coming from taxes, largely falls under the command of other actors: social partners, local authorities, non-profit organizations, and voluntary collective schemes, recipients themselves via savings or market insurance; and the same is true for welfare provision. This leaves much room for social and civil dialogue in Europe (see Salais and Villeneuve 2002)—whose implications and development are part of the European Social Agenda—to address work and welfare issues.

References

ADEMA, W. and EINERHAND, M. (1998). 'The Growing Role of Private Social Benefits'. *OECD Labor Market and Social Policy Occasional Papers*, 32. Paris: OECD.

—— EINERHAND, M., EKLIND, B., LOTZ, J., and PEARSON, M. (1996). 'Net Public Social Expenditure'. *OECD Labor Market and Social Policy Occasional Papers*, 19. Paris: OECD.

ATKINSON, T., CANTILLON B., MARLIER, E., and NOLAN, B. (2002). *Social Indicators: the EU and Social Inclusion*. Oxford: Oxford University Press.

ESPING-ANDERSEN, G. (1990). *The Three Worlds of Welfare Capitalism*. Cambridge: Polity Press.

—— with GALLIE, D., HEMERIJCK, A., and MYLES, J. (2002). *Why We Need a New Welfare State*. Oxford: Oxford University Press.

International Social Security Association (ISSA) (2000). *Social Security Worldwide Database*. Geneva: ISSA.

MUFFELS, R. and FOUARGE, D. (2002). 'Labor Market Attachment, Income Poverty and Consumption Deprivation. How Successful Are Employment Regimes to Cope with Exclusion', in R. Muffels and P. Tsakloglou (eds), *Social Exclusion in Europe: An Empirical Analysis*. Aldershot: Edward Elgar, forthcoming.

Observatoire national de la pauvreté et de l'exclusion (2002). *Rapport 2001–2002*. Paris: La Documentation française.

OECD (1998). *Social Expenditure Database (SOCX)*. Paris: OECD.

—— (1999). *Fighting Against Exclusion*. 3 vols. Paris: OECD.

Rawls, J. (1971). *A Theory of Justice*. Cambridge, MA: Harvard University Press.

Revue économique (1989). 'L'économie des conventions', special issue, 40/2, March.

Salais, R. (1989). 'L'analyse économique des conventions du travail'. *Revue économique*, 40, March: 199–240.

—— (1998). 'Le travail à l'épreuve de ses produits', in A. Supiot (ed.), *Le travail en perspectives*. Paris: LGDJ, 45–68.

—— and Raveaud, G. (2002). 'Rethinking the Concept of Social Exclusion: Towards a "Capabilities" Approach'. Submitted to the *Journal of Social European Policy*.

—— and Villeneuve, R. (eds) (2002). *Europe and the Politics of Capabilities*, forthcoming.

Sen, A. (1983). 'Poor, Relatively Speaking', *Oxford Economic Papers*, 35: 153–69.

—— (1985). 'Commodities and Capabilities'. *North-Holland Lectures in Economics*, 7. Amsterdam: North Holland.

—— (1990). 'Justice: Means versus Freedom'. *Philosophy and Public Affairs*, 19/2: 111–21.

Storper, M. (2000). 'Conventions and the Genesis of Institutions', in L. Burlamaqui, A. C. Castro, and H.-J. Chang (eds), *Institutions and the Role of the state*. Aldershot: Edward Elgar.

Storper, M. and Salais, R. (1997). *Worlds of Production. The Action Frameworks of the Economy*. Cambridge, MA: Harvard University Press.

Supiot, A. (ed.) (2001). *Beyond Employment. Transformation of Work and the Future of Labor Law in Europe*. Oxford: Oxford University Press.

Townsend, P. (1985). 'A Sociological Approach to the Measurement of Poverty. A Reply to Sen'. *Oxford Economic Papers*, 37: 659–68.

Wagner, P. (1994). 'Dispute, Uncertainty and Institution in Recent French Debates'. *The Journal of Political Philosophy*, 2: 270–89.

13

Sovereignty and Solidarity: EU and US

JOSHUA COHEN AND CHARLES F. SABEL

13.1. Some Stylized Facts About the EU's Democratic Vocation

In a world that still venerates democracy's principles but regularly despairs of its practice, the nascent political order of the European Union is a crucial test case. Can the ideal of self-government be extended to this new setting, with its welter of problem-solving committees, processes, and reflection groups that appear to lie beyond the reach of popular direction and accountability? What does the prospect of this extension tell us about the possibilities of popular sovereignty and redistributive solidarity when politics extends beyond current national political boundaries? And what does it tell us about the possibilities of democracy itself?

To address these questions, we begin with a stylized description of the European Union. Although the elements of the description are not completely uncontentious, they command sufficient agreement that they must be respected by any theoretical characterization of what the European Union is and what it might become.

Judged simply by its ability to survive, the EU is a success. 'Unity impossible, collapse improbable', is the grudging acknowledgment of a British observer inclined to Euro-skepticism (Garton Ash 2001: 60–7). In a dynamic environment, where the basic terms of collaboration remain uncertain but paralysis would soon lead to breakdown, existence itself is an achievement. In particular the European Union is managing to reconcile two tasks, each of which is extremely demanding even without the constraints imposed by pursuit of the other. Thus it is achieving an integrated market by eliminating obstacles to internal trade—in particular by mutual recognition of norms of commercial exchange (as urged by the European Court of Justice),[1] and by their harmonization through other means—while also protecting public health and safety, avoiding regulatory races to the bottom and possibly initiating some races to the top. To be sure, outcomes differ by policy area, with greater harmonization, and at a higher level, in safety devices for machines than in highway or railroad transport, and more in transport than in taxation. But areas that seemed intractable ten years ago—such as transport, education, immigration, and asylum—are no longer so. And areas such as taxation—that seemed indissolubly linked to the traditions and practices of individual Member States, and natural instruments of competitive conflict—now seem at least in principle possible arenas of harmonization.[2] Whatever the precise extent of regulation, dark predictions of a new laissez-faire order, established beyond the reach of existing national regulatory regimes, have been overturned by events.

Moving from policy to process, the European Union is producing the regulatory setting for the integrated market through new forms of rule-making issuing in open-ended rules. One well-studied example is *comitology*. This system of expert committees, appointed by the Member States, works with the Commission and drafts regulatory proposals for areas such as telecommunications equipment, foodstuffs, cosmetics, or pressure vessels. In principle decision-making in these committees is by qualified majority vote. In practice they operate through deliberation—(self-)reflective debate by which participants reason about proposals and are open to changing their own initial preferences—aimed at consensus. Committee deliberations are driven by the comparison of differences among current regulatory systems in the Member States. Such comparisons permit identification of best practices that serve as the starting point for a detailed, harmonized regime. Because the Commission is formally implementing decisions of the Council, and the committees are formally assisting the Commission, comitology preserves, though just barely, the appearance that a sovereign lawgiver—the European Union in the guise of the Commission and the Council—is setting the rules (Joerges, Ladeur, and Vos 1997; Van Schendelen 1998; Joerges and Vos 1999; Christiansen and Kirchner 2000).

A more recent and encompassing version of this kind of regulatory device—a decentralized specification of standards, disciplined by systematic comparison—is the Open Method of Coordination (OMC). In the OMC Member States agree to formulate national action plans to further, say,

---

[1] Case 120/78 *Rewe-Zentrale AG v. Bundesmonopolverwaltung für Branntwein (Cassis de Dijon)* (1979) ECR 649; Case C-212/97 *Centros Ltd. v. Erhvervs-og Selkskabssttryrelsen* (1999) ECR I-1459.

[2] For an overview and references to detailed studies of developments in these policy areas see Héritier (1999).

employment promotion. These plans integrate, and adjust their policies in related, but typically distinct areas such as training, the operation of the labor market, taxation, and aspects of social security. The plans are periodically criticized by a panel of expert officials from other Member States in light of other plans, and each country's performance is judged against its own goals, the performance of the others, and its response to earlier rounds of criticism. The exact mechanisms by which the OMC is applied differ between policy areas, especially with regard to the thoroughness of peer review and the sanctions for lax response by Member States. These (sometimes significant) differences aside, the goal here too is mutual correction, not uniformity, and here too peak-level consultation among experts grows out of and reflects back upon a broader process of consultation. The extent to which that consultation ramifies into the larger society—the extent to which deliberation by policymakers is connected to broader democratic debate and practice—is an open question.[3]

The OMC formalizes and makes manifest a form of policy-making that the European Union has applied to encourage an integrated approach to economic development regionally and social inclusion—as a response to grinding poverty—locally. With regard to social inclusion, for example, the European Union typically funds at the municipal level a public–private partnership whose members are drawn from NGOs and the relevant statutory authorities (the welfare department, the training service, and so on). Organized as a not-for-profit corporation, this partnership solicits proposals to combat social exclusion from local groups, which may themselves be public–private partnerships organized as non-profits. The most promising proposals are selected and reviewed periodically in the light of their ability to achieve their goals, and the achievements of other projects in the parent company's jurisdiction. In addition to monies provided by the European Union, funding for projects often includes resources formally allocated to the statutory agencies and placed at the disposition of the local partnership by board members with the approval of their home department. The performance of the parent company is, ideally, evaluated by comparison of its projects to those of its peers nationally and within the European Union. But practice and ideal typically have only a nodding acquaintance in this regard. As in the case of the OMC, integrated programs that reflect the peculiarities of their contexts emerge through iterated, critical comparison of local initiative (Sabel 1996; Geddes and Benington 2001).

The European Court of Justice (ECJ) has tolerated these innovations in regulatory process, despite their tenuous connection to the constitutional

---

[3] See the introduction and the chapters by Trubek and Mosher and Goetschy, this volume.

structure, such as it is, of the European Union (or any other advanced democracy, for that matter). In particular, the ECJ has not substantially limited the cascading delegation of authority by the European Union or Member States to experts or public–private partnerships, and from them to actors in civil society. Instead, the ECJ has from time to time sought to regularize, if not 'constitutionalize' them. Thus the ECJ requires that comitological deliberations be generally transparent to the public, respect the full range of reasonable argument, and strictly apply certain other rules of procedure.[4] The ECJ has arguably itself encouraged a roughly analogous form of rule making by occasionally using its case law jurisprudence to articulate frameworks within which the parties, after extensive collaboration with affected interests, must construct concrete solutions. Is this de facto collaboration between the ECJ and the Commission a marriage of convenience, an expression of judicial deference or defeat, or an intimation of an emerging (if imperfectly grasped) understanding of a new form of democratic constitutionalism?[5]

So the European Union is having some success in reconciling market integration and protection of public health and safety, creating integrative actors regionally and locally, and fostering deliberative policy-making in the regulatory surround of the single market. Moreover, the Commission and the ECJ (a de facto constitutional court) are amicably cohabitating. Nevertheless, the EU manifestly suffers from a 'democratic deficit'.

Most notably, it has failed to engage the attention of a European electorate. Turnout for elections to the European Parliament has declined steadily from some 60 percent of the eligible voters a decade ago to some 50 percent today, and would decline further still were it not for compulsory voting laws. Neither has it fomented, beyond the formalities of elections, the creation of an engaged European public sphere or a European demos, debating the future of a European polity.

Indeed, the European Union has failed to give its political institutions even the gross outward trappings of constitutionality. It is unclear, for example, whether the European Union legislature is the Council, comprising representatives of the Member States, or the European Parliament, with its represented deputies. More exactly, it is clear that whenever the co-decision procedure applies—and it is the most common option—Council and Parliament are co-equal in the legislative process (see Article 251 EC). A further complication arises from the Commission's agenda-setting powers. Is it an administrative or

---

[4] Case T-188/97 *Rothmans International BV* v. *Commission* [1999] ECR II-02463; see for a more recent and ambitious effort to 'constitutionalize' EU regulatory processes, the opinion of advocate General Jacobs C-50/00P, *Union de Pequeños Agricoltores* v. *Council of the European Union*, delivered 21 March 2002.

[5] For an excellent anthology of current research on the ECJ, see de Búrca and Weiler (2001).

executive organ of government? It is commonly and correctly remarked that the European Union would not admit itself to membership, because it lacks the conventional features of representative democracy required of applicant countries.[6]

Now the stylization gets more complicated and for that reason more interesting. While the European Union faces a democratic deficit, it is not entirely unaccountable, and not only because national level accountability is inherited at the EU level. In the 1990s the Member States have convened themselves in a nearly continuous series of 'intergovernmental' conferences (IGCs) and semi-annual European Council sessions, supplemented by the periodic formation of high-level reflection groups. These overlapping meetings would be called an extended constitutional convention if the result, or aim, had been to establish a document with the foundational character of a constitution (Smith 2002). Instead the main results have been, by traditional standards, meta-constitutional on the one hand and sub-constitutional, verging on the operational, on the other. Meta-constitutionally the IGCs and their offspring have explicitly authorized the European Union to extend its competence to areas such as health, education, and protection against discrimination not contemplated in the treaties establishing the European Union. Through the (non-binding) Charter of Fundamental Rights they have taken a step towards eventually founding or conditioning the law of the EU treaties and the ECJ on a jurisprudence of human rights, including those that begin to give substance to the idea of 'Social Europe'. Sub-constitutionally, or, if you like, extra-constitutionally, they have produced innovations such as the OMC (Craig and de Búrca 1999/2003). Is it political blockage or insight into the limits of the traditional notions of the separation of powers that hinders efforts at the intermediate level? Why the continuing oversight of the Member States has not issued in constitutionally conventional (re)form is, in any case, another open question.

The traditional social partners—labor unions and employers associations—can also be said to be actively acquiescing in, and in some measure validating, the new EU order. This claim seems of course absurd from the vantage point of German, British, or French experience. In these large countries the European Union, and globalization more generally, is seen as shaking the foundations of the labor movement. But in the small countries, such as Ireland, Portugal, the Netherlands, or Denmark, labor participates in various social pacts that make it, with capital, a partner in national adjustment to the new, EU context. Whether these pacts are durable, and whether

---

[6] On the complexity of the institutional relations see, for example the reviews of literature by Scully (2001) and Tsebelis and Garrett (2001).

they create 'new actors' in the sense of the EU regions and localities noted above, or rejuvenate traditional, neo-corporatist arrangements, are also open questions.[7]

These limits on the size of the democratic deficit notwithstanding, EU governance in general, and the success of its innovative rule making in particular, depend on the participation of experts who are not accountable by the familiar methods of legislative oversight or judicial review. Technical experts are crucial to the committees of comitology and the OMC. But these technical experts play a novel role. Efforts to integrate discrete solutions in new regional and local institutions and in the OMC explicitly obligate participating experts to revisit their assumptions in the light of the experience of peers in related disciplines. Comitology teaches a similar lesson about the ambiguity and insufficiency of disciplinary knowledge by exposing experts to disparate solutions that an apparently homogeneous body of professional knowledge—their home field—warrants. Whether this opening by experts to outsiders in processes of practical deliberation extends to inclusion of laypersons—even as knowledgeable 'clients' or 'expert users'—in the circle of decision-making is an open question. Whether such inclusion, assuming it exists, is extensive enough to influence our understanding of democratic participation and accountability is more open still.

Despairing of the see-saw character and sheer opacity of the debate about the European Union's democratic accountability, moved by concern for popular control, or simply anxious to forestall 'populist' rejection of globalization in one region, the European Union's elites have, finally, convened a constitutional convention in Brussels. Its current focus of attention on conventional proposals and its compulsive sideways glances at the European Union's own unconventional practices together capture the yearning for normalcy and the thrall of experimentation that grips the Union today.

For now debate in the convention focuses on normalizing the European Union by endowing it with the two classic elements of democratic constitutions dating to the French and American Revolutions: a statement of inalienable rights (enumerated recently in the Charter of Fundamental Rights of the European Union) and a _Kompetenzkatalog_ delimiting the powers and privileges of the various branches and levels of government. The most salient such catalog is the German proposal to restructure the European Union on the model of the Bundesrepublik, with a bicameral legislature consisting of a parliament of Euro deputies elected by direct vote of the citizens and

---

[7] For an account emphasizing the influence of monetary constraints on bargaining structures see Iversen, Pontusson, and Soskice (2000). For explanations focusing on new roles for the social actors as agents of welfare state reform see Green-Pedersen, van Kersbergen, and Hemerijck (2001).

a senate with members appointed by the governments of the Member States.[8]

But off stage there is acknowledgement and discussion of the two de facto abnormal efforts at constitutional reform noted above: the IGC and the OMCs. Both are constitutional insofar as they plainly allow the Member States, as masters of the European Union's founding treaties, to extend the competence and transform the decision-making processes of the European Union in ways not currently authorized by treaty provisions. Both, but most especially the OMCs, are constitutionally anomalous in that they foster integration across levels of government and between branches of government: they connect what the *Kompetenzkatalog* would sunder. More worrisome still, from the traditional perspective, the OMCs might come to shape the more detailed understanding of rights, rather than merely 'implementing' them: subject to international treaty provisions, the right to asylum in the European Union could be shaped as much by the interpretation of practice through the OMC as by decisions of the ECJ.

The connections between the traditional debate and consideration of the abnormal constitutional projects are more intimate than appears. The experienced politicians attending the Convention are well aware that even cosmetic democratization of the formal relations among EU institutions could easily limit the effectiveness of current methods of decision-making. Allowing the European Parliament to enhance its control of the Commission by electing some proportion of Commissioners, for example, would likely set off strategic games in both institutions that could undermine the Commission's crucial role as a convening 'neutral' in comitological and other regulatory processes. More generally, and unintended or higher-order consequences aside, political operatives know that cosmetic solutions face a deep problem. A fundamental constitutional defect of the European Union, from the traditional point of view, is the delegation or dispersion of state authority from formal organs of government to non-state actors. Reforms of gross constitutional framework that leave this 'defect' untouched will change only appearances. But the 'defect' also appears to be the source of regulatory success. So really eliminating it— by turning current regulatory arrangements into the administrative agencies of a newly constitutionalized Eurostate—may buy gains in conventional democracy at the cost of problem-solving efficacy.[9] In any case, given the dangers of inadvertently subverting problem-solving by cosmetic reform, and the

---

[8] The speech of the German foreign minister, Joschka Fischer, in Berlin on 12 May 2000, that opened the current constitutional debate, refers to the goal of a 'European Federation' in the first sentence.

[9] A good statement of the mismatch between the innovative thrust of EU governance and efforts to democratize the European Union on the model of classic administrative state is Dehousse (2002*a*).

persistence of traditional differences regarding how to accomplish even the latter—the French are famously allergic to the word 'federalism' when sounded with a Germanic accent[10]—the convention is much more likely to produce constitutional rectification than a constitution.

So what is the European Union? We suggest four answers, each based on a reading of the stylized description considered thus far: the European Union as technocracy, as association of associations, as Eurodemocracy founded on a transnational public sphere, and as deliberative polyarchy. Each provides a different way to understand the relationship between arenas of deliberative problem-solving and democratic possibilities. Each draws on a distinctive idea of sovereignty in relation to solidarity. This relation in turn suggests a characteristic understanding of regulation and redistribution and the connection between them. Each pairs with a distinct concept of democracy. Finally, each reading of the European Union also suggests a corresponding reading of US experience. In presenting the views we will be at pains to put the best face on each without disguising our preference for the fourth polyarchic understanding. As you might expect, the first three readings run afoul of the stylized facts, while the last—and in particular, its democratic potential—is hostage to the eventual answers to the open questions.

13.2. No Sovereignty, No Solidarity: The EU as Technocracy

The technocratic view currently dominates European discussion of the European Union, at least among the intellectuals, and quite probably among Eurocrats as well. It assumes that there can be no democratic sovereignty in the European Union because democracy requires a demos; and there is, as the Bundesverfassungsgericht has famously determined, no European demos.[11] The demos is a precondition for popular sovereignty in this view because unless the citizens are as one, united by language, history, and sentiment, they lack the coherence of judgment and will need to personify themselves in the legislature. As it is the people's will, reposed in the legislature and providing the democratic substitute for the will of the monarch, which gives substance and validity to the law, there can be no democracy without a people, and—on this first reading—no people without distinctive bonds of history and sentiment.

---

[10] In replying to Fischer's speech before the Bundestag on 27 June 2001 the French President, Jacques Chirac uses the word 'federal' only in pronouncing the official title of one of his hosts, the Bundespräsident. For the texts of the speeches see Dehousse (2002*b*).

[11] Maastricht decision of the Bundesverfassungsgericht, Judgement of 12 October 1993, 89 BverGE 155.

As with democracy, so with solidarity.[12] Underlying the technocratic view is the idea that we are capable of sympathy only with others who are substantially like ourselves. A demos is founded on a solidarity of sentiment, an identification of citizens with each other, and sense of common belonging, which allows the sharing of material things precisely because such sharing is not selfless—in the limit, not a self-sacrifice for others, but an expression of a larger sense of self. The demos is thus the precondition not only of the nation but of the welfare state; without the demos, conversely, we let the market take the hindmost.

On these assumptions the successes and failures of the European Union are the marks of technocracy at work. Regulation succeeds where it does—in setting rules for machinery safeguards which protect workers from accidents, not machine-tool makers from imports—because rules make orderly markets, and orderly markets advance the interests of citizens as producers and consumers. Regulation is less possible—in certain areas of pollution prevention, for instance—when it threatens the competitive advantage of producers in a position to oppose it without providing benefits to citizens, which might move to overcome the opposition. (When, as noted earlier, efforts to regulate succeed despite the apparent logic of interests, this is because political forces at the national and EU levels can accidentally align to favor outcomes that the parties would not have reached in institutional settings of their own choosing.) Redistribution, understood as the correction of market outcomes, and thus wholly distinct from market-defining regulation, can occur by accident. Rule systems may have redistributive consequences, even without redistributive aims, for example, as a result of political bargains, in the form of side payments to particular groups to induce compliance with rules whose enforcement they can disrupt and whose costs they fear. But redistribution is never systematic, the expression of solidarity and sharing, or a sense of fairness or justice that transcends minimal entitlements to personal liberty and security. Hence 'Social Europe' will always remain a meta-constitutional aspiration, not a reality.

In this world the master skill is expertise in effective rule making in the specialized domains requiring regulation; and power flows as a result to the technocrats who possess it. Comitology and the OMC are effective not because they compel comparisons of difference but rather because they subtract decision-making from the public and entrust cloistered experts to sort through intramural disputes that are circumscribed by a technical consensus that excludes real alternatives (if those exist at all). The collaboration of Commission and ECJ assures the dominance of market-making regulation

---

[12] The following views are most ably developed by Fritz Scharpf. See for example Scharpf (1999).

over redistribution, occasional political (mis-)alignments notwithstanding.[13] The new regionalism and the policies to combat social exclusion are payoffs to a potentially disruptive periphery dressed up as policy innovations. The social partners, labor unions in particular, 'acquiesce' in all this, when they do, because there is a gun (the threat of capital flight) to their head.

All of this is not necessarily undemocratic, because technocracy exercised to the benefit of those whose lives it governs, and recognized as beneficial by its beneficiaries, can be thought of as achieving the democratic value of government for the people. Moreover, the Europe as technocracy view goes together with a minimalist, principal-agent understanding of representative democracy. In this view a polity is a democracy just in case its principal-citizens can vote out their agent-officials whenever they judge the performance of the latter to be unsatisfactory. If, having this recourse, the principals nonetheless allow crucial aspects of their lives to be governed by technocrats—perhaps because the technocrats are having some regulatory success—the outcome is properly seen not as usurpation by an elite, but rather as an expression of democracy's recognition of what it can efficiently manage by its own methods (Moravcsik 2001; 2002). When European commentators fret that EU citizens need to be more visibly in control of their agents, American commentators may take the relative calm of EU politics as a sign that all is in a possibly precarious equilibrium, which might be perturbed by further discussion of democracy, even the minimalist, principal-agent kind.

The United States figures in this account principally as a model for organizing the administrative state on a continental scale, under conditions of diversity. The success of the New Deal administrative agencies such as the Securities and Exchange Commission show in this view that it is possible and, broadly speaking, profitable to entrust market making to insulated technicians (Majone 2000).

The most conspicuous shortcoming of this view is that it systematically underpredicts the scope and level of regulation in general, and social regulation in particular, of which the European Union is capable. The articulation of emergent standards for employment promotion and even the reform of the welfare state through OMC are at odds with an understanding of the European Union as a market-making technocracy. Explaining away such anomalies as the outcome of unusual political alignments looks more like a compensating fallacy—correcting one erroneous assertion with another—than a fruitful elaboration of the original view. Indeed the idea that there would be at least some efforts at market correction and redistribution accompanying the creation of a single market should have come as no surprise.

---

[13] For a clear formulation of the desirability of this distinction, see Majone (1998).

After all, the idea that the orderly functioning of society requires political efforts to correct market imbalances antedates the practice of democracy in Western Europe—and the relatively homogeneous peoples now associated with nation states. And if it is surprising because of the assumption that such correction requires strong national solidarities, so much the worse for that assumption.

In addition to mischaracterizing the scope of regulation, the technocratic reading mischaracterizes the character of EU regulation. It is now a commonplace of progressive legal criticism to unmask the politics underneath allegedly technocratic regulation. But the political character of EU regulation is openly acknowledged by the participants. The differences in beliefs and values that make recourse to comitology and OMC necessary undercut any clear distinction between political and technical considerations, and *a fortiori* any idea that regulation is about finding and imposing a single, technically correct solution. (Indeed we will want to argue later that the political character of OMC and comitology—that they are not simply means for implementing legislatively fixed values and goals—invites consideration of how to craft a new form of democracy, integrated closely with these regulatory processes.)

Apart from underpredicting 'social regulation' and mischaracterizing EU regulation as technocratic, this first reading is founded on a wildly optimistic and empirically unfounded faith in the power of technocracy. Here the references to the New Deal and the US administrative state—the goal towards which, in this first reading, the EU, *faute de mieux*, is tending and should be striving—are particularly revealing. In American eyes the state of that state is sorry, certainly nothing to emulate. The US administrative process is almost invariably described as 'ossified': agencies simply cannot make new rules, even where there is near universal agreement of the need to do so. Commentators are happy to apportion the blame among all the actors: the courts made it easier for affected interests to have a say in administrative proceedings in the 1960s and 1970s, thereby turning the agencies into minilegislatures. Congress passed highly detailed statutes—the Clean Air and Water Acts—that deprived agencies of the flexibility needed to adjust to the changing circumstances. The executive imposed review requirements—cost–benefit analysis—that made it easy for private actors and dissidents with government itself to frustrate administrative action, and so on.[14] Thus from the US point of view, at least as we understand it, emulation of the United States, conventionally taken as the paragon of technocracy, will make things better for the European Union only by accident. A theory that suggests

---

[14] The consensus has recently been summarized in Kagan (2001).

otherwise diverts attention from just what, on the basis of US experience and the 'facts' listed above, needs to be explained: that the European Union is succeeding at regulatory tasks, at least as well as others, by use of novel means—the method of benchmarking comparisons in comitology and OMC—which do not seem to respect the distinction between market-making and social-protection policies.

Given these objections we pass on from the reading of the European Union as a technocracy, and consider the Union as an association of associations.

13.3. The EU as an Association of Associations

The second, associative reading of the 'facts' is much more resolutely European than the first in the sense of seeing the European Union as the extension or generalization of distinctively (though not uniquely) European ideas of political conviviality and democracy. It takes its inspiration on the one hand from such 'complex' nations as Switzerland or Belgium. In these consociational democracies diverse ethnic groups agree a common citizenship on condition that each obtains, as a group, the right veto powers that protect it against predation by the others.[15] On the other hand it is inspired by systems of neo-corporatism, in which peak organizations representing, say, labor and capital, bargain within a framework created by the state to reconcile the interests of their members in a way consistent with the common good (Schmitter 1977).

The associative view inherits from its consociational and neo-corporatist inspirations the idea of sovereignty as plural. Unity of judgment and will is not found at the level of the demos, but in quasi-natural or, perhaps, primordial groups—ethnic, religious, occupational, gender-based, political, and so on. Within each group members identify with each other as do citizens of the demotic nation. Groups are bound to each other, and thus drawn into encompassing political formations, by a solidarity of complementarity: labor and capital are mutually dependent, even if they compete in trying to capture the gains of their cooperation. The Swiss cantons are divided by language and faith, but historically united in resisting intruders in the name of a common freedom that none can secure alone. The solidarity of complementarity that results is too calculating to count as selfless, but too constitutive of the actors, too central to their being, to be purely self-serving.

---

[15] For the historical background, see Te Brake (1998). For the experience of US and EU federalism viewed against this historical backdrop, see Goldstein (2001).

Regulation and redistribution collapse, at the limit, into each other in this view. The rules of conduct and the rules of sharing are decided together, simultaneously or nearly so, in the continuing bargaining between the plurally sovereign groups. Indeed the state acknowledges and validates the sovereign character of the groups, and the limits on its own pretensions to (unitary) sovereignty, precisely by lending its legitimacy to the bargaining regime that in effect constitutionalizes private groups, allowing them to make rules and redistribute wealth in the public's name. Or, looked at from the perspective of the groups themselves, the state is the association of associations, their coordinating instrument, not their sovereign master.

Democracy in this conception is social democracy: the view that democracy can only be an effective form of self-rule by openly taking as much account of what differentiates citizens as members of different social groups as of what they share as members of the same polity. But the more the legislature enacts the program of social democracy, passing powers to social groups, the less central it remains to law making. Carl Schmitt, no friend of democracy in any form, took particular delight in contrasting the pretense of parliamentary sovereignty in the Weimar Republic with the reality of corridor deals among the parties of Weimar social democracy (Schmitt 1985).

From the point of view of this Euro-centric argument the United States is a contrast pole or antipode. Capitalism in Europe in this view is organized by bargaining among peak associations. The market prevails in the United States, with employers and employees essentially bargaining as individuals. European politics acknowledges enduring difference by granting groups veto rights over fundamental decisions and enfranchising minorities through proportional voting. The United States favors first-past-the-post elections where the majority winner takes all, and the US Supreme Court debates incessantly whether the mention of minorities, even with the express intention of protecting them from discrimination, violates constitutional guarantees to equal respect for all citizens.[16] Where the first reading treats the New Deal as the advent of the administrative state, the second scarcely acknowledges that it occurred at all, the (neo-corporatist) Wagner Act notwithstanding. (Whether this historical omission is relevant to the understanding of the current situation, or the larger juxtaposition of organized and unorganized capitalism is, of course, a nice question.) Just as ossification is the centerpiece of discussion of the administrative process in the US, so is the demise of the Wagner Act central to discussion of the labor law regime (Barenberg 1994).

---

[16] For these distinctions from the vantage point of political science, see Lijphart (1999). For the distinction as viewed from political economy, see Hall and Soskice (2001).

As applied to the reading of the European Union, the associative thesis suggests that no demos is not necessarily a problem. If Switzerland, Austria, the Netherlands, and (on good days) Belgium can manage nationhood in the sense of full participation in the world order without benefit of traditional nationality, why cannot the European Union manage the same? The argument applies *a fortiori* if devolution of British sovereignty to Scotland, Wales, and Northern Ireland is a harbinger of a general return to the pre-Westphalian heritage of a complexly national Europe. Dropping the demos as a precondition of political will or self-government broadly speaking in turn opens the way to thinking of the EU as a Europe *à géométrie variable*: an association of (the associations of) monetary Europe, security Europe, the Europe of the regions, social Europe, and others to come, whose respective Member States overlap without ever fully coinciding. The European Union on this reading is not a political accident but a congeries of potentially meshing political projects that can succeed separately and together precisely because they are not all of a piece.

This reading, moreover, begins to make sense of 'facts' that the first treats as spurious. Why has a decade or more of constitutional convening not produced a constitution? Because the Member States were working through the rules of 'functional representation' for the many Europes of the European Union, not aiming to constitute a (supranational) nation on the model of the French and American revolutions. What is the meaning of the resurgence of social partnership among the small nations? The European Union, having disrupted organized capitalism by substituting one central bank for many, is now sufficiently stable so that the social partners can reorganize themselves again.

But the interpretative possibilities that this reading opens by relaxing the grip of the no-demos assumption and admitting the feasibility of a polycentric European Union is obstructed again by the assumptions it makes regarding the sovereign character of the social actors that count. The 'functional representatives' are presumed to (almost) already exist with something like the internal cohesion and well-ordered capacity for self-determination of an occupational group. The problem for politics is, as suggested a moment ago, creating a regime that identifies and legitimates them, typically by authorizing and stabilizing bargaining relations among complementary groups.

The second reading thus shifts attention to the creation and conditions of legitimacy of the bargaining regime—the social pact as the real key to political democracy—and away from what might be thought of as the inputs and outputs of the latter: the formation of the actors and the complex of rights, regulations and redistributive rules that they may agree. This is why one of the most interesting associative accounts of the European Union, Schmitter's

(2000) *How to Democratize the European Union*, devotes only a paragraph to regulatory outcomes, including 'equal treatment of women and part-time workers, better consumer and environmental protection, emergency medical care and legal help when traveling within the European Union, fair competitive practices between firms, uniform conditions for company formation, minimal health and safety standards'. These 'aspects of "market membership"', moreover, 'have only a limited impact on the quality of "political citizenship"', which depends on the public's control of the formation of the bargaining regime itself (*ibid.*: 33–4).

But what if the actors and the regime that connects them are both in some sense the product of the rule-making or regulatory process, rather than being preconditions for it? Then the associative reading would be confusing cause and effect, along the way trivializing outcomes—rules and rights—that have profound effects on everyday life and form the starting point in turn for the (re)-elaboration of what might amount to or take the place of constitutional regimes. Put another way, it would be to look for mono-directional causality where we should be searching for reciprocal influence. The OMC seems to work by such a process, and comitology and the new social pacts may do so as well. And what if such a 'processual' regime led to actors whose membership was too open to revision to be consistent with the notion of an occupational group or a 'functional' sovereign? There is more than a hint of such openness in the social inclusion partnerships, the OMC, and, again, perhaps comitology and social compacting.

These troubles with the stylized facts suggest that the associative view has stopped mid-stream. Dropping the idea of unitary sovereignty, of the people personified as the starting point for political will and accountability, allows us to make sense of the European Union as an open political project rather than the plaything of technocrats. But making the protagonists of the many Europes of the EU sovereign lords of their little realms makes it hard to come to grips with their most innovative achievements, in both regulation and political construction.

The difficulties with the first two readings suggest two possibilities. The first is to preserve a unitary democratic sovereignty, drop the assumption that democracy requires a substantive demos, and connect democracy instead with a public sphere founded on open discussion among equal persons—a discussion freed from overriding group solidarities and everyday practical entanglements, about the broad purposes to which collective power should be devoted. Put otherwise, the idea would be to achieve a form of old-style democracy, but on more cosmopolitan terms. The second is to drop the assumption of singular sovereignty as well as the assumption of a substantive demos, and to imagine a world where sovereignty is plural, and politics is not founded on the kind of cohesion we associate with the nation or the occupation: that is, to achieve a new form of democracy that frees cosmopolitanism itself from its traditional and self-defeating disengagement from practical problems. We consider these readings in turn.

13.4. The EU as Emerging Eurodemocracy

A third reading of the European Union as an emerging Europolity is animated by a more ambitious idea of democracy than the first two. In this view, democracy is neither reduced to minimal electoral control of distant officials, as in the technocratic conception, nor limited to a fair arrangement for group bargaining, as in the associative interpretation. Instead current developments are seen as intimating both the need for and the possibility of a new public sphere: an agora for our day that both comprises and transforms the public spheres of existing states so as to provide communicative direction to a new Eurodemocracy.[17] Put another way, the creation of the Europolity promises to restore the unitary sovereignty of the traditional state (the goal of the first view) while restoring effective democratic power to society itself (the goal of the second), and to do both without delivering the citizens into the power of bureaucrats or interest groups.

At the core of the Europolity view is the assumption that the increasing complexity and diversity of the European Union drive public debate to focus more on the matters of principle governing life among free and equal citizens, and less on situations of fact. As new market and regulatory arrangements take hold across existing political boundaries, and individuals and groups see the fateful import of these arrangements, the public-sphere view expects a corresponding shift in the public debate about the exercise of collective power. Given a background of assured rights of participation, communication, and association, deliberation between and among equal citizens—and the parties, movements, and groups they form—will concentrate more on the Europolity and less on national politics. Moreover, as the Europolity shifts from a collection of functionally specific problem-solving agencies to a genuine polity, deliberation will focus more on the guiding principles and values for the polity, and less on concrete policy.[18] The more cautious advocates of the enlarged public sphere may doubt that the new, transnational solidarities will displace traditional national attachments or

---

[17] For background, see Habermas (1989). And for a more recent application of these ideas to the EU, see Habermas (1996).   [18] See Weiler (1999), pp. 324–57; *idem* (2001).

prove robust enough to create anything approaching a free-standing polity. But whether they see the new public sphere as a complement or substitute for current loyalties, proponents of this view expect more cosmopolitan solidarities to emerge as surely from the newly encompassing political institutions as, historically, nations emerged as creations of states, rather than as their prior subjects.

In the most boldly idealized form of a new Eurodemocracy, popular sovereignty does not reside in a substantively defined demos. Sovereignty emerges rather in the dispersed process of informal discussion about broad principles and programs. The values formed in this procedurally defined sovereignty become authoritative in laws enacted by an empowered European Parliament that translates values into laws. These laws are then implemented by agencies under the Parliament's watchful eye. European courts protect the rights of democratic process required for the formation of the people's will, and ensure that agencies faithfully carry out the legal expression of the results of discussion as expressed through elections.

Regulation and redistribution depend in this view not on technical necessity or bargaining, but rather on the implications of the communicative principles informing the new public sphere. Commitment to unconstrained deliberation among equals is said to entail commitment to providing citizens with the capacities actually needed to deliberate. So construction of the new public sphere will grow from and contribute to the realization that citizens require a whole range of resources—from schools to new mass media—in order to participate in the public life that guides their collective endeavors. If there is any historical precedent for this ideal, it is the early nineteenth century United States, with its famously boisterous civil society and its simple, limited machinery of state (Habermas 2001).

As this historical reference suggests (and its self-consciously radical understanding of democracy notwithstanding), this public sphere interpretation is surprisingly conventional, even nostalgic in its understanding of politics. This nostalgia is particularly ill-suited to the novel facts about regulatory policy and process sketched in our stylized facts. Because the difficulties will be familiar from the technocratic view, we pass them quickly in review.

First and foremost, the public-sphere interpretation shares an implausible conception of the administrative state with the technocratic view. Both draw a sharp division between an arena of public deliberation that confines its attention to and fixes the content of broad goals and priorities, and administrative agencies that, in the ideal case, faithfully implement those goals by choosing effective means to their achievement. Both assume a sharp distinction between setting goals and choosing means. On both views, the regulatory state can be made consistent with democracy by ensuring that elected officials, acting on behalf of citizens, present clear rules and standards to agencies, and that those agencies confine their activity to the efficient implementation of those rules and standards, subject to external monitoring.

Quite apart from the EU setting, this conception of a depoliticized administration of standards set out ex ante is widely discredited. 'Agency' problems are the notorious weak link in the minimalist views of democracy that accept any duly elected legislative authority as a legitimate 'principal'. In aiming to realize both a greater articulation of the public will, and a tighter connection between that will and technical decision making, the project of a new public-sphere theory can only increase the gap between what is expected of the technicians and what they deliver. More concretely, with EU political deliberation now so concentrated in regulatory processes that involve substantial elements of delegation and thus lying beyond the reach of conventional legislative oversight, the public sphere conception is so far removed from evolving practice that it cannot serve as a guide to reform.

Indeed, it may be that awareness of this impracticability explains the distinctive vacillations of proponents of this view. Born aloft by hopeful expectation of a cosmopolitan democracy, they soon sink in despair of fulfilling that expectation, only to be propelled upward again by enthusiasm for experiments in deliberation whose disconnection from practice, routine or emerging, is seen as a precondition of their success.

What, then, of the possibility of a practical cosmopolitanism that does not sacrifice its dedication to democratic principle by actually engaging in problem-solving?

13.5. The EU as Deliberative Polyarchy

Consider now a world in which sovereignty—legitimate political authorship—is neither unitary nor personified, and politics is about addressing practical problems and not simply about principles, much less performance or identity. In this world, a public is simply an open group of actors, nominally private or public, which constitutes itself as such in coming to address a common problem, and reconstitutes itself as efforts at problem solving redefine the task at hand. The polity is the public formed of these publics: this encompassing public is not limited to a list of functional tasks (police powers) enumerated in advance, but understands its role as empowering members to address such issues as need their combined attention.[19]

---

[19] On this conception of the public see Dewey (1927). This section develops arguments advanced in Cohen and Sabel (1997); Dorf and Sabel (1998); and Gerstenberg and Sabel (2002).

Solidarity here rests neither on a sentiment of identity nor on a complementarity rooted in the division of labor. Rather it is both moral and practical. Moral, in that individuals recognize one another as moral agents entitled to be treated as equals; practical, in that they are bound to each other by the recognition that each is better able to learn what he or she needs to master problems through collaboration with the others whose experiences, orientations, and even most general goals differ from his or her own—a recognition that both express and reinforce a sense of human commonality that extends beyond existing solidarities. Such practical attachment is fostered by a pervasively uncertain world, where even the strongest have reasons to favor a division of investigative labor to incurring the risks of choosing and executing a solution alone. In such a world the practical benefits that flow from constant testing and reexamination of assumptions and practices that define a public provide a powerful motive to participate in collaborative problem-solving on equal terms. Conversely, the cultural homogeneity and intellectual closure of the demos and occupational group obstruct cooperation in this setting as much as they enabled it in more stable ones. Solidarity in the sense of mutual capacitating by equals cannot be placed on the spectrum reaching from selfish calculation to selfless abandon because actors' preferences and identities change in the course of their joint reasoning. And its deliberation is practical— about solving problems—rather than dispassionate, senatorial reflection on clashes among deep principles, as in the traditions of civic republicanism or the upper reaches of Madisonian democracy.

When sovereignty resides in a public that comprises practical publics and solidarity is capacitating, rule making is open—the creation of frameworks within which actors are encouraged to experiment with local solutions, on the condition they pool what they learn with others—and redistribution follows rule making. If actors could devise precise rules, or even confidently delegate responsibility for doing so, they might well band with their likes or complements as the case might be and spare themselves the evident inconvenience of deliberating about difference. But the world is not with them. So the best they can do is authorize the search for best practices, promising solutions, by those in a position to judge their promise and domain of applicability, and periodically revise the general framework of investigation as results warrant.

If rule making is principally about empowering publics to explore and test solutions, so, too, is redistribution. The most promising way of avoiding unacceptable market outcomes is to explore collaboratively the sources of the risks and reduce them by re-ordering markets accordingly. This kind of risk reduction flows into regulation and becomes nearly indistinguishable from it when the latter is taken as market-making subject to the protection of public health and safety broadly understood. The web of connections resulting from this kind of regulation might (indeed very probably does) redistribute resources from one group to another. But such redistribution would be the consequence of a solution adopted first and foremost to address common problems—above all, the problem of maintaining the ability to address together, as equals, unforeseen problems—not correct specific social or economic imbalances: standards requiring that citizens be provided with 'adequate' or 'current state of the art' environmental protection, employment policies, workplace health and safety, and education and vocational training—where the understanding of 'adequate' and 'current' is redefined in the light of experience in the respective areas—would have this result.

The OMC as applied to the development of a European Employment Strategy (EES) shows how the formation of a public relies on, but continuously perturbs and reshapes public entities and groups in civil society. It suggests as well the general architecture of the background institutions that make possible the generation of publics.

To see the relation between the activity of forming a public and the actors thus formed consider the EES that has emerged from the Amsterdam Treaty and from the 'jobs summit' in Luxembourg in November 1997 as a flow chart. Initial Employment Guidelines are proposed by the Commission acting chiefly through the Employment Committee (EMCO), an advisory body composed of two officials from each Member State and two Commission officials. In formulating its proposals EMCO consults the European social partners—the peak associations of labor and capital—the European Parliament, the Economic and Social Committee, and the Committee of the Regions. The Commission then forwards the proposed guidelines to the Council, which must approve them by a qualified majority. Member States respond to the guidelines by elaborating annual National Action Plans (NAPs) on employment. Ideally, these NAPs integrate and correct policies in such disparate areas as vocational training and continuing education, taxation, the collection of statistics, and so on. The Commission compares and reviews the NAPs, while the Member States, acting through EMCO subject their actual labor market performance to a peer review. A Joint Report on Employment, prepared by the Commission and the Council, benchmarks the employment policies of the Member States and identifies best practices. The Council can, by qualified majority vote recommend that Member States that show badly in these comparisons conform their policies to the guidelines. The guidelines themselves are revised every year, and the process as a whole is reviewed every four to five years in light of experience.

One predictable outcome of the EES is attempts by the interests it threatens to manipulate the process itself. Member States and their ministers do not typically relish criticism by their peers, especially not when such criticism may provoke unrest among their domestic constituents and collaborators. A process as formal as the EES offers numerous occasions for self-protective interventions: the formulation of guidelines and the choice of peer reviewers are obvious opportunities. Early returns of reviews of the EES in action suggest that anxious members do sometimes seek shelter this way.

But another predictable outcome of the formulation of general guidelines and NAPs, and revision of each in the light of the other, is unpredictability: obligated to explain their choices and performance, and exposed to the justifications and achievements of others in like circumstances, the actors must expect to find their constitution—their relation to their key constituents, to each other, and to the policies they pursue—open to challenge from within and without. Some of these challenges will arise as routine response to EES questions: How does a Member State's continuing and vocational education program comport with its tax structure and pension system? What should be done about a mismatch? Will some of the challenges emerge as higher order effects of the process itself? How does participation in the formulation and revision of the NAP affect trade union federations at the national level and influence labor's understanding of the social welfare state? What are its effects on the strategies of trade unions at the local level, and their relation to the national federation?

It is next to certain that reactions will differ within and across nations. Try to imagine a mechanism that could ensure uniformity in the current, volatile environment. It is also likely that some of these reactions will cohere into alternatives to familiar models of social partnership and interest-group representation. In the new Irish social pacts, for example, the central labor and employers' federations are less focused on questions of wages and hours than before. Instead they aim to provide information and services to local branches participating in the continuing reorganization of firms, helping members manage careers on local labor markets, or participating in local programs of social inclusion—all of which entail new political combinations that potentially reshape the identity of 'labor' (O'Donnell and O'Reardon 2000).

The EES does not, of course, ensure this outcome or any other. But it makes it easier for those who want such changes to identify and learn from each other, and harder for those who oppose them for reasons that they or their current organization, rather than the public, succeed in their obstinacy. Or that at least is the result that will come to light if private and public actors are formed on the lines suggested by the third reading.

The EES in turn depends on an organizational infrastructure whose general architecture was anticipated above in the descriptions of comitology and social inclusion programs: local, or, more exactly, lower-level actors (nation-states or national peak organizations of various kinds within the European Union; regions, provinces or sub-national associations within these, and so on down to whatever neighborhood is relevant to the problem at hand) are given autonomy to experiment with their own solutions to broadly defined problems of public policy. In return they furnish higher-level units with rich information regarding their goals as well as the progress they are making towards achieving them. They agree as well to respect the framework rights of democratic procedure and substance as these are elaborated in the course of experimentation itself. The periodic pooling of results reveals the defects of parochial solutions, and allows the elaboration of standards for comparing local achievements, exposing poor performers to criticism from within and without, and making of good (temporary) models for emulation.

It is the pervasiveness of this new architecture in the European Union, as well as its dependence on a center—though a 'center' that has nothing to do with the apex of a hierarchy—that causes us to speak of a deliberative polyarchy, rather than, say, a new form of anarchy. In anarchy the alignment of interests and incentives among the actors results in spontaneous coordination without the need for a center to compel provision of information, facilitate the pooling of the information provided, discipline those who abuse the grant of autonomy to victimize some within their own jurisdiction, or take advantage of outsiders acting in good faith. Traditional examples are the market of the neo-classical textbook or the Proudhonian federation, in which *'les industries sont sœurs'* (Proudhon 1863: 113). Contemporary versions are found in the social law of George Gurvitch, which descends directly from Proudhon (Gurvitch 1932), and certain versions of systems theory, in which the 'sub-systems' of law and economics mutually 'irritate' each other, causing an adjustment without need for mutual understanding between the adjusting parts (Teubner 2000).

In deliberative polyarchy, problem-solving depends not on harmony and spontaneous coordination, but on the permanent disequilibrium of incentives and interests imperfectly aligned, and on the disciplined, collaborative exploration of the resulting differences. As both the exploration and the sanctioning depend on mutual checking by decentralized actors facilitated by the central provision of the relevant infrastructure—think of the process by which NAPs are criticized—we term the European Union's practical deliberations polyarchic.

But what democracy, if any, might this be or become? Democracy is deliberative when collective decisions are founded not on a simple aggregation of interests, but on arguments from and to those governed by the decision, or their representatives. But deliberation, understood as reasoning about how best to address a practical problem, is not intrinsically democratic: it can be conducted within cloistered bodies that make fateful choices, but are inattent-ive to the views or the interests of large numbers of affected parties—without being connected to open public debate and practice. So deliberative poly-archy can be democratic only if the deliberation is democratized. But what might it be to democratize a deliberative polyarchy?

The question is hard to answer because so much conventional thinking about democracy—whether deliberative or aggregative, minimalist and elect-oralist or founded on more the demanding idea of a public sphere—assumes a central authority that operates over a territory, monopolizes the legitimate use of force in that territory, and has a wide range of policy competences—employment, environment, health, product safety, domestic security, research/development, and so forth. In this setting, we have democracy when policy-makers are held accountable to citizens through regular competitive elections, against a background of basic liberties of speech and association, in which citizens debate issues and choose representatives, and representatives make policies and hold officials accountable for the articulation and imple-mentation of those policies. The political architecture of deliberative poly-archy is different, and its democratization must take a correspondingly unconventional form.

Stepping back, then, from familiar forms of democratic polity, we have a democratic form of deliberative polyarchy when its dispersed and coordi-nated deliberative decision-making is subjected to what Frank Michelman calls the 'full blast' of diverse opinions and interests in society (Michelman 1999). Meeting the full-blast condition requires open-ended, informed dis-cussion about the decisions taken by separate units and the coordinating center. But what makes for democracy is not simply the fact of discussion, but that those discussions shape subsequent decisions. To meet these full-blast requirements, then, a deliberative polyarchy must be located in surroundings that meet five conditions. Thus, full-blast political discussion requires assured protections of basic rights of speech, association, and participation. Moreover, deliberation and decision must proceed under a norm of trans-parency that invites and informs wider public participation in policy argu-ment. Furthermore, that public discussion must have the right content and focus, which means that it must be attentive to coordination across units as well as decisions by the separate units; in the case of OMC, this means EU-level policy coordination, as well as national policies. So the full-blast condition is not satisfied simply by the fact of separate discussions about national policy, together with administrative coordination across jurisdictions. In addition, the democratic form of deliberative polyarchy requires mechanisms of accountability that connect deliberative decisions, in particular, policy areas with wider public discussion about those areas.

And, to ensure that such accountability respects the equality of those subject to the decisions, a democratic background of deliberative polyarchy includes an individual right to contest decisions.

A deliberative polyarchy that meets these full-blast conditions not only achieves the democratic ideal of accountability and responsiveness to those who are subject to its decisions; it is also more plausibly an epistemic or learning democracy than the principal-agent view of the first reading, the corporatist understanding of the second, and the deliberation-about-principles of the third. Recall that the defining feature of the European Union on the deliberative, polyarchic reading is to transform diversity and difference from an obstacle to cooperative investigation of possibilities into a means for accelerating and widening such enquiry. Comparison of different projects by publics that are themselves diverse in their composition (peer evaluators, standard-setting bodies, and so on, down to localities and neighborhoods) makes it possible to examine each concept both in the mirror of the others and from the varying angles presented by differing points of view. This kind of examination has been shown in many settings to bring to light deep flaws in individual projects that remain long undetected when they are pursued in isolation, and to reveal novel possibilities that are missed when many projects are pursued simultaneously but in willful indifference to each other. Although deliberative polyarchy is not intrinsically democratic, when it is focused on practicality it seems tailor-made to encourage the exploration of diversity in a way that exposes decision makers to its 'full blast'.

Seen as a method of revising designs in the light of their realization, moreover, it is clear why deliberative polyarchy is especially well suited to this task. Assume that ends and means are mutually defining: that understanding the content of ends requires inquiring into means, and that understanding the content of means requires inquiring into ends. Deliberative polyarchy revises (sets of) ends in the light of (sets of) means and vice versa. It provides a general, and, judging by our two examples, broadly applicable and inclusive model for realizing the epistemic promise of deliberative democracy.

But how broad? How inclusive? Surely neither all-encompassing with respect to domain of application, nor all-inclusive—fully engaging all potentially affected interests—within any domain. Deliberative democracy is often suspected, rightly, of being exclusive, or outright elitist: and when deliberation is the province of a professional problem-solving elite (of legislators, administrators, or judges) it is frankly exclusive. Distrust of deliberation is thus distrust of the exclusionary power of professionals, certified or not. It seems justified in that the very source of professional autonomy—the professional's ability to bring expertise to bear on complex, singular cases—does seem tied to an unaccountable aloofness from clients, let alone the public.

Thus in professions, as in crafts, learners acquire skill by applying familiar techniques to well understood problems under the supervision of accomplished masters. The real teaching of law or medicine is done not in the classroom, but in the clinic—the analog to the apprentices' shop—or in the early years, as resident or associate, on the job. When the routine is of a second nature, the learner takes on novel problems, achieving mastery herself when these can be solved without supervision. The knowledge of problem-solving techniques acquired this way is tacit: professionals, like craftspersons, can make refined judgments about the quality of work, yet not be able to say with precision how it is done. Indeed, because professional dignity is tied to autonomy, and autonomy to freedom from supervision, inquiry into what a professional does can easily appear a veiled accusation of incompetence or worse. Thus the professional's autonomy—the ability to solve complex problems without the support, and free of the limits of hierarchy—goes hand in hand with distance from clients, other kinds of professionals, and even one's own colleagues.

Through the use of comparisons of performance and the formulation of various responses to the problems such comparisons reveal, deliberative polyarchy potentially transforms the professions: it reduces their technocratic pretense, and reveals the dependence of expert judgment on assessments of ends as well as means. By making tacit knowledge of problem-solving explicit, or explicable, in a way that disrupts the traditional hierarchy of skill within each, it may open the boundaries that separate it from the others and the larger public.

But this is, of course, speculative. The facts of the democratic vocation of deliberative polyarchy are inconclusive and equivocal, if not contradictory. One fundamental fact is that the extent to which deliberative polyarchy ramifies past the technical elite into civil society is an open question. Another is that the regulatory successes of the European Union have gone hand in hand with the spread of parallel governments. So the democratization of deliberative polyarchy remains a project, whose precise institutional commitments have not yet been fixed. To be so in the sense of the 'full-blast' conditions it must be broadly inclusive, both in the scope of its deliberations and in the arrangements of public accountability. It must also be officialized, openly acknowledged as part of the legitimate process by which a self-governing people make their laws.

A concomitant of—perhaps, indeed, a condition for—the democratization of deliberative polyarchy is an understanding of constitutionalism as the continuing activity of assessing a polity's practices in the light of its deep commitments, and vice versa. Constitutionalism in this sense begets not a constitution of enumerated powers and rights, but more activity like itself: constitutionalism.

Indeed, insofar as this kind of constitutionalism respects the constraint of the joint determination of means and ends, it is by conventional standards anti-constitutional. Thus the separation of powers among the branches and levels of government and allocation of authority as between, say, the federal and state levels cannot be fixed in advance. Doing so would be to choose procedural means without attention to substantive ends. Neither can the content of the system of rights be fully fixed in advance. Doing so would fix ends without attention to the means for realizing them. Can this kind of constitutionalism possibly secure the accountability of government and the efficacy of rights?

The problem of accountability seems fairly tractable, at least in comparison to the task of making sense of experimentalist rights. Deliberative polyarchy makes official actors transparent and answerable to each other and the public in ways that severely limit unaccountability. Our Madisonian constitution takes the branches and levels of government to be natural units, and makes their rivalry for power the source of our protection against the self-aggrandizement of government. Deliberative, polyarchical constitutionalism might be called neo-Madisonian in that it uses the polyarchical competition of purpose-built and re-configurable problem-solving units to the same end.

If accountability is not an insurmountable problem, can polyarchic constitutionalism make assertion of constitutional values definite enough to bound behavior, yet open enough to admit of re-elaboration by, literally, the means of practice? More generally, on the full-blast view, the exploration of democracy itself emerges from the elaboration of starting commitments under the pressure of the full blast of social diversity. So on that view it must be true that the particular rights, or clusters of these, that inform and define democracy as a whole are shaped the same way. In other words, the precise content of rights is, in the full-blast view, emergent: without free expression, there is no democracy; but the elaboration of the content of that right in light of alternative specifications is part of democracy's work.

Consider again the OMC. Think of this as constitutionalism without, or instead of a constitution. OMC-style re-elaborations of employment, welfare, and education and tax policies are what the European Union's Member States are doing instead of creating a constitution on the French or American models. Taken together, these policies are at the heart of what a state does. Perhaps this benchmarking all the way up is a novel path to a constitution, or at least a way of making justiciable the elaborate charter of the rights securing democracy. Or it may be that benchmarking all the way up just keeps going, and the forms of practical deliberation it engages become at one and the same time a form of problem solving and new method of articulating constitutional values. This fourth reading of EU constitutionalism is, if you like, not simply a theory about what has been happening, but an interpretation with a practical intent: it suggests the kinds of participation we ought to be looking for, where we might find it, and how to think about making participation officially accountable if and when it is found.

Finally, the fourth reading calls attention to aspects of US experience that also link fluid problem solving and new forms of accountability in strikingly similar ways. We presented deliberative polyarchy as a kind of construct, a way of reading the stylized facts that makes sense of a pattern that confounds conventional interpretations even in raising troubling questions of its own. We might as well have said that it constitutes the accidental discovery of a promising response to a broad class of current situations in which inaction is unacceptable but omnibus solutions are plainly unworkable. There are many such situations in the United States as well, and many responses that recall the essentials of the European Union read as a deliberative polyarchy.

Consider developments in education first and foremost, and also the reorganization of police departments, social services, and others besides: the areas at the core of the broad, now apparently humbled movement for general institutional reform that Chayes three decades ago called public law (Chayes 1976, 1982).

The differences between public law and what we will call, mindful of a family resemblance, the new public law parallel those between the familiar constitutionalism of the administrative state and the continuing constitutionalism of the OMC. Public-law courts aimed to establish the acceptable minimum standards of institutional performance—the wattage of bulbs in prison cells, to take an extreme but not exceptional case. New public-law judges today declare their commitment to the vindication of broad, open-ended constitutional values or legislative mandates. Thus the supreme courts of Texas and Kentucky, referring to their respective state constitutions, insist that schools provide an 'adequate' education for all children, even if virtually every school, school district, and the state department of education must be restructured to meet the adequacy standard.[20] In cases of police abuse, courts, referring to recent federal legislation, make it the responsibility of police departments themselves to detect and correct a 'pattern or practice' of abusive behavior.[21]

This commitment to open-ended, expansive values becomes an effective discipline for broad reform because it is accompanied by a shift in the responsibility for and the focus of the monitoring of institutional performance.

---

[20] See on the movement from 'equity' to 'adequacy' claims in school-reform litigation, and generally for the developments in Texas reported below, Liebman and Sabel (forthcoming 2003).

[21] For a review of the relevant literature see Garrett (2001).

In public law the court convened an *ad hoc* group, drawn from parties and outside experts, to monitor periodically the reforming institution. The monitors' report, addressed to the judge, comprehensively evaluated the institution's compliance with the minimal standards. Today monitoring is continuous, not episodic. This routine monitoring is a continuing responsibility of the reforming institution itself, not an exceptional engagement by the court and its adjuncts. The monitoring focuses on key indicators of the reforming institutions' overall performance, particularly with respect to constitutionally aggrieved groups, not on a comprehensive evaluation of the progress of reform. And the monitoring results are addressed at least as much to the staff and clients of the reforming institution, and often to the public at large, as to the judge.

For example, it is the responsibility of the Texas Education Agency (TEA) to report regularly on the performance of public school children in grades 3–10 on certain standardized tests of proficiency in reading and mathematics. Disaggregated by school and by ethnic and socio-economic groups within schools, and organized to permit comparisons of each school to the 39 others in the state that it most resembles on these dimensions, these results are reported publicly. In still more finely disaggregated form they are reported to school and district officials, and by the latter to teachers. Parents, administrators at the school, district, and state levels can monitor the progress of individual schools and districts. The Supreme Court of Texas can as well determine whether the TEA, and beyond it the state legislature, are meeting their obligations both to monitor the performance of individual schools and to respond in case poorly performing ones fail to improve at an acceptable rate.

Thus, despite their commitment to open-ended values and their disinclination to limit the scope of reform, the courts today are much less involved in the management of institutional reorganization than their public-law predecessors. Where public law invited courts to in effect create *ad hoc* public agencies to set standards and provide designs for meeting them, courts today leave the substantive elaboration of the constitutional standards, and the means for satisfying them, to the primary actors. In this sense the new reform movements, unlike public law, are not court-centric. In imposing on the primary actors a continuing obligation to monitor themselves, the courts induce novel forms of self-critical cooperation between these latter and other public and private parties. Designs for reform arise from this vigilant cooperation, and the courts' ability to evaluate it. It is this new division of labor among the branches of government and between them and civil society—a new separation of powers—that makes judicial affirmation of need-based claims to something so vague and so fundamental as an adequate education into an effective, justiciable right to disentrench current practices and seek, account-ably, for better ones.

Or, put in a way that closes the circle of our argument, US courts are creating the equivalent of a constitutional OMC. Deliberative polyarchy as a serious possibility on both sides of the Atlantic? This fourth reading, you may say, abuses the license to speculate provided by the open questions. But then democracy, history shows, is a kind of collective license to answer, by means that affirm our values and our obligations to each other, questions we never imagined being asked.

References

BARENBERG, M. (1994). 'Democracy and Domination in the Law of the Workplace Cooperation: From Bureaucratic to Flexible Production'. *Columbia Law Review*, 94/3: 753–983.

CHAYES, A. (1976). 'The Role of the Judge in Public Law Litigation'. *Harvard Law Review*, 89/7: 1281–1316.

—— (1982). 'Public Law Litigation and the Burger Court'. *Harvard Law Review*, 96/1: 4–60.

CHRISTIANSEN, T. and KIRCHNER, E. (eds) (2000). *Committee Governance in the European Union*. Manchester: Manchester University Press.

COHEN, J. and SABEL C. F. (1997). 'Directly-deliberative Polyarchy'. *European Law Journal*, 3/4: 313–40.

CRAIG, P. and DE BÚRCA, G. (eds) (1999/2003). *The Evolution of EU Law*. 1st edn 1999; revised edn forthcoming 2003. Oxford: Oxford University Press.

DE BÚRCA, G. and WEILER, J. H. H. (eds) (2001). *The European Court of Justice*. Oxford: Oxford University Press.

DEHOUSSE, R. (2002*a*). 'Misfits: EU Law and the Transformation of European Governance'. *Jean Monnet Working Paper* 2/02. Available at http://www.jeanmonnetprogram.org/papers/02/020201.rtf

—— (ed.) (2002*b*). *Une constitution pour l'Europe?* Paris: Presses des Sciences Po.

DEWEY, J. (1927). *The Public and its Problems*. New York: H. Holt and Company.

DORF, M. C. and SABEL C. F. (1998). 'A Constitution of Democratic Experimentalism'. *Columbia Law Review*, 98/2: 267–473.

GARTON ASH, T. (2001). 'The European Orchestra'. *New York Review of Books*, 48/8: 60–7.

GARRETT, B. (2001). 'Remedying Racial Profiling'. *Columbia Human Rights Law Review*, 33/1: 41–148.

GEDDES, M. and BENINGTON, J. (eds) (2001). *Local Partnerships and Social Exclusion in the European Union*. London: Routledge.

GERSTENBERG, O. and SABEL, C. F. (2002). 'Directly Deliberative Polyarchy: An Institutional Ideal for Europe?', in C. Joerges and R. Dehousse (eds), *Good Governance in Europe's Integrated Market*. Oxford: Oxford University Press, 289–341.

GOLDSTEIN, L. (2001). *Constituting Federal Sovereignty: The European Union in Comparative Context*. Baltimore: Johns Hopkins University Press.

GREEN-PEDERSEN, C., VAN KERSBERGEN, K., and HEMERIJCK, A. (2001). 'Neo-liberalism, the "Third Way" or What? Recent Social Democratic Welfare Polices in Denmark and the Netherlands'. *Journal of European Public Policy*, 8/2: 307–25.

GURVITCH, G. (1932). *L'idée du droit social*. Paris: Recueil Sirey.

HABERMAS, J. (1989). *The Structural Transformation of the Public Sphere: An Inquiry into a Category of Bourgeois Society.* Translated by T. Burger. Cambridge, MA: MIT Press.

—— (1996). *Between Facts and Norms: Contributions to a Discourse Theory of Law and Democracy.* Translated by W. Rehg. Cambridge, MA: MIT Press.

—— (2001). *On the Pragmatics of Social Interaction: Preliminary Studies in the Theory of Communicative Action.* Translated by B. Fultner. Cambridge, MA: MIT Press.

HALL, P. A. and SOSKICE, D. (2001). *Varieties of Capitalism: Institutional Foundations of Comparative Advantage.* Oxford: Oxford University Press.

HÉRITIER, A. (1999). *Policy-making and Diversity in Europe: Escaping Deadlock.* Cambridge: Cambridge University Press.

IVERSEN, T., PONTUSSON, J., and SOSKICE, D. (2000). *Unions, Employers, and Central Banks: Macroeconomic Coordination and Institutional Change in Social Market Economies.* New York: Cambridge University Press.

JOERGES, C., LADEUR, K.-H., and VOS, E. (eds) (1997). *Integrating Scientific Expertise into Regulatory Decision-making: National Traditions and European Innovations.* Schriftenreihe des Zentrums für Europäische Rechtspolitik an der Universität Bremen (ZERP), Bd. 23. Baden-Baden: Nomos.

—— and VOS, E. (eds) (1999). *EU Committees: Social Regulation, Law and Politics.* Oxford: Hart.

KAGAN, E. (2001). 'Presidential Administration'. *Harvard Law Review*, 114/8: 2245–315.

LIEBMAN, J. and SABEL, C. F. (2003). 'A Public Laboratory Dewey Never Imagined'. Forthcoming in *New York University Review of Law & Social Change.*

LIJPHART, A. (1999). *Patterns of Democracy.* New Haven, CT: Yale University Press.

MAJONE, G. (1998). 'Europe's "Democratic Deficit": The Question of Standards'. *European Law Journal*, 4/1: 5–28.

MAJONE, G. (2000). 'The Credibility Crisis of Community Regulation'. *Journal of Common Market Studies*, 38/2: 273–302.

MICHELMAN, F. I. (1999). *Brennan and Democracy.* Princeton, NJ: Princeton University Press.

MORAVCSIK, A. (2001). 'Federalism in the European Union: Rhetoric and Reality', in K. Nicolaidis and R. Howse (eds), *The Federal Vision: Legitimacy and Levels of Governance in the European Union and the United States.* Oxford: Oxford University Press, 161–87.

MORAVCSIK, A. (2002). 'If It Ain't Broke, Don't Fix It!; Beware Europe's Rhetoric (and America's Fears) About What It Wants to Be. Focus On What It Is'. *Newsweek*, March 4: 15.

O'DONNELL, R. and O'REARDON, C. (2000). 'Social Partnership in Ireland's Economic Transformation', in G. Fajertag and P. Pochet (eds), *Social Pacts in Europe—New Dynamics.* Brussels: European Trade Union Institute/Observatoire Social Européen, 237–56.

PROUDHON, P.-J. (1863). *Du principe fédératif et de la nécessité de reconstituer le parti de la révolution.* Paris: E. Dentu.

SABEL, C. F. (1996). *Local Partnerships and Social Innovation: Ireland.* Paris: OECD.

SCHARPF, F. W. (1999). *Governing in Europe: Effective and Democratic?* Oxford/New York: Oxford University Press.

SCHMITT, C. (1985). *The Crisis of Parliamentary Democracy.* Translated by E. Kennedy. Cambridge, MA: MIT Press.

SCHMITTER, P. C. (2000). *How to Democratize the European Union—and Why Bother? Governance in Europe.* Lanham, MD: Rowman & Littlefield.

—— (ed.) (1977). 'Corporatism and Policy-making in Contemporary Western Europe'. Special issue of *Comparative Political Studies*, 10/1.

SCULLY, R. (2001). 'The European Parliament as a Non-legislative Actor'. *The Journal of European Public Policy*, 8/1: 162–9.

SMITH, B. (2002). *Constitution Building in the European Union: The Process of Treaty Reforms*. The Hague: Kluwer.

TE BRAKE, W. P. (1998). *Shaping History: Ordinary People in European Politics, 1500–1700*. Berkeley, CA: University of California Press.

TEUBNER, G. (2000). 'Contracting Autonomies: The Many Autonomies of Private Law'. *Social and Legal Studies*, 9/3: 399–418.

TSEBELIS, G. and GARRETT, G. (2001). 'The Institutional Foundations of Intergovernmentalism and Supranationalism in the European Union'. *International Organization*, 55/2: 357–90.

VAN SCHENDELEN, M. P. C. M. (ed.) (1998). *EU Committees as Influential Policymakers*. Aldershot: Ashgate.

WEILER, J. H. H. (1999). *The Constitution of Europe: 'Do the New Clothes Have an Emperor?' and Other Essays on European Integration*. Cambridge: Cambridge University Press.

——(2001). 'The Commission as Euro-sceptic: A Task-oriented Commission for a Project-based Union. A Comment on the First Version of the White Paper'. Available at http://www.jeanmonnetprogram.org/papers/01/013401.html.

14

Governing Work and Welfare in a Global Economy

ALAIN SUPIOT

14.1. Introduction

In Europe as in the United States, the 'globalization' of the economy has led to a reduction in the importance of law in mastering transformations of work and employment. In the United States, it is the notion of 'governance' which is most often used to this effect, while in continental Europe '*régulation*' (*Regulierung, regolazione*) is preferred to distinguish it from conventional '*réglementation*' (*Regelung, regolamentazione*) (cf. Clam and Martin 1998). But beyond these semantic differences, we are dealing with a similar phenomenon which is expressed through new ways of elaborating and implementing rules governing work and employment. European social policy offers numerous examples of this, such as the technique of lawmaking through collective agreements introduced under the Maastricht Treaty (Articles 138 and 139 of the Treaty of European Union) and that of the employment 'guidelines', authorized by the Treaty of Amsterdam (Article 128 TEU) or again the 'Open Method of Coordination' (Articles 130 and 140 TEU), conceived and developed since the Lisbon Summit of March 2000. Similar developments can be observed at both national and international levels, where alternative means of '*régulation*' are energetically sought. These combine in varying degrees the enunciation of general principles or guidelines, 'benchmarking' (periodic assessment on the basis of common indicators), and new forms of collective bargaining.

This distancing of '*réglementation*' and 'government' in favor of '*régulation*' or 'governance' can be placed within the perspectives outlined after the Second World War by the theorists of cybernetics. These combine the idea of

This text is based on a contribution presented at the France/ILO meetings organized in Annecy in January 2001. I would like to thank the ILO for permitting me to publish it here as it is especially suited to inclusion in this book.

governance (the word cybernetic comes from the Greek *kubernetes*: the pilot who takes the helm or *gouvernail* in French) with that of regulation (inherent in every homeostatic system)[1] to create a general science of information and commun-ication which would protect us from entropic disorder.[2] In line with these prophecies, the rapid development of information technology is accompan-ied today by the dilution of law in a theory of communication which can be seen not only in sociology (especially the works of Jürgen Habermas and his procedural concept of law) (cf. Habermas 1984, 1989, 1996), but also in economics, notably in the work of the so-called '*Régulation School*' (cf. Boyer and Saillard 2002).

From a legal point of view *régulation* appears to be an attempt to combine the two contrasting types of rules which have been opposed in the West since the birth of modern science (cf. Supiot 1994: 183 ff.). On the one hand we have legal rules, which draw their strength from a shared belief in the values they are meant to express (order, justice, freedom, equality, private owner-ship, etc.), and on the other we have technical rules, which draw their strength from scientific knowledge of the facts they are meant to represent. Technical rules are one-dimensional (they belong to the world of facts) and are thus practical (having to reflect the diverse nature of those facts), evolv-ing (having to keep pace with progress in knowledge) and refutable (allow-ing contradictions or technical alternatives). Their validity is entirely dependent on their effectiveness. By contrast, legal rules are two-dimensional (being designed to make the world as it is into the world as it should be). They are therefore general and abstract (the diverse nature of facts must be subsumable to them), permanent and binding (they are not subject to the

---

[1] In the mechanical sciences, '*régulation*' means the spontaneous adjustment of a machine to the purposes assigned to it. This has experienced the most remarkable developments with the arrival of information technology: computers are able not only to obey orders, but also to adjust their behavior instantaneously to environmental conditions. In respect of a car conceived in line with this principle, it would suffice to state a destination for the car to automatically work out the route and speed necessary to get its passengers there in the shortest time possible. This example of the automatic pilot, already widely used in navigation by sea and air, helps us to understand the distinction between the notions of '*réglementation*' and '*régulation*' found in the majority of European languages. '*Réglementer*' is to impose rules, whilst '*réguler*' is to ensure respect for the rules necessary for the homeostatic functioning of an organization. According to cybernetic theory, only adequate '*régulation*' and not strict '*réglementation*', can protect society from entropic disorder, that is to say the tendency of nature to distort what is ordered and destroy what is comprehensible (Wiener 1964; for the relationship between law and technique, cf. Supiot (2002)). In this text we have kept the French word '*régulation*' in italics to distinguish it from '*réglementation*' and avoid confusion with the English word 'regulation'.

[2] Cf. Wiener (1954). A notion coming from thermodynamics, entropy (from the Greek ἐντροπή, cause of evolution) means the spontaneous tendency that each ordered system has to disintegrate. Entropy is at its greatest when disintegration is total. Entropy is the scientific wording of an old biblical knowledge: 'Both go to the same place, both come from the dust, and both return to dust'. (*Ecclesiastes* 3: 20).

requirements of truth). Their legitimacy is based not on scientific knowledge of the world, but on the fact that they form part of a system of rules which is itself based on ideal values.

In its desire to substitute the administration of things for the government of men, the West in modern times has attempted to reconcile these two types of rules. It has done this in two ways: first, by reducing the law to a simple technique which has nothing to do with values and should be judged by its effectiveness; and second, by placing scientific knowledge of man and nature at the heart of its system of values. Since it resulted in man being treated as an object, this attempt to manage the world scientifically produced some monstrous results (the Holocaust, the Gulag, Hiroshima), from which we do not yet appear to have learnt all the necessary lessons. This is why we cannot be too careful about ideas which, like that of *régulation*, apply modes of thought drawn from the natural sciences to human affairs. If we stick to its primary meaning, *régulation* approaches living beings as machines, whose mechanisms for adapting to their environment can be formalized.[3] Understood in this sense, the *régulation* of society would involve three steps: first, identify the mutual adaptation mechanisms which govern human behavior (this is what economic or socio-economic analysis does); then express knowledge of these mechanisms in the form of behavioral rules; finally, try to ensure that human behavior obeys those rules. The law appears in this program only as a possible, and fairly outdated, way of formalizing the natural laws identified by scientific and technical knowledge, in other words as a mere tool from which all traces of dogmatism have been removed. The knowledge of experts based in regulatory authorities would enable political disputes and conflicts of interest to be avoided and would, as it were, rise above the old opposition between state and market. Harmony through calculation would thus gradually replace the arbitrariness of laws.

Not only would this approach to *régulation* be dangerous, but it would also be doomed to failure. The dynamics of calculation on which the modern world is founded have developed on the basis of a shared belief in a number of unprovable values. We must not forget that the *lex mercatoria*, the merchants' law developed in medieval times, was made by good Christians united in their belief in a God who guaranteed promises given. It was the shared belief in this third-party guarantor which created the confidence essential for trade beyond frontiers. Trusts were invented for knights heading off for the crusades, and limited companies came from the model of the Franciscan Order, recipient of money which the monks were not allowed to own. In

---

[3] The concept of '*régulation*' was borrowed from the mechanical sciences by molecular biology before it spread into the vocabulary of the social sciences: cf. Lecourt (ed.) (1999) on 'Régulation'.

modern times the West has, admittedly, secularized these ideas and made the state the ultimate guardian of personal identity and promises. But there is still a distinction between what we might broadly term the sphere of belief and the sphere of calculation. The sphere of belief is the sphere of what is qualitative and unprovable; it was largely dealt with by laws, public consultation and the state. The sphere of calculation, of what is quantitative, was dealt with by contracts, negotiation, and the market. In order to calculate you have to be able to forget the diverse nature of objects and beings and focus only on their fundamental, quantitative characteristics. This ability to forget, which is necessary for calculating interest as for scientific calculations, is possible because human reason has another side which deals with anything that resists the abstract nature of numbers. Even today our calculations still depend on a number of beliefs that we regard as universal truths and which are prerequisites for the process of globalization (faith in scientific discovery, human rights, the value of the dollar).

It is only because the state has taken charge of the incalculable aspects of human life that the market could be viewed as a mechanism of self-*régulation* and be seen in abstract terms, as a separate entity from the people making the contracts and the objects to which they relate (Supiot 2000*b*). State and market, law and contract, thus become inseparably linked. In an increasingly complex and international world, the division of roles between law and contract is changing. On the one hand there are ever-increasing demands on law and the state to deal with everything not covered by the simple logic of calculation. For example, we expect the public authorities to protect us against the incalculable risks generated by economic and technical 'development' which go beyond the statistical limits of insurance contracts. This is precisely why the 'precautionary principle' has emerged. But the public authorities can only meet these demands if the legitimacy of the law is based on expert knowledge, often institutionalized in the form of independent authorities. On the other hand, because of the limits of the state's cognitive abilities, issues until recently covered by the law are now handled through contracts and negotiation. This is what is known as the 'proceduralization' of law, whose most overlooked aspect is that specific, qualitative issues previously regulated by laws are now covered by contracts. But contracts, therefore, can no longer be seen as abstract relationships distinct from the identity of the contracting parties and the particular nature of the goods and services or even persons to whom they relate. Each type of product or service requires its own '*régulation*' or even its own regulatory authority (water, food, telecommunications, medicines, finance, aviation, products of the human body, etc.), which applies its technical knowledge of those products and services while at the same time weighing up the interests involved. The regulatory authority thus acts as a new type of magistracy, which like a judge, takes decisions by referring both to knowledge of the facts and to value judgments.

In other words, *régulation* certainly does not mean the disappearance of that 'third party' which characterizes what we in the West call 'the law' (*le Droit*) (cf. Kojève 2000). Without this dogmatic reference, which both engenders and symbolizes belief in a world order, no institutional structure could survive. It is simply that the modern world prefers to see this 'third party' as a great regulator rather than as the divine figure of a 'great watchmaker' or the legal figure of the state. But we should bear in mind that neither God nor states have disappeared from the global institutional stage. There can be no *régulation* without a regulator, and there have always been many who aspire to that role.

This reassuring interpretation of social *régulation* is the one I shall use as the basis for our discussion. Construed in this way *régulation* does not mean reducing social life to a set of calculations for mutual adaptation or the programmed disappearance of the non-quantifiable and non-provable values which are inherent in our legal structures. It might therefore help us to get away from the 'occidento-centrism' which is inherent in the very concept of law and to place the structures of the nation-state in the broader context of that dogmatic imperative which is common to all civilizations.[4] Since states are no longer able to define or impose the imperative of 'decent work' (Somavia 1999), this must be expressed through other institutional channels, particularly at the international level.

Redefined in this way, the concept of *régulation* provides a suitable framework for tackling the problems currently facing labor law. This law incorporates 'regulatory' mechanisms for transforming relationships based on strength into legal relationships. By permitting workers' representation and collective action, it recognizes a veritable right to challenge the law; on the other hand, it channels these collective forces to promote the ongoing development of the law. These mechanisms are what we now call 'social dialogue', which actually refers to a wide range of instruments for confronting employers' and workers' interests: rights to information, to consultation, to strike, to representation, to negotiation. Of course, we can criticize the imprecision of this concept, which is perhaps inevitable in view of the diverse and constantly changing industrial relations systems it is designed to cover. But it might also

---

[4] In Western history 'dogma' and 'dogmatic' are linked to knowledge by tradition spread throughout the concepts of 'Medicine' and 'Jurisprudence' (cf. Herberger 1981). Their modern heuristic use is due to the works of Pierre Legendre (1983, 1999, 2001). The dogmatic imperative, today as yesterday, and in the West as elsewhere, means that human reason supposes the existence of a 'place of legal truth, postulated and laid out as such. The 'globalization' of markets does not escape from this imperative (see Supiot 2000).

be said that it goes straight to the very heart of the matter by getting us to think of social linkages as linkages of speech. In order to have a dialogue we must speak the same language or use interpreters. Dialogue is therefore never reduced to a binary relationship, since it always requires the existence of a common language, a 'third party' which Plato, in the *Cratylus*, calls the legislator of language. In the case of social dialogue this common language is primarily determined by states and, to a lesser extent, by international organizations, in other words by public authorities. Dialogue also presupposes that the speakers are capable of making their views understood. And in the case of social dialogue it is the law which creates these interlocutors and which channels their forces, by organizing the representation of the interests concerned and recognizing their capacity for action.

Thus, the concept of *régulation* cannot mean the disappearance of the 'third party' which characterizes states governed by the rule of law. Instead it suggests that this 'third party', whether it be the state, judges or international organizations, no longer has a monopoly on issuing rules, since rules are also generated by the mechanism which balances the forces operating on the labor markets. If we are to consider new forms of *régulation*, therefore, we must examine the two conditions required for the very existence of any *régulation*: the presence of a regulator (I), and a balance in the forces regulated (II).

14.2. No *Régulation* without a Regulator

States remain the keystone of our institutions both nationally and internationally. But they are being universally destabilized, internally by the centrifugal forces of decentralization, and externally by the centripetal forces of internationalization. We must therefore start from the metamorphoses of the state to identify the new foundations of a possible regulation of work.

14.2.1. *Metamorphoses of the State*

The state is not an everlasting and universal institutional form; it was invented by the West in medieval times. The idea of a state that never dies has its roots in the notion of the body mystical, with the theory of the two bodies of the king, as described by Ernst Kantorowicz (1963). Although severed from its religious roots by the Enlightenment and the French Revolution, the state nevertheless continued to be viewed as a super-person, the personification of a power which transcended individual interests (what German lawyers called

Herrschaft and the French called *puissance publique*). The legitimacy of this public authority was challenged in the nineteenth century by the industrial revolution and the ensuing political and trade union struggles which ensued. From its very beginnings the market economy undermined the traditional forms of local solidarity on which pre-industrial societies were founded. This breakdown was first seen in Europe and the United States and then moved on to affect every other country to varying degrees as the world became Westernized.

The destabilization of social links based on family, geographical or occupational proximity appeared at the start of the nineteenth century as a *sine qua non* of modernity. It undermined the legitimacy of the state, whose role and very existence were already starting to be challenged at that time. The first response to that challenge was that of the totalitarian ideologies, which viewed the state as a mere tool in the hands of a single party acting in the name of what were claimed to be scientific laws governing social life (racial laws, historical laws, etc.). The state lost its legitimacy, which passed to other symbols that were supposed to represent the motor of societies: race, class, etc. This response was a catastrophic failure, and we must never forget the lessons we have learnt from it. An alternative response, on the other hand, was to restore the legitimacy of the state by giving it new responsibilities. Instead of merely being in charge of governing people and representing a dominant power, it became the servant of people's welfare.

The state thus claimed to guarantee people's well-being, in what became known as the 'welfare state', the '*Sozialstaat*' or '*l'État providence*'. This welfare state involved two aspects, which developed to varying degrees depending on the country concerned. The first were public services, in other words people were given new rights—rights to health care, education, etc.—which added the concept of social citizenship to that of political citizenship. The second was wage-earning status (employment), in other words a series of security rights that came with being an employed worker. Depending on the country in question, those security rights might be directly defined by law or might be the result of collective bargaining which was authorized or organized by law. But in every case mandatory rules were included in the contract of employment and formed the basis for national labor legislation (cf. Supiot 1994; Castel 1995). The invention of the welfare state enabled the dual trend towards individualization and interdependence, which was developing in industrial societies, to be controlled. But at the same time as it permitted these trends to be controlled, it also accelerated them. Bringing men and women into broad networks of solidarity such as social security, for example, freed them from local solidarities while at the same time making them increasingly interdependent at a national level.

Today, the open frontiers which have been the response to a whole series of factors (economic, political and technical) with which we are all familiar are overturning the national frameworks on which social life has been constructed. In turn, national solidarities are being challenged by what we call globalization and by relocalization and reterritorialization. Globalization and localization are the two inseparable faces of world economic strategies that are based on the exploitation of local competitive advantages. This dual trend towards internationalization and localization has paradoxical effects on labor markets, subjecting them to quantitative pressures to reduce labor costs, which place labor at a lower value than capital, and at the same time to qualitative pressures to improve work skills as a result of the demand for innovation and greater quality in product and service markets (see Reich 1991; Storper and Salais 1997). These trends are beneficial for some workers (usually the most highly skilled) and harmful for others (usually the least skilled), and they challenge the accepted forms of national solidarity, including, of course, labor law.

The state is thus caught in a vise. On an international level 'globalization' is producing a legal system in which international competition law, which is supposed to embody the common interest of all different nations, is being forced upon states, which are deemed to express merely local solidarities, acceptable only if they do not interfere with the free movement of goods and capital. In this *neo-liberal* perspective, competition law is operating as constitutional law on a global scale, and the international trade institutions are challenging the states for the role of 'third party' guaranteeing trade. But unfortunately competition law is not constitutional law. The international economic system turns a blind eye to the social problems it creates, which ultimately become the responsibility of states whose scope for action has also shrunk. Internally states are facing growing demands for security, solidarity and decentralization as the destabilizing effects of globalization are felt. Their response has often been to negotiate with or consult the represent-atives of different categories of interests. With such practices, which have been labeled *neo-corporatist*, defining the general interest is no longer the prerogative of the state, but becomes the product of a relationship of force between individual interests. The state is thus no longer a neutral arbiter, but an interested party engaged in 'social dialogue'.

Neo-corporatism and neo-liberalism have combined in practice to make the state a mere tool which is subject to a rationality which transcends it, whether the economy at an international level or society at a domestic level. Thus it is that states, which remain the subjects of law *par excellence* on the international stage, are losing some of their substance, or even most of it in the case of the weakest and poorest countries, which are caught between structural adjustment plans forced upon them by international financial institutions and the informal economy which assures the survival for many of their denizens, and which thereby become almost reduced to the role of extras, without any real grip on the economy or society proper.

However, it is unlikely that the space vacated by the retreat of the state will remain empty for long. The myth expounded in the West that society is being ground down to a dust made up of rational individuals maximizing their interests ignores the basics of anthropology. Human reason is never a direct product of individual consciousness: it is the product of the institutions which allow each person to make sense of her own existence, give her a place in society and enable her to express her own talent. Professional identity—the performance of decent work—is therefore something very different from just an economic asset: it is the condition for the economy's existence, its very nucleus. For if there is to be trade in products, if there is to be a market, there must first of all be workers who produce and exchange. In turn, involvement in that exchange is a condition for the preservation of those professional identities. 'Economic laws' thus assume that a world exists where everyone is assured of her identity. Once that identity is no longer guaranteed by the state, people are forced to base it on something else: religion, ethnicity, region, tribe, sect, and so on. This leads to new identity-based demands which destabilize states even more quickly and pave the way for violent conflict between reference groups, of which there are many national and international examples today. This sort of retreat to identity and the violence it causes undermine confidence, encourage protectionism and thus jeopardize the economic globalization of which they are a product. This is why we need to ask what could be the new foundations for *régulation* in an economy and a world which are open to trade.

14.2.2. *The New Foundations of* Régulation

The developments I have just described show both that '*regulation*' cannot exist without regulatory institutions, and that the state has lost its monopoly over that role. This is changing the ways of thinking which allowed us to conceptualize the 'third party' and to oppose it to rights-bearing individuals. In an institutional universe organized around the state, the terms state and market, law and contract, public and private all represent polar opposites. Today, each of those pairs is undergoing a shift which should help to define the new foundations of *régulation*. Where we used to oppose the private and the public, we must also now oppose the social and the economic. Where we used to distinguish between law and contract we must now distinguish between principles and procedures. And lastly, where the state, vis-à-vis the market, combined power and authority, these two attributes, which were previously in the hands of a single great regulator, now need to be separated.

14.2.2.1. *The Social and the Economic*

In the welfare state model, private interests are subordinated to respect for the universal values expressed in the public domain. In other words, the public encompasses the private. However, with the opening-up of frontiers and the subordination of states to a global or regional commercial order, it is now the private which encompasses the public. National solidarities operating within states are thus becoming subordinate to the principles of free competition on which international markets are founded. Social rights only have substance in respect of a given claimant, in other words at a local or national level, whereas economic rights (of ownership, contract, etc.) exercised on the markets acquire universal scope with globalization. The only reference able to transcend nationality is therefore the market. This reference, which was the principal factor in the creation of the European Community, is supposedly intended to extend gradually to cover all products and services in every country. Harmony through calculation, which is the principal factor in commercial trade, would then be able to encompass all of humanity. The old distinction between public and private is thus overtaken by the distinction between economic rights ('rights of...') and social rights ('rights to...'). Like the 'private', the 'social' is a local, individual factor logically subordinate to the 'economic', which at an international level is taking over the pre-eminent place previously occupied by the 'public' in domestic law. But this is all at the cost of a reversal in the values attributed to the private and the public: commercial law is regarded as global law *par excellence*, whereas public law becomes merely the expression of local solidarities. This approach is reflected in the case law of the European Court of Justice (ECJ), which defines an enterprise as 'every entity engaged in an economic activity, regardless of its legal status and the way in which it is financed'.[5] The concept of economic activity thus becomes a dogmatic category, indicating any activity that can be carried out by a private entity, regardless of whether it is carried out in the private or public sector of a Member State.[6]

This definition prompted the ECJ to analyze the solidarity operating within national social security schemes as an exception to the principles of free competition, and one to be interpreted restrictively.[7] The Court has likewise analyzed collective bargaining agreements as a restriction on

---

[5] ECJ, *Höfner and Elser*, Case C-41/90 [1991] ECR I-1979, para. 21; *Fédération française des sociétés d'assurance and others*, Case C-244/94 [1995] ECR I-4013, para. 14; *Albany*, Case C-67/96, judgment of 21 September 1999, para. 77.

[6] ECJ, judgment in *Höfner and Elser*, paras 21 and 24.

[7] ECJ, Cases C-159 and 160/91, *Poucet & Pistre*, [1993] ECR I-664, *Droit Social* 1993, 488, note P. Laigre and commentary J.-J. Dupeyroux; ECJ judgment of 16 November 1995, Case C-244/94 (Coreva), *Droit Social* 1996, 82, note P. Laigre; ECJ judgment of 26 March 1996, Case C-238/94 (Garcia), *Droit Social* 1996, 707.

competition between participating enterprises, only exempting them from the ban on cartel agreements insofar as their objectives were concerned with social policy.[8] The same reasoning was applied to public service monopolies. These monopolies are tolerated to the extent necessary 'to correct the imbalance between profitable sectors of activity and less profitable sectors (which justifies) a limiting of the ability of private businesses to compete in sectors which are economically profitable'.[9]

The force of this thesis (consistent with the utilitarian philosophy which gave rise to economic ideology (see the seminal work by Louis Dumont (1977, 1985)) stems from the fact that the market is the only institution which excludes all discriminating factors except money. It is the only one to practice the idea of universal formal equality. By contrast, all institutions built on the principle of solidarity put the collective interest before the individual interest, and the interest of group members before that of persons outside the group. This thesis thus usefully reminds us that any legal methodology in respect of solidarity rests on a ranking of the interests involved. It is not convincing, however, in the radical separation it makes between economic rights (which may be universal) and social rights (which are by their nature particular). The distinction is purely ideological: any legal relationship must have both an economic and a social dimension.[10] So it must be seen for what it is: not a scientific given but a dogmatic construct to which new rights can be attached, not only at national level but also, and especially, at an international level. The establishment of an international market causes social rights to be seen as necessary exceptions to the rules of competition law.

So one must be careful to distinguish between the scientific value of separating the economic from the social—which is zero—and its dogmatic value—which is considerable. This distinction underlies the legal structures which have come about as a result of globalized markets. It is found not only in EU law but also in domestic law[11] and international law.[12] And EU law shows that the consideration of social rights can counterbalance the rules of free competition, not only nationally but at a supranational level too. This is

---

[8] ECJ judgment of 21 December 1999 in *Albany*, paras 60 ff.

[9] ECJ judgment of 19 May 1993 (Corbeau), *AJDA* 1993, 865, note F. Hamon, quoted § 17.

[10] The work relationship, for example, is indissolubly an economic and a social relationship. Markets are constituted legally in conditions which depend very much on 'social' (national) factors.

[11] In English law employment matters are regarded as a 'non-commercial' issue which does not have to be taken into account when subcontractors are selected for a public service (cf. Deakin 1998).

[12] The World Bank is required to ensure that sums from any type of loan are used with due attention to economic and yield factors and disregarding political influences or considerations or any other influences or considerations which are not economic in nature (cf. Maupain 2000).

an extremely interesting way of building an international social order which will act as a counterweight to the economic order.

14.2.2.2. *Principles and Procedure*

In the royal or sovereign conception of the state, there are two levels of legal obligation, corresponding to two major types of rules: on the one hand that of law, which is deliberate and unilateral, reflecting the general interest, and on the other hand that of contract, which is negotiated, bilateral and reflects individual interests. This clear distinction was first blurred by the invention in labor law of a 'hybrid' between law and contract—the collective agreement. The welfare state, being unwilling or unable to regulate the details of employment relations, allowed or encouraged this hybrid to develop, either outside the legal framework as such (the English solution) or as an alternative to legislative action (the Nordic solution), or again as a complement to the provisions of the law (the French or German solution). But these systems do not undermine the legislator's monopoly over the definition of the general interest: while collective agreements go some way towards setting norms and standards, their purpose remains private in nature, limited to collective definition of the various obligations incumbent on the parties to an employment contract. Things were taken a step further when governments, keen to establish the legitimacy of the law, insisted on prior negotiations or consultations designed to prepare its contents. This practice of 'negotiated law' represents a far more serious challenge to the distinction between law and contract. In this case the purpose of negotiating is to legislate and the sole purpose of the law is to give legal force to an agreement.

This trend towards 'contractualization' was also encouraged by the dominant economic ideology. As early as the nineteenth century the great English jurist Henry Summer Maine (1870: 285) observed that

the bias indeed of most persons trained in political economy is to consider the general truth on which their science reposes as entitled to become universal, and, when they apply it as an art, their efforts are ordinarily directed to enlarging the province of Contract and to curtailing that of Imperative Law, except so far as law is necessary to enforce the performance of Contracts.

To say that the contract is universal or that the market is universal amounts to more or less the same thing, because without a contract there is no conceivable market, and where there is a contract there is negotiation, and so the possibility of a deal and a market. Consequently the necessary corollary of a globalized market economy would be a decline in positive law in favor of contracts. So while it had not always been so, the contract would be on the way to becoming a universal category, indicating that the Western understanding of man and society might be applied worldwide. This, at least, is the *credo* of globalization which celebrates at once the virtues of free trade and the contract, seen as flexible, egalitarian and liberating, as opposed to the constraints of governments and shortcomings of the law, which is seen as rigid, one-sided and oppressive. Any law which is not the result of an agreement has thus become suspect, and every effort is made to ensure that obligations are defined consensually.

In fact, the vocabulary of contracts is spreading to all areas of human life, including the public domain. And this trend affects labor law above all. A feature common to all the developed nations over the last thirty years has been that contracts are preferred to laws in the area of labor legislation. At EU level this radical trend is reflected in the promotion of 'social dialogue' in the construction of European social law. This vague concept has brought together the two political variants of contractualism: the right-wing variant which stresses the individual contract of employment, and the left-wing variant which places the emphasis on the collective agreement. The 'social dialogue' culminated in a major institutional innovation in the Treaty of Amsterdam.[13] Building on the terms of the Maastricht Social Agreement, this Treaty formalized the idea that subsidiarity should apply in regulating the labor market, that is, the law should take second place to collective bargaining.[14] Thus collective bargaining totally replaces parliamentary debate as the expression of democracy, as the ECJ rightly observed.[15]

On closer examination, however, the current trend is more than a new retreat of the law in the face of contract. What we are seeing is rather a change which affects them both. The law is relinquishing the job of establishing substantive rules, but is instead concentrating on affirming principles and laying down procedures. And these procedures pass on to contracts the burden of the qualitative issues being offloaded by the law, and in so doing profoundly alter their nature. Far from relinquishing their role as an initiator, states are seeking to reaffirm it in new ways. On the one hand they are still responsible for non-quantifiable common goods which are not subject to price coordination (health, education environment); but on the other hand the economy and society have become too complex for them to manage these common goods themselves. Neocorporatist methods borrowed to identify a way out of this dilemma lead to an impasse since these common goods cannot be reduced to the outcome of bargaining amongst interest groups. Thus the

---

[13] Article 138 (new numbering) Treaty of the European Community.

[14] On this 'horizontal' dimension of the subsidiarity principle, see Bercusson (1996).

[15] European Court of First Instance, judgment of 17 June 1998, Case T-135/96 (UEAPME), *Droit Social* 1999, 53, commentary Marie-Ange Moreau, see § 89.

trend today is away from a state which manages social matters and towards a state which acts as the guardian of solidarity. This redefinition of the role of the state, and more generally of government, is apparent in two ways. On the one hand the state no longer aspires to do everything itself. Instead of playing a direct part in negotiations or concertation on the neo-corporatist model, it confines itself to laying down the procedures according to which these negotiations should be conducted by others. But, on the other hand, it defines the general principles which these negotiations must help to implement. Thus the state is at once withdrawing, disengaging from the management of social affairs, and reaffirming its role as the guardian of the common good.

This form of *régulation* is increasingly successful and there are many examples of it. In domestic policy there have been numerous labor law reforms reflecting the intervention of the legislator, who sets a general objective or principle, and that of collective bargaining which implements this principle or these objectives (this has been the case in France with all the major labor laws adopted since 1986, from the abolition of government authorization for redundancies to adoption of the 35-hour week). Similar action has been taken at EU level with the 'Luxembourg Process', which sets 'guidelines' for Member States' employment policies and fixes a procedure requiring Member States and the social partners to tailor these guidelines to specific national conditions. Council Directive 94/45 of September 22, 1994 did the same with businesses, requiring multinational companies to establish a works council or a procedure for informing and consulting their employees. At an international level the International Labor Organization (ILO) did something similar, adopting in 1998 a Declaration on Fundamental Principles and Rights at Work which requires all Member States 'to respect, to promote and to realize [these principles] in good faith'.

So these new forms of governance in no way signify a return to the minimal state, simply abandoning social affairs to the private sector. They express themselves rather in a policy of 'government by objectives' which allows the social partners to choose the ways and means of attaining those objectives. The problem, if this policy is to succeed, is how to define objectives which are accepted by all. One can involve the social partners in that process (e.g. with the lawmaking negotiations introduced by the Maastricht Social Agreement). One can also, and this is doubtless the most novel feature of these new forms of governance, base the legitimacy of these objectives on the presumed expertise of specialists. This 'expertise' is then institutionalized by the setting up of regulatory authorities which are independent of both the state and the social partners. But in that case the functions of power and authority previously unified in the state alone tend to become separated.

14.2.2.3. Power and Authority

In the West, the distinction between power and authority goes back a long way. In Roman law, as we know, '*potestas* is the ability to act and *auctoritas* is the ability to dictate the actions of another person'.[16] Following the advent of Christianity, this distinction informed the debate on the respective prerogatives of the Pope and the Emperor.[17] This debate was to some extent closed by the secularization of the state, which combined power and authority, albeit at the cost of a separation of its legislative, executive, and judicial powers. Thereafter, the distinction between power and authority weakened and gave way to other contrasts—between state and nation, state and civil society, state and market—which fed the institutional debate. But it is resurfacing today with the issue of '*régulation*', which produces the different functions of 'operator' (who has the power to act) and 'regulator' (who has authority over this power). This distinction rests on a simple idea: the welfare state has inherited the function of grand market regulator, but it is also an economic player which can with impunity break the laws of the market or turn them to its advantage (as it can with other freedoms such as freedom of information). Where this risk of confusion exists it is thus appropriate to deprive the state of one or other of these functions (or both, in more radical versions of this thesis). The function of *régulation* will then be entrusted to an authority set up specially to that end.

The opening up of markets has thus been accompanied by a proliferation of regulatory authorities which are independent of state control.[18] At a national level these authorities have prospered with the privatization (or opening up to competition) of public enterprises and services and the liberalization of capital movements. Most of these authorities are specialized and are responsible for a specific product or service (electricity, telecommunications, television, the stock exchange, medicinal products, etc.). 'Market' authorities are the most numerous (see Frison-Roche, *forthcoming*), but authorities have also been set up to help regulate a number of public services (health, hospitals), to safeguard certain freedoms (data protection) or to explain government decisions on major social issues (ethical review committees). At an international level there are also a number of authorities specialized in the

---

[16] de Noailles 1949: 250 and 1947: 223 ff., esp. 274. On the origin of the concept see Benveniste (1969: 148–51).

[17] On this point cf. the famous letter sent in 494 to the Byzantine Emperor by Pope Gelasius, which distinguishes *auctoritas sacralis pontificum et regalis potestas* (see full text translated into French by G. Dagron (1996: 310 ff.).

[18] There is an abundant literature on this. For a study of comparative law, see Lomgobardi (1995: 171, 383). For France: see the Public Report 2001 of the Conseil d'État (2001: 253–452); Colliard and Timsit (1988); Autin (1988); Jodeau Grymberg, Bonnat and Pecheur (2000: 3–14).

régulation of a given service (e.g. aviation), but most strikingly, independent authorities have also been created at this level with a general remit to regulate markets. The body with the longest and greatest experience of this is undoubtedly the European Commission, but the World Trade Organization (WTO) was set up to pursue the same objective, on a wider stage but with more restricted powers.

The powers of regulatory authorities are as diverse as the areas they cover, but they have two features in common: they draw their legitimacy from the scientific or technical expertise of their members and they are held to be independent of both government and private operators. This independence is often questioned; the shadow of the state looms ever large (e.g. in the matter of appointments) and private lobbies are never far away. And the remit of authorities always goes beyond simple technical expertise, requiring them to make value judgments and to rule on disputes rather like a scientific, technical or economic magistracy. For both these reasons the tendency is to require these authorities to observe broad procedural principles as derived from the European Convention on Human Rights and Fundamental Freedoms.[19] In other words, they are being directed back to the essence of legal methodology.

This re-emergence of 'authorities' prompts us to remember the important question which in France gave rise to the essential concept of social law (*Droit Social*) in the late 1930s. The lawyers who created this body of law had realized that social conflict cannot be resolved using ordinary judicial methods, whereby a dispute is measured against a previously defined rule (whether that rule is contained in a law or a legal precedent). Most of the time the whole point of social conflict is to get a new rule adopted. This is why these jurists had placed such faith in the creation of a social magistracy, which had considerable socio-economic powers and was able, by ruling on disputes, to build up a body of social law which was genuinely geared to changes in the world of work and not to the relationship between economic or political forces (Laroque 1954). Paradoxically this idea is flourishing today in the economic rather than the social sphere. Thus there is an imbalance between the economic sphere, in which authorities predominate, and the social sphere in which there are none, which produces an opposition between the social and the economic with all its perverse effects. The authorities responsible for markets do not see it as their job to address the social dimension of the problems they deal with. That does not mean that this dimension does not exist, but that there is no one to authorize states to invoke social considerations as

---

[19] Cass. Com., 18 June 1996 (Conso), *B. civ.* No. 179; Ass. plén., 5 February 1999, (Oury), *B. civ.* No. 1; La position du Conseil d'Etat est très en retrait: Cons. d'Et., Ass., 3 December 1999 (Didier); see Ribs and Schwartz (2000); Brisson (1999).

a way of limiting the effects of competition law. This leads to decisions which can, at a single stroke of the pen, destroy the livelihood of entire societies, above all the poorest.[20]

There are two ways of escaping such follies. The first would be to 'de-specialize' regulatory authorities and enable them to take equal account of the economic and social aspects of cases they are required to adjudicate. This would mean moving towards more broadly based authorities, including specialist groups within them. But the example of this which we already have, the European Commission, points up the limitations of this solution: notwithstanding laudable efforts and considerable achievements, the Commission's Directorate-General for Employment and Social Affairs has never had as much influence as the Directorate-General for Competition. The other way is to set up authorities with special responsibility for regulating the social dimension of markets. These authorities could rule on disputes where a state or a trade union believed that the application of competition law infringed fundamental social principles or, conversely, cases in which a state or a company thought that specific social legislation constituted an unfair barrier to free trade. There might also be a role for such authorities in regulating the forces operating within the labor market and ensuring that a proper balance was maintained between them.

14.3. No *Régulation* without a Balance of Forces

The old corporations were swept away by the Industrial Revolution, but as no lasting institutional vacuum can persist between the state and individuals, new players emerged to replace them on the legal stage. The large modern enterprise was the first focus of attention, with the introduction of legislation on commercial companies. In the area of labor law, the old journeyman guilds gave way to unions, for individual trades first, and later for whole industries. Hence, the development of a level of collective action, that of employment relations, whose existence is guaranteed by the ILO conventions on trade union freedom.

Just as the welfare state is structured differently from one country to the next, collective labor relations too are treated differently in national legal systems. But notwithstanding this diversity, collective worker representation has always been modeled on the organization of employers' economic power,

---

[20] The dispute over bananas now before the WTO or the definition of (cocoa-free!) chocolate adopted by the European Union are good examples of this kind of decision which are more evocative of techno-crime than the exercise of authority.

since its aim has always been to maintain a balance of forces with management. Consequently problems of action, representation and negotiation manifest themselves differently in labor law and in civil (or common) law. This difference may be summed up as follows: civil law takes the 'players' (i.e. legal persons) as its starting point in defining the legal frameworks for their actions and negotiations (i.e. the law on representation and contracts). In dealing with the question of representation in the negotiation of a contract, for example, civil law will take as its initial given the existence of a person to be represented and will then decide how that person is to be represented and her interests defended. In collective labor relations the exact opposite obtains. Here one starts with the frameworks for action and collective bargaining (i.e. from a given organization of work) and then defines 'players' (i.e. collective legal persons, with power to negotiate), and this definition of legally empowered representatives precedes and determines the identification of the groups represented. This is true firstly of the economic activity of employers: the first sense of the word enterprise or 'undertaking' describes the action of one who exercises her freedom to act, that is, the action (under)taken, and only in a secondary and derived sense does it describe the legal organization which is the consequence of that action, that is, the business or company formed. It is also true of collective action by the workforce, which has to tailor itself to employers' forms of economic activity: trade unions are primarily a means of collective action and they organize labor around the requirements of such action.

So in seeking to understand the factors which are transforming collective labor relations, one cannot start from a given set of enterprises and trade unions and then study the new forms in which disputes or agreements arise. We have to take the opposite approach, looking first at the new forms of economic activity to discover what has caused the imbalance between economic and social forces (Section 14.3.1), before we can decide how that balance might be restored (Section 14.3.2).

14.3.1. *Upsetting the Balance between Economic and Social Forces*

Large firms are no longer homogeneous work communities obeying the orders of a single boss within the laws of a single state. They are adopting new structures and adapting to a new environment, while workers' collective action, by contrast, remains a prisoner of the past.

14.3.1.1. *New Structures*
The pyramid model of the large industrial firm with its integrated hierarchical structure covering the entire process of manufacturing a product was

mirrored by the organization of all workers involved in that production into industrial unions, eliminating craft-based professional identities. Depending on whether or not firms were organized into sectors, the industrial unions' center of gravity lay at sectoral or company level. The forms of worker representation necessarily mimicked the ways that capital dictated that work should be organized.

Forms of work organization have undergone fundamental transformations over the last twenty years. Technical progress, the opening-up of frontiers to international competition, the growth of knowledge and the division of labor have all had the same destabilizing effects on businesses as on states. The difference between states and firms has less to do with their structure than with their point of reference. The state takes as its reference qualitative values transcending the interests of capital; it is responsible for people's destiny and it takes a long-term, lifetime view. A firm's reference is to quantitative, capital-based values; it is responsible for providing products or services and it takes the short-term view dictated by markets. But like states, large firms are finding it impossible to take all decisions at the top, and are having to invent new ways of governing people. Like states, they are facing enormous problems in justifying their existence, which in their case have resulted in greater authority for shareholders and less power for managers. As with states, those in charge have had to redefine their role by fixing general objectives but leaving details of their implementation to individual and collective negotiation not only with the workforce, but also with subcontractors whose numbers are burgeoning in the new network-based organization. It is even the case that independent authorities are found in companies, both in the financial field (market authorities; auditors) and in the product field (standard-setting and certification agencies). The original meaning of the word 'enterprise' (the act of undertaking) has returned, to the detriment of its derived meaning (the institution resulting from that act). Hence, the large firm can no longer be construed as a homogeneous work community subordinated to its boss and functioning under national law. It forms part of a network, that is, a polycentric structure with international branches and fluid boundaries, each element of which is both autonomous and required to serve the interests of the whole.

These developments call into question the traditional categories of labor law. This applies in the first instance to the concept of 'subordination' (the boundary between dependent and self-employed work is becoming blurred) (Supiot 2000a), but it also applies to the notions of 'employer' (the point of entrepreneurial decision-making is fanning out into groups and networks), 'branch of activity' (the refocusing of companies on their main business and the farming out of other activities mean that collective employment status is being refocused around the core business, thus restricting the coverage of sectoral agreements), 'employment' (the status of the workforce is becoming fragmented, with the decentralization of collective bargaining and the development of peripheral employment: precarious forms of employment, part-time work, etc.), and the 'collective agreement' (whose meaning is changing as collective bargaining functions are extended).

14.3.1.2. *New Environment*

These changes in company structure are compounded by an upheaval in their environment. The opening up of markets to international competition is having ambivalent effects in most cases. On the one hand, it *emancipates* firms from the powers of states. The mobility of capital, goods and people, coupled with the resources of transportation and information technology, also enables them to place states in a position of economic competition by choosing to establish themselves on the territory of those which impose the fewest constraints, while taking advantage of the resources of those which offer the best material and intellectual infrastructure. Supported in this respect by the market authorities, they are even able to make states pander to their appetites and oblige governments to dismantle laws which would restrict their profitability. On the other hand, 'globalization' makes companies increasingly *vulnerable*. The free movement of goods leads to the disappearance of their captive markets. The free movement of capital exposes them to speculative takeovers and to the volatility of the capital they mobilize. The free circulation of information compounds these risks by exposing them to the critical gaze of consumers, shareholders and environmental pressure groups.

Such upheavals have led the biggest companies to arm themselves against these new risks. Vis-à-vis their shareholders they have adopted a policy of openness by subjecting themselves to the rules of corporate governance[21] and to the demands of so-called 'value creation' (albeit at the expense of the company's 'human resources'). Vis-à-vis consumers they have improved their techniques for controlling public opinion by gaining a hold on the major media, either directly (financial control) or indirectly (financing of advertising). Finally they have learned how to curry favor with politicians and intellectuals by winning them over to the company's values, or even by simply buying them, as witnessed by the countless corruption scandals which are universally tarnishing public life (Mény 1992).

---

[21] See for the United States the report of the American Law Institute *Principles of Corporate Governance*; for the United Kingdom the *Code of Best Practice* which resulted from the work of the Cadbury Commission; and in France, the Viénot (1999) report. Cf. a presentation of these texts by Tunc (1994: 59–72); also Decoopman (1996: 105 ff.).

These profound changes in companies' modes of economic action render the institutional framework of social dialogue largely inoperable. This was essentially conceived as a face-to-face interaction between employers and trade unions under the watchful eye of the state. The mechanisms of representation, negotiation and collective action are entirely oblivious to anything that has to do with the products of labor, their intended recipients and public information. The balance of forces between the economic action of companies and the collective action of workers, which is necessary for 'social *régulation*', is thus disrupted, and it is the latter which loses out. One of the great tasks facing labor lawyers in years to come will be to invent ways of restoring that balance, many possibilities for which are already available in practice.

14.3.2. *Possibilities for Re-establishing a Balance of Economic and Social Forces*

The great challenge facing trade unionism today is how to adapt to new forms of corporate organization. It too will probably not be able to escape the network approach. The pyramid structure of mass trade unionism is likely to be replaced by an approach which coordinates various types of representative units located as near as possible to the genuine centers of corporate decision-making (not just firms and sectors, but also international centers, groups, company networks, districts, trades, etc.). This development is essential if the unions are to cope with the expansion and fragmentation of the interests that they represent: the interests not just of skilled male workers employed by large companies in developed countries, but also those of workers in insecure or part-time jobs, women, the unemployed, pensioners, those employed by sub-contractors, those who are partially self-employed, etc. It is also essential if the unions are to cope with the expansion of the functions of collective bargaining, which no longer merely covers wage levels and working hours, but also addresses issues of general interest with the development of negotiations on jobs, the organization of working hours and the development of labor law (legislative bargaining).

Thus the whole complex of law governing collective labor relations needs to be reconsidered. Negotiation, representation and collective action form a tripod structure on which social dialogue must be based. Indeed no collective bargaining is conceivable without the involvement of legal persons appointed to represent the interests concerned and endowed with the resources needed to have an effective influence on the terms of the negotiations. These three dimensions of collective employment relations are closely bound up with one another and are all affected by the new organization of labor in the world. The key element here is probably not so much to introduce new regulations as to adapt the legislation governing collective labor relations to take account of the new forms of corporate organization. Various steps have already been taken in this direction, in particular concerning worker representation in groups of enterprises. There are already tentative openings allowing collective bargaining to break out of the straitjacket of sectors and companies and to develop in new fields (districts, networks, the international level). Nothing, or hardly anything, has been done as yet on the collective action front: the right to strike should be re-examined, as it too can no longer continue to be viewed as a binary interaction between an employer and his employees (Supiot 2001).

But from the point of view of the new forms of governance in the global economy, it is better to focus on the social forces capable of restoring a minimum balance between economic rights and social rights at an international level. According to Manuel Castells (1998), the only countervailing forces able to play a role in the new world economic order are identity movements alien to the organizing principles of the network society (Castells 1997, 1998; on the rising power of new 'identity groups' see Piore 1995). If this hypothesis, which is strongly supported by the observation of current events, is correct, any hope of regulating this globalized order will no doubt have to be abandoned, and we shall have to wait for major political, social, or ecological disasters to end the one-party dominance of free trade over the institutions of world commerce.[22] Even so it is possible that there are ways, albeit very limited ones, of restoring a balance of forces, based on the very logic behind the new economic organization. In order to gain access to them we would have to extend the scope for action and collective representation to areas currently barred to them, to bring them out of the closed arena in which they are locked by an institutional conception of firms which no longer corresponds to present-day forms of economic action. Two types of method can be employed here. The first involves using the new freedoms inherent in globalization: the freedom of choice enjoyed by consumers and investors, together with freedom of information, offer ways to influence the social policies of entrepreneurs. The second involves the reverse: restraining global competition law by emphasizing the distinction between the economic and social fields and by strengthening the authority of institutions concerned with social affairs. In both cases, however the objective is the same: giving workers back the ability to take collective action in fields which currently lie abandoned, without any sort of counterweight for firms' economic initiatives. Many routes could be explored in this direction. I will

---

[22] I draw this very evocative characterization of the political nature of these institutions from Faux (2000).

confine my remarks to three fields which appear particularly promising for this revitalization of collective action: information, consumption and finance.

14.3.2.1. *Targeting Information*

The new information technologies and control of the media have become powerful instruments in the hands of companies. These new powers call for counter-powers, both within and outside firms.

Within companies the gap has widened between the information resources available to employers, thanks to new information technology (intranet networks), and those which the law affords to the workers' representatives, who remain penned inside the legal confines of the company and have to rely on traditional forms of communication (handbills, notice boards). Use by workers of information technology outside their employer's control has already given rise to litigation. It should become accepted that, wherever employers use computerized networks to convey information to their employees, the employees' representatives should also have access to these networks in accordance with arrangements to be laid down by law or agreement. The same network approach should also apply when it comes to the economic information available to the staff representatives. It must be possible for contacts to be established between the employees of the contracting company and those of its sub-contractors.

Outside the company, workers' freedom of expression concerning their work needs to be spelt out in detail. The information which the trade unions give the public must be able to cover not only working conditions, but also the company's products. The radical separation maintained in the industrial world between work and its products is no longer justified today. In a 'tertiarized' economy, work is concerned more with signs than with things. Hence, the activity of the worker cannot be dissociated from the product of that activity and consideration of the product necessarily affects the employment relationship. Legal precedent has begun to draw certain consequences from this concerning the rights of workers' representatives to information and consultation.[23] Moreover, work in the 'post-industrial' era is no longer concerned solely with what in civil law are called 'generic objects' (*choses de genre*, Article 1246 of the Civil Code), that is, mass-produced articles which are interchangeable and independent of the skill of the workers. It gives increasing prominence to 'specific items' (*corps certains*), that is, quality

---

[23] Soc. 28 November 2000, *Semaine soc.* of 11 December 2000, to be published in *Bulletin civil* (obligation to consult the works council about the launch of a new insurance product which is bound to affect the way in which workers are paid).

products for which the company must provide an assurance of safety and traceability.[24] This tends to mean that the link is restored between the professional skills of the worker and the qualities of the product, a link which Taylorism had sought to break. With these developments, products are once again being considered within the contractual domain, justifying the fact that counterweights have been introduced to the monopoly which companies enjoyed on the information provided on their own products. The need for this has been recognized in consumer law, which gives consumers the right to information (see Calais-Auloy and Steinmetz 2000). For its part, Article XX of GATT (1994) allows any member of the WTO to take measures necessary to prevent the import of 'articles manufactured in prisons' and for the 'protection of the health or life of persons' or for the 'conservation of non-renewable natural resources'.[25] Leaving aside the debate on the social clause in international trade agreements, the principle that the public has the right to information on the social and environmental dimensions of products seems to be indisputable, and indeed undisputed, today.

This right presupposes that the trade unions also have a right to inform the public about these dimensions (Société française de droit de l'environnement 1994: 153). Various initiatives have been taken on these lines by associations or unions posting information on the Internet about the social policies of big companies, particularly their relations with subcontractors in developing countries (Fung *et al.* 2001). The companies in question have reacted by issuing codes of conduct and social labels, the effectiveness and sincerity of which are open to question in the absence of reliable certification procedures covering their content and application along the lines of those that apply to ISO standards. This is why some people are calling for the introduction of a market in the social certification of good practice, whose idea is to draw both certifying bodies and certified firms into a virtuous circle (Fung *et al.* 2001). Notwithstanding the value of these initiatives and proposals, it is reasonable to argue that two conditions must be met without which public information will be vulnerable to all kinds of manipulation. The first, which has already been mentioned, is the existence at an international level of proper social *régulation* authorities which would guarantee the validity of the information

---

[24] See European directive No. 85/374, 25 July 1985 establishing liability for defective goods (Taylor 1999).

[25] On the application of these measures as regards the environment, see Monier (2000) and the much more critical stance adopted by Howse and Regan (2000). This article could have important implications for the social field, placing emphasis on the notion of 'protection of the health and life of persons', the dynamics of which have always informed the development of labor law (cf. 'La dynamique du corps (protection physique et transformations du droit du travail et de la sécurité sociale'), in *Scritti in onore di Gino Giugni*, Bari: Caccuci, 1999, 2: 1621–46)

disseminated. The second is to give trade unions and consumers' associations the financial resources to provide social information for the public. Funds could be set up for this purpose fed by a levy consisting of a percentage of firms' advertising budgets. Without this kind of financing the public will never hear the other side of the argument and will only ever receive the one-sided propaganda of the companies dominating the markets.

14.3.2.2. *Targeting Demand*

The scope for states to take measures restricting freedom of competition on social grounds was mentioned briefly above (Section 14.2.2.3). This also presupposes the involvement of social *régulation* authorities able to ensure that such measures should promote the equalization of working conditions throughout the world and do not serve to protect the richest countries which would prefer to close their borders to both workers and products from the poorest countries. It is worth reflecting here that the ILO is particularly well placed to become that authority. Such an authority could be called on to intervene, either directly or by way of a complaint to the market economic authorities (e.g. the WTO's Dispute Settlement Body).

Concerning trade union action in this field, it is appropriate to go back to the origins of the right to take collective action. This was originally an immunity granted to trade unions which took collective action against an enterprise in the legitimate pursuit of social protection. This immunity resulted in France from the abolition of the offence of 'coalition' in 1864 and in the USA from the Hunt ruling (Mass. 1842) and the Clayton Act (1914). The transition from coalition to strike reflected the binary structure (employer/ employees; capital/ labor) imposed on labor law by the industrial model, a structure which does not allow for any consideration of products or consumers or of disputes between dominant and subordinate employers. But in the new world economic order, pre-industrial forms of collective action are making a come-back, and with them the quest for an alliance of workers and consumers to target the Achilles heel of the big companies: sensitivity to demand for their products. The expression *par excellence* of this alliance is the boycott. This is a formidable weapon which is making its reappearance in the current social arena. Last month, for example, the threat of a boycott was enough for Coca-Cola, in the dock for many months over racial discrimination against black workers, to decide in favor of a settlement which will cost it $192.5 million. In France the mere threat of a boycott of its products led Total to give a public undertaking to contribute to repairing the damage caused by the *Erika* disaster; an effect out of all proportion to what would have been the consequences if the seamen aboard the vessel, recruited under a social flag of convenience and screened from the main contractor by a chain of subcontractors, had gone on strike.

The arguments advanced to condemn in principle recourse to the boycott do not carry much weight. Some would say that this 'Anglo-Saxon' form of struggle is foreign to European culture (*Le Monde*, 18 November 2000).[26] But must not the internationalization of businesses (and their alignment with the rules of corporate governance) go hand-in-hand with the internationalization of means of collective action? Boycotts would risk causing businesses losses, which could be harmful to employment. But does not every collective action, starting with the strike, have the effect, if it is successful, of causing loss to businesses and thus putting jobs at risk because of competition? Conversely, one can clearly see why there is a renewal of interest in the boycott: it is capable of joining together, across national frontiers, the interests of workers, consumers and environmentalists, it repositions the products of work at the heart of collective disputes, it is impervious to stratagems aiming at making work precarious or changing its location; the boycott is thus well suited to the new forms of economic domination. One can also clearly see the risks peculiar to this type of action. The boycott can become an ineffective weapon if it is used too often or limits itself to a single country or a small circle of activists. It can also be a destructive weapon which unjustly strikes a business as a result of disinformation campaigns. More so than the strike, it lends itself to possible manipulation in particular by competitors.

Recognition of the right to boycott and its incorporation into international legislation is thus firmly on the agenda. There is no doubt as to its legal status as far as the rules of free trade are concerned: within the meaning of Article 85 of the Treaty of Rome it counts among the 'concerted actions... which have as their object or effect the prevention, restriction or distortion of competition'. The French courts even subject it to harsher treatment than an agreement between firms or the abuse of a dominant position, since they do not even require proof that the call for a boycott has had a significant effect to declare it unlawful.[27] However, this prohibition should not be applicable to action taken by workers' trade unions (see in this regard du Cheyron du Pavillon 1991). In a recent case the Paris Court had referred to it a ruling of the Competition Council against unions which had taken concerted action to prevent a firm from engaging the services of a printer not covered by the collective agreement. The Court pointed out that the rules of competition law only applied to economic agents pursuing an activity on the market in question, and ruled that the Competition Council was not qualified to pronounce

---

[26] This assertion is historically incorrect: in continental Europe, the boycott was one of the means of protest favored by anarcho-syndicalism. But it is true that in contra-distinction to European unions, American unions have never ceased to have recourse to it.

[27] Cass. com. 10 March 1998, *Bull. civ.* No 95; see J.-D. Bretzner: 'Le boycottage face à l'impérialisme' du seuil de sensibilité', *D.* 2000, Chr. 441.

on the action of the trade unions, which were not operators on product markets.[28] We can see here that the legal concept of 'economic agent' allows an area to be defined which falls outside the purview of competition law and the jurisdiction of the economic market authorities. This does not mean that any form of concerted action must be deemed lawful, but it does mean that they are legal in principle and that measures relating to them at international level must be the prerogative of social market authorities.

14.3.2.3. *Targeting Finance*

I mention this third field of collective action by workers merely for the record. Like consumers, shareholders can also be sensitive to information about companies' social policies. Here too campaigns have been launched, particularly on the Internet, to promote 'ethical investment opportunities' (for France see *Alternatives économiques* 1999: 160). The development of a savings scheme or of wage funds managed by workers' representatives could be one of the points considered in the social strategies of firms. However, this is a field where specific national concerns feature very prominently. These sorts of ideas have aroused most interest in the English-speaking world. There is a whole body of British and American doctrine promoting a much wider view of the interests which must be taken into account in the running of companies (see Ireland 1996; Deakin and Hughes 1997). Alongside the interests of the shareholders, those of other 'stakeholders' in the business should also be taken into account, the first in line being the workers. Noting the devastating social consequences of strategies based solely on profit in a deregulated global environment (see Craypo 1997: 10), this interpretation of corporate governance retains its instruments, but uses them for the benefit of all the stakeholders in the company (workers, consumers, etc.). This means, for example, that workers who pay into a pension fund may demand that the fund should require firms in which it holds shares to take account of social and not just financial requirements (Ghuilarducci, Hawley and Williams 1997: 26). In the same way, the introduction of non-executive directors could serve to represent the interests of the workers or consumers as well as those of the shareholders alone.

These ideas do not make much headway in countries like France, which have never really succeeded in developing a popular share-owning culture. They are not easily compatible with the German concept of codetermination, which is based upon a clear division of roles between the shareholders' representatives and those of the workforce and has no place for the 'unnatural' phenomenon of the worker-shareholder. More generally finance as a weapon

---

[28] CA Paris, 29 February 2000, *Dr. ouv.* 2000, 143, commentary by G. Lyon-Caen.

is linked to the development of pension funds and cannot therefore play a major role in countries which remain attached to unfunded pensions based on general taxation.

14.4. Conclusion

In the world order which evolved out of the industrial revolution, nation-states became the keystone of the organization of societies and the guarantors of their cohesion. Admittedly the manner in which states fulfilled this role differed greatly from one country to the other. In some cases, they took direct control of the organization of the social security system, while relying on collective bargaining for the organization of labor relations, as for example in the United Kingdom after 1945. In others, like that of France, they were able to codify labor relations considerably, while delegating the management of social security to unions and employers. However, the rules and institutions necessary for the functioning of the labor market were always developed within the framework of the nation-state. Hence, the development of national models of labor relations and social security rights.

Nowadays, the opening up of borders is shaking the foundations of these national frameworks of social life. National solidarities have themselves been called into question, by globalization on the one hand and by relocalization and reterritorialization on the other. Globalization and localization are the two inseparable faces of global economic strategies based on the valorization of local competitive advantages. The effects of this double movement of internationalization and regionalization on the legal framework of employment and social welfare are ambivalent. On the one hand they free firms from the supervision of national laws and encourage the deregulation of labor relations. On the other hand they expose firms and their employees to new risks which render inevitable the elaboration of new types of legal rules. Faced with these changes, some already proclaim the withering away of states, emptied of their relevance, by the combination of 'local' and 'global'. But this idea of a world in which there would be only the 'local' and the 'global', has an imperial stamp that does not stand up to a legal analysis of the contemporary world. Nothing permits us to say that national laws are going to lose the major role which has always been theirs in employment relations. This role is simply changing and becoming more complex. It no longer consists in simply establishing the rules of the game at national level, but rather in incorporating local and global norms into national models. These transformations cannot work harmoniously unless each country accepts that it has as much to learn from others as to teach them and that legal concepts cannot be exported like goods. Undoubtedly there is no dialogue between cultures, but, at best, a mutual learning process based on a well-understood interest. At an international level this mutual learning process presupposes the avoidance of imposing rules of Western origin on the whole world (this is the great weakness of the campaign for social clauses in trade agreements). Rather one should invest an international social authority, recognized by all, with the power to settle on a case by case basis, social disputes arising from the development of international trade. Only this casuistical method, so dear to Common Law countries, can gradually give substance to the universal principles that the Civil Law culture demands. Much more than law or contract, it is the figure of the judge which has a universal scope. It is thus an international social judge that the globalization of the economy needs, if we want to prevent it from giving rise to a resurgence of identity-based fundamentalisms.

References

Alternatives économiques (1999). *Les placements éthiques*, special issue, 2nd edn.

ALI (American Law Institute) (1993). 'Principles of Corporate Governance'. *The Business Lawyer*, August, 1267–1744.

AUTIN, J.-L. (1988). 'Du juge administratif aux autorités administratives indépendantes: un autre mode de régulation'. *Revue de droit public*.

BENVENISTE, E. (1969). *Le vocabulaire des institutions indo-européennes*. Vol. 2 Paris: Minuit (English translation: *Indo-European Language and Society*. Florida: University of Miami Press, 1973).

BERCUSSON, B. (1996). *European Labor Law*. London: Butterworths.

BOYER, R. and SAILLARD, Yv. (2002). *Regulation Theory: The State of the Art* (trans Carolyn Shread), London: Routledge *(orig.: Théorie de la régulation : l'État des savoirs*, Paris: La Découverte, 1995).

BRETZNER, J.-D. (2000). 'Le boycottage face à l'"impérialisme" du seuil de sensibilité'. *Recueil Dalloz* , Chronique 441.

The Committee on Corporate Governance (2000). 'The Combined Code: Principles of Good Governance and Code of Best Practice'. Derived from the Committee's Final Report and from the Cadbury and Greenbury Reports. London: The Committee on Corporate Governance.

CALAIS-AULOY, J. and STEINMETZ, F. (2000). *Droit de la consommation*. Paris: Dalloz, 5th edn.

CASTEL, R. (1995). *Les métamorphoses de la question sociale. Une chronique du salariat*. Paris: Fayard.

CASTELLS, M. (1998). *End of Millennium*. Oxford: Blackwell (Fr. trans. *Fin de millénaire*, Paris: Fayard, 1999).

—— (1997). *The Power of Identity*. Oxford: Blackwell.

CLAM, J. and MARTIN, G. (eds) (1998) *Les transformations de la régulation juridique*. Paris: LGDJ.

COLLIARD, C.-A. and TIMSIT, G. (1988). *Les autorités administratives indépendantes*, Paris: PUF.

CONSEIL D'ÉTAT (2001). *Les autorités administratives indépendantes.* Public Report 2001. Paris: La Documentation française, 253–452.

CRAYPO, C. (1997). 'The Impact of Changing Corporate Strategies on Communities, Unions and Workers in The United States of America', in S. Deakin and A. Hughes (eds), *Enterprise and Community, New Directions in Corporate Governance.* Oxford: Blackwell, 10–25.

DAGRON, G. (1996). *Empereur et prêtre.* Paris: Gallimard.

DEAKIN, S. (1998). 'Privatization, Enterprise Restructuring and Labor Law in Britain', French translation in A. Supiot (ed.), *Le travail en perspectives*, Paris: LGDJ, 391–401.

——and HUGHES A. (eds) (1997). *Enterprise and Community: New Directions in Corporate Governance.* Oxford: Blackwell.

DECOOPMAN, N. (1996). 'Du gouvernement des entreprises à la gouvernance', in J. Chevalier *et al. La gouvernabilité.* Paris: PUF, 105–13.

DU CHEYRON DU PAVILLON, A. (1991). 'Le boycottage', in *Les activités et les biens de l'entreprise, Mélanges J. Déruppé*, Paris: Litec.

DUMONT, L. (1977). *From Mandeville to Marx: The Genesis and Triumph of Economic Ideology.* Chicago: University of Chicago Press.

——(1985). *Homo aequalis I. Genèse et épanouissement de l'idéologie économique*, 2nd edn. Paris: Gallimard.

FAUX, J. (2000). Toward a Global 'New Deal'. Paper for the conference on Work and Social Citizenship in a Global Economy, WAGEnet, University of Wisconsin-Madison, November.

FRISON-ROCHE, M.-A. *Droit, finance, autorité*, Paris: PUF, *forthcoming.*

FUNG, A., O'ROURKE, D., and SABEL, C. (2001). 'Realizing Labor Standards: How Transparency, Competition, and Sanctions Could Improve Working Conditions Worldwide'. *Boston Review*, February–March.

GHILARDUCCI, T., HAWLEY, J., and WILLIAMS, A. (1997). 'Labour's Paradoxical Interests and the Evolution of Corporate Governance', in S. Deakin and A. Hughes (eds), *Enterprise and Community. New Directions in Corporate Governance.* Oxford: Blackwell, 26–43.

HABERMAS, J. (1984). *The Theory of Communicative Action*, 2 Vols. (trans Thomas McCarthy), Boston: Beacon Press, 1984, 1989 (orig.: *Theorie des kommunikativen Handelns*, Frankfurt am Main.: Suhrkamp, 1981).

——(1996). *Between Facts and Norms: Contributions to a Discourse Theory of Law and Democracy.* Trans. by W. Rehg. Cambridge, Mass.: MIT Press (orig.: *Faktizität und Geltung. Beiträge zur Diskurstheorie des Rechts und des demokratischen Rechtsstaats*, Frankfurt am Main.: Suhrkamp, 1992).

HERBERGER, M. (1981). *Dogmatik. Zur Geschichte von Begriff und Methode in Medizin und Jurisprudenz*, Frankfurt/M.: Vittorio Klostermann.

HOWSE, R. and REGAN, D. (2000). 'The Product/Process Distinction—An Illusory Basis for Disciplining "Unilateralism" in Trade Policy'. *European Journal of International Law*, 11/2: 249–89.

IRELAND, P. (1996). 'Corporate Governance, Stakeholding and the Company : Towards a Less Degenerate Capitalism?' *Journal of Law and Society*, 287–320.

JODEAU GRYMBERG, M., BONNAT, C., and PÊCHEUR, B. (2000). 'Les autorités administratives indépendantes', *Cahiers de la Fonction publique et de l'administration*, 190: 3–14.

KANTOROWICZ, E. (1963). *The King's Two Bodies: A Study in Medieval Political Theology.* Princeton, NJ: Princeton University Press.

KOJÈVE, A. (2000). *Outline of a Phenomenology of Right* (trans, with an introductory essay and notes, by Bryan-Paul Frost and Robert Howse; ed. Bryan-Paul Frost), Lanham, MD.: Rowman & Littlefield (orig.: *Esquisse d'une phénoménologie du droit*, Paris: Gallimard, 1981).

LAROQUE, P. (1954). 'Contentieux social et juridiction sociale'. *Droit Social*, 271–80.

LE MONDE, 18 November 2000.

LECOURT, D. (ed.) (1999). *Dictionnaire d'histoire et de philosophie des sciences*. Paris: PUF.

LEGENDRE, P. (1983). *L'empire de la vérité. Introduction aux espaces dogmatiques industriels*. Paris: Fayard.

—— (1999). *Sur la question dogmatique en Occident*. Paris: Fayard.

—— (2001). *De la Société comme Texte. Linéaments d'une anthropologie dogmatique*. Paris: Fayard.

LOMGOBARDI, N. (1995). 'Autorités administratives indépendantes et position institutionnelle de l'administration publique'. *Revue française de droit administratif*, 11/1: 171–77; 11/2: 383–9.

MAINE, H. S. (1870). *Ancient Law. Its Connection with the Early History of Society and Its Relation to Modern Ideas*, 1861, with an introduction by Theodore W. Dwight, 1st American edn. from 2nd London edn., New York: Charles Scribner, 1864.

MAUPAIN, F. (2000). 'L'OIT devant le défi de la Mondialisation—de la réglementation à la régulation internationale du Travail?', in P. de Senarclens (ed.), *Maîtriser la mondialisation*. Paris: Presses de Sciences Po, 147–91.

MÉNY, Y. (1992). *La corruption de la République*. Paris: Fayard.

MONIER, P. (2000). 'L'environnement dans la jurisprudence de l'OMC'. *Les notes bleues de Bercy*, 186: July 1–4, and 1–15.

NOAILLES, P. DE (1947). *Fas et Jus. Études de droit romain*. Paris: Les Belles Lettres.

—— (1949). *Du droit sacré au droit civil*. Paris: Sirey.

PIORE, M. J. (1995). *Beyond Individualism*. Cambridge, MA: Harvard University Press.

REICH, R. (1991). *The Work of Nations*. New York: Alfred A. Knopf.

RIBS, J. and SCHWARTZ, R. (2000). 'L'actualité des sanctions administratives infligées par les autorités administratives indépendantes'. *Gaz. Pal.* July 28, 3–11.

Société française de droit de l'environnement (1994). *Droit du travail et droit de l'environnement*. Paris: Litec.

SOMAVIA, J. (1999). 'Decent Work'. Report of the ILO Director-General, 87th session of the International Labour Conference. Geneva: ILO.

STORPER, M. and SALAIS, R. (1997). *Worlds of Production*, Cambridge, MA: Harvard University Press (French version: *Les mondes de production*. Paris: Eds de l'EHESS, 1993).

SUPIOT, A. (1994). *Critique du droit du travail*. Paris: PUF.

—— (2000a). 'Les nouveaux visages de la subordination'. *Droit Social*, 2: 131–45, February.

—— (2000b). 'The Dogmatic Foundation of the Market', *Industrial Law Journal*, 29/4: 331–45.

—— (2001). 'Revisiter les droits d'action collective'. *Droit Social*, 687–704.

—— (2002). 'Travail, droit et technique'. *Droit Social*, 1: January, 13–25.

TAYLOR, S. (1999). *L'harmonisation communautaire de la responsabilité du fait des produits défectueux. Etude comparative du droit anglais et du droit français* Paris: LGDJ.

TUNC, A. (1994). 'Le gouvernement des sociétés anonymes. Le mouvement de réforme aux Etats-Unis et au Royaume-Uni'. *Revue internationale de droit comparé*, 1: 59–72.

VIÉNOT, M. *et al.* (1999). 'Recommendations of the Committee on Corporate Governance'. Paris: Committee on Corporate Governance. Available at www.medef.fr/fr/Frame.htm?CDI_gouv_enterprise.htm.

WIENER, N. (1954). *The Human Use of Human Beings (Cybernetics and Society)*. 2nd edn. Boston: Houghton Mifflin & Co.

—— (1964). *God and Golem Inc.* Cambridge: MIT Press.

INDEX

Printed in the United Kingdom
by Lightning Source UK Ltd.
108229UKS00001B/135